# healthy cooking
## Taste of Home
# annual recipes

RDA ENTHUSIAST BRANDS, LLC
GREENDALE, WI

# healthy cooking
### Taste of Home
#### annual recipes

23

92

113

**EDITORIAL**
**EDITOR-IN-CHIEF** Catherine Cassidy
**CREATIVE DIRECTOR** Howard Greenberg
**EDITORIAL OPERATIONS DIRECTOR** Kerri Balliet

**MANAGING EDITOR/PRINT & DIGITAL BOOKS**
Mark Hagen
**ASSOCIATE CREATIVE DIRECTOR**
Edwin Robles Jr.

**EDITOR** Heather Ray
**ART DIRECTOR** Jessie Sharon
**CONTRIBUTING LAYOUT DESIGNER**
Siya Motamedi
**EDITORIAL PRODUCTION MANAGER**
Dena Ahlers
**COPY CHIEF** Deb Warlaumont Mulvey
**COPY EDITORS** Mary-Liz Shaw, Joanne Weintraub
**CONTRIBUTING COPY EDITOR** Valerie Phillips

**CHIEF FOOD EDITOR** Karen Berner
**FOOD EDITORS** James Schend;
Peggy Woodward, RD
**ASSOCIATE FOOD EDITOR** Krista Lanphier
**RECIPE EDITORS** Mary King; Annie Rundle;
Jenni Sharp, RD; Irene Yeh
**CONTENT OPERATIONS MANAGER**
Colleen King
**CONTENT OPERATIONS ASSISTANT**
Shannon Stroud
**EXECUTIVE ASSISTANT** Marie Brannon

**TEST KITCHEN AND FOOD STYLING MANAGER**
Sarah Thompson
**TEST COOKS** Nicholas Iverson (lead), Matthew Hass,
Lauren Knoelke
**FOOD STYLISTS** Kathryn Conrad (senior),
Shannon Roum, Leah Rekau
**PREP COOKS** Megumi Garcia, Melissa Hansen,
Bethany Van Jacobson

**PHOTOGRAPHY DIRECTOR** Stephanie Marchese
**PHOTOGRAPHERS** Dan Roberts, Jim Wieland
**PHOTOGRAPHER/SET STYLIST**
Grace Natoli Sheldon
**SET STYLISTS** Stacey Genaw, Melissa Haberman,
Dee Dee Jacq

**BUSINESS ANALYST** Kristy Martin
**BILLING SPECIALIST** Mary Ann Koebernik

**BUSINESS**
**VICE PRESIDENT, CHIEF SALES OFFICER**
Mark S. Josephson
**VICE PRESIDENT, BUSINESS DEVELOPMENT
& MARKETING** Alain Begun
**GENERAL MANAGER, TASTE OF HOME
COOKING SCHOOL** Erin Puariea

**VICE PRESIDENT, DIGITAL EXPERIENCE
& E-COMMERCE** Jennifer Smith
**VICE PRESIDENT, DIRECT TO CONSUMER
MARKETING** Dave Fiegel

**THE READER'S DIGEST ASSOCIATION, INC.**
**PRESIDENT AND CHIEF EXECUTIVE OFFICER**
Robert E. Guth
**VICE PRESIDENT, CHIEF OPERATING OFFICER,
NORTH AMERICA** Howard Halligan
**PRESIDENT & PUBLISHER, BOOKS** Harold Clarke
**VICE PRESIDENT, NORTH AMERICAN
OPERATIONS** Philippe Cloutier
**VICE PRESIDENT, CHIEF MARKETING OFFICER**
Leslie Doty
**VICE PRESIDENT, NORTH AMERICAN HUMAN
RESOURCES** Phyllis E. Gebhardt, SPHR
**VICE PRESIDENT, CHIEF TECHNOLOGY
OFFICER** Rob Hilliard
**VICE PRESIDENT, CONSUMER MARKETING
PLANNING** Jim Woods

**COVER PHOTOGRAPHY**
**PHOTOGRAPHER** Dan Roberts
**FOOD STYLIST** Leah Rekau
**SET STYLIST** Dee Dee Jacq

© 2014 RDA ENTHUSIAST BRANDS, LLC
5400 S. 60TH ST., GREENDALE WI 53129

INTERNATIONAL STANDARD BOOK NUMBER: 978-1-61765-270-7
INTERNATIONAL STANDARD SERIAL NUMBER: 1944-7736
COMPONENT NUMBER: 117900032H00

**PICTURED ON THE FRONT COVER:** Chocolate Eclair Delight (p. 258), Tenderloin with Cremini-Apricot Stuffing (p. 113), Roasted Tomato & Garlic Soup (p. 56) and Citrus-Spiced Roast Chicken (p. 117).

**PICTURED ON THE BACK COVER:** Garden Orzo Risotto (p. 69), Balsamic-Glazed Beef Skewers (p. 99), Grilled Halibut Steaks (p. 95) and Lemon Breakfast Parfaits (p. 83).

# Contents

Get inspired to try something new, fresh and healthy. With more than 400 satisfying recipes to choose from, you'll find everything you need for casual weeknight dinners, holiday entertaining, vegetarian cooking and more.

Chicken Gyros, 46

# Keep It Simple

The *Healthy Cooking Annual Recipes* collection makes preparing good-for-you meals easier than ever.

Those who work with me know I have a sweet tooth—one that requires a daily dose of chocolate. Considering I spend my days hand-selecting healthy recipes for books like this one (notice there are three dessert chapters), that may come as a surprise to some readers.

But as a registered dietitian, I'm a firm believer that all foods can and should be enjoyed in moderation—and that includes one of my favorite recipes, Chocolate Lover's Pudding (p. 248). To me, it exemplifies how easy it is to make from-scratch desserts using only a handful of basic ingredients.

The same approach can be applied to savory snacks and home-style dinners. By focusing on fresh whole foods, you'll find you don't need to add a lot of extras to make the kinds of meals you crave. With recipes like the Spud-Stuffed Peppers on p. 104 and the Caribbean Chicken Stir-Fry on p. 91 that use only five ingredients, taste amazing, and are loaded with protein and fiber, you can put a comforting, healthy dinner on the table tonight.

In fact, inside the pages of this year's *Healthy Cooking Annual Recipes*, you'll find hundreds of meals like the ones above. For breakfast, lunch, dinner and, of course, dessert, let this collection be your go-to source for dishes that are not only low-maintenance and simple, but healthy, too.

Happy cooking,

*Peggy Woodward, RD*

Peggy Woodward, RD
Food Editor

## Nutrition Fact Nuggets

**NUTRITIONAL GUIDELINES**
All the recipes in our *Healthy Cooking Annual Recipes* cookbook fit the lifestyle of health-conscious cooks and families. The recipes represent a variety of foods that fit into any meal plan within the standards of the USDA's "MyPlate" plan for moderately active adults (see the Daily Nutrition Guide on p. 5).

**FACTS**
- Whenever a choice of ingredients is given in a recipe (such as ⅓ cup of sour cream or plain yogurt), the first ingredient listed is always the one calculated in the Nutrition Facts.
- When a range is given for an ingredient (such as 2 to 3 teaspoons), we calculate the first amount given.
- Only the amount of a marinade absorbed during preparation is calculated.
- Optional ingredients are not included in our calculations.

**DIABETIC EXCHANGES**
All recipes in *Healthy Cooking Annual Recipes* have been reviewed by a registered dietitian. Diabetic Exchanges are assigned to recipes in accordance with guidelines from the American Diabetic Association and the Academy of Nutrition and Dietetics.

The majority of recipes in this cookbook are suitable for diabetics, but please check the Diabetic Exchanges to make sure the recipe is in accordance with your doctor's instructions and fits your particular dietary guidelines.

**SPECIAL DIET INDICATORS**
To help those on restricted diets easily find dishes to suit their needs, we clearly indicate recipes that are particularly low in fat, sodium or carbohydrates as well as those that contain no meat. You will find these colored special diet indicators directly after the recipe title where appropriate:

**F** One serving contains 3 fat grams or less
**S** One serving contains 140 milligrams sodium or less
**C** One serving contains 15 grams carbohydrates or less
**M** Recipe contains no meat

101

79

54

229

# The Year's Best Tips

People are always asking us to lighten up their recipes and offer advice on cooking healthier meals at home. Check out our favorite tricks to share:

When it comes to cheese, opt for a strong-tasting variety, like goat cheese or blue cheese. You can get away with using less of an ingredient if it has a bold flavor.
**GOAT CHEESE & HAM OMELET, P. 79**

For tacos and wraps, instead of 10-inch tortillas, use 8- or 6-inch ones. Ten-inch tortillas have more than 200 calories before any fillings are added.
**OPEN-FACED TURKEY TACOS, P. 101**

For sausage dinners, think of sausage as the flavor component instead of the main protein source. Replace half (or more) of the sausage with plain lean ground beef or turkey instead.

For soups and stews, use no-salt-added canned tomatoes; rinse canned beans to cut the sodium by 40 percent; and try a combination of water and reduced-sodium broth for the base.
**TURKEY SAUSAGE BEAN SOUP, P. 54**

For baking, substitute applesauce or, better yet, mashed ripe bananas for half the fat (butter or oil). When you do this, you generally can cut down on sugar, too. The sweetness from the fruit puree makes up for it.
**APPLESAUCE BROWNIES, P. 229**

## DAILY NUTRITION GUIDE

| | Women 25-50 | Women over 50 | Men 50-65 |
|---|---|---|---|
| **CALORIES** | 2,000 | 1,800 | 2,400 |
| **FAT** | 67 g or less | 60 g or less | 80 g or less |
| **SATURATED FAT** | 22 g or less | 20 g or less | 27 g or less |
| **CHOLESTEROL** | 300 mg or less | 300 mg or less | 300 mg or less |
| **SODIUM** | 2,300 mg or less | 1,500 mg or less | 1,500 mg or less |
| **CARBOHYDRATES** | 300 g | 270 g | 360 g |
| **FIBER** | 20-30 g | 20-30 g | 30-40 g |
| **PROTEIN** | 50 g | 45 g | 60 g |

This chart is only a guide. Requirements vary, depending on age, weight, height and amount of activity.
Children's dietary needs vary as they grow.

11

12

17

# Starters & Snacks

❝Upgrade your appetizer spread with this easy asparagus dip. If any pesto mayonnaise is left, it makes a flavorful sandwich spread.❞

**—JANIE COLLE** HUTCHINSON, KS
*about her recipe, Asparagus with Basil Pesto Sauce, on page 26*

# Around the World Tapenade F C M

Don't dirty a dish—let the food processor do the work for this easy tapenade. Spread onto crackers or toasted baguette slices, it makes a fantastic appetizer.

—**KIM RILA** LEESBURG, VA

**START TO FINISH:** 10 MIN. • **MAKES:** 16 APPETIZERS

- ½ cup chopped roasted sweet red pepper
- ½ cup pitted Greek olives
- ¼ cup chopped poblano pepper
- 2 tablespoons lemon juice
- 2 tablespoons olive oil
- 1 tablespoon minced fresh parsley
- 1 tablespoon capers, drained
- 2 garlic cloves, minced
- ¼ teaspoon dried thyme
- 16 slices French bread baguette (½ inch thick), toasted

In a food processor, combine the first nine ingredients; cover and process until blended. Spoon 1 tablespoon tapenade onto each baguette slice.

**NOTE** *Wear disposable gloves when cutting hot peppers; the oils can burn skin. Avoid touching your face.*

**PER SERVING** *63 cal., 3 g fat (trace sat. fat), 0 chol., 183 mg sodium, 7 g carb., trace fiber, 1 g pro.* **Diabetic Exchanges:** *½ starch, ½ fat.*

AROUND THE WORLD TAPENADE

 **top tip**

## Hostess Gift

In total, the Around the World Tapenade recipe makes about a cup's worth. Spooned into an 8-ounce mason jar or other airtight container, it makes a lovely hostess gift for parties.

CHICKEN NUGGETS WITH APRICOT SAUCE

# Chicken Nuggets with Apricot Sauce F S C

Satisfying a hungry crowd is easy with these oven-baked morsels. The bite-sized coated chicken pieces are served with an incredible sauce that combines apricot preserves and mustard.

—**MICHELLE KRZMARCZICK** REDONDO BEACH, CA

**PREP:** 25 MIN. • **BAKE:** 10 MIN. • **MAKES:** 2 DOZEN ( 1 CUP SAUCE )

- 1 cup buttermilk, divided
- 1 pound boneless skinless chicken breasts, cut into 1-inch cubes
- ¾ cup all-purpose flour
- 1 cup crushed cornflakes
- ½ teaspoon onion powder
- ½ teaspoon garlic salt
- ¼ teaspoon salt
- ¼ teaspoon dried oregano
- ⅛ teaspoon pepper
- 2 eggs
- 1 cup apricot preserves
- 2 tablespoons prepared mustard

**1.** Pour ½ cup buttermilk into a large resealable plastic bag; add chicken. Seal bag and turn to coat. Place flour in another resealable plastic bag. In a third bag, combine the cornflakes, onion powder, garlic salt, salt, oregano and pepper. In a shallow bowl, whisk eggs and the remaining buttermilk.

**2.** Drain chicken; add to flour and shake to coat. Coat with egg mixture, then add to cornflake mixture and shake to coat. Arrange chicken in a greased 15-in. x 10-in. x 1-in. baking pan.

**3.** Bake at 350° for 10-15 minutes or until juices run clear. In a small bowl, combine apricot preserves and mustard. Serve with chicken.

**PER SERVING** *91 cal., 1 g fat (trace sat. fat), 28 mg chol., 134 mg sodium, 15 g carb., trace fiber, 5 g pro.* **Diabetic Exchanges:** *1 lean meat, 1 starch.*

## Sesame Pork Appetizers 🄵🄲

The honey marinade gives this hearty pork appetizer added flavor. It's served with an Asian-inspired dipping sauce that would also be good with salmon or chicken.

—**JOYCE MOYNIHAN** LAKEVILLE, MN

**PREP:** 15 MIN. + MARINATING • **BAKE:** 40 MIN.
**MAKES:** 2 DOZEN (½ CUP SAUCE)

- ½ cup sherry or chicken broth
- 1 tablespoon reduced-sodium soy sauce
- 2 pork tenderloins (¾ pound each)
- ½ cup honey
- ½ cup sesame seeds

**DIPPING SAUCE**

- ⅓ cup reduced-sodium soy sauce
- 1 green onion, finely chopped
- 1 tablespoon sherry or chicken broth
- 1 tablespoon sesame oil
- 1 garlic clove, minced
- ½ teaspoon minced fresh gingerroot

**1.** In a large resealable plastic bag, combine sherry and soy sauce; add pork. Seal bag and turn to coat; refrigerate for 8 hours or overnight.

**2.** Drain and discard marinade; pat pork dry. Place honey and sesame seeds in separate shallow bowls. Roll pork in honey, then sesame seeds. Place on a rack in a shallow roasting pan. Bake at 350° for 40-45 minutes or until a thermometer reads 160°. Let stand for 5 minutes before slicing.

**3.** Meanwhile, in a small bowl, combine sauce ingredients. Serve with pork.

**PER SERVING** *70 cal., 3 g fat (trace sat. fat), 16 mg chol., 155 mg sodium, 5 g carb., trace fiber, 6 g pro.* **Diabetic Exchange:** *1 lean meat.*

SESAME PORK APPETIZERS

CREAMY FETA-SPINACH DIP

## Creamy Feta-Spinach Dip 🄲🄼

Garlic and feta make a powerfully tasty pair in this addictive dip. I first tried it at a party and had to drag myself away from the bowl!

—**ELISSA ARMBRUSTER** MEDFORD, NJ

**PREP:** 15 MIN. + CHILLING • **MAKES:** 2 CUPS (8 SERVINGS)

- 1 cup (8 ounces) fat-free plain yogurt
- ¾ cup crumbled feta cheese
- 2 ounces reduced-fat cream cheese, cubed
- ¼ cup reduced-fat sour cream
- 1 garlic clove, minced
- 1½ cups finely chopped fresh spinach
- 1 teaspoon dill weed
- ⅛ teaspoon pepper
  Fresh vegetables and/or sliced bread

**1.** Line a strainer with four layers of cheesecloth or one coffee filter; place over a bowl. Place yogurt in prepared strainer; cover yogurt with edges of cheesecloth. Refrigerate for 2 hours or until yogurt has thickened to the consistency of whipped cream.

**2.** Transfer yogurt to a food processor (discard liquid from bowl). Add the feta cheese, cream cheese, sour cream and garlic; cover and process until smooth.

**3.** Transfer to a small bowl. Stir in the spinach, dill and pepper. Cover and refrigerate until chilled. Serve with vegetables and/or bread.

**PER SERVING** *68 cal., 4 g fat (3 g sat. fat), 14 mg chol., 158 mg sodium, 4 g carb., 1 g fiber, 5 g pro.* **Diabetic Exchanges:** *½ starch, ½ fat.*

**WATERMELON CUPS**

# Watermelon Cups F S C M

This lovely appetizer is almost too pretty to eat! Sweet watermelon cubes hold a refreshing topping that showcases cucumber, red onion and fresh herbs.

—TASTE OF HOME TEST KITCHEN

**START TO FINISH:** 25 MIN.
**MAKES:** 16 APPETIZERS

- 16 seedless watermelon cubes (1 inch)
- ⅓ cup finely chopped cucumber
- 5 teaspoons finely chopped red onion
- 2 teaspoons minced fresh mint
- 2 teaspoons minced fresh cilantro
- ½ to 1 teaspoon lime juice

**1.** Using a small melon baller or measuring spoon, scoop out the center of each watermelon cube, leaving a ¼-in. shell (save pulp for another use).
**2.** In a small bowl, combine the remaining ingredients; spoon into watermelon cubes.
**PER SERVING** *7 cal., trace fat (trace sat. fat), 0 chol., 1 mg sodium, 2 g carb., trace fiber, trace pro.* **Diabetic Exchange:** *Free food.*

# Strawberry Salsa F S C M

This fun, fresh-tasting salsa is strawberry-sweet with just a hint of heat. It really adds a punch to tortilla chips and has wonderful color and visual appeal.

—NANCY WHITFORD EDWARDS, NY

**PREP:** 20 MIN. + CHILLING
**MAKES:** 4 CUPS (16 SERVINGS)

- 1½ cups sliced fresh strawberries
- 1½ cups chopped sweet red pepper
- 1 cup chopped green pepper
- 1 cup seeded chopped tomato
- ¼ cup chopped Anaheim pepper
- 2 tablespoons minced fresh cilantro
- ½ teaspoon salt
- ½ teaspoon crushed red pepper flakes
- ¼ teaspoon pepper
- 2 tablespoons plus 2 teaspoons honey
- 2 tablespoons lemon juice

In a large bowl, combine the first nine ingredients. In a small bowl, combine honey and lemon juice; gently stir into strawberry mixture. Cover and chill for at least 4 hours. Stir just before serving. Serve with a slotted spoon.
**NOTE** *Wear disposable gloves when cutting hot peppers; the oils can burn skin. Avoid touching your face.*
**PER SERVING** *25 cal., trace fat (trace sat. fat), 0 chol., 76 mg sodium, 6 g carb., 1 g fiber, 1 g pro.* **Diabetic Exchange:** *½ starch.*

**STRAWBERRY SALSA**

## Tomato-Basil Bruschetta F C M

It's easy to double this great recipe for a crowd. You can make the tomato topping ahead, or keep it simple and serve it as a dip for French bread slices.

—**MARIE COSENZA** CORTLANDT MANOR, NY

**START TO FINISH:** 25 MIN.
**MAKES:** ABOUT 2 DOZEN

- 3 plum tomatoes, chopped
- ⅓ cup thinly sliced green onions
- 4 tablespoons olive oil, divided
- 1 tablespoon minced fresh basil or 1 teaspoon dried basil
- 1 tablespoon red wine vinegar
- ½ teaspoon dried oregano
- ¼ teaspoon salt
- ⅛ teaspoon pepper
- 1 loaf (1 pound) French bread, cut into ½-inch slices
- 2 garlic cloves, peeled and halved

**1.** In a small bowl, combine the tomatoes, onions, 2 tablespoons oil, basil, vinegar, oregano, salt and pepper; set aside.
**2.** Lightly brush both sides of bread slices with remaining oil. Arrange on ungreased baking sheets. Broil 3-4 in. from the heat for 2-3 minutes on each side or until golden brown.
**3.** Rub garlic over bread slices. With a slotted spoon, top each slice with tomato mixture.
**PER SERVING** *84 cal., 3 g fat (trace sat. fat), 0 chol., 162 mg sodium, 12 g carb., 1 g fiber, 3 g pro.* **Diabetic Exchange:** *1 starch.*

GARBANZO-STUFFED MINI PEPPERS

 **Did you know?**

Garbanzo beans, also known as chickpeas, are the most widely consumed legume in the world. In addition to being high in protein, iron and fiber, they are low in fat and cholesterol, making them ideal for turning salads and soups into main-dish vegetarian meals. In fact, one cup of chickpeas can give you 30 percent of your daily protein.

## Garbanzo-Stuffed Mini Peppers F S C M

Mini peppers are so colorful and they're the perfect size for a two-bite appetizer. They have all the crunch of a pita chip, without the extra calories.

—**CHRISTINE HANOVER** LEWISTON, CA

**START TO FINISH:** 20 MIN.
**MAKES:** 32 APPETIZERS

- 1 teaspoon cumin seeds
- 1 can (15 ounces) garbanzo beans or chickpeas, rinsed and drained
- ¼ cup fresh cilantro leaves
- 3 tablespoons water
- 3 tablespoons cider vinegar
- ¼ teaspoon salt
- 16 miniature sweet peppers, halved lengthwise
  Additional fresh cilantro leaves

**1.** In a dry small skillet, toast cumin seeds over medium heat 1-2 minutes or until aromatic, stirring frequently. Transfer to a food processor. Add garbanzo beans, cilantro, water, vinegar and salt; pulse until blended.
**2.** Spoon into pepper halves. Top with additional cilantro. Refrigerate until serving.
**PER SERVING** *15 cal., trace fat (trace sat. fat), 0 chol., 36 mg sodium, 3 g carb., 1 g fiber, 1 g pro.*

"I like to make these game-day appetizer meatballs with blue cheese or ranch salad dressing for dipping. If I make them for a meal, I often skip the dressing and serve with blue cheese polenta on the side."

—AMBER MASSEY ARGYLE, TX

BUFFALO CHICKEN MEATBALLS

## Buffalo Chicken Meatballs F S C

**PREP:** 15 MIN. • **BAKE:** 20 MIN.
**MAKES:** 2 DOZEN

- ¾ cup panko (Japanese) bread crumbs
- ⅓ cup plus ½ cup Louisiana-style hot sauce, divided
- ¼ cup chopped celery
- 1 egg white
- 1 pound lean ground chicken
  Reduced-fat blue cheese or ranch salad dressing, optional

**1.** Preheat oven to 400°. In a large bowl, combine bread crumbs, ⅓ cup hot sauce, celery and egg white. Add chicken; mix lightly but thoroughly.

**2.** Shape into twenty-four 1-in. balls. Place on a greased rack in a shallow baking pan. Bake 20-25 minutes or until cooked through.

**3.** Toss meatballs with remaining hot sauce. If desired, drizzle with salad dressing just before serving.

**PER SERVING** *35 cal., 1 g fat (trace sat. fat), 14 mg chol., 24 mg sodium, 2 g carb., trace fiber, 4 g pro.*

## Healthy Steamed Dumplings F S C

My family loves Chinese food, but it's hard to find healthy choices in restaurants or at the grocery store. So instead, I make these healthy dumplings. Preparing them is a great family activity. With many hands helping out, filling the dumplings goes quickly. When we are done, we have lots of dumplings to put in the freezer for later.
—**MELODY CRAIN** HOUSTON, TX

**PREP:** 45 MIN. • **COOK:** 10 MIN./BATCH
**MAKES:** 4 DOZEN

- 1 cup finely shredded Chinese or napa cabbage
- ¼ cup minced fresh cilantro
- ¼ cup minced chives
- 1 egg, lightly beaten
- 3 tablespoons rice vinegar
- 1 tablespoon sesame oil
- 4 garlic cloves, minced
- 1 teaspoon ground ginger
- 1 teaspoon Chinese five-spice powder
- 1 teaspoon salt
- ½ teaspoon pepper
- ½ teaspoon grated lemon peel
- 1¾ pounds lean ground turkey
- 50 pot sticker or gyoza wrappers
- 6 cabbage leaves
  Sweet chili sauce, optional

**1.** In a large bowl, combine the first 12 ingredients. Add turkey; mix lightly but thoroughly.

**2.** Place 1 tablespoon of filling in the center of one wrapper. (To prevent remaining wrappers from drying out, keep them covered with a damp towel until ready to use.) Moisten entire edge with water. Fold wrapper over filling to form a semicircle. Press edges firmly to seal, pleating the front side to form three to five folds.

**3.** Holding sealed edges, stand each dumpling on an even surface; press to flatten bottom. Curve ends to form a crescent shape. Repeat with remaining wrappers and filling.

**4.** Line a steamer basket with six cabbage leaves. In batches, arrange dumplings 1 in. apart over cabbage; place basket in a large saucepan over 1 in. of water. Bring to a boil; cover and steam for 6-8 minutes or until cooked through. Discard cabbage. If desired, serve with chili sauce.

**FREEZE OPTION** *Cover and freeze cooled dumplings on waxed paper-lined baking sheets until firm. Transfer to a resealable plastic freezer bag. To use, microwave dumplings, covered, for 30-45 seconds or until heated through.*

**PER SERVING** *43 cal., 2 g fat (trace sat. fat), 17 mg chol., 79 mg sodium, 3 g carb., trace fiber, 3 g pro.*

HEALTHY STEAMED DUMPLINGS

## Iced Skinny Hazelnut Latte F S M

After trying a friend's iced hazelnut latte, I was hooked. This homemade version has less than 150 calories.

—**MARIE FIBELSTAD** STORM LAKE, IA

**START TO FINISH:** 10 MIN.
**MAKES:** 4 SERVINGS

- 3 cups fat-free milk, divided
- ¼ cup hazelnut Belgian cafe coffee drink mix
- 2 tablespoons refrigerated hazelnut coffee creamer
  Crushed ice

Place 1 cup milk in a large microwave-safe bowl. Microwave, uncovered, on high for 1-2 minutes or until hot. Stir in drink mix until dissolved. Add coffee creamer and remaining milk. Serve over ice.

**PER SERVING** *135 cal., 2 g fat (trace sat. fat), 4 mg chol., 125 mg sodium, 22 g carb., 0 fiber, 7 g pro.* **Diabetic Exchanges:** *1 starch, ½ fat-free milk.*

ICED SKINNY HAZELNUT LATTE

PORK SATAY

## Pork Satay C

Cilantro gives this delightful dish freshness, while the sesame oil and Thai chili sauce add layers of Asian flavors that pair perfectly with peanut butter.

—**TASTE OF HOME TEST KITCHEN**

**PREP:** 20 MIN. + MARINATING
**COOK:** 10 MIN.
**MAKES:** 20 SERVINGS

- ⅓ cup reduced-sodium soy sauce
- 2 green onions, sliced
- 3 tablespoons brown sugar
- 3 tablespoons minced fresh cilantro
- 3 tablespoons Thai chili sauce
- 2 tablespoons sesame oil
- 2 teaspoons minced garlic
- 1 pound pork tenderloin, cut into ¼-inch slices
- ⅓ cup creamy peanut butter
- 3 tablespoons hot water
- 2 teaspoons lime juice

**1.** In a small bowl, combine the first seven ingredients. Set aside ¼ cup for dipping sauce. Pour remaining sauce into a large resealable plastic bag; add the pork. Seal bag and turn to coat; refrigerate 30 minutes.

**2.** Drain and discard marinade. Thread pork slices onto 20 metal or soaked wooden skewers. Place skewers on a greased 15-in. x 10-in. x 1-in. baking pan. Broil 3-4 in. from heat 3-4 minutes on each side or until meat juices run clear.

**3.** Meanwhile, for sauce, combine peanut butter and water in a small bowl until smooth. Stir in lime juice and reserved soy sauce mixture. Serve with pork.

**PER SERVING** *73 cal., 4 g fat (1 g sat. fat), 13 mg chol., 172 mg sodium, 4 g carb., trace fiber, 6 g pro.* **Diabetic Exchanges:** *1 lean meat, ½ fat.*

## ? Did you know?

Ever wonder what all those drinks on the menu at your local cafe are? The Iced Skinny Hazelnut Latte at left is a fun take on the popular coffee shop order, but a real latte consists of one part espresso and two parts steamed milk. Add chocolate to that and you've got yourself a cafe mocha. A cafe Americano, on the other hand, is equal parts hot water and espresso, and a cafe au lait is one part coffee, one part steamed milk.

# Polenta Mushroom Appetizers F C

Everyday ingredients—you probably have most if not all in your kitchen—are used to create a fantastic but different appetizer.
—**META WEST** ABILENE, KS

**PREP:** 40 MIN. + COOLING • **BAKE:** 15 MIN.
**MAKES:** 32 APPETIZERS

- 2  **cups chicken broth**
- 2  **cups 2% milk**
- ½  **teaspoon salt**
- 1  **cup cornmeal**
- ¼  **cup grated Parmesan cheese**

**MUSHROOM TOPPING**

- ½  **pound thinly sliced fresh mushrooms**
- 3  **tablespoons olive oil**
- 1  **tablespoon butter**
- 6  **garlic cloves, minced**
- 1  **teaspoon minced fresh thyme or ¼ teaspoon dried thyme**
- ½  **teaspoon salt**
- ¼  **teaspoon pepper**
- 2  **tablespoons white wine or additional chicken broth**
- 1  **tablespoon lemon juice**
- ¼  **cup grated Parmesan cheese**

**1.** In a large heavy saucepan, bring broth, milk and salt to a boil. Reduce heat to a gentle boil; slowly whisk in cornmeal. Cook and stir with a wooden spoon for 15-20 minutes or until polenta is thickened and pulls away from sides of the pan. Stir in cheese.
**2.** Spread into a greased 11-in. x 7-in. baking dish. Cool to room temperature, about 30 minutes. Cut polenta into 16 pieces, then cut each diagonally in half to make 32 triangles; place on a greased baking sheet. Bake at 350° for 12-15 minutes or until light golden brown.
**3.** For mushrooms, saute mushrooms in oil and butter until tender. Add the garlic, thyme, salt and pepper; cook 1 minute longer. Add wine and lemon juice; cook and stir until liquid is almost absorbed.
**4.** Top each triangle with 1½ teaspoons mushrooms; sprinkle appetizers with cheese. Serve warm.
**PER SERVING** *47 cal., 2 g fat (1 g sat. fat), 3 mg chol., 165 mg sodium, 5 g carb., trace fiber, 2 g pro.*

POLENTA MUSHROOM APPETIZERS

## Garlic Pumpkin Seeds C M

What to do with all those pumpkin seeds scooped out of your soon-to-be jack-o'-lanterns? This yummy microwave recipe will have folks eating 'em up by the handfuls! Save a few for yourself before they're gone.
—**IOLA EGLE** BELLA VISTA, AR

**START TO FINISH:** 25 MIN. • **MAKES:** 2 CUPS (8 SERVINGS)

- 1 tablespoon canola oil
- ½ teaspoon celery salt
- ½ teaspoon garlic powder
- ½ teaspoon seasoned salt
- 2 cups fresh pumpkin seeds

**1.** In a small bowl, combine the oil, celery salt, garlic powder and seasoned salt. Add pumpkin seeds; toss to coat. Spread a quarter of the seeds in a single layer on a microwave-safe plate. Microwave, uncovered, on high for 1 minute; stir.
**2.** Microwave 2-3 minutes longer or until seeds are crunchy and lightly browned, stirring after each minute. Repeat with remaining pumpkin seeds. Serve warm, or cool before storing in an airtight container.
**NOTE** *This recipe was tested in a 1,100-watt microwave.*
**PER SERVING** *87 cal., 5 g fat (1 g sat. fat), 0 chol., 191 mg sodium, 9 g carb., 1 g fiber, 3 g pro.* **Diabetic Exchanges:** *1 fat, ½ starch.*

## Little Mexican Pizzas F M

These little pizzas are perfect for lunch, snacks or parties. Whole wheat English muffins offer more fiber than regular pizza crust.
—**LINDA EGGERS** ALBANY, CA

**START TO FINISH:** 25 MIN. • **MAKES:** 1 DOZEN

- 1 package (13 ounces) whole wheat English muffins, split
- ¾ cup fat-free refried beans
- ¾ cup salsa
- ⅓ cup sliced ripe olives
- 2 green onions, chopped
- 2 tablespoons canned chopped green chilies
- 1½ cups (6 ounces) shredded part-skim mozzarella cheese

**1.** Spread cut sides of muffins with refried beans; top with salsa, olives, onions, chilies and cheese.
**2.** Place on baking sheets; broil 4-6 in. from the heat for 2-3 minutes or until cheese is melted.
**PER SERVING** *129 cal., 3 g fat (2 g sat. fat), 8 mg chol., 368 mg sodium, 17 g carb., 2 g fiber, 7 g pro.* **Diabetic Exchanges:** *1 starch, 1 lean meat.*

## Lean Green Smoothie 🄵🅂🄼

Kids love the unusual color of this frosty and flavorful smoothie. It's fine-tuned to their liking with bananas, creamy yogurt and (shh!)—spinach.

—**MADISON MAYBERRY** AMES, IA

**START TO FINISH:** 10 MIN. • **MAKES:** 4 SERVINGS

 ¾ **cup fat-free milk**
 1½ **cups (12 ounces) fat-free vanilla yogurt**
 1 **cup ice cubes**
 1 **cup fresh spinach**
 1 **ripe medium banana**
 2 **tablespoons lemon juice**

In a blender, combine all ingredients; cover and process for 30 seconds or until smooth. Pour into chilled glasses; serve immediately.
**PER SERVING** *99 cal., trace fat (trace sat. fat), 4 mg chol., 24 mg sodium, 19 g carb., 1 g fiber, 5 g pro. **Diabetic Exchanges:** 1 fat-free milk, ½ fruit.*

## Tex-Mex Popcorn 🄵🄲🄼

Spicy Southwest seasoning makes this snackin' good popcorn ideal for any fiesta.

—**KATIE ROSE** PEWAUKEE, WI

**START TO FINISH:** 15 MIN. • **MAKES:** 4 QUARTS (16 SERVINGS)

 ½ **cup popcorn kernels**
 3 **tablespoons canola oil**
 ½ **teaspoon cumin seeds**
 **Refrigerated butter-flavored spray**
 ¼ **cup minced fresh cilantro**
 1 **teaspoon salt**
 1 **teaspoon chili powder**
 ½ **teaspoon garlic powder**
 ⅛ **teaspoon smoked paprika**

**1.** In a Dutch oven over medium heat, cook the popcorn kernels, oil and cumin seeds until oil begins to sizzle. Cover and shake for 2-3 minutes or until popcorn stops popping.
**2.** Transfer to a large bowl; spritz with butter-flavored spray. Add remaining ingredients and toss to coat. Continue spritzing and tossing until popcorn is coated.
**PER SERVING** *44 cal., 3 g fat (trace sat. fat), 0 chol., 150 mg sodium, 5 g carb., 1 g fiber, 1 g pro. **Diabetic Exchanges:** ½ starch, ½ fat.*

CANNELLINI BEAN HUMMUS

# Cannellini Bean Hummus S C M

My version of hummus features a tasty nuttiness from tahini—a peanut butter-like paste made from ground sesame seeds. The beans pack a lot of protein, so it's a healthy snack for kids.

—**MARINA CASTLE** CANYON COUNTRY, CA

**START TO FINISH:** 5 MIN.
**MAKES:** 1¼ CUPS (10 SERVINGS)

- 2 garlic cloves, peeled
- 1 can (15 ounces) white kidney or cannellini beans, rinsed and drained
- ¼ cup tahini
- 3 tablespoons lemon juice
- 1½ teaspoons ground cumin
- ¼ teaspoon salt
- ¼ teaspoon crushed red pepper flakes
- 2 tablespoons minced fresh parsley
  Pita breads, cut into wedges

1. Place garlic in a food processor; cover and process until minced. Add the beans, tahini, lemon juice, cumin, salt and pepper flakes; cover and process until smooth.
2. Transfer to a small bowl; stir in parsley. Refrigerate until serving. Serve with pita wedges.
**PER SERVING** *78 cal., 4 g fat (1 g sat. fat), 0 chol., 114 mg sodium, 8 g carb., 2 g fiber, 3 g pro.* **Diabetic Exchanges:** *1 fat, ½ starch.*

# Shrimp & Cucumber Rounds F S C

I always make these appetizers for our get-togethers. They're easy to prepare and a snappy addition to any party.

—**KELLY ALANIZ** EUREKA, CA

**START TO FINISH:** 25 MIN.
**MAKES:** 3 DOZEN

- ½ pound cooked shrimp, peeled, deveined and finely chopped
- ½ cup reduced-fat mayonnaise
- 2 green onions, thinly sliced
- 1 celery rib, finely chopped
- 1 teaspoon dill pickle relish
  Dash cayenne pepper
- 1 medium English cucumber, cut into ¼-inch slices

In a small bowl, combine the first six ingredients. Spoon onto cucumber slices. Serve immediately.
**PER SERVING** *20 cal., 1 g fat (trace sat. fat), 11 mg chol., 38 mg sodium, 1 g carb., trace fiber, 1 g pro.* **Diabetic Exchange:** *Free food.*

# Avocado Shrimp Salsa F S C

**START TO FINISH:** 25 MIN.
**MAKES:** 6 CUPS (24 SERVINGS)

- 1 pound cooked small shrimp, peeled, deveined and chopped
- 2 medium tomatoes, seeded and chopped
- 2 medium ripe avocados, peeled and chopped
- 1 cup minced fresh cilantro
- 1 medium sweet red pepper, chopped
- ¾ cup thinly sliced green onions
- ½ cup chopped seeded peeled cucumber
- 3 tablespoons lime juice
- 1 jalapeno pepper, seeded and chopped
- 1 teaspoon salt
- ¼ teaspoon pepper
  Tortilla chips

In a large bowl, combine the first 11 ingredients. Serve with tortilla chips.
**NOTE** *Wear disposable gloves when cutting hot peppers; the oils can burn skin. Avoid touching your face.*
**PER SERVING** *52 cal., 3 g fat (trace sat. fat), 33 mg chol., 133 mg sodium, 3 g carb., 1 g fiber, 5 g pro.* **Diabetic Exchanges:** *1 lean meat, ½ fat.*

"This is salsa Southern-style! It's delicious scooped up with tortilla chips or atop grilled chicken breasts or pork chops. You can even eat it as a chunky side dish to your favorite entree."
—**MARIA RIVIOTTA-SIMMONS** RIO RANCHO, NM

AVOCADO SHRIMP SALSA

# Garden Spring Rolls F S M

My family loves Asian food, and this recipe captures the health benefits of nutritious veggies without any loss of vitamins from cooking. Even kids will gobble up raw veggies in the form of a spring roll dipped into a sauce.

—**TERRI MERRITTS** NASHVILLE, TN

**START TO FINISH:** 30 MIN.
**MAKES:** 8 SERVINGS

- 3 **cups shredded cabbage or romaine lettuce**
- ¼ **cup Thai chili sauce**
- 8 **spring roll wrappers or rice papers (8 inches)**
- 1 **small sweet red pepper, thinly sliced**
- ½ **cup thinly sliced sweet onion**
- 1 **small ripe avocado, peeled and thinly sliced**
- 4 **fresh basil leaves, thinly sliced**
  **Additional Thai chili sauce, optional**

**1.** In a small bowl, combine cabbage and chili sauce; toss to coat. Fill a shallow bowl with water. Soak a spring roll wrapper in the water just until pliable, 30-45 seconds (depending on thickness of rice paper); remove, allowing excess water to drip off.

**2.** Place on a flat surface. Layer cabbage mixture, red pepper and onion down the center; top with avocado and basil. Fold both ends over filling; fold one long side over the filling, then roll up tightly. Place seam side down on a serving platter. Repeat with remaining ingredients.

**3.** Cover with damp paper towels until serving. Cut rolls diagonally in half; serve with additional Thai chili sauce if desired.

**PER SERVING** *97 cal., 3 g fat (trace sat. fat), 0 chol., 105 mg sodium, 16 g carb., 2 g fiber, 2 g pro.* ***Diabetic Exchanges:*** *1 starch, ½ fat.*

GARDEN SPRING ROLLS

## Virgin Hurricanes [F][S][C][M]

Revelers of all ages will take delight in this non-alcoholic version of the punch-like refresher often called "Mardi Gras in a glass."

**—TASTE OF HOME TEST KITCHEN**

**START TO FINISH:** 10 MIN.
**MAKES:** 9 SERVINGS (¾ CUP EACH)

- 2 **cups passion fruit juice**
- 1 **cup unsweetened pineapple juice**
- 1 **cup orange juice**
- ¾ **cup lemon juice**
- 2 **cups carbonated water**
  **Ice cubes**
  **Pineapple wedges and maraschino cherries**

Combine the juices in a pitcher. Just before serving, stir in carbonated water. Pour into hurricane or highball glasses filled with ice. Garnish with pineapple wedges and cherries.

**PER SERVING** *61 cal., trace fat (trace sat. fat), 0 chol., 6 mg sodium, 15 g carb., trace fiber, trace pro.* **Diabetic Exchange:** *1 fruit.*

GRILLED SHRIMP WITH SPICY-SWEET SAUCE

VIRGIN HURRICANES

## Grilled Shrimp with Spicy-Sweet Sauce [F][C]

Just the right amount of spice adds a zip to the plump and juicy shrimp in this five-ingredient appetizer.

**—SUSAN HARRISON** LAUREL, MD

**START TO FINISH:** 30 MIN.
**MAKES:** 15 SERVINGS (⅓ CUP SAUCE)

- 3 **tablespoons reduced-fat mayonnaise**
- 2 **tablespoons sweet chili sauce**
- 1 **green onion, thinly sliced**
- ¾ **teaspoon Sriracha Asian hot chili sauce or ½ teaspoon hot pepper sauce**
- 45 **uncooked large shrimp (about 1½ pounds), peeled and deveined**
- ¼ **teaspoon salt**
- ¼ **teaspoon pepper**

**1.** In a small bowl, mix mayonnaise, chili sauce, green onion and Sriracha. Sprinkle shrimp with salt and pepper. Thread three shrimp onto each of 15 metal or soaked wooden skewers.

**2.** Moisten a paper towel with cooking oil; using long-handled tongs, rub on grill rack to coat lightly. Grill shrimp, covered, over medium heat or broil 4 in. from heat 3-4 minutes on each side or until shrimp turn pink. Serve with sauce.

**PER SERVING** *56 cal., 2 g fat (trace sat. fat), 61 mg chol., 156 mg sodium, 2 g carb., trace fiber, 8 g pro.* **Diabetic Exchange:** *½ lean meat.*

## Moroccan Stuffed Mushrooms F S C M

Coriander and cumin update the familiar stuffed mushrooms. And the addition of couscous makes them filling and delicious.

**—RAYMONDE BOURGEOIS** SWASTIKA, ON

**PREP:** 45 MIN. • **BAKE:** 10 MIN.
**MAKES:** 2 DOZEN

- 24 **medium fresh mushrooms**
- ½ **cup chopped onion**
- ⅓ **cup finely shredded carrot**
- 1 **teaspoon canola oil**
- 1 **garlic clove, minced**
- ½ **teaspoon salt**
- ½ **teaspoon ground cumin**
- ¼ **teaspoon ground coriander**
- ¾ **cup vegetable broth**
- 2 **tablespoons dried currants**
- ½ **cup uncooked couscous**
- 2 **tablespoons minced fresh parsley**
- 2 **tablespoons minced fresh mint**

**1.** Remove stems from mushrooms and finely chop stems; set caps aside. In a large nonstick skillet, saute the onion, carrot and chopped stems in oil until crisp-tender.
**2.** Add the garlic, salt, cumin and coriander. Cook and stir for 1 minute. Add broth and currants; bring to a boil. Stir in couscous. Remove from the heat; cover and let stand for 5-10 minutes or until broth is absorbed. Fluff with a fork. Stir in parsley and mint. Stuff into mushroom caps.
**3.** Place on a foil-lined baking sheet. Bake at 400° for 10-15 minutes or until mushrooms are tender.
**PER SERVING** *25 cal., trace fat (trace sat. fat), 0 chol., 81 mg sodium, 5 g carb., 1 g fiber, 1 g pro.*

MOROCCAN STUFFED MUSHROOMS

TOMATO-SQUASH APPETIZER PIZZA

## Tomato-Squash Appetizer Pizza F C M

I was looking for quick weeknight meals that would use the fresh herbs from my windowsill garden when I decided to create this seasonal flatbread pizza. To my surprise, I discovered it also made a fabulous appetizer.

**—ANDREA TOVAR** NEW YORK, NY

**START TO FINISH:** 30 MIN.
**MAKES:** 24 PIECES

- 1 **loaf (1 pound) frozen bread dough, thawed**
- ¼ **teaspoon salt**
- 1 **tablespoon olive oil**
- 1½ **cups (6 ounces each) shredded part-skim mozzarella cheese**
- 1 **large yellow summer squash, sliced**
- 1 **large tomato, sliced**
- 4 **teaspoons shredded Parmesan cheese**
- ¼ **teaspoon pepper**
- 1 **teaspoon each minced fresh basil, oregano and chives**

**1.** Roll dough into a 14-in. x 8-in. rectangle. Transfer to a greased baking sheet. Prick dough thoroughly with a fork. Sprinkle with salt. Bake at 425° for 8-10 minutes or until lightly browned.
**2.** Brush crust with oil. Top with mozzarella cheese, squash, tomato, Parmesan cheese, pepper and herbs. Bake 5-10 minutes longer or until cheese is melted.
**PER SERVING** *81 cal., 3 g fat (1 g sat. fat), 4 mg chol., 169 mg sodium, 10 g carb., 1 g fiber, 4 g pro.* **Diabetic Exchanges:** *1 fat, ½ starch.*

CHILLED PEA SOUP SHOOTERS

## Chilled Pea Soup Shooters F C

Served in espresso cups, sake cups or shot glasses, these soup shooters look as good as they taste.

—TASTE OF HOME TEST KITCHEN

**PREP:** 20 MIN. + CHILLING
**MAKES:** 2 DOZEN

- 1 package (16 ounces) frozen peas, thawed
- 1 cup chicken broth
- ¼ cup minced fresh mint
- 1 tablespoon lime juice
- 1 teaspoon ground cumin
- ¼ teaspoon salt
- 1½ cups plain yogurt

**CURRY CRAB**

- 2 tablespoons minced fresh mint
- 4 teaspoons lime juice
- 4 teaspoons canola oil
- 2 teaspoons red curry paste
- ⅛ teaspoon salt
- 1 cup lump crabmeat, drained

**1.** Place the peas, broth, mint, lime juice, cumin and salt in a blender. Cover and process until smooth. Add yogurt; process until blended. Refrigerate for at least 1 hour.

**2.** Meanwhile, in a small bowl, whisk the mint, lime juice, oil, curry paste and salt. Add crabmeat; toss gently to coat. Chill until serving.

**3.** To serve, pour soup into shot glasses; garnish with crab mixture.

**PER SERVING** *40 cal., 1 g fat (trace sat. fat), 20 mg chol., 216 mg sodium, 4 g carb., 1 g fiber, 3 g pro.* **Diabetic Exchange:** *½ starch.*

## Rosemary Walnuts S C M

My Aunt Mary started making this recipe years ago, and each time we visited her she would have a batch ready for us. The use of cayenne adds an unexpected zing to the savory combo of rosemary and walnuts. When you need a good hostess gift, double the batch.

—RENEE CIANCIO NEW BERN, NC

**START TO FINISH:** 20 MIN
**MAKES:** 2 CUPS (8 SERVINGS)

- 2 cups walnut halves
  Cooking spray
- 2 teaspoons dried rosemary, crushed

- ½ teaspoon kosher salt
- ¼ to ½ teaspoon cayenne pepper

**1.** Place walnuts in a small bowl. Spritz with cooking spray. Add the seasonings; toss to coat. Place in a single layer on a baking sheet.

**2.** Bake at 350° for 10 minutes. Serve warm.

**PER SERVING** *166 cal., 17 g fat (2 g sat. fat), 0 chol., 118 mg sodium, 4 g carb., 2 g fiber, 4 g pro.* **Diabetic Exchange:** *3 fat.*

## Cucumber Fruit Salsa F S C M

We always have way more cucumbers and tomatoes coming out of our garden than we can handle. This is one of the many recipes I found to use them up in a delightful way. If you want to make this ahead, stir in the banana and peach right before serving.

—ANNA DAVIS HALF WAY, MO

**PREP:** 25 MIN. + CHILLING
**MAKES:** 24 SERVINGS (¼ CUP EACH)

- 1 large cucumber, finely chopped
- 2 medium green peppers, finely chopped
- 2 medium tomatoes, finely chopped
- 1 medium peach, peeled and finely chopped
- 1 small banana, finely chopped
- 1 small red onion, finely chopped
- 1 small navel orange, segmented and chopped
- 2 tablespoons lemon juice
- 1 tablespoon minced fresh cilantro
- 1 tablespoon minced fresh parsley
- 1 garlic clove, minced
- ¼ teaspoon salt
- ¼ teaspoon hot pepper sauce
- ⅛ teaspoon pepper

In a large bowl, combine all ingredients. Refrigerate at least 30 minutes to allow flavors to blend.

**PER SERVING** *15 cal., trace fat (trace sat. fat), 0 chol., 26 mg sodium, 4 g carb., 1 g fiber, trace pro.* **Diabetic Exchange:** *Free food.*

CUCUMBER FRUIT SALSA

## Salsa Verde F S C M

This salsa is fresh and creamy! It's great as a chip dip or as a topper for tacos and other Mexican dishes. You can adjust the spiciness as you want.

**—NANETTE HILTON** LAS VEGAS, NV

**PREP:** 15 MIN. + CHILLING • **MAKES:** 2½ CUPS (10 SERVINGS)

- 8 tomatillos, husks removed
- 1 medium ripe avocado, peeled and pitted
- 1 small onion, halved
- 1 jalapeno pepper, peeled and pitted
- ⅓ cup fresh cilantro leaves
- ½ teaspoon salt
    Tortilla chips

**1.** In a large saucepan, bring 4 cups water to a boil. Add tomatillos. Reduce heat; simmer, uncovered, for 5 minutes. Drain.

**2.** Place the avocado, onion, jalapeno, cilantro, salt and tomatillos in a food processor. Cover and process until blended. Refrigerate until chilled. Serve with chips.

**NOTE** *Wear disposable gloves when cutting hot peppers; the oils can burn skin. Avoid touching your face.*

**PER SERVING** *42 cal., 3 g fat (trace sat. fat), 0 chol., 121 mg sodium, 3 g carb., 2 g fiber, 1 g pro.* **Diabetic Exchange: 1 fat.**

## Raspberry-Lime Yogurt Dip for Fresh Fruit F S C M

We know that fresh, seasonal fruit is the essence of beauty itself. For an added touch when serving, a dipping sauce of sweet raspberries and tart lime juice makes a good thing even better.

**—CLARA COULSON MINNEY** WASHINGTON COURT HOUSE, OH

**PREP:** 15 MIN. • **MAKES:** 1¾ CUPS (7 SERVINGS)

- 1 cup fresh or frozen unsweetened raspberries, thawed and drained
- 1¼ cups reduced-fat plain Greek yogurt
- ⅓ cup packed brown sugar
- 1 tablespoon lime juice
- ½ teaspoon grated lime peel
    Assorted fresh fruit

Place raspberries in a blender; cover and process until smooth. Strain and discard seeds. In a large bowl, whisk the yogurt, brown sugar, lime juice, lime peel and raspberry puree until blended. Chill until serving. Serve with fruit.

**PER SERVING** *78 cal., 1 g fat (trace sat. fat), 2 mg chol., 23 mg sodium, 14 g carb., trace fiber, 4 g pro.* **Diabetic Exchange: 1 starch.**

## Minty Tea Punch F S C M

Forget sugary (and boring) sodas for your next potluck and treat your family and friends to a homemade punch. Serve in mason jars with striped paper straws and really "wow" the crowd.
—**CRYSTAL BRUNS** ILIFF, CO

**PREP:** 15 MIN. + CHILLING • **MAKES:** 12 SERVINGS (¾ CUP EACH)

- 8 **cups water, divided**
- 12 **mint sprigs**
- 4 **individual tea bags**
- 1 **cup orange juice**
- ¼ **cup lemon juice**
- ½ **cup sugar**
  **Ice cubes**
  **Orange and lemon slices, optional**

1. In a large saucepan, bring 3 cups water to a boil. Remove from heat; add mint and tea bags. Steep, covered, 3-5 minutes according to taste. Discard mint and tea bags.
2. Stir in orange and lemon juices, sugar and remaining water. Transfer to a pitcher; refrigerate until cold. Serve over ice; add orange and lemon slices if desired.
**PER SERVING** *43 cal., 0 fat (0 sat. fat), 0 chol., trace sodium, 11 g carb., trace fiber, trace pro.* **Diabetic Exchange:** *½ starch.*

## Roasted Grape Tomatoes F S C M

Everyone loves this mouthwatering starter that needs just a few ingredients. We appreciate that it's a fast, simple way to use up extra tomatoes from our garden.
—**LINDA GREEN** ARDMORE, OK

**START TO FINISH:** 25 MIN. • **MAKES:** 4 CUPS (16 SERVINGS)

- ½ **cup cider vinegar**
- ¼ **cup packed brown sugar**
- 2 **tablespoons canola oil**
- 4 **garlic cloves, minced**
- ½ **teaspoon salt**
- ½ **teaspoon pepper**
- 1 **pound grape tomatoes**
- 1 **tablespoon minced fresh parsley**
  **Assorted crackers and Gouda cheese slices**

1. In a large bowl, whisk the first six ingredients. Add tomatoes; toss to coat. Transfer to a greased 15-in. x 10-in. x 1-in. baking pan. Sprinkle with parsley.
2. Bake, uncovered, at 375° for 12-14 minutes or until softened, stirring occasionally. Serve with crackers and cheese.
**PER SERVING** *36 cal., 2 g fat (trace sat. fat), 0 chol., 78 mg sodium, 5 g carb., trace fiber, trace pro.*

## Spicy Peanuts C M

It's always nice to have something simple for guests to nibble on while mingling. These special peanuts are just the thing. Crushed red pepper flakes and chili powder turn up the heat on this classic party fare.

**—PHYLLIS SCHMALZ** KANSAS CITY, KS

**START TO FINISH:** 15 MIN.
**MAKES:** 4½ CUPS (18 SERVINGS)

- 3 tablespoons olive oil
- 1 tablespoon crushed red pepper flakes
- 1 can (12½ ounces) Spanish peanuts (skin on)
- 1 can (12 ounces) salted peanuts
- 4 garlic cloves, minced
- 1 teaspoon chili powder
- ¼ teaspoon salt

**1.** In a large heavy skillet, heat oil and pepper flakes over medium heat for 1 minute. Add peanuts and garlic. Cook and stir for 3-5 minutes or until lightly browned. Drain on paper towels.

**2.** Transfer to a large bowl. Sprinkle with chili powder and salt; toss to coat. Cool completely. Store in an airtight container.

**PER SERVING** *246 cal., 21 g fat (3 g sat. fat), 0 chol., 202 mg sodium, 8 g carb., 4 g fiber, 10 g pro.*

SPICY PEANUTS

"Upgrade your appetizer spread with this easy asparagus dip. If any pesto mayonnaise is left, it makes a flavorful sandwich spread." **—JANIE COLLE** HUTCHINSON, KS

ASPARAGUS WITH BASIL PESTO SAUCE

## Asparagus with Basil Pesto Sauce C M

**START TO FINISH:** 15 MIN.
**MAKES:** 12 SERVINGS

- ¾ cup reduced-fat mayonnaise
- 2 tablespoons prepared pesto
- 1 tablespoon grated Parmesan cheese
- 1 tablespoon minced fresh basil
- 1 teaspoon lemon juice
- 1 garlic clove, minced
- 1½ pounds fresh asparagus, trimmed

**1.** In a small bowl, mix the first six ingredients until blended; refrigerate until serving.

**2.** In a Dutch oven, bring 12 cups water to a boil. Add asparagus in batches; cook, uncovered, 2-3 minutes or until crisp-tender. Remove and immediately drop into ice water. Drain and pat dry. Serve with sauce.

**PER SERVING** *72 cal., 6 g fat (1 g sat. fat), 6 mg chol., 149 mg sodium, 3 g carb., 1 g fiber, 1 g pro.* **Diabetic Exchange:** *1½ fat.*

**BARBECUE GLAZED MEATBALLS**

# Barbecue Glazed Meatballs F S C

Stock your freezer with these meatballs and you'll always have an appetizer on hand for unexpected guests. We even like to eat them as a main dish with rice or noodles on busy weeknights.

**—ANNA FINLEY** COLUMBIA, MO

**PREP:** 30 MIN. • **BAKE:** 15 MIN.
**MAKES:** 8 DOZEN

- 2 cups quick-cooking oats
- 1 can (12 ounces) fat-free evaporated milk
- 1 small onion, finely chopped
- 2 teaspoons garlic powder
- 2 teaspoons chili powder
- 3 pounds lean ground beef (90% lean)

**SAUCE**
- 2½ cups ketchup
- 1 small onion, finely chopped
- ⅓ cup packed brown sugar
- 2 teaspoons liquid smoke, optional
- 1¼ teaspoons chili powder
- ¾ teaspoon garlic powder

**1.** Preheat oven to 400°. In a large bowl, combine oats, milk, onion and spices. Add beef; mix lightly but thoroughly. Shape into 1-in. balls.
**2.** Place meatballs on a greased rack in shallow baking pans. Bake 15-20 minutes or until cooked through. Drain on paper towels.
**3.** In a Dutch oven, combine sauce ingredients. Bring to a boil over medium heat, stirring constantly. Reduce heat; simmer, uncovered, 2-3 minutes or until slightly thickened. Add meatballs; heat through, stirring gently.

**FREEZE OPTION** *Freeze cooled meatball mixture in freezer containers. To use, partially thaw in refrigerator overnight. Microwave, covered, on high in a microwave-safe dish until heated through, gently stirring and adding a little water if necessary.*

**PER SERVING** *42 cal., 1 g fat (trace sat. fat), 9 mg chol., 93 mg sodium, 4 g carb., trace fiber, 3 g pro.*

33

34

40

# Salads & Dressings

66 For even more flavor, mix field greens and crisp, crumbled bacon into this appealing veggie salad. Or whisk a tablespoon of honey into the dressing. Guests will love it! 99

**—LAURA MCALLISTER** MORGANTON, NC
*about her recipe, Roasted Vegetable Salad, on page 36*

# Rice Noodle Salad ᴹ

This salad is easy, sweet, spicy, nutty and light. Many friends request this for get-togethers, and our family enjoys it at least once a month for dinner. To make it a main dish, I add marinated and grilled teriyaki chicken.

**—KRISTA FRANK** RHODODENDRON, OR

**START TO FINISH:** 25 MIN. • **MAKES:** 8-10 SERVINGS

- 1 **package (8.8 ounces) thin rice noodles**
- 2 **cups fresh spinach, cut into strips**
- 1 **large carrot, shredded**
- ½ **cup pineapple tidbits**
- ¼ **cup minced fresh cilantro**
- 1 **green onion, chopped**

**SESAME PEANUT DRESSING**
- ¼ **cup unsalted peanuts**
- ¼ **cup water**
- ¼ **cup lime juice**
- 2 **tablespoons soy sauce**
- 1 **tablespoon brown sugar**
- 1 **tablespoon canola oil**
- 1 **teaspoon sesame oil**
- ½ **teaspoon ground ginger**
- ¼ **teaspoon crushed red pepper flakes**

**1.** Cook noodles according to package directions. Meanwhile, in a large salad bowl, combine the spinach, carrot, pineapple, cilantro and onion.

**2.** In a blender, combine the dressing ingredients; cover and process until blended. Drain noodles and rinse in cold water; drain well. Add to spinach mixture. Drizzle with dressing and toss to coat.

**PER SERVING** *149 cal., 4 g fat (1 g sat. fat), 0 chol., 238 mg sodium, 26 g carb., 1 g fiber, 2 g pro.* **Diabetic Exchanges:** *1½ starch, 1 fat.*

MINTY WATERMELON SALAD

RICE NOODLE SALAD

# Minty Watermelon Salad ꜰ ꜱ ᴄ ᴹ

My 4-year-old twin grandchildren love to cook and create in the kitchen with me. Last summer, the three of us were experimenting with watermelon and cheese and that's where this recipe began. It's great for neighborhood gatherings, picnics or as a healthy snack on a hot summer day.

**—GWENDOLYN VETTER** ROGERS, MN

**PREP:** 20 MIN. + CHILLING • **MAKES:** 8 SERVINGS

- 6 **cups cubed watermelon**
- ½ **cup thinly sliced fennel bulb**
- ⅓ **cup crumbled feta cheese**
- 2 **tablespoons minced fresh mint**
- 2 **tablespoons thinly sliced pickled onions**
- ½ **teaspoon pepper**

In a large bowl, combine all ingredients. Refrigerate, covered, at least 1 hour.

**PER SERVING** *45 cal., 1 g fat (1 g sat. fat), 2 mg chol., 65 mg sodium, 11 g carb., 1 g fiber, 1 g pro.* **Diabetic Exchange:** *½ fruit.*

## Strawberry Vinaigrette F S C M

Fruity and tangy, this sweet salad dressing is just as delicious tossed with mixed greens as it is drizzled over chicken salad.
—**CAROLYN MCMUNN** SAN ANGELO, TX

**START TO FINISH:** 10 MIN. • **MAKES:** 2½ CUPS

- 1 **package (16 ounces) frozen unsweetened strawberries, thawed**
- 6 **tablespoons lemon juice**
- ¼ **cup sugar**
- 2 **tablespoons cider vinegar**
- 2 **tablespoons olive oil**
- ⅛ **teaspoon poppy seeds**

1. Place the strawberries in a blender; cover and process until pureed. Add lemon juice and sugar; cover and process until blended. While processing, gradually add vinegar and oil in a steady stream; process until thickened. Stir in poppy seeds.

2. Transfer to a bowl or jar; cover and store in the refrigerator.

**PER SERVING** *31 cal., 1 g fat (trace sat. fat), 0 chol., 1 mg sodium, 5 g carb., trace fiber, trace pro.* **Diabetic Exchange:** *½ starch.*

DILL GARDEN SALAD

STRAWBERRY VINAIGRETTE

## Dill Garden Salad C M

I love to cut up whatever fresh vegetables I have on hand and mix them with this tasty dressing and fresh dill. This salad shows up on our table several times a week during the summer.
—**BETHANY MARTIN** LEWISBURG, PA

**START TO FINISH:** 15 MIN. • **MAKES:** 6 SERVINGS

- 3 **cups chopped English cucumbers**
- 1 **large tomato, seeded and cut into ½-inch pieces**
- 1 **small sweet red pepper, chopped**
- 2 **tablespoons chopped sweet onion**
- 3 **tablespoons reduced-fat mayonnaise**
- 4 **teaspoons olive oil**
- 2 **teaspoons rice vinegar**
- 2 **teaspoons sugar**
- ½ **teaspoon salt**
- ¼ **teaspoon garlic powder**
- ¼ **teaspoon pepper**
- 2½ **teaspoons snipped fresh dill**

In a large bowl, combine cucumbers, tomato, red pepper and onion. In a small bowl, whisk mayonnaise, oil, vinegar, sugar, salt, garlic powder and pepper until blended. Stir in dill. Spoon dressing over salad; toss to coat.

**PER SERVING** *75 cal., 6 g fat (1 g sat. fat), 3 mg chol., 260 mg sodium, 6 g carb., 1 g fiber, 1 g pro.* **Diabetic Exchanges:** *1 vegetable, 1 fat.*

CONFETTI JICAMA SALAD

## Confetti Jicama Salad C M

I love jicama dipped in citrus and sprinkled with salt and jalapenos. So when I needed to bring a salad to a Fourth of July picnic, I decided to use this crunchy vegetable to make a spicy new dish.

—JAN LYSAK-RUIZ YUCAIPA, CA

**PREP:** 35 MIN. + CHILLING
**MAKES:** 6 SERVINGS

- ½ medium jicama, peeled and julienned
- 1⅓ cups julienned seedless cucumber
- 1 each small sweet red, orange and yellow peppers, julienned
- ½ cup thinly sliced red onion
- 3 green onions, chopped

DRESSING

- ⅓ cup minced fresh cilantro
- 1 jalapeno pepper, seeded and finely chopped
- 2 tablespoons lime juice
- 2 tablespoons orange juice concentrate
- 2 tablespoons olive oil
- 1 garlic clove, minced
- 1 teaspoon sugar
- ½ teaspoon salt
- ¼ teaspoon pepper
- ⅛ teaspoon cayenne pepper

1. In a large bowl, combine the jicama, cucumber, peppers and onions.
2. In a small bowl, whisk the cilantro, jalapeno, lime juice, juice concentrate, oil, garlic and seasonings. Pour over salad; toss to coat. Cover and refrigerate for at least 1 hour. Stir before serving.
**NOTE** *Wear disposable gloves when cutting hot peppers; the oils can burn skin. Avoid touching your face.*
**PER SERVING** *96 cal., 5 g fat (1 g sat. fat), 0 chol., 203 mg sodium, 13 g carb., 4 g fiber, 1 g pro.* **Diabetic Exchanges:** *2 vegetable, 1 fat.*

 **Did you know?**

Also known as a Mexican yam, jicama is a member of the potato family. It can be peeled and eaten raw or chopped up for salads. While it tastes similar to an apple, it does not turn brown after being cut.

## Mom's Gingered Apple Salad M

**START TO FINISH:** 15 MIN.
**MAKES:** 6 SERVINGS

- 3 medium apples, chopped
- 1 can (8 ounces) water chestnuts, drained and finely chopped
- 2 celery ribs, finely chopped
- ½ cup dried cranberries
- 3 tablespoons crystallized ginger, finely chopped
- ½ cup vanilla yogurt
- ¼ cup reduced-fat mayonnaise
- 2 tablespoons sugar
- ¼ to ½ teaspoon ground ginger
- ⅛ teaspoon salt
- ¼ cup chopped pecans, toasted

1. In a large bowl, combine the first five ingredients. Combine the yogurt, mayonnaise, sugar, ginger and salt; pour over apple mixture and toss to coat. Chill until serving.
2. Just before serving, sprinkle with pecans.
**PER SERVING** *213 cal., 7 g fat (1 g sat. fat), 5 mg chol., 161 mg sodium, 38 g carb., 4 g fiber, 2 g pro.*

"Here's a refreshing twist on the classic Waldorf salad. Sprinkled with ginger, dried cranberries and water chestnuts, this combo is quick and delicious."
—REBEKAH RADEWAHN WAUWATOSA, WI

MOM'S GINGERED APPLE SALAD

SHRIMP VEGGIE SALAD

## Shrimp Veggie Salad 🄲

My family loves to have potluck barbecues during the summer. With several backyard gardens in the family, you can be sure one of us will bring a variation (with added hot sauce) of this salad.

—**KAREN GOODNATURE** LOMPOC, CA

**START TO FINISH:** 20 MIN.
**MAKES:** 12 SERVINGS (1 CUP EACH)

- 1 pound peeled and deveined cooked medium shrimp
- 3 medium tomatoes, seeded and cut into ½-inch pieces
- 2 medium cucumbers, quartered and sliced
- 1 small red onion, chopped
- ½ cup chopped fresh cilantro
- 4 green onions, chopped
- 2 jalapeno peppers, seeded and minced
- 2 tablespoons lemon juice
- ½ teaspoon salt
- 2 medium ripe avocados, peeled and cubed

Combine the first nine ingredients in a large bowl. Gently stir in avocado. Serve immediately.
**PER SERVING** *108 cal., 5 g fat (1 g sat. fat), 57 mg chol., 160 mg sodium, 7 g carb., 3 g fiber, 9 g pro.* **Diabetic Exchanges:** *1 lean meat, 1 vegetable, 1 fat.*

## Tangerine Tabbouleh 🄼

Citrus really comes through in this interesting mix of fruit, nuts and chickpeas. It makes a hearty and flavorful side dish that's perfect with grilled chicken, pork or beef.

—**VIVIAN LEVINE** SUMMERFIELD, FL

**PREP:** 35 MIN. + CHILLING
**MAKES:** 8 SERVINGS

- 1 cup bulgur
- 1 cup boiling water
- 1 can (15 ounces) garbanzo beans or chickpeas, rinsed and drained
- 2 tangerines, peeled, sectioned and chopped
- ⅔ cup chopped dates
- ½ cup pistachios, coarsely chopped
- ⅓ cup dried cranberries
- ½ cup tangerine juice
- 2 tablespoons olive oil
- 1 teaspoon grated tangerine peel
- ¼ teaspoon ground ginger
- ⅛ teaspoon salt

1. Place bulgur in a large bowl. Stir in water. Cover and let stand for 30 minutes or until most of the liquid is absorbed. Drain well.

2. Stir in the garbanzo beans, tangerines, dates, pistachios and cranberries. In a small bowl, combine the tangerine juice, oil, tangerine peel, ginger and salt. Pour over bulgur mixture and toss to coat. Cover and refrigerate for at least 1 hour. Stir before serving.
**PER SERVING** *261 cal., 8 g fat (1 g sat. fat), 0 chol., 142 mg sodium, 44 g carb., 8 g fiber, 7 g pro.*

TANGERINE TABBOULEH

BALSAMIC HERB VINAIGRETTE

## Balsamic Herb Vinaigrette S C M

The best part about making your own salad dressing is knowing exactly what you're putting on your greens. Most commercial versions have ingredients many people can't even pronounce.

—EDGAR WRIGHT SILVER SPRING, MD

**START TO FINISH:** 25 MIN.
**MAKES:** 2¼ CUPS

- ½ cup balsamic vinegar
- ½ cup honey
- 1 tablespoon minced fresh basil
- 1½ teaspoons onion powder
- 1½ teaspoons snipped fresh dill
- 1½ teaspoons minced fresh oregano
- 1½ teaspoons minced fresh thyme
- 1 garlic clove, peeled
- ½ teaspoon white pepper
- ½ teaspoon prepared mustard
- 1½ cups canola oil

In a blender, combine the first 10 ingredients; cover and process until blended. While processing, gradually add the oil in a steady stream. Cover and refrigerate until serving.
**PER SERVING** 2 tablespoons equals 199 cal., 19 g fat (1 g sat. fat), 0 chol., 4 mg sodium, 9 g carb., trace fiber, trace pro.

## Curry-Cranberry Spinach Salad M

I sometimes switch up this salad by using dried apricots or pineapple and arugula or other sturdy greens.

—TRISHA KRUSE EAGLE, ID

**START TO FINISH:** 10 MIN.
**MAKES:** 5 SERVINGS

- 5 cups fresh baby spinach
- ¼ cup pine nuts
- 3 tablespoons dried cranberries
- 1 tablespoon sesame seeds
- ¼ cup packed brown sugar
- ¼ cup rice vinegar
- ¼ cup olive oil
- 1 tablespoon soy sauce
- 2 teaspoons dried minced onion
- ½ teaspoon curry powder
- ¼ teaspoon salt

In a large salad bowl, combine the spinach, pine nuts, cranberries and sesame seeds. In a small bowl, whisk the remaining ingredients. Drizzle over salad and toss to coat.
**PER SERVING** 214 cal., 15 g fat (2 g sat. fat), 0 chol., 332 mg sodium, 19 g carb., 1 g fiber, 3 g pro.

## Summer Garden Couscous Salad

This makes the most of summer's bounty. I used to prepare it with a mayonnaise dressing, but lightened it with lemon vinaigrette. It's even better.

—PRISCILLA YEE CONCORD, CA

**START TO FINISH:** 30 MIN.
**MAKES:** 9 SERVINGS

- 3 medium ears sweet corn, husks removed
- 1 cup reduced-sodium chicken broth or vegetable broth
- 1 cup uncooked couscous
- 1 medium cucumber, halved and sliced
- 1½ cups cherry tomatoes, halved
- ½ cup crumbled feta cheese
- ¼ cup chopped red onion
- 3 tablespoons minced fresh parsley
- 3 tablespoons olive oil
- 3 tablespoons lemon juice
- 1 teaspoon dried oregano
- ¾ teaspoon ground cumin
- ½ teaspoon salt
- ½ teaspoon pepper

1. Place corn in a Dutch oven; cover with water. Bring to a boil; cover and cook for 6-9 minutes or until tender. Meanwhile, in a small saucepan, bring broth to a boil. Stir in couscous. Remove from the heat; cover and let stand for 5-10 minutes or until water is absorbed. Fluff with a fork and set aside to cool slightly.

2. In a large bowl, combine the cucumber, tomatoes, cheese, onion and parsley. Drain corn and immediately place in ice water. Drain and pat dry; cut the kernels from the cobs. Add to cucumber mixture. Stir in couscous.

3. In a small bowl, whisk the oil, lemon juice and seasonings. Pour over couscous mixture; toss to coat. Serve immediately or cover and refrigerate until chilled.
**PER SERVING** 171 cal., 6 g fat (1 g sat. fat), 3 mg chol., 265 mg sodium, 25 g carb., 3 g fiber, 6 g pro. **Diabetic Exchanges:** 1½ starch, 1 fat.

SUMMER GARDEN COUSCOUS SALAD

ROASTED VEGETABLE SALAD

## Roasted Vegetable Salad M

For even more flavor, mix field greens and crisp, crumbled bacon into this appealing veggie salad. Or whisk a tablespoon of honey into the dressing. Guests will love it!

**—LAURA MCALLISTER** MORGANTON, NC

**PREP:** 30 MIN. • **BAKE:** 20 MIN.
**MAKES:** 12 SERVINGS (⅔ CUP EACH)

- 1 **pound small red potatoes, quartered**
- 2 **medium ears sweet corn, halved**
- ½ **pound baby portobello mushrooms, halved**
- 1 **medium sweet red pepper, cut into strips**
- 2 **medium leeks (white portion only), cut into 2-inch lengths**
- ¼ **cup plus 2 tablespoons olive oil, divided**
- ½ **teaspoon salt**
- ¼ **teaspoon pepper**
- ½ **pound fresh asparagus, cut into 2-inch lengths**
- 2 **garlic cloves, minced**
- ½ **teaspoon crushed red pepper flakes**
- 2 **cups cubed French bread**
- 10 **cherry tomatoes, halved**
- 1 **cup (4 ounces) crumbled feta cheese**
- 1 **cup thinly sliced fresh basil leaves**

**DRESSING**
- ⅓ **cup olive oil**
- ¼ **cup red wine vinegar**

**1.** In a large bowl, combine the first five ingredients. Drizzle with ¼ cup oil; sprinkle with salt and pepper and toss to coat. Place in two greased 15-in. x 10-in. x 1-in. baking pans. Bake at 425° for 20-25 minutes or until potatoes are tender.

**2.** Meanwhile, in a large skillet, saute asparagus in remaining oil until tender. Add garlic and pepper flakes; cook 1 minute longer.

**3.** Cut corn from cobs; place in a large bowl. Stir in the bread, tomatoes, cheese, basil, asparagus and roasted vegetable mixture. Combine oil and vinegar; drizzle over mixture and toss to coat.

**PER SERVING** *210 cal., 14 g fat (3 g sat. fat), 5 mg chol., 239 mg sodium, 17 g carb., 3 g fiber, 5 g pro.*

## Add Some Crunch

Make homemade croutons by cutting leftover French bread into cubes. Place them in a bowl and drizzle them with 1 tablespoon of melted butter and 1 tablespoon of olive oil (per 8-ounce loaf). Add seasonings such as ½ teaspoon of garlic salt. Place cubes in a single layer on an ungreased pan and bake at 400° for about 15-20 minutes or until golden brown. Cool and store in an airtight container.

## Picnic Sweet Potato Salad C

**START TO FINISH:** 30 MIN. • **MAKES:** 13 SERVINGS (¾ CUP EACH)

- 4 medium sweet potatoes, peeled and cubed
- 3 medium apples, chopped
- 6 bacon strips, cooked and crumbled
- ¼ cup chopped onion
- 3 tablespoons minced fresh parsley
- ½ teaspoon salt
- ¼ teaspoon pepper
- ⅔ cup canola oil
- 2 tablespoons red wine vinegar

**1.** Place sweet potatoes in a Dutch oven and cover with water. Bring to a boil. Reduce heat; cover and cook for 10-15 minutes or just until tender. Drain.

**2.** Transfer to a large bowl; cool to room temperature. Add the apples, bacon, onion, parsley, salt and pepper to the potatoes. In a small bowl, whisk oil and vinegar. Pour over salad; toss gently to coat. Chill until serving.

**PER SERVING** *169 cal., 12 g fat (2 g sat. fat), 3 mg chol., 163 mg sodium, 13 g carb., 2 g fiber, 2 g pro.* **Diabetic Exchanges:** *2 fat, 1 starch.*

"A homemade vinaigrette coats this colorful salad chock-full of sweet potato cubes. It's ideal for warm-weather picnics and patio parties, but my family loves it year round!" **—MARY MARLOWE LEVERETTE** COLUMBIA, SC

PICNIC SWEET POTATO SALAD

EASY GARDEN TOMATOES

## Easy Garden Tomatoes C M

Simple as it is, this is one of my favorite dishes, and my family loves it. I made three batches the first time, and a few stray olive slices were the only things left on the platter.
**—HEATHER AHRENS** COLUMBUS, OH

**START TO FINISH:** 15 MIN. • **MAKES:** 6 SERVINGS

- 3 large tomatoes, thinly sliced
- 1 large red onion, thinly sliced
- ⅓ cup olive oil
- ¼ cup red wine vinegar
- 2 garlic cloves, minced
- 1 tablespoon minced fresh basil or 1 teaspoon dried basil
- 1½ teaspoons minced fresh oregano or ½ teaspoon dried oregano
- ¾ cup crumbled feta cheese
- 1 can (2¼ ounces) sliced ripe olives, drained

Arrange tomatoes and onion on a serving platter. In a small bowl, whisk the oil, vinegar, garlic, basil and oregano; drizzle over salad. Top with cheese and olives. Chill until serving.

**PER SERVING** *184 cal., 16 g fat (3 g sat. fat), 8 mg chol., 234 mg sodium, 8 g carb., 2 g fiber, 4 g pro.*

## Mixed Greens with Creamy Honey Mustard Dressing F C M

The dressing for this salad is one of my favorites. It's a good balance of ingredients and coats the greens well.
—**PHYLLIS SCHMALZ** KANSAS CITY, KS

**START TO FINISH:** 10 MIN. • **MAKES:** 2 SERVINGS (¾ CUP DRESSING)

- 4 **cups spring mix salad greens**
- ¼ **cup julienned carrot**
- ¼ **cup grape tomatoes**
- ½ **cup reduced-fat plain yogurt**
- 2 **tablespoons white wine vinegar**
- 2 **tablespoons Dijon mustard**
- 2 **tablespoons honey**

In a serving bowl, combine the salad greens, carrot and tomatoes. In a small bowl, whisk the remaining ingredients. Serve with salad. Refrigerate leftover dressing.
**PER SERVING** *69 cal., 1 g fat (trace sat. fat), 1 mg chol., 175 mg sodium, 14 g carb., 3 g fiber, 3 g pro.* **Diabetic Exchanges:** *1 vegetable, ½ starch.*

## Romaine and Walnut Salad S C M

A super-quick dressing jazzes up this easy salad of romaine, tomato, mushrooms and walnuts.
—**BEVERLY NICHOLS** MIDLAND, TX

**START TO FINISH:** 10 MIN. • **MAKES:** 3 SERVINGS

- 2 **cups hearts of romaine salad mix**
- 1 **plum tomato, sliced**
- ¼ **cup sliced fresh mushrooms**
- 3 **tablespoons chopped walnuts**
- 2 **tablespoons red wine vinegar**
- 4½ **teaspoons canola oil**
- 1 **tablespoon honey**
- ⅛ **teaspoon ground mustard**

In a small bowl, combine the romaine, tomato, mushrooms and walnuts. In another bowl, whisk the remaining ingredients. Pour over salad; toss to coat.
**PER SERVING** *146 cal., 12 g fat (1 g sat. fat), 0 chol., 5 mg sodium, 10 g carb., 2 g fiber, 2 g pro.* **Diabetic Exchanges:** *2 fat, ½ starch.*

## Maple Salad Dressing C M

Sweet and tangy like French dressing but with a little kick from horseradish, this is something you'll want to drizzle on everything from pork, chicken and fish to salad and roasted vegetables.
—**JANET LAWTON** ST. ALBANS, VT

**START TO FINISH:** 10 MIN. • **MAKES:** 1¼ CUPS

- 7 **tablespoons maple syrup**
- ¼ **cup cider vinegar**
- ¼ **cup ketchup**
- 3 **tablespoons plus 1 teaspoon canola oil**
- 2 **tablespoons water**
- ½ **teaspoon prepared horseradish**
- ¼ **teaspoon salt**
- ⅛ **teaspoon celery salt**

In a small bowl, whisk all the ingredients. Cover and refrigerate until serving.
**PER SERVING** *2 tablespoons equals 85 cal., 5 g fat (trace sat. fat), 0 chol., 156 mg sodium, 11 g carb., trace fiber, trace pro.* **Diabetic Exchanges:** *1 starch, 1 fat.*

## No-Fuss Avocado Onion Salad S C M

My mother could take a simple salad and make it incredibly delicious, like this one, which is a favorite of mine.
—**MARINA CASTLE** CANYON COUNTRY, CA

**START TO FINISH:** 20 MIN. • **MAKES:** 12 SERVINGS

- 3 **medium ripe avocados, peeled and thinly sliced**
- 1 **large sweet onion, halved and thinly sliced**
- ⅓ **cup olive oil**
- ¼ **cup stone-ground mustard**
- 2 **tablespoons lemon juice**
- 1 **tablespoon honey**

Arrange avocados and onion on a large platter. In a small bowl, whisk the remaining ingredients; drizzle over vegetables.
**PER SERVING** *147 cal., 13 g fat (2 g sat. fat), 0 chol., 108 mg sodium, 8 g carb., 3 g fiber, 1 g pro.* **Diabetic Exchanges:** *2 fat, ½ starch.*

## Layered Garden Bean Salad F C M

For easy entertaining, cover and refrigerate this salad a few hours before guests arrive so you don't have to bother with last-minute assembly. Turn it into a light lunch by adding sliced rotisserie chicken, salmon or tuna.

—MELISSA WHARTON CINCINNATI, OH

**START TO FINISH:** 20 MIN.
**MAKES:** 16 SERVINGS (1 CUP EACH)

- 2 **cups shredded romaine**
- 2 **cans (15 ounces each) black beans, rinsed and drained**
- 2 **tablespoons chopped red onion**
- 2 **cups frozen corn, thawed**
- 2 **English cucumbers, chopped**
- 4 **medium tomatoes, chopped**
- ½ **cup reduced-fat ranch salad dressing**
- 1 **teaspoon cumin seeds**

In a 4-qt. glass bowl, layer the first six ingredients. In a small bowl, mix salad dressing and cumin seeds; drizzle over salad.

**PER SERVING** *93 cal., 2 g fat (trace sat. fat), 2 mg chol., 180 mg sodium, 15 g carb., 4 g fiber, 4 g pro.* **Diabetic Exchange:** *1 starch.*

SPINACH PENNE SALAD

LAYERED GARDEN BEAN SALAD

## Spinach Penne Salad M

This beautiful salad will shine as is, or you can double the vinaigrette and use half to marinate and grill chicken breasts to serve on top.

—BENICE SILVER CARMEL, IN

**START TO FINISH:** 30 MIN.
**MAKES:** 10 SERVINGS

- 1 **package (16 ounces) uncooked whole wheat penne pasta**

**VINAIGRETTE**
- ½ **cup olive oil**
- ½ **cup white wine vinegar**
- ⅓ **cup grated Parmesan cheese**
- 1 **tablespoon Dijon mustard**
- 2 **garlic cloves, minced**
- 1 **teaspoon dried oregano**
- ¼ **teaspoon salt**
- ¼ **teaspoon pepper**

**SALAD**
- 1 **package (6 ounces) fresh baby spinach**
- 3 **medium tomatoes, seeded and chopped**
- ¾ **cup (6 ounces) crumbled feta cheese**
- 4 **green onions, thinly sliced**
- ½ **cup sliced ripe or Greek olives**

1. In a Dutch oven, cook pasta according to package directions. Drain and rinse in cold water; drain again.
2. Meanwhile, in a small bowl, whisk the vinaigrette ingredients. In a large bowl, combine the pasta, spinach, tomatoes, feta cheese, onions and olives. Add vinaigrette; toss to coat. Serve immediately.

**PER SERVING** *327 cal., 15 g fat (3 g sat. fat), 7 mg chol., 233 mg sodium, 38 g carb., 7 g fiber, 11 g pro.*

### ? Did you know?

Spinach is an excellent source of many vitamins and minerals, including folic acid—a B vitamin that our bodies use to make new cells.

## Mimi's Lentil Medley

I made this one summer evening by putting together what I had on hand. It turned out so well, I brought it to our family picnic.

—MARY ANN HAZEN ROCHESTER HILLS, MI

**PREP:** 40 MIN. • **MAKES:** 8 SERVINGS

- 1 cup dried lentils, rinsed
- 2 cups water
- 2 cups sliced fresh mushrooms
- 1 medium cucumber, cubed
- 1 medium zucchini, cubed
- 1 small red onion, chopped
- ½ cup chopped sun-dried tomatoes (not packed in oil)
- ½ cup rice vinegar
- ¼ cup minced fresh mint
- 3 tablespoons olive oil
- 2 teaspoons honey
- 1 teaspoon dried basil
- 1 teaspoon dried oregano
- 4 cups fresh baby spinach, chopped
- 1 cup (4 ounces) crumbled feta cheese
- 4 bacon strips, cooked and crumbled

**1.** In a small saucepan, bring lentils and water to a boil. Reduce heat; cover and simmer for 20-25 minutes or until tender. Drain and rinse in cold water.

**2.** Transfer to a large bowl. Add the mushrooms, cucumber, zucchini, onion and tomatoes. In a small bowl, whisk the vinegar, mint, oil, honey, basil and oregano. Drizzle over lentil mixture; toss to coat. Add the spinach, cheese and bacon; toss to combine.

**PER SERVING** *226 cal., 9 g fat (3 g sat. fat), 11 mg chol., 299 mg sodium, 25 g carb., 10 g fiber, 12 g pro.* **Diabetic Exchanges:** *2 fat, 1 starch, 1 vegetable.*

MIMI'S LENTIL MEDLEY

"This is the kind of salad you can keep in the fridge for a couple days and it gets even better. I just add the sunflower seeds before serving to keep the crunch."

—TRISHA KRUSE EAGLE, ID

COLESLAW WITH POPPY SEED DRESSING

## Coleslaw with Poppy Seed Dressing F S C M

**PREP:** 20 MIN. + CHILLING
**MAKES:** 12 SERVINGS

- 4½ cups shredded cabbage
- 6 large carrots, shedded
- 8 green onions, chopped
- 1 cup fat-free poppy seed salad dressing
- ⅓ cup sunflower kernels

In a large bowl, combine cabbage, carrots and green onions. Drizzle with dressing; toss to coat. Refrigerate, covered, at least 1 hour. Sprinkle with sunflower kernels.

**PER SERVING** *83 cal., 2 g fat (trace sat. fat), 3 mg chol., 102 mg sodium, 14 g carb., 2 g fiber, 2 g pro.* **Diabetic Exchanges:** *1 vegetable, ½ starch, ½ fat.*

47

52

55

# Soups & Sandwiches

❝This soup recipe is a family favorite handed down from my great-grandmother. I've tweaked it a bit to add some of my current favorites like celery root. Serve it with a side salad and some artisan bread for a wonderful, hearty family dinner.❞

**—TERREL PORTER-SMITH** LOS OSOS, CA
*about her recipe, Turkey Sausage Bean Soup, on page 54*

## Seafood Cioppino 🄵🄲

If you're looking for a great seafood recipe to create in your slow cooker, this classic fish stew is just the ticket. It's full to the brim with clams, crab, fish and shrimp, and is fancy enough to be an elegant meal.
—LISA MORIARTY WILTON, NH

**PREP:** 20 MIN. • **COOK:** 4½ HOURS
**MAKES:** 8 SERVINGS (2½ QUARTS)

- 1 can (28 ounces) diced tomatoes, undrained
- 2 medium onions, chopped
- 3 celery ribs, chopped
- 1 bottle (8 ounces) clam juice
- 1 can (6 ounces) tomato paste
- ½ cup white wine or vegetable broth
- 5 garlic cloves, minced
- 1 tablespoon red wine vinegar
- 1 tablespoon olive oil
- 1 to 2 teaspoons Italian seasoning
- ½ teaspoon sugar
- 1 bay leaf
- 1 pound haddock fillets, cut into 1-inch pieces
- 1 pound uncooked small shrimp, peeled and deveined
- 1 can (6 ounces) lump crabmeat, drained
- 1 can (6 ounces) chopped clams
- 2 tablespoons minced fresh parsley or 2 teaspoons dried parsley flakes

In a 4- or 5-qt. slow cooker, combine the first 12 ingredients. Cover and cook on low for 4-5 hours. Stir in the haddock, shrimp, crabmeat and clams. Cover and cook 30 minutes longer or until fish flakes easily with a fork and shrimp turn pink. Stir in parsley. Discard bay leaf.

**PER SERVING** *205 cal., 3 g fat (1 g sat. fat), 125 mg chol., 483 mg sodium, 15 g carb., 3 g fiber, 29 g pro.* **Diabetic Exchanges:** *3 lean meat, 2 vegetable.*

CHICKEN TORTELLINI SOUP

SEAFOOD CIOPPINO

## Chicken Tortellini Soup

Put a fun twist on chicken noodle soup by making it with cheese tortellini and a simple blend of Italian seasonings.
—JEAN ATHERLY RED LODGE, MT

**START TO FINISH:** 30 MIN.
**MAKES:** 8 SERVINGS (ABOUT 2 QUARTS)

- 2 cans (14½ ounces each) chicken broth
- 2 cups water
- ¾ pound boneless skinless chicken breasts, cut into 1-inch cubes
- 1½ cups frozen mixed vegetables
- 1 package (9 ounces) refrigerated cheese tortellini
- 2 celery ribs, thinly sliced
- 1 teaspoon dried basil
- ½ teaspoon garlic salt
- ½ teaspoon dried oregano
- ¼ teaspoon pepper

**1.** In a large saucepan, bring broth and water to a boil; add chicken. Reduce heat; cook for 10 minutes.

**2.** Add the remaining ingredients; cook 10-15 minutes longer or until chicken is no longer pink and vegetables are tender.

**PER SERVING** *170 cal., 4 g fat (2 g sat. fat), 37 mg chol., 483 mg sodium, 20 g carb., 3 g fiber, 14 g pro.* **Diabetic Exchanges:** *2 lean meat, 1 starch.*

## Beef Pitas with Yogurt Sauce

**START TO FINISH:** 25 MIN.
**MAKES:** 4 SERVINGS

- 1 cup (8 ounces) fat-free plain yogurt
- ¼ cup minced fresh parsley
- 1 garlic clove, minced
- ⅛ teaspoon plus ½ teaspoon salt, divided
- 1 teaspoon dried oregano
- 1 teaspoon minced fresh rosemary
- ¼ teaspoon pepper
- 1 pound beef top sirloin steak, cut into thin strips
- 4 teaspoons olive oil, divided
- 1 large sweet onion, sliced
- 4 whole pita breads, warmed

**1.** In a small bowl, mix yogurt, parsley, garlic and ⅛ teaspoon salt. Sprinkle oregano, rosemary, pepper and remaining salt over beef.

**2.** In a large nonstick skillet, heat 2 teaspoons oil over medium-high heat. Add onion; cook and stir 4-6 minutes or until tender. Remove from pan.

**3.** In same skillet, heat remaining oil over medium-high heat. Add beef; cook and stir 3-4 minutes or until no longer pink. Serve with pita breads, onions and yogurt mixture.

**PER SERVING** *405 cal., 10 g fat (2 g sat. fat), 47 mg chol., 784 mg sodium, 45 g carb., 2 g fiber, 33 g pro.* **Diabetic Exchanges:** *3 starch, 3 lean meat, 1 fat.*

GRILLED FISH SANDWICHES

## Grilled Fish Sandwiches 🅕

These fish fillets are seasoned with lime juice and lemon pepper before being charbroiled on the grill. A simple mayonnaise and honey-mustard sauce sets them apart from the rest.
—**VIOLET BEARD** MARSHALL, IL

**START TO FINISH:** 30 MIN.
**MAKES:** 4 SERVINGS

- 4 cod fillets (4 ounces each)
- 1 tablespoon lime juice
- ½ teaspoon lemon-pepper seasoning
- ¼ cup fat-free mayonnaise
- 2 teaspoons Dijon mustard
- 1 teaspoon honey
- 4 hamburger buns, split
- 4 lettuce leaves
- 4 tomato slices

**1.** Brush both sides of fillets with lime juice; sprinkle with lemon pepper. Moisten a paper towel with cooking oil; using long-handled tongs, lightly coat the grill rack. Grill fillets, covered, over medium heat or broil 4 in. from the heat for 4-5 minutes on each side or until fish flakes easily with a fork.

**2.** In a small bowl, combine the mayonnaise, mustard and honey. Spread over the bottom of each bun. Top with a fillet, lettuce and tomato; replace bun tops.

**PER SERVING** *241 cal., 3 g fat (1 g sat. fat), 49 mg chol., 528 mg sodium, 28 g carb., 2 g fiber, 24 g pro.* **Diabetic Exchanges:** *3 lean meat, 2 starch.*

"Begin a Greek menu with our tasty version of a traditional gyro made with sauteed onions and tender beef. I top it with an easy-to-make yogurt sauce that doubles as a dip for warmed pita."
—**DANIEL ANDERSON** PLEASANT PRAIRIE, WI

BEEF PITAS WITH YOGURT SAUCE

FLAVORFUL SOUTHWESTERN CHILI

## Flavorful Southwestern Chili

This treasured recipe comes from my grandmother. The chili is full of flavor, freezes beautifully and makes a complete last-minute meal. I top it with grated cheddar cheese and chopped black olives and serve tortilla chips on the side.

**—JENNY GREEAR** HUNTINGTON, WV

**START TO FINISH:** 30 MIN. • **MAKES:** 10 SERVINGS (2½ QUARTS)

- 2 **pounds lean ground beef (90% lean)**
- 1½ **cups chopped onions**
- 2 **cans (14½ ounces each) diced tomatoes, undrained**
- 1 **can (15 ounces) pinto beans, rinsed and drained**
- 1 **can (15 ounces) tomato sauce**
- 1 **package (10 ounces) frozen corn, thawed**
- 1 **cup salsa**
- ¾ **cup water**
- 1 **can (4 ounces) chopped green chilies**
- 1 **teaspoon ground cumin**
- ½ **teaspoon garlic powder**

**1.** In a Dutch oven, cook beef and onions over medium heat until meat is no longer pink; drain. Stir in the remaining ingredients. Bring to a boil. Reduce heat; simmer, uncovered, for 15 minutes.

**2.** Serve desired amount. Cool the remaining chili; transfer to freezer containers. May be frozen for up to 3 months.

**TO USE FROZEN CHILI** *Thaw in the refrigerator. Place in a saucepan; heat through.*

**PER SERVING** *245 cal., 7 g fat (3 g sat. fat), 44 mg chol., 580 mg sodium, 22 g carb., 5 g fiber, 22 g pro.* **Diabetic Exchanges:** *3 lean meat, 1 starch, 1 vegetable.*

## Chicken Gyros

These yummy Greek specialties are a cinch to prepare at home. Just take tender chicken, coat it in a creamy cucumber-yogurt sauce, then tuck it into pita pockets. Some folks like lettuce and diced tomato on top.

**—TASTE OF HOME TEST KITCHEN**

**PREP:** 20 MIN. + MARINATING • **COOK:** 10 MIN. • **MAKES:** 2 SERVINGS

- ¼ **cup lemon juice**
- 2 **tablespoons olive oil**
- ¾ **teaspoon minced garlic, divided**
- ½ **teaspoon ground mustard**
- ½ **teaspoon dried oregano**
- ½ **pound boneless skinless chicken breasts, cut into ½-inch strips**
- ½ **cup chopped peeled cucumber**
- ⅓ **cup plain yogurt**
- ¼ **teaspoon dill weed**
- 2 **whole pita breads**
- ½ **small red onion, thinly sliced**

**1.** In a large resealable plastic bag, combine the lemon juice, oil, ½ teaspoon garlic, mustard and oregano; add chicken. Seal bag and turn to coat; refrigerate for at least 1 hour. In a small bowl, combine the cucumber, yogurt, dill and remaining garlic; cover and refrigerate until serving.

**2.** Drain and discard marinade. In a large nonstick skillet, cook and stir the chicken for 7-8 minutes or until no longer pink. Spoon onto pita breads. Top with yogurt mixture and onion; fold in half.

**PER SERVING** *1 gyro equals 367 cal., 9 g fat (2 g sat. fat), 68 mg chol., 397 mg sodium, 39 g carb., 2 g fiber, 30 g pro.* **Diabetic Exchanges:** *3 lean meat, 2½ starch, 1 fat.*

CHICKEN GYROS

## Hearty Vegetable Barley Soup

My mom picked up this barley soup recipe in her fitness class and passed it to me. It's loaded with goodness! Sometimes I substitute ground turkey as the meat and use chicken bouillon instead of beef flavored.

—**EMILY MELTON** PROPHETSTOWN, IL

**PREP:** 20 MIN. • **COOK:** 45 MIN. • **MAKES:** 5 SERVINGS

½ **pound lean ground beef (90% lean)**
5 **cups water**
1 **can (14½ ounces) diced tomatoes, undrained**
1 **small onion, chopped**
1 **celery rib, sliced**
1 **medium carrot, sliced**
2 **teaspoons reduced-sodium beef bouillon granules**
1 **bay leaf**
1 **garlic clove, minced**
½ **teaspoon salt**
½ **teaspoon dried basil**
¼ **teaspoon pepper**
2 **cups frozen mixed vegetables**
¾ **cup quick-cooking barley**

1. In a Dutch oven, cook beef over medium heat until no longer pink; drain. Add the water, tomatoes, onion, celery, carrot, bouillon, bay leaf, garlic, salt, basil and pepper. Bring to a boil. Reduce heat; cover and simmer for 20 minutes.
2. Stir in mixed vegetables and barley; return to a boil. Reduce heat; cover and simmer 10-15 minutes longer or until vegetables and barley are tender. Discard bay leaf.
**PER SERVING** 233 cal., 5 g fat (2 g sat. fat), 28 mg chol., 527 mg sodium, 35 g carb., 9 g fiber, 15 g pro. **Diabetic Exchanges:** 2 starch, 1 lean meat, 1 vegetable.

## Ranch Chicken Salad Sandwiches

My husband, who is diabetic, takes lunch to work with him every day. We love chicken salad, and I created a low-fat version that we both feel good about.

—**BOBBIE SCROGGIE** SCOTT DEPOT, WV

**START TO FINISH:** 15 MIN. • **MAKES:** 6 SERVINGS

¼ **cup reduced-fat mayonnaise**
3 **tablespoons fat-free ranch salad dressing**
3 **tablespoons fat-free sour cream**
1 **tablespoon lemon juice**
⅛ **teaspoon pepper**
2 **cups cubed cooked chicken breast**
½ **cup thinly sliced celery**
2 **tablespoons diced sweet red pepper**
1 **tablespoon chopped green onion**
6 **hamburger buns, split**
6 **lettuce leaves**
6 **slices tomato**

In a small bowl, combine the mayonnaise, ranch dressing, sour cream, lemon juice and pepper. Stir in the chicken, celery, red pepper and onion until combined. Spoon ⅓ cup onto each bun bottom; top with lettuce and tomato. Replace bun tops.
**PER SERVING** 257 cal., 7 g fat (1 g sat. fat), 41 mg chol., 456 mg sodium, 29 g carb., 2 g fiber, 18 g pro. **Diabetic Exchanges:** 2 starch, 2 lean meat, ½ fat.

RANCH CHICKEN SALAD SANDWICHES

## Turkey & Swiss with Herbed Greens

A simple-to-make dressing lends a burst of flavor to an otherwise ordinary sandwich.

**—PAM NORBY** AMERY, WI

**START TO FINISH:** 30 MIN. • **MAKES:** 8 SERVINGS

- 2 tablespoons balsamic vinegar
- 1 tablespoon olive oil
- ½ teaspoon dried oregano
- ¼ teaspoon garlic powder
- ¼ teaspoon dried basil
- 4 cups torn mixed salad greens
- 2 tablespoons finely chopped onion
- 16 slices multigrain bread
- ¾ pound thinly sliced deli turkey
- 8 slices Swiss cheese
- 2 large tomatoes, sliced

1. In a large bowl, whisk the vinegar, oil, oregano, garlic powder and basil. Add salad greens and onion; toss to coat.
2. On eight slices of bread, layer the turkey, cheese, tomatoes and salad greens. Top with remaining bread.
**PER SERVING** *297 cal., 12 g fat (6 g sat. fat), 40 mg chol., 686 mg sodium, 28 g carb., 5 g fiber, 20 g pro.* **Diabetic Exchanges:** *2 starch, 2 lean meat, 1 fat.*

## Chilled Melon Soup F S M

Looking for something to put pizzazz in a summer luncheon? Try this pretty, refreshing soup with a kick of cayenne pepper to get the conversation going.

**—MARY LOU TIMPSON** COLORADO CITY, AZ

**PREP:** 25 MIN. + CHILLING • **MAKES:** 6 SERVINGS

- ¾ cup orange juice
- 1 cup (8 ounces) plain yogurt
- 1 medium cantaloupe, peeled, seeded and cubed
- 1 tablespoon honey
- ¼ teaspoon salt
- ¼ teaspoon ground nutmeg
- ⅛ teaspoon cayenne pepper
- 6 mint sprigs

Place the orange juice, yogurt and cantaloupe in a blender; cover and process until pureed. Add the honey, salt, nutmeg and cayenne; cover and process until smooth. Refrigerate for at least 1 hour before serving. Garnish with mint sprigs.
**PER SERVING** *82 cal., 2 g fat (1 g sat. fat), 5 mg chol., 126 mg sodium, 16 g carb., 1 g fiber, 2 g pro.* **Diabetic Exchange:** *1 fruit.*

## Special Egg Salad ⓜ

This recipe proves you don't have to sacrifice flavor to eat lighter. These yummy, satisfying egg salad sandwiches are sure to be well-received whenever you serve them.

**—JUDY NISSEN** SIOUX FALLS, SD

**PREP:** 15 MIN. + CHILLING • **MAKES:** 6 SERVINGS

- 3 ounces reduced-fat cream cheese
- ¼ cup fat-free mayonnaise
- ½ teaspoon sugar
- ¼ teaspoon onion powder
- ¼ teaspoon garlic powder
- ⅛ teaspoon salt
- ⅛ teaspoon pepper
- 6 hard-cooked eggs, chopped
- 12 slices whole wheat bread, toasted
- 6 lettuce leaves

In a small bowl, beat the cream cheese until smooth. Beat in the mayonnaise, sugar, onion powder, garlic powder, salt and pepper; fold in the eggs. Cover and refrigerate for 1 hour. Serve on toast with lettuce.

**PER SERVING** *259 cal., 10 g fat (4 g sat. fat), 225 mg chol., 528 mg sodium, 30 g carb., 4 g fiber, 13 g pro.* **Diabetic Exchanges:** *2 starch, 1½ fat, 1 lean meat.*

## Hearty Split Pea Soup Ⓕ

For a different spin on split pea soup, try this recipe. The flavor is peppery rather than smoky.

**—BARBARA LINK** RANCHO CUCAMONGA, CA

**PREP:** 15 MIN. • **COOK:** 1½ HOURS
**MAKES:** 12 SERVINGS (3 QUARTS)

- 1 package (16 ounces) dried split peas
- 8 cups water
- 2 medium potatoes, peeled and cubed
- 2 large onions, chopped
- 2 medium carrots, chopped
- 2 cups cubed fully cooked lean ham
- 1 celery rib, chopped
- 5 teaspoons reduced-sodium chicken bouillon granules
- 1 teaspoon dried marjoram
- 1 teaspoon poultry seasoning
- 1 teaspoon rubbed sage
- ½ to 1 teaspoon pepper
- ½ teaspoon dried basil

In a Dutch oven, combine all ingredients; bring to a boil. Reduce heat; cover and simmer for 1¼ to 1½ hours or until peas and vegetables are tender.

**PER SERVING** *198 cal., 2 g fat (trace sat. fat), 9 mg chol., 440 mg sodium, 32 g carb., 11 g fiber, 15 g pro.* **Diabetic Exchanges:** *2 starch, 1 lean meat.*

## Curried Chicken Sloppy Joes

**PREP:** 20 MIN. • **COOK:** 30 MIN.
**MAKES:** 10 SERVINGS

- 1¼ pounds ground chicken
- 1 cup chopped sweet onion
- ½ cup chopped sweet orange pepper
- 2 garlic cloves, minced
- 1 tablespoon olive oil
- 2 teaspoons curry powder
- 1 teaspoon minced fresh gingerroot
- ½ teaspoon coarsely ground pepper
- ¼ teaspoon salt
- 1 can (14½ ounces) petite diced tomatoes, undrained
- 1 medium tart apple, peeled and diced
- ½ cup golden raisins
- 3 tablespoons mango chutney
- ¼ cup reduced-fat mayonnaise
- 1 tablespoon Dijon mustard
- 10 whole wheat hamburger buns, split

1. In a large nonstick skillet, cook chicken over medium heat until no longer pink; drain and set aside.
2. In the same skillet, cook the onion, pepper and garlic in oil until tender. Stir in the curry, ginger, pepper and salt; cook 1 minute longer.
3. Stir in the tomatoes, apple and raisins; bring to a boil. Reduce heat; simmer, uncovered, for 6-8 minutes. Stir in the chutney, mayonnaise, mustard and chicken; heat through. Serve on buns.

**PER SERVING** *288 cal., 10 g fat (2 g sat. fat), 40 mg chol., 486 mg sodium, 39 g carb., 5 g fiber, 14 g pro.* **Diabetic Exchanges:** *2 starch, 2 lean meat, 1 vegetable, ½ fat.*

"These delicious sloppy joes pack a burst of unexpected flavors in every bite. For potlucks, keep the chicken mixture warm in a slow cooker and allow everyone to help themselves."—**JAMIE MILLER** MAPLE GROVE, MN

CURRIED CHICKEN SLOPPY JOES

LIMA BEAN OKRA SOUP

## Lima Bean Okra Soup **F M**

This soup's unique flavor comes from the wonderful combination of vegetables with a hint of sweet spices. Every serving is loaded with nutrition and color.

—**CLARA COULSON MINNEY**
WASHINGTON COURT HOUSE, OH

**PREP:** 20 MIN. • **COOK:** 15 MIN.
**MAKES:** 7 SERVINGS

- 1 medium green pepper, chopped
- 1 medium onion, chopped
- ¼ teaspoon whole cloves
- 1 tablespoon butter
- 3 cups vegetable broth
- 3 cups chopped tomatoes
- 2½ cups sliced fresh or frozen okra, thawed
- 1 cup frozen lima beans, thawed
- ½ cup fresh or frozen corn, thawed
- ½ to 1 teaspoon salt
- ¼ to ½ teaspoon ground allspice
- ¼ teaspoon pepper
- ⅛ teaspoon cayenne pepper

1. In a large saucepan, saute the green pepper, onion and cloves in butter until vegetables are tender. Discard cloves.
2. Stir in the remaining ingredients. Bring to a boil. Reduce heat; cover and simmer for 15-20 minutes or until beans are tender.

**PER SERVING** *96 cal., 2 g fat (1 g sat. fat), 4 mg chol., 601 mg sodium, 17 g carb., 5 g fiber, 4 g pro.* **Diabetic Exchanges:** *1 starch, 1 vegetable.*

## Mushroom Barley Soup F

After tinkering with three different recipes, I came up with this warming rich, dark brown broth with hearty mushrooms, barley and onions. It's a beefy-tasting soup for my meat-loving husband, completely vegan for me and healthy for both of us. It can simmer all day in a slow cooker or be served up right after preparation.

—REBEKAH WHITE SEASIDE, OR

**PREP:** 15 MIN. • **COOK:** 45 MIN.
**MAKES:** 7 SERVINGS

- 1 large onion, chopped
- 1 tablespoon olive oil
- 2 cups sliced fresh mushrooms
- 2 garlic cloves, minced
- 7 cups reduced-sodium chicken broth
- 2 cups water
- ½ cup medium pearl barley
- 2 tablespoons reduced-sodium soy sauce
- 1 teaspoon dried thyme
- ¼ teaspoon pepper

**1.** In a large saucepan, saute onion and mushrooms in oil until vegetables are tender. Add garlic; cook 1 minute longer.

**2.** Stir in the remaining ingredients. Bring to a boil. Reduce heat; simmer, uncovered, for 45-50 minutes or until barley is tender.

**PER SERVING** *101 cal., 2 g fat (trace sat. fat), 0 chol., 746 mg sodium, 16 g carb., 3 g fiber, 6 g pro.*

MUSHROOM BARLEY SOUP

ITALIAN CHICKEN SALAD SANDWICHES

## Italian Chicken Salad Sandwiches

My whole family loves this recipe. The Italian pickled vegetables give it a distinctive taste. I also serve it on a bed of lettuce, or as an appetizer on crackers.

—GIOVANNA KRANENBERG

MAHNOMEN, MN

**START TO FINISH:** 15 MIN.
**MAKES:** 2 SERVINGS

- ⅔ cup shredded cooked chicken breast
- 3 tablespoons shredded carrot
- 3 tablespoons finely chopped celery
- 2 tablespoons mild giardiniera, chopped
- 2 teaspoons finely chopped onion
- 1 small garlic clove, minced
- ¼ cup fat-free mayonnaise
  Dash pepper
- 4 slices sourdough bread
- 2 lettuce leaves

In a small bowl, combine the first six ingredients. Add mayonnaise and pepper; toss to coat. Spoon ½ cup salad onto two bread slices; top with lettuce and remaining bread.

**PER SERVING** *302 cal., 4 g fat (1 g sat. fat), 43 mg chol., 732 mg sodium, 43 g carb., 3 g fiber, 23 g pro.* **Diabetic Exchanges:** *3 starch, 2 lean meat.*

### top tip

## Relish the Flavor

Giardiniera is an Italian relish consisting of pickled vegetables such as carrots, bell peppers, cauliflower, celery and more. Look for a jar of it in the condiment aisle, near the pickles and canned olives.

## Pumpkin Harvest Beef Stew

By the time the stew is done simmering and a batch of bread finishes baking, the house smells absolutely wonderful.

**—MARCIA O'NEIL** CEDAR CREST, NM

**PREP:** 25 MIN. • **COOK:** 6½ HOURS
**MAKES:** 6 SERVINGS

- 1 tablespoon canola oil
- 1 beef top round steak (1½ pounds), cut into 1-inch cubes
- 1½ cups cubed peeled pie pumpkin or sweet potatoes
- 3 small red potatoes, peeled and cubed
- 1 cup cubed acorn squash
- 1 medium onion, chopped
- 2 cans (14½ ounces each) reduced-sodium beef broth
- 1 can (14½ ounces) diced tomatoes, undrained
- 2 bay leaves
- 2 garlic cloves, minced
- 2 teaspoons reduced-sodium beef bouillon granules
- ½ teaspoon chili powder
- ½ teaspoon pepper
- ¼ teaspoon ground allspice
- ¼ teaspoon ground cloves
- ¼ cup water
- 3 tablespoons all-purpose flour

**1.** In a large skillet, heat oil over medium-high heat. Brown beef in batches; remove with a slotted spoon to a 4- or 5-qt. slow cooker. Add the pumpkin, potatoes, squash and onion. Stir in the broth, tomatoes and seasonings. Cover and cook on low for 6-8 hours or until meat is tender.

**2.** Remove bay leaves. In a small bowl, mix water and flour until smooth; gradually stir into stew. Cover and cook on high for 30 minutes or until liquid is thickened.

**PER SERVING** *258 cal., 6 g fat (1 g sat. fat), 67 mg chol., 479 mg sodium, 21 g carb., 4 g fiber, 29 g pro.* **Diabetic Exchanges:** *3 lean meat, 1 starch, 1 vegetable, ½ fat.*

PUMPKIN HARVEST BEEF STEW

## Singapore Satay Sandwiches

My grandkids think this shredded chicken is the best thing under a bun. The peanut butter flavor and fresh fruit and veggie toppings make it a fun, packable sandwich for lunches.

**—DIANE HALFERTY** CORPUS CHRISTI, TX

**START TO FINISH:** 30 MIN.
**MAKES:** 6 SERVINGS

- 1½ pounds boneless skinless chicken breasts
- 1 teaspoon steak seasoning
- 1 tablespoon canola oil
- 3 tablespoons reduced-fat chunky peanut butter
- ¼ cup unsweetened apple juice
- 2 tablespoons lime juice
- 2 tablespoons reduced-sodium soy sauce
- 2 teaspoons hot pepper sauce
- 6 kaiser rolls, split
- 2 cups torn romaine
- 1 cup shredded carrots
- ½ cup julienned peeled cucumber
- 6 tablespoons unsweetened crushed pineapple

**1.** Sprinkle chicken on both sides with steak seasoning. In a large skillet, cook chicken in oil for 4-7 minutes on each side or until juices run clear. Transfer to a cutting board and shred.

**2.** In a large microwave-safe bowl, melt peanut butter. Whisk in the apple juice, lime juice, soy sauce and hot pepper sauce. Add chicken and toss to coat.

**3.** Spoon ½ cup chicken mixture onto roll bottoms; top with romaine, carrots, cucumber and pineapple. Replace roll tops.

**NOTE** *This recipe was tested with McCormick's Montreal Steak Seasoning. Look for it in the spice aisle.*

**PER SERVING** *388 cal., 11 g fat (2 g sat. fat), 63 mg chol., 759 mg sodium, 41 g carb., 3 g fiber, 31 g pro.* **Diabetic Exchanges:** *3 starch, 3 lean meat, 1 fat.*

SINGAPORE SATAY SANDWICHES

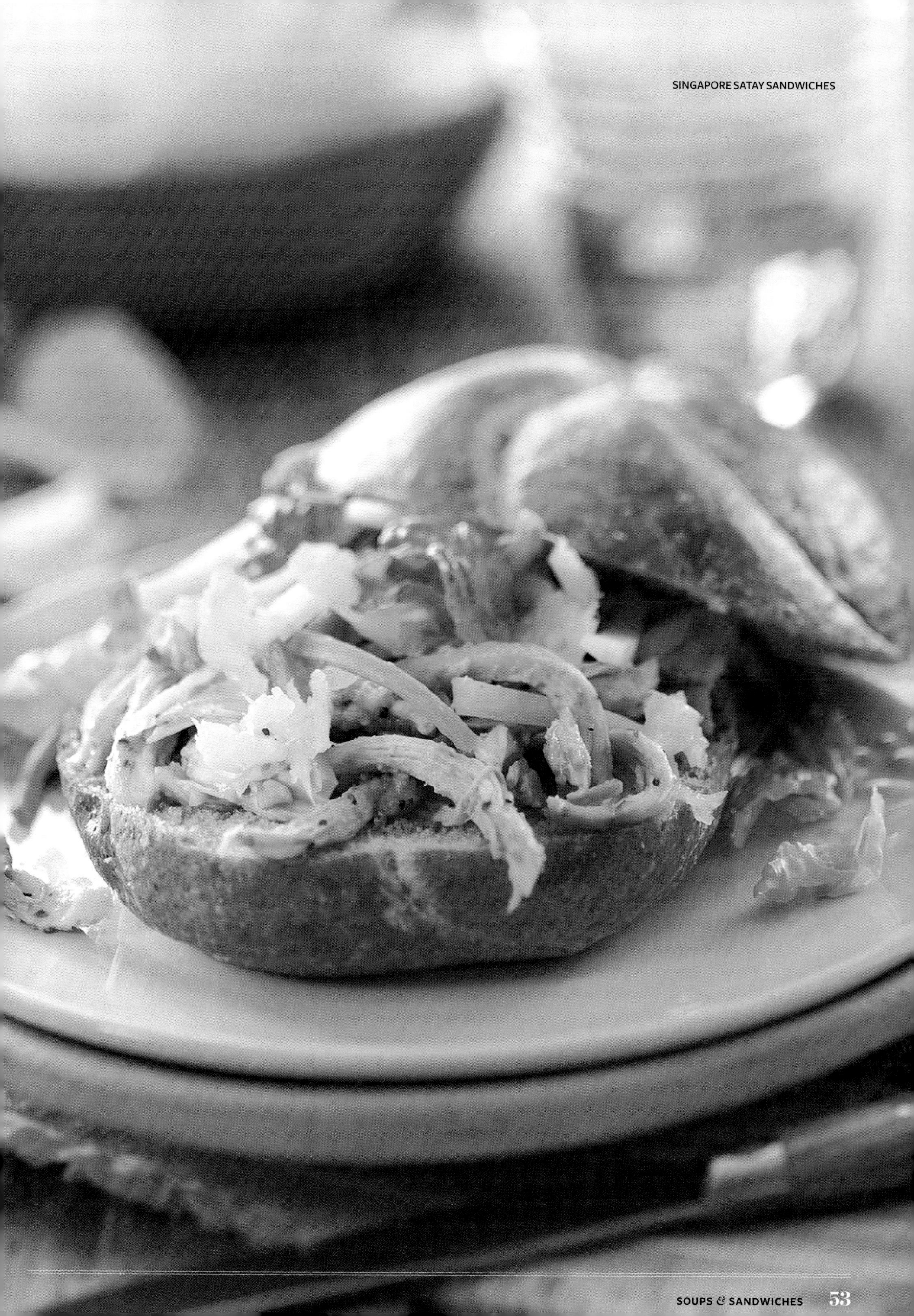

TURKEY SAUSAGE BEAN SOUP

## Turkey Sausage Bean Soup

This soup recipe is a family favorite handed down from my great-grandmother. I've tweaked it a bit to add some of my current favorites like celery root. Serve it with a side salad and some artisan bread for a wonderful, hearty family dinner.
—**TERREL PORTER-SMITH** LOS OSOS, CA

**PREP:** 15 MIN. • **COOK:** 25 MIN. • **MAKES:** 8 SERVINGS (2 QUARTS)

- 4 **Italian turkey sausage links, casings removed**
- 1 **large onion, chopped**
- 1 **cup chopped fennel bulb**
- 1 **cup chopped celery root or peeled turnip**
- 1 **can (14½ ounces) no-salt-added diced tomatoes, undrained**
- 3 **cups water**
- 4 **bay leaves**
- 1 **tablespoon reduced-sodium beef base**
- 2 **teaspoons Italian seasoning**
- ½ **teaspoon pepper**
- 2 **cans (15 ounces each) white kidney or cannellini beans, rinsed and drained**
   **Shaved Parmesan cheese, optional**

**1.** In a Dutch oven, cook sausage, onion, fennel and celery root over medium heat 4-5 minutes or until sausage is no longer pink, breaking into crumbles; drain. Stir in tomatoes, water, bay leaves, beef base, Italian seasoning and pepper.
**2.** Bring to a boil. Reduce heat; simmer, covered, 20 minutes or until vegetables are tender. Stir in the beans; heat through. Remove bay leaves. If desired, top servings with cheese.
**FREEZE OPTION** *Freeze soup without cheese in freezer containers. To use, partially thaw in refrigerator overnight. Heat through in a saucepan, stirring occasionally. If desired, top with cheese.*
**PER SERVING** *168 cal., 4 g fat (1 g sat. fat), 20 mg chol., 585 mg sodium, 22 g carb., 6 g fiber, 11 g pro.* **Diabetic Exchanges:** *1½ starch, 1 medium-fat meat.*

## Grilled Turkey Sandwiches

These sandwiches are a welcome change from the usual hamburger or grilled chicken sandwich. The herbed marinade makes the meat so juicy and tender.
—**MARY DETWEILER** MIDDLEFIELD, OH

**PREP:** 20 MIN. + MARINATING • **GRILL:** 10 MIN. • **MAKES:** 6 SERVINGS

- ½ **cup chicken broth**
- ¼ **cup olive oil**
- 4½ **teaspoons finely chopped onion**
- 1 **tablespoon white wine vinegar**
- 2 **teaspoons dried parsley flakes**
- ½ **teaspoon salt**
- ½ **teaspoon rubbed sage**
- ⅛ **teaspoon pepper**
- 6 **turkey breast cutlets (about 1 pound)**
- 6 **whole wheat hamburger buns, split**
- 6 **lettuce leaves**
- 6 **tomato slices**

**1.** In a large resealable plastic bag, combine the first eight ingredients; add turkey. Seal bag and turn to coat; refrigerate for 12 hours or overnight, turning occasionally.
**2.** Drain and discard marinade. Moisten a paper towel with cooking oil; using long-handled tongs, lightly coat the grill rack.
**3.** Prepare grill for indirect heat, using a drip pan. Place turkey over drip pan and grill, covered, over indirect medium heat or broil 4 in. from the heat for 3-4 minutes on each side or until no longer pink. Serve on buns with lettuce and tomato.
**PER SERVING** *286 cal., 12 g fat (2 g sat. fat), 47 mg chol., 387 mg sodium, 24 g carb., 4 g fiber, 23 g pro.* **Diabetic Exchanges:** *2 lean meat, 2 fat, 1½ starch.*

GRILLED TURKEY SANDWICHES

GRECIAN GOLD
MEDAL WRAPS

## Grecian Gold Medal Wraps

**START TO FINISH:** 20 MIN. • **MAKES:** 4 SERVINGS

- ½ cup canned white kidney or cannellini beans, rinsed and drained
- ⅓ cup crumbled feta cheese
- ⅓ cup fat-free plain yogurt
- ¼ cup chopped red onion
- 2 teaspoons lemon juice
- 2 small tomatoes, chopped
- 4 whole wheat tortillas (8 inches), room temperature
- 1 package (6 ounces) ready-to-use grilled chicken breast strips
- ⅔ cup torn romaine
- 2 tablespoons chopped pitted Greek olives

In a small bowl, mash beans with a fork. Stir in the feta cheese, yogurt, onion and lemon juice. Fold in tomatoes. Spread ¼ cup onto each tortilla. Top with chicken, romaine and olives; roll up.

**PER SERVING** *279 cal., 7 g fat (2 g sat. fat), 33 mg chol., 774 mg sodium, 33 g carb., 5 g fiber, 18 g pro.* **Diabetic Exchanges:** *2 starch, 2 lean meat, 1 fat.*

## Southwestern Chicken Soup F C

Here's the perfect recipe for a busy week, because the slow cooker does most of the work for you!
—**HAROLD TARTAR** WEST PALM BEACH, FL

**PREP:** 10 MIN. • **COOK:** 7 HOURS
**MAKES:** 10 SERVINGS (2½ QUARTS)

- 1¼ pounds boneless skinless chicken breasts, cut into thin strips
- 1 tablespoon canola oil
- 2 cans (14½ ounces each) reduced-sodium chicken broth
- 1 package (16 ounces) frozen corn, thawed
- 1 can (14½ ounces) diced tomatoes, undrained
- 1 medium onion, chopped
- 1 medium green pepper, chopped
- 1 medium sweet red pepper, chopped
- 1 can (4 ounces) chopped green chilies
- 1½ teaspoons seasoned salt, optional
- 1 teaspoon ground cumin
- ½ teaspoon garlic powder

1. In a large skillet, saute chicken in oil until lightly browned. Transfer to a 5-qt. slow cooker. Stir in the remaining ingredients.
2. Cover and cook on low for 7-8 hours or until chicken and vegetables are tender. Stir before serving.

**PER SERVING** *143 cal., 3 g fat (1 g sat. fat), 31 mg chol., 364 mg sodium, 15 g carb., 3 g fiber, 15 g pro.* **Diabetic Exchanges:** *2 lean meat, 1 starch.*

SOUTHWESTERN
CHICKEN SOUP

## Low-Fat Shrimp Chowder 🄵

This yummy chowder is full of shrimp and vegetables, so it satisfies hearty appetites. The skim milk and reduced-sodium broth help keep it on the surprisingly healthy side. It tastes even better the next day, after the flavors have melded overnight.

—MICHELLE CONLEY EVANSTON, WY

**PREP:** 20 MIN. • **COOK:** 20 MIN.
**MAKES:** 8 SERVINGS

- 1 pound red potatoes, peeled and cubed
- 2½ cups reduced-sodium chicken broth
- 3 celery ribs, chopped
- 8 green onions, chopped
- ½ cup chopped sweet red pepper
- 1½ cups fat-free milk
- ¼ cup all-purpose flour
- ½ cup fat-free evaporated milk
- 1½ pounds uncooked medium shrimp, peeled and deveined
- 2 tablespoons minced fresh parsley
- ½ teaspoon paprika
- ½ teaspoon Worcestershire sauce
- ⅛ teaspoon cayenne pepper
- ⅛ teaspoon pepper

**1.** In a large saucepan, bring the potatoes, broth, celery, onions and red pepper to a boil. Reduce heat; cover and simmer for 13-15 minutes or until vegetables are tender. Stir in milk. Gently mash vegetables with a potato masher, leaving some chunks of potatoes.

**2.** Combine flour and evaporated milk until smooth; gradually stir into potato mixture. Bring to a boil; cook and stir for 2 minutes or until thickened. Stir in the remaining ingredients. Return to a boil. Cook and stir for 2-3 minutes or until shrimp turn pink.

**PER SERVING** 192 cal., 2 g fat (trace sat. fat), 130 mg chol., 334 mg sodium, 21 g carb., 2 g fiber, 23 g pro. **Diabetic Exchanges:** 2 lean meat, 1 starch.

## Roasted Tomato & Garlic Soup

This is a wonderful way to use the last of the season's tomatoes and garlic in a creamy, rich soup. Serve it as a meal starter or on its own with fresh-baked bread for a light lunch.

—LIZZIE MUNRO BROOKLYN, NY

**PREP:** 55 MIN. • **COOK:** 30 MIN.
**MAKES:** 4 SERVINGS

- 3 whole garlic bulbs
- 3 tablespoons olive oil, divided
- 2½ pounds large tomatoes, quartered and seeded
- ¼ teaspoon salt, divided
- ¼ teaspoon pepper, divided
- 1 medium onion, chopped
- 5 garlic cloves, minced
- 1 tablespoon minced fresh or 1 teaspoon dried thyme
- 2 cups chicken stock
- ½ cup half-and-half cream

**1.** Preheat oven to 350°. Remove papery outer skin from garlic bulbs, but do not peel or separate the cloves. Cut off top of garlic bulbs, exposing individual cloves; drizzle with 2 tablespoons oil. Wrap in foil.

**2.** Place tomatoes in a 15-in. x 10-in. x 1-in. foil-lined baking pan; sprinkle with ⅛ teaspoon each salt and pepper. Bake garlic bulbs and tomatoes 40-45 minutes or until cloves are soft and tomatoes are tender. Unwrap and cool 10 minutes.

**3.** In a large saucepan, heat remaining oil over medium heat. Add onion; cook and stir until tender. Add minced garlic, thyme and tomatoes. Squeeze baked garlic from skin; add to pan. Add stock; bring to a boil. Reduce heat; simmer, uncovered, 20-25 minutes

or until flavors are blended, breaking up tomatoes with a spoon.

**4.** Remove soup from heat; cool slightly. Process in batches in a blender until smooth. Return soup to the pan; add cream and remaining salt and pepper. Heat through.

**PER SERVING** 252 cal., 14 g fat (4 g sat. fat), 15 mg chol., 438 mg sodium, 27 g carb., 5 g fiber, 8 g pro. **Diabetic Exchanges:** 2½ fat, 1½ starch.

HUMMUS & VEGGIE WRAP UP

## Hummus & Veggie Wrap Up 🄼

I had a sandwich similar to this once when I stopped at a diner while on a long walk. I enjoyed it so much that I modified it to my own taste, and now I have it for lunch on a regular basis. Everyone at work wants to know how to make it.

—MICHAEL STEFFENS INDIANAPOLIS, IN

**START TO FINISH:** 15 MIN.
**MAKES:** 1 SERVING.

- 2 tablespoons hummus
- 1 whole wheat tortilla (8 inches)
- ¼ cup torn mixed salad greens
- 2 tablespoons finely chopped sweet onion
- 2 tablespoons thinly sliced cucumber
- 2 tablespoons alfalfa sprouts
- 2 tablespoons shredded carrot
- 1 tablespoon balsamic vinaigrette

Spread hummus over tortilla. Layer with salad greens, onion, cucumber, sprouts and carrot. Drizzle with vinaigrette. Roll up tightly.

**PER SERVING** 235 cal., 8 g fat (1 g sat. fat), 0 chol., 415 mg sodium, 32 g carb., 5 g fiber, 7 g pro. **Diabetic Exchanges:** 2 starch, 1 fat.

LOW-FAT SHRIMP CHOWDER

## Zesty Chicken Soup  ▣

This spicy chicken soup is chock-full of chicken and vegetables. Best of all, it freezes nicely, making a second meal with little effort!

—**GWEN NELSON** CASTRO VALLEY, CA

**PREP:** 25 MIN. • **COOK:** 40 MIN.
**MAKES:** 10 SERVINGS (3¾ QUARTS)

- 1¼ pounds boneless skinless chicken breasts
- 4 cups water
- 1 medium onion, chopped
- 2 celery ribs, chopped
- 4 garlic cloves, minced
- 1 tablespoon canola oil
- 1 can (14½ ounces) Mexican diced tomatoes
- 1 can (14½ ounces) diced tomatoes
- 1 can (8 ounces) tomato sauce
- 1 cup medium salsa
- 3 medium zucchini, halved and sliced
- 2 medium carrots, sliced
- 1 cup frozen white corn
- 1 can (4 ounces) chopped green chilies
- 3 teaspoons ground cumin
- 2 teaspoons chili powder
- 1 teaspoon dried basil
  Shredded cheddar cheese and tortilla chips, optional

**1.** Place chicken in a Dutch oven or soup kettle; add water. Bring to a boil; reduce heat. Cover and simmer for 10-15 minutes or until chicken juices run clear. Remove chicken; cut into ½-in. cubes. Return to cooking liquid.
**2.** In a large skillet, saute onion, celery and garlic in oil until tender; add to the Dutch oven. Stir in the tomatoes, tomato sauce, salsa, zucchini, carrots, corn, chilies, cumin, chili powder and basil. Bring to a boil. Reduce heat; cover and simmer for 20-25 minutes or until vegetables are tender.
**3.** Garnish with cheese and tortilla chips if desired. Soup may be frozen for up to 3 months.
**PER SERVING** *152 cal., 3 g fat (1 g sat. fat), 31 mg chol., 518 mg sodium, 16 g carb., 5 g fiber, 14 g pro.* **Diabetic Exchanges:** *2 vegetable, 1 lean meat, ½ starch.*

## Rustic Autumn Soup

This recipe is a great way to use the harvest of fall. The flavors of root vegetables really shine when combined with the subtle sweetness of apple.

—**GREG HAGELI** ELMHURST, IL

**PREP:** 30 MIN. • **COOK:** 25 MIN.
**MAKES:** 13 SERVINGS (3¼ QUARTS)

- 5 medium parsnips, chopped
- 5 medium carrots, chopped
- 2 medium onions, chopped
- 1 medium sweet potato, peeled and chopped
- 1 medium turnip, peeled and chopped
- ½ medium tart apple, peeled and chopped
- 2 tablespoons chopped roasted sweet red pepper
- 2 celery ribs, chopped
- 3 cans (14½ ounces each) reduced-sodium chicken broth
- 2 bay leaves
- 1 garlic clove, minced
- 1 teaspoon dried tarragon
- ½ teaspoon salt
- ½ teaspoon pepper
- 2 cups half-and-half cream
  Optional garnish: additional cooked finely chopped carrots, parsnips and/or apples, fresh chives

**1.** In a Dutch oven, combine the first 14 ingredients. Bring to a boil. Reduce heat; cover and simmer for 20-25 minutes or until tender. Discard bay leaves. Cool slightly.
**2.** In a blender, process soup in batches until smooth. Return all to the pan; add cream and heat through. Garnish with additional cooked vegetables and/or apples and chives.
**PER SERVING** *134 cal., 4 g fat (3 g sat. fat), 18 mg chol., 384 mg sodium, 20 g carb., 4 g fiber, 4 g pro.* **Diabetic Exchanges:** *1 starch, 1 fat.*

### ❓ Did you know?

There are two main types of bay leaves: Turkish bay leaves, the most common variety, and California bay leaves, which are twice as strong and tend to be longer and thinner.

ZESTY CHICKEN SOUP

COLORADO LAMB CHILI

## Colorado Lamb Chili

This hearty and spicy stew is wonderful with fresh hot rolls and your favorite green salad.

—**KAREN GORMAN** GUNNISON, CO

**PREP:** 20 MIN. • **COOK:** 1½ HOURS
**MAKES:** 6 SERVINGS (2¼ QUARTS)

- 1 **pound lamb stew meat, cut into 1-inch pieces**
- 2 **tablespoons canola oil, divided**
- 1 **large onion, chopped**
- 1 **large sweet yellow pepper, chopped**
- 4 **garlic cloves, minced**
- 1 **can (30 ounces) black beans, rinsed and drained**
- 1 **can (28 ounces) diced tomatoes, undrained**
- 1 **can (14½ ounces) reduced-sodium beef broth**
- 1 **tablespoon dried oregano**
- 1 **tablespoon chili powder**
- 1 **tablespoon brown sugar**
- 2 **teaspoons Worcestershire sauce**
- 1 **teaspoon ground cumin**
- ½ **teaspoon fennel seed, crushed**
  **Sliced green onions, chopped tomatoes and corn chips, optional**

**1.** In a Dutch oven, brown lamb in 1 tablespoon oil. Remove and set aside.
**2.** In the same pan, saute onion and pepper in remaining oil until tender. Add garlic; cook 1 minute longer. Add the beans, tomatoes, broth, oregano, chili powder, brown sugar, Worcestershire sauce, cumin and fennel. Return lamb to the pan.
**3.** Bring to a boil. Reduce heat; cover and simmer for 1¼ to 1½ hours or until lamb is tender. Garnish each

## Doubling Up

When doubling a recipe that cooks for a long period of time, keep in mind that flavorful spices such as garlic and chili powder will intensify. To balance out the flavors, add only 50 percent more spices, instead of adding twice as much.

ROAST BEEF GARDEN PITAS

serving with green onions, tomatoes and corn chips if desired.
**PER SERVING** *325 cal., 9 g fat (2 g sat. fat), 51 mg chol., 646 mg sodium, 36 g carb., 9 g fiber, 25 g pro.* **Diabetic Exchanges:** *3 lean meat, 2 starch, 1 vegetable, 1 fat.*

## Roast Beef Garden Pitas

Showcasing lots of fresh veggies coated with horseradish mayonnaise, these packed pitas appeal to all. Men especially will like the hearty combination.

—**NICOLE FILIZETTI** JACKSONVILLE, FL

**START TO FINISH:** 20 MIN.
**MAKES:** 3 SERVINGS

- 3 **whole wheat pita pocket halves**
- ⅓ **pound thinly sliced deli roast beef**
- ¼ **cup chopped fresh broccoli**
- ¼ **cup frozen corn, thawed**
- ¼ **cup chopped seeded peeled cucumber**
- 2 **tablespoons shredded carrot**
- 2 **tablespoons finely chopped celery**
- 2 **tablespoons thinly sliced green onion**

**DRESSING**

- 1½ **teaspoons prepared horseradish**
- 1½ **teaspoons mayonnaise**
- 1½ **teaspoons reduced-fat sour cream**
- ½ **teaspoon Dijon mustard**
- ⅛ **teaspoon salt**
- ⅛ **teaspoon pepper**

**1.** Line pita halves with roast beef. In a small bowl, combine the broccoli, corn, cucumber, carrot, celery and onion.
**2.** In another bowl, combine the dressing ingredients. Pour over vegetable mixture; toss to coat. Fill pita halves.
**PER SERVING** *172 cal., 5 g fat (1 g sat. fat), 30 mg chol., 579 mg sodium, 20 g carb., 3 g fiber, 14 g pro.* **Diabetic Exchanges:** *2 lean meat, 1 starch, ½ fat.*

## Spicy Turkey Burgers

The hot pepper sauce comes through nicely to spark the flavor of these tender turkey patties. It's a good low-fat burger without the typical boring taste of low-fat foods.
—**MAVIS DIMENT** MARCUS, IA

**START TO FINISH:** 25 MIN. • **MAKES:** 4 SERVINGS

- ½ cup chopped onion
- 2 tablespoons reduced-fat plain yogurt
- 1 tablespoon snipped fresh dill or 1 teaspoon dill weed
- 1½ teaspoons hot pepper sauce
- ½ teaspoon salt
- 1 garlic clove, minced
- 1 pound lean ground turkey
- 4 kaiser rolls, split
- 4 lettuce leaves
- 4 tomato slices

1. In a large bowl, combine the onion, yogurt, dill, hot pepper sauce, salt and garlic. Crumble turkey over mixture; mix well. Shape into four patties, each about ¾-in. thick.
2. Grill, uncovered, over medium-hot heat for 6-8 minutes on each side or until a thermometer reads 165° and juices run clear. Serve on rolls with lettuce and tomato.

**PER SERVING** *357 cal., 12 g fat (3 g sat. fat), 90 mg chol., 766 mg sodium, 34 g carb., 2 g fiber, 27 g pro.* **Diabetic Exchanges:** *3 lean meat, 2 starch.*

SPICY TURKEY BURGERS

JUMPIN' ESPRESSO BEAN CHILI

## Jumpin' Espresso Bean Chili M

Chili is a hearty dish I love experimenting with. This meatless version I created is low in fat, but high in flavor. Everyone tries to guess the secret ingredient; no one ever thinks it's coffee.
—**JESSIE APFEL** BERKELEY, CA

**PREP:** 15 MIN. • **COOK:** 35 MIN. • **MAKES:** 7 SERVINGS

- 3 medium onions, chopped
- 2 tablespoons olive oil
- 2 tablespoons brown sugar
- 2 tablespoons chili powder
- 2 tablespoons ground cumin
- 1 tablespoon instant coffee granules
- 1 tablespoon baking cocoa
- ¾ teaspoon salt
- 2 cans (14½ ounces each) no-salt-added diced tomatoes
- 1 can (15 ounces) black beans, rinsed and drained
- 1 can (15 ounces) kidney beans, rinsed and drained
- 1 can (15 ounces) garbanzo beans or chickpeas, rinsed and drained
  Sour cream, thinly sliced green onions, shredded cheddar cheese and pickled jalapeno slices, optional

1. In a Dutch oven, saute the onions in oil until tender. Add the brown sugar, chili powder, cumin, coffee granules, cocoa and salt; cook and stir for 1 minute.
2. Stir in tomatoes and beans. Bring to a boil. Reduce heat; cover and simmer for 30 minutes or until heated through. Serve with sour cream, onions, cheese and jalapeno slices if desired.

**PER SERVING** *272 cal., 6 g fat (1 g sat. fat), 0 chol., 620 mg sodium, 45 g carb., 12 g fiber, 12 g pro.* **Diabetic Exchanges:** *2½ starch, 2 vegetable, 1 lean meat.*

## Easy Gazpacho 🄲

**PREP:** 25 MIN. + CHILLING • **MAKES:** 4 SERVINGS

- 2 cups Clamato juice
- 3 plum tomatoes, seeded and finely chopped
- ½ cup finely chopped green pepper
- ½ cup finely chopped seeded cucumber
- ½ cup finely chopped celery
- ¼ cup finely chopped onion
- 2 tablespoons olive oil
- 2 tablespoons red wine vinegar
- 2 teaspoons minced fresh parsley
- 1 teaspoon minced chives
- 1 garlic clove, minced
- ½ teaspoon pepper
- ½ teaspoon Worcestershire sauce
- ¼ teaspoon salt
  Salad croutons, optional

In a large bowl, combine the Clamato juice, tomatoes, green pepper, cucumber, celery, onion, oil, vinegar, parsley, chives, garlic, pepper, Worcestershire sauce and salt. Cover and refrigerate for at least 4 hours. Serve with croutons if desired.

**PER SERVING** *114 cal., 7 g fat (1 g sat. fat), 0 chol., 611 mg sodium, 11 g carb., 1 g fiber, 1 g pro.* **Diabetic Exchanges:** *1½ fat, 1 vegetable.*

EASY GAZPACHO

"I really enjoy gazpacho a lot. Sometimes I make this on Sunday evening and then take it to school for lunch all week. The crunchy vegetables in the tomato base just add a healthy item to my menu."
—**SUSAN FERRELL** TAMPA, FL

SPINACH CHICKEN POCKETS

## Spinach Chicken Pockets

The tender chicken mixture that's tucked into these pita pockets has a cumin zip and refreshing cucumber-and-yogurt flavor. A favorite at my house, this sandwich is great alone or served with soup or salad.
—**MITZI SENTIFF** ANNAPOLIS, MD

**START TO FINISH:** 30 MIN. • **MAKES:** 4 SERVINGS

- ¾ pound boneless skinless chicken breast halves
- ½ cup reduced-fat plain yogurt
- 2 tablespoons reduced-fat mayonnaise
- 1 tablespoon Dijon mustard
- ¼ teaspoon ground cumin
- ⅛ teaspoon cayenne pepper
- 2 cups fresh baby spinach
- ½ cup chopped seeded cucumber
- 2 green onions, sliced
- 4 pita breads (6 inches), halved

1. In a large nonstick skillet coated with cooking spray, cook chicken over medium heat for 10-12 minutes on each side or until juices run clear. Remove; slice chicken thinly and cool.
2. Meanwhile, in a small bowl, combine the yogurt, mayonnaise, mustard, cumin and cayenne; set aside. In a large bowl, combine the spinach, cucumber, onions and chicken.
3. Drizzle with yogurt mixture; toss to coat. Microwave pita breads for 15-20 seconds or until warmed. Fill each half with ½ cup chicken mixture.

**PER SERVING** *317 cal., 6 g fat (1 g sat. fat), 51 mg chol., 552 mg sodium, 39 g carb., 2 g fiber, 25 g pro.* **Diabetic Exchanges:** *2 starch, 2 lean meat, 1 fat.*

65

69

72

# Side Dishes

**“** This is one of my family's special-occasion dishes. We all love the fresh taste of asparagus, and we know it's healthy, too. **”**

**—JENNIFER CLARK** BLACKSBURG, VA
*about her recipe, Fresh Asparagus with Pecans, on page 66*

# Springtime Barley

While working as a sorority house mother, I occasionally filled in for the cook. The girls just loved when I made this healthy springtime medley.

—**SHARON HELMICK** COLFAX, WA

**START TO FINISH:** 30 MIN. • **MAKES:** 4 SERVINGS

- 1 **small onion, chopped**
- 1 **medium carrot, chopped**
- 1 **tablespoon butter**
- 1 **cup quick-cooking barley**
- 2 **cups reduced-sodium chicken broth, divided**
- ½ **pound fresh asparagus, trimmed and cut into 1-inch pieces**
- ¼ **teaspoon dried marjoram**
- ⅛ **teaspoon pepper**
- 2 **tablespoons shredded Parmesan cheese**

**1.** In a large skillet, saute onion and carrot in butter until crisp-tender. Stir in the barley; cook and stir for 1 minute. Stir in 1 cup broth. Bring to a boil. Reduce heat; cook and stir until most of the liquid is absorbed.

**2.** Add asparagus. Cook for 15-20 minutes or until barley is tender and liquid is absorbed, stirring occasionally and adding more broth as needed. Stir in marjoram and pepper; sprinkle with cheese.

**PER SERVING** *226 cal., 5 g fat (2 g sat. fat), 9 mg chol., 396 mg sodium, 39 g carb., 9 g fiber, 9 g pro.* **Diabetic Exchanges:** *2 starch, 1 vegetable, ½ fat.*

SPRINGTIME BARLEY

LEMON HERB QUINOA

# Lemon Herb Quinoa F M

My family is turning to quinoa more and more these days. It's a super grain that's packed with protein and vitamins. Plus, it can be paired with any kind of main course.

—**JENN TIDWELL** FAIR OAKS, CA

**START TO FINISH:** 25 MIN. • **MAKES:** 4 SERVINGS

- 2 **cups water**
- 1 **cup quinoa, rinsed**
- ½ **teaspoon salt, divided**
- 1 **tablespoon minced fresh basil**
- 1 **tablespoon minced fresh cilantro**
- 1½ **teaspoons minced fresh mint**
- 1 **teaspoon grated lemon peel**

**1.** In a small saucepan, bring water to a boil. Add quinoa and ¼ teaspoon salt. Reduce heat; cover and simmer for 12-15 minutes or until liquid is absorbed.

**2.** Remove from the heat. Add the basil, cilantro, mint, lemon peel and remaining salt; fluff with a fork.

**NOTE** *Look for quinoa in the cereal, rice or organic food aisle.*

**PER SERVING** *160 cal., 2 g fat (trace sat. fat), 0 chol., 304 mg sodium, 29 g carb., 3 g fiber, 6 g pro.* **Diabetic Exchange:** *2 starch.*

# Peanut Ginger Pasta M

Ginger and peanut butter add a sweet-nutty depth of flavor that no one suspects could be this good. The combination is amazing!

—**ALLIL BINDER** SPOKANE, WA

**START TO FINISH:** 30 MIN. • **MAKES:** 4 CUPS

- 2 tablespoons lime juice
- 1 tablespoon reduced-sodium soy sauce
- 1 teaspoon water
- ½ teaspoon sesame oil
- 3 tablespoons peanut butter
- 1¼ teaspoons minced fresh gingerroot
- 1¼ teaspoons grated lime peel
- 1 garlic clove, minced
- ¼ teaspoon salt
- ⅛ teaspoon pepper
- 4 ounces uncooked whole wheat linguine
- 1 cup chopped fresh broccoli
- 1 medium carrot, grated
- ½ medium sweet red pepper, thinly sliced
- 1 green onion, chopped
- 1 tablespoon minced fresh basil

**1.** In a blender, combine the first 10 ingredients; cover and process until blended. Set aside.

**2.** In a large saucepan, cook linguine according to package directions, adding broccoli during the last 5 minutes. Cook until broccoli is tender; drain.

**3.** In a large bowl, combine the carrot, red pepper, onion and basil. Add linguine, broccoli and lime juice mixture; toss to coat.

**PER SERVING** *191 cal., 7 g fat (1 g sat. fat), 0 chol., 366 mg sodium, 29 g carb., 5 g fiber, 7 g pro.* **Diabetic Exchanges: 2 starch, ½ fat.**

PEANUT GINGER PASTA

"I used to hate sweet potatoes as a child, mostly because they came out of a can. When I heard of the many health benefits, my husband and I began trying fresh sweet potatoes. We liked to make fries with different toppings, like cinnamon and sugar, or cayenne pepper. Then we discovered how awesome they are with blue cheese." —**KATRINA KRUMM** APPLE VALLEY, MN

SWEET POTATO FRIES WITH BLUE CHEESE

# Sweet Potato Fries with Blue Cheese M

**START TO FINISH:** 25 MIN. • **MAKES:** 2 SERVINGS

- 1 tablespoon olive oil
- 2 medium sweet potatoes, peeled and cut into ½-in.-thick strips
- 1 tablespoon apricot preserves
- ¼ teaspoon salt
- 3 tablespoons crumbled blue cheese

In a large skillet, heat oil over medium heat. Add potatoes; cook 12-15 minutes or until tender and lightly browned, turning occasionally. Add preserves and stir to coat. Sprinkle with salt. Remove to serving plate; top with cheese.

**PER SERVING** *246 cal., 11 g fat (3 g sat. fat), 9 mg chol., 487 mg sodium, 34 g carb., 3 g fiber, 5 g pro.*

## Dilly Grilled Veggies S C M

Use any combination of vegetables in this versatile side dish. I like to include cauliflower, carrots, green peppers and onions, too!
—**FRAN SCOTT** BIRMINGHAM, MI

**START TO FINISH:** 30 MIN. • **MAKES:** 6 SERVINGS

- 2 **cups sliced fresh mushrooms**
- 2 **cups sliced fresh zucchini**
- 2 **cups fresh broccoli florets**
- ½ **medium sweet red pepper, cut into strips**
- 2 **tablespoons olive oil**
- 2 **tablespoons minced fresh dill or 2 teaspoons dill weed**
- ⅛ **teaspoon garlic salt**
- ⅛ **teaspoon pepper**

**1.** Place vegetables on a double thickness of heavy-duty foil (about 18-in. square). Drizzle with oil; sprinkle with dill, garlic salt and pepper. Fold foil around vegetables and seal tightly.
**2.** Grill, covered, over medium heat for 15 minutes or until vegetables are tender. Open foil carefully to allow steam to escape.
**PER SERVING** *61 cal., 5 g fat (1 g sat. fat), 0 chol., 49 mg sodium, 4 g carb., 2 g fiber, 2 g pro.* **Diabetic Exchanges:** *1 vegetable, 1 fat.*

## Fresh Asparagus with Pecans C M

This is one of my family's special-occasion dishes. We all love the fresh taste of asparagus, and we know it's healthy, too!
—**JENNIFER CLARK** BLACKSBURG, VA

**PREP:** 15 MIN. + MARINATING • **MAKES:** 4 SERVINGS

- 1 **pound fresh asparagus, trimmed**
- ¼ **cup cider vinegar**
- ¼ **cup reduced-sodium soy sauce**
- 2 **tablespoons sugar**
- 2 **tablespoons olive oil**
- 3 **tablespoons chopped pecans, toasted**

**1.** In a large skillet, bring 3 cups water to a boil. Add asparagus; cover and boil for 3 minutes. Drain and immediately place asparagus in ice water. Drain and pat dry.
**2.** In a large resealable plastic bag, combine the vinegar, soy sauce, sugar and oil. Add the asparagus; seal bag and turn to coat. Refrigerate for up to 3 hours.
**3.** Drain and discard marinade. Sprinkle asparagus with pecans.
**PER SERVING** *77 cal., 6 g fat (1 g sat. fat), 0 chol., 164 mg sodium, 5 g carb., 1 g fiber, 2 g pro.* **Diabetic Exchanges:** *1 vegetable, 1 fat.*

## Cranberry Wild Rice Ⓢ Ⓜ

Nuts are a wonderful source of protein and nutrition, so I always look for ways to include them in my dishes. The addition of cranberries in this recipe makes it perfect for fall.
—**DAWN E. BRYANT** THEDFORD, NE

**PREP:** 15 MIN. • **COOK:** 50 MIN. • **MAKES:** 4 SERVINGS

- 4 **cups water**
- ¾ **cup uncooked wild rice**
- 1 **small red onion, chopped**
- ½ **cup chopped dried cranberries**
- 1 **teaspoon dried thyme**
- 1 **tablespoon olive oil**
- 3 **garlic cloves, minced**
- 2 **tablespoons pine nuts, toasted**

**1.** In a large saucepan, bring water and rice to a boil. Reduce heat; simmer, uncovered, for 50-60 minutes or until rice is tender.

**2.** In a large skillet, saute the onion, cranberries and thyme in oil until onion is tender. Add garlic; cook 1 minute longer. Drain rice if needed; stir in onion mixture and pine nuts.

**PER SERVING** *238 cal., 6 g fat (1 g sat. fat), 0 chol., 1 mg sodium, 42 g carb., 3 g fiber, 6 g pro.*

## Garbanzo Bean Medley Ⓜ

This Italian-style side dish is quick, flavorful and satisfying. Sprinkle some feta cheese on top for a change of pace.
—**DENISE NEAL** YORBA LINDA, CA

**START TO FINISH:** 10 MIN. • **MAKES:** 4 SERVINGS

- 1 **small zucchini, cubed**
- 1 **teaspoon olive oil**
- 2 **teaspoons minced garlic**
- 1 **can (15 ounces) garbanzo beans or chickpeas, rinsed and drained**
- 1 **can (14½ ounces) diced tomatoes, undrained**
- 1 **teaspoon Italian seasoning**
- ¼ **teaspoon crushed red pepper flakes, optional**
- ¼ **cup shredded Parmesan cheese**

In a small skillet, saute zucchini in oil until tender. Add garlic; saute 1 minute longer. Stir in the garbanzo beans, tomatoes, Italian seasoning and pepper flakes if desired; heat through. Sprinkle with cheese.

**PER SERVING** *157 cal., 5 g fat (1 g sat. fat), 4 mg chol., 354 mg sodium, 23 g carb., 6 g fiber, 7 g pro.* **Diabetic Exchanges:** *1 starch, 1 lean meat, 1 vegetable.*

## Roasted Peppers 'n' Cauliflower C M

Roasting really enhances the taste of this cauliflower-red pepper-onion dish. The nicely seasoned veggies are great with nearly any main course.

—CHERYL WILT EGLON, WV

**PREP:** 10 MIN. • **BAKE:** 30 MIN.
**MAKES:** 6 SERVINGS

- 1 medium head cauliflower, broken into florets
- 2 medium sweet red peppers, cut into strips
- 2 small onions, cut into wedges
- 2 tablespoons olive oil
- ½ teaspoon salt
- ½ teaspoon pepper
- 1 tablespoon grated Parmesan cheese
- 1 tablespoon minced fresh parsley

**1.** Place the cauliflower, red peppers and onions in a shallow roasting pan. Add the oil, salt and pepper; toss to coat. Bake, uncovered, at 425° for 20 minutes.

**2.** Stir; bake 10 minutes longer or until vegetables are tender and lightly browned. Transfer to a serving bowl; sprinkle with Parmesan cheese and parsley.

**PER SERVING** *88 cal., 5 g fat (1 g sat. fat), 1 mg chol., 243 mg sodium, 10 g carb., 4 g fiber, 3 g pro.* **Diabetic Exchanges:** *2 vegetable, 1 fat.*

HONEY-THYME BUTTERNUT SQUASH

ROASTED PEPPERS 'N' CAULIFLOWER

## Honey-Thyme Butternut Squash M

Instead of potatoes, try whipping up mashed butternut squash with honey, butter and thyme. More than a festive side, this 30-minute dish will be a new fall favorite for weeknight meals.

—BIANCA NOISEUX BRISTOL, CT

**START TO FINISH:** 30 MIN.
**MAKES:** 10 SERVINGS

- 1 large butternut squash (about 5 pounds), peeled and cubed
- ¼ cup butter, cubed
- 3 tablespoons half-and-half cream
- 2 tablespoons honey
- 2 teaspoons dried parsley flakes
- ½ teaspoon salt
- ⅛ teaspoon dried thyme
- ⅛ teaspoon coarsely ground pepper

**1.** In a large saucepan, bring 1 in. of water to a boil. Add squash; cover and cook for 10-15 minutes or until tender.

**2.** Drain. Mash squash with the remaining ingredients.

**PER SERVING** *145 cal., 5 g fat (3 g sat. fat), 14 mg chol., 161 mg sodium, 26 g carb., 7 g fiber, 2 g pro.* **Diabetic Exchanges:** *1½ starch, 1 fat.*

 **Did you know?**

If stored properly away from light and in a cool, dry place (not the refrigerator), a whole, uncooked butternut squash will last up to a month.

## Garden Orzo Risotto M

**START TO FINISH:** 30 MIN.
**MAKES:** 6 SERVINGS

- 1 small zucchini, chopped
- 1 shallot, chopped
- 2 tablespoons olive oil
- 2 garlic cloves, minced
- 1 cup uncooked whole wheat orzo pasta
- 2 cups vegetable broth
- 1 cup 2% milk
- 1 package (6 ounces) fresh baby spinach
- 2 medium tomatoes, seeded and chopped
- ¼ cup minced fresh basil
- ⅓ cup grated Parmesan cheese
  Salt and pepper to taste

**1.** In a large saucepan, saute zucchini and shallot in oil until almost tender. Add garlic; cook 1 minute longer. Add the orzo, broth and milk. Bring to a boil. Reduce heat to medium-low; cook and stir for 10-15 minutes or until liquid is almost absorbed.

**2.** Stir in the spinach, tomatoes and basil; cook and stir until spinach is wilted. Remove from the heat; stir in the cheese, salt and pepper.

**PER SERVING** *202 cal., 7 g fat (2 g sat. fat), 7 mg chol., 429 mg sodium, 27 g carb., 6 g fiber, 8 g pro.* **Diabetic Exchanges:** *1 starch, 1 vegetable, 1 fat.*

GARDEN ORZO RISOTTO

"No one will believe this rich, creamy dish was prepared in less than 30 minutes! I developed the recipe when my garden tomatoes, zucchini and basil were coming on strong. Using orzo instead of arborio rice makes the risotto so much easier to prepare." —**CINDY BEBERMAN** ORLAND PARK, IL

ACORN SQUASH WITH APRICOT SAUCE

## Acorn Squash with Apricot Sauce S M

With its mild flavor, acorn squash is the perfect base for crunchy walnuts and sweet apricots. I like to double the sauce so I can serve it with my breakfast oatmeal the next day.

—**JUDY PARKER** MOORE, OK

**PREP:** 10 MIN. • **BAKE:** 55 MIN.
**MAKES:** 4 SERVINGS

- 2 small acorn squash
- 2 tablespoons brown sugar
- ¼ teaspoon ground cinnamon
- 2 tablespoons butter
- 1 cup orange juice
- ½ cup dried apricots, coarsely chopped
- ½ cup chopped walnuts, optional

**1.** Cut squash in half; discard seeds. Cut a thin slice from bottom of squash with a sharp knife to allow it to sit flat. Place hollow side up in a greased 15-in. x 10-in. x 1-in. baking pan; add ½ in. of hot water.

**2.** Combine brown sugar and cinnamon; sprinkle over squash. Dot with butter. Cover and bake at 375° for 55-65 minutes or until tender.

**3.** Meanwhile, in a small saucepan, combine orange juice and apricots. Bring to a boil. Reduce heat; simmer, uncovered, for 15 minutes or until apricots are tender. Transfer to a blender; cover and process until smooth. Serve with squash; sprinkle with walnuts if desired.

**PER SERVING** *241 cal., 6 g fat (4 g sat. fat), 15 mg chol., 50 mg sodium, 48 g carb., 5 g fiber, 3 g pro.*

VEGGIE KABOBS WITH GINGERED YOGURT

## Veggie Kabobs with Gingered Yogurt

This is a great way to serve vegetables and add color to any meal. But the really fun part is the gingered yogurt dip.

—MARIE RIZZIO INTERLOCHEN, MI

**PREP:** 20 MIN. • **GRILL:** 15 MIN.
**MAKES:** 4 SERVINGS

- 1 carton (8 ounces) reduced-fat plain yogurt
- 2 green onions, finely chopped
- 1 teaspoon grated fresh gingerroot
- 1 teaspoon honey
- ½ teaspoon ground mustard
- 1 garlic clove, minced
- ¼ teaspoon salt
- 2 large sweet red peppers, cut into eight pieces
- 1 large zucchini, cut into eight slices
- 1 medium eggplant, peeled and cut into eight slices
- 1 large green pepper, cut into eight pieces
- 4 teaspoons canola oil

**1.** In a small bowl, combine the yogurt, onions, ginger, honey, mustard, garlic and salt. Cover and refrigerate until serving.

**2.** On four metal or soaked wooden skewers, alternately thread the red peppers, zucchini, eggplant and green pepper; brush with oil. Grill, covered, over medium heat for 15-18 minutes or until vegetables are tender, turning occasionally. Serve with yogurt sauce.
**PER SERVING** *162 cal., 6 g fat (1 g sat. fat), 3 mg chol., 197 mg sodium, 24 g carb., 6 g fiber, 6 g pro.* **Diabetic Exchanges:** *1½ starch, 1 fat.*

## Garden Zucchini & Corn Saute

This is great with any barbecue main dish, and it's also the perfect filling for a brunch omelet. It's even good cold as a salad.

—TRISHA KRUSE EAGLE, ID

**START TO FINISH:** 25 MIN.
**MAKES:** 4 SERVINGS

- 2 medium zucchini, thinly sliced
- ⅓ cup sliced onion
- 1½ teaspoons olive oil
- ¾ cup fresh whole kernel corn
- 2 garlic cloves, minced
- ½ teaspoon sugar

- ¼ teaspoon salt
- ¼ teaspoon lemon-pepper seasoning

In a large skillet, saute zucchini and onion in oil until crisp-tender. Add corn and garlic; saute 2 minutes longer or until vegetables are tender. Sprinkle with sugar, salt and lemon pepper.
**PER SERVING** *72 cal., 2 g fat (trace sat. fat), 0 chol., 192 mg sodium, 13 g carb., 2 g fiber, 2 g pro.* **Diabetic Exchanges:** *1 vegetable, ½ starch.*

## Lentil White Bean Pilaf

Vegetarians will be happy to see this hearty meatless grain pilaf on the holiday buffet table. I like to make this when I have extra cooked lentils, barley, quinoa and rice on hand.

—JULI MEYERS HINESVILLE, GA

**PREP:** 35 MIN. • **COOK:** 15 MIN.
**MAKES:** 10 SERVINGS

- 1 cup dried lentils, rinsed
- ½ cup quick-cooking barley
- ½ cup quinoa, rinsed
- ⅓ cup uncooked long grain rice
- ½ pound sliced baby portobello mushrooms
- 3 medium carrots, finely chopped

- 3 celery ribs, finely chopped
- 1 large onion, finely chopped
- ¼ cup butter, cubed
- 3 garlic cloves, minced
- 2 teaspoons minced fresh rosemary or ½ teaspoon dried rosemary, crushed
- ½ cup vegetable broth
- ½ teaspoon salt
- ½ teaspoon pepper
- 2 cups canned white kidney or cannellini beans, rinsed and drained

**1.** Cook the lentils, barley, quinoa and rice according to package directions; set aside.

**2.** In a Dutch oven, saute the mushrooms, carrots, celery and onion in butter until tender. Add garlic and rosemary; cook 1 minute longer. Add broth, salt and pepper, stirring to loosen browned bits from pan. Stir in beans and the cooked lentils, barley, quinoa and rice; heat through.
**NOTE** *Look for quinoa in the cereal, rice or organic food aisle.*
**PER SERVING** *259 cal., 6 g fat (3 g sat. fat), 12 mg chol., 290 mg sodium, 41 g carb., 11 g fiber, 11 g pro.*

LENTIL WHITE BEAN PILAF

SMOKY GRILLED CORN ON THE COB

## Lemon Crumb-Topped Broccoli F S C M

Dress up broccoli with a lemony bread-crumb topping. You'll be surprised with the delicious result and delighted with the positive reaction from guests.

—**PATRICIA NIEH** PORTOLA VALLEY, CA

**START TO FINISH:** 20 MIN. • **MAKES:** 4 SERVINGS

- 1 **garlic clove, minced**
- 1 **teaspoon olive oil**
- 1 **slice multigrain bread, toasted and crumbled**
- ½ **teaspoon grated lemon peel**
- 2 **tablespoons minced fresh parsley**
- 3 **cups fresh broccoli florets**
- 1 **tablespoon water**
- 2 **tablespoons lemon juice**

**1.** In a small skillet, saute garlic in oil for 30 seconds. Stir in bread crumbs and lemon peel; cook 1 minute longer. Remove from the heat. Stir in parsley; set aside.

**2.** Place broccoli and water in a microwave-safe bowl. Cover and microwave on high for 2-3 minutes or until crisp-tender; drain. Drizzle with lemon juice; toss to coat. Sprinkle with crumb mixture.

**NOTE** *This recipe was tested in a 1,100-watt microwave.*
**PER SERVING** *45 cal., 2 g fat (trace sat. fat), 0 chol., 47 mg sodium, 7 g carb., 2 g fiber, 2 g pro.* **Diabetic Exchange: 1 vegetable.**

## Smoky Grilled Corn on the Cob M

We love corn and are always looking for new ways to enjoy it. This tastes great right off the grill, but leftovers are delicious in salads and tacos. I like to let the corn cool, cut it off the cob, then top it with butter and fresh cracked pepper.

—**RACHEL KIRTLEY** VICKSBURG, MI

**PREP:** 15 MIN. + SOAKING • **GRILL:** 25 MIN. • **MAKES:** 6 SERVINGS

- 6 **medium ears sweet corn**
- 2 **tablespoons olive oil**
- 1 **teaspoon chili powder**
- 1 **teaspoon smoked paprika**
- ½ **teaspoon seasoned salt**
- ⅛ **teaspoon cayenne pepper**

**1.** Carefully peel back corn husks to within 1 in. of bottoms; remove silk. Brush corn with oil. In a small bowl, combine remaining ingredients; sprinkle over corn. Rewrap corn in husks; secure with kitchen string. Place in a Dutch oven; cover with cold water. Soak 20 minutes; drain.

**2.** Grill corn, covered, over medium heat 25-30 minutes or until tender, turning often.

**PER SERVING** *120 cal., 6 g fat (1 g sat. fat), 0 chol., 145 mg sodium, 18 g carb., 3 g fiber, 3 g pro.* **Diabetic Exchanges: 1 starch, 1 fat.**

LEMON CRUMB-TOPPED BROCCOLI

SAUSAGE CORN BREAD DRESSING

## Sausage Corn Bread Dressing 🖪

You wouldn't know it from tasting it, but my holiday corn bread dressing has only 3 grams of fat per serving. Made with turkey sausage, herbs, fruit and veggies, it's a healthy alternative to traditional dressing recipes.

**—REBECCA BAIRD** SALT LAKE CITY, UT

**PREP:** 30 MIN. • **BAKE:** 50 MIN. • **MAKES:** 16 SERVINGS

- 1 **cup all-purpose flour**
- 1 **cup cornmeal**
- ¼ **cup sugar**
- 3 **teaspoons baking powder**
- 1 **teaspoon salt**
- 1 **cup buttermilk**
- ¼ **cup unsweetened applesauce**
- 2 **egg whites**

**DRESSING**
- 1 **pound turkey Italian sausage links, casings removed**
- 4 **celery ribs, chopped**
- 1 **medium onion, chopped**
- 1 **medium sweet red pepper, chopped**
- 2 **medium tart apples, chopped**
- 1 **cup chopped roasted chestnuts**
- 3 **tablespoons minced fresh parsley**
- 2 **garlic cloves, minced**
- ½ **teaspoon dried thyme**
- ½ **teaspoon pepper**
- 1 **cup reduced-sodium chicken broth**
- 1 **egg white**

**1.** For corn bread, combine the first five ingredients in a large bowl. Combine the buttermilk, applesauce and egg whites; stir into dry ingredients just until moistened.

**2.** Pour into a 9-in. square baking dish coated with cooking spray. Bake at 400° for 20-25 minutes or until a toothpick inserted near the center comes out clean. Cool on a wire rack.

**3.** In a large nonstick skillet, cook the sausage, celery, onion and red pepper over medium heat until meat is no longer pink; drain. Transfer to a large bowl. Crumble corn bread over mixture. Add the apples, chestnuts, parsley, garlic, thyme and pepper. Stir in broth and egg white.

**4.** Transfer to a 13-in. x 9-in. baking dish coated with cooking spray. Cover and bake at 325° for 40 minutes. Uncover; bake 10 minutes longer or until lightly browned.

**NOTE** *Dressing can be prepared as directed and used to stuff a 10- to 12-pound turkey.*

**PER SERVING** *157 cal., 3 g fat (1 g sat. fat), 18 mg chol., 464 mg sodium, 24 g carb., 2 g fiber, 8 g pro.* **Diabetic Exchanges:** *1½ starch, 1 lean meat.*

## ❓ Did you know?

In Louisiana and Texas, it's not uncommon for stuffing to be prepared with rice, while in other parts of the South, corn bread replaces white bread. Wild rice is a popular stuffing ingredient in the Midwest, and along the Eastern seaboard, oysters make an appearance.

## Garlic Roasted Green Beans with Lemon & Walnuts Ⓒ Ⓜ

I first tasted roasted green beans in a Chinese restaurant and fell in love with the texture and flavor. This is my Americanized version, and it's always a big hit at our holiday table.

—LILY JULOW LAWRENCEVILLE, GA

**START TO FINISH:** 25 MIN.
**MAKES:** 8 SERVINGS

- 2 pounds fresh green beans, trimmed
- 2 shallots, thinly sliced
- 6 garlic cloves, crushed
- 2 tablespoons olive oil
- ¾ teaspoon salt
- ¼ teaspoon pepper
- 2 teaspoons grated lemon peel, divided
- ½ cup chopped walnuts, toasted

**1.** Preheat oven to 425°. In a large bowl, combine green beans, shallots and garlic; drizzle with oil and sprinkle with salt and pepper. Transfer to two 15-in. x 10-in. x 1-in. baking pans coated with cooking spray.

**2.** Roast 15-20 minutes or until tender and lightly browned, stirring occasionally. Remove from oven; stir in 1 teaspoon lemon peel. Sprinkle with walnuts and the remaining lemon peel.

**NOTE** *To toast nuts, spread in a 15-in. x 10-in. x 1-in. baking pan. Bake at 350° for 5-10 minutes or until lightly browned, stirring occasionally. Or, spread in a dry nonstick skillet and heat over low heat until lightly browned, stirring occasionally.*

**PER SERVING** *119 cal., 8 g fat (1 g sat. fat), 0 chol., 229 mg sodium, 11 g carb., 4 g fiber, 3 g pro.* **Diabetic Exchanges: 2 vegetable, 1½ fat.**

EASY BEANS & POTATOES WITH BACON

## Easy Beans & Potatoes with Bacon

I love the combination of green beans with bacon, so I created this recipe. It's great for when you have company because you can start the side dish in the slow cooker and continue preparing the rest of your dinner.

—BARBARA BRITTAIN SANTEE, CA

**PREP:** 15 MIN. • **COOK:** 6 HOURS
**MAKES:** 10 SERVINGS

- 8 bacon strips, chopped
- 1½ pounds fresh green beans, trimmed and cut into 2-inch pieces (about 4 cups)
- 4 medium potatoes, peeled and cubed (½ inch)
- 1 small onion, halved and sliced
- ¼ cup reduced-sodium chicken broth
- ½ teaspoon salt
- ¼ teaspoon pepper

**1.** In a large skillet, cook bacon over medium heat until crisp, stirring occasionally. Remove to paper towels with a slotted spoon; drain, reserving 1 tablespoon drippings. Cover and refrigerate bacon until serving.

**2.** In a 5-qt. slow cooker, combine the remaining ingredients; stir in reserved drippings. Cover and cook on low for 6-8 hours or until potatoes are tender. Stir in bacon; heat through.

**PER SERVING** *116 cal., 4 g fat (1 g sat. fat), 8 mg chol., 256 mg sodium, 17 g carb., 3 g fiber, 5 g pro.* **Diabetic Exchanges: 1 starch, 1 fat.**

GARLIC ROASTED GREEN BEANS WITH LEMON & WALNUTS

## Grilled Sweet Potato Wedges

When an entire meal can be cooked outside on the grill and I don't need to heat up the kitchen, you better believe I'm going to love it. Next time you're grilling out, try a side of grilled fries.
—**NATALIE KNOWLTON** KAMAS, UT

**START TO FINISH:** 30 MIN.
**MAKES:** 8 SERVINGS

- 4 large sweet potatoes, peeled and cut into ½-inch wedges
- ½ teaspoon garlic salt
- ¼ teaspoon pepper

**DIPPING SAUCE**

- ½ cup reduced-fat mayonnaise
- ½ cup fat-free plain yogurt
- 1 teaspoon ground cumin
- ½ teaspoon seasoned salt
- ½ teaspoon paprika
- ½ teaspoon chili powder

**1.** Place potatoes in a large saucepan and cover with water. Bring to a boil. Reduce heat; cover and simmer for 4-5 minutes or until crisp-tender. Drain; pat dry with paper towels. Sprinkle potatoes with garlic salt and pepper.
**2.** Grill, covered, over medium heat for 10-12 minutes or until tender, turning once. In a small bowl, combine the mayonnaise, yogurt and seasonings. Serve with sweet potatoes.
**PER SERVING** *166 cal., 5 g fat (1 g sat. fat), 6 mg chol., 349 mg sodium, 28 g carb., 3 g fiber, 3 g pro.* **Diabetic Exchanges:** *1½ starch, 1 fat.*

PEAS A LA FRANCAISE

GRILLED SWEET POTATO WEDGES

## Peas a la Francaise

I love these buttery peas, and consider this recipe a favorite. It features tiny pearl onions touched with thyme and chervil, and its presentation is lovely.
—**CHRISTINE FRAZIER** AUBURNDALE, FL

**START TO FINISH:** 30 MIN.
**MAKES:** 12 SERVINGS (½ CUP EACH)

- 1½ cups pearl onions, trimmed
- ¼ cup butter, cubed
- ¼ cup water
- 1 tablespoon sugar
- 1 teaspoon salt
- ¼ teaspoon dried thyme
- ¼ teaspoon dried chervil
- ¼ teaspoon pepper
- 2 packages (16 ounces each) frozen peas, thawed
- 2 cups shredded lettuce

**1.** In a Dutch oven, bring 6 cups water to a boil. Add pearl onions; boil for 3 minutes. Drain and rinse in cold water; peel and set aside.
**2.** In the same saucepan, melt butter over medium heat. Stir in the onions, water, sugar and seasonings. Add peas and lettuce; stir until blended. Cover and cook for 6-8 minutes or until vegetables are tender. Serve with a slotted spoon.
**PER SERVING** *112 cal., 4 g fat (2 g sat. fat), 10 mg chol., 315 mg sodium, 15 g carb., 4 g fiber, 4 g pro.* **Diabetic Exchanges:** *1 starch, 1 fat.*

82

83

86

# Good Mornings

"As a busy working mom, I need breakfast that requires minimal prep. I often combine the egg mixture in advance and refrigerate overnight. Then all I have to do in the morning is heat up my skillet. My favorite part is the goat cheese filling, which gets nice and creamy from the heat of the omelet."

ANNE DIETERLE ROCHESTER HILLS, MI
her recipe, Goat Cheese & Ham Omelet, on page 79

## Hash Brown Nests with Portobellos and Eggs

Hash browns make a fabulous crust for the individual egg quiches. They look fancy, but are actually easy to make. They've been a hit at holiday brunches and other special occasions.

—**KATE MEYER** BRENTWOOD, TN

**PREP:** 30 MIN. • **BAKE:** 15 MIN.
**MAKES:** 12 SERVINGS

- 3 **cups frozen shredded hash brown potatoes, thawed**
- 3 **cups chopped fresh portobello mushrooms**
- ¼ **cup chopped shallots**
- 2 **tablespoons butter**
- 1 **garlic clove, minced**
- ½ **teaspoon salt**
- ¼ **teaspoon pepper**
- 2 **tablespoons sour cream**
- 1 **tablespoon minced fresh basil**
  **Dash cayenne pepper**
- 7 **eggs, beaten**
- ¼ **cup shredded Swiss cheese**
- 2 **bacon strips, cooked and crumbled**
  **Additional minced fresh basil, optional**

**1.** Press ¼ cup hash browns onto the bottom and up the sides of 12 greased muffin cups; set aside.

**2.** In a large skillet, saute mushrooms and shallots in butter until tender. Add garlic, salt and pepper; cook 1 minute longer. Remove from the heat; stir in sour cream, basil and cayenne.

**3.** Divide eggs among potato-lined muffin cups. Top with mushroom mixture. Sprinkle with Swiss cheese and bacon.

**4.** Bake at 400° for 15-18 minutes or until eggs are completely set. Garnish with additional basil if desired. Serve warm.

**PER SERVING** *101 cal., 6 g fat (3 g sat. fat), 134 mg chol., 187 mg sodium, 5 g carb., 1 g fiber, 6 g pro.* **Diabetic Exchanges:** *1 medium-fat meat, ½ fat.*

CANTALOUPE BANANA SMOOTHIES

## Cantaloupe Banana Smoothies

This is one of my favorite flavor combinations for a smoothie. Cool and fruity, a full glass satisfies my cravings for sweets and munchies.

—**JANICE MITCHELL** AURORA, CO

**START TO FINISH:** 10 MIN.
**MAKES:** 3 SERVINGS

- ½ **cup fat-free plain yogurt**
- 4½ **teaspoons orange juice concentrate**
- 2 **cups cubed cantaloupe**
- 1 **large firm banana, cut into 1-inch pieces and frozen**
- 2 **tablespoons nonfat dry milk powder**
- 2 **teaspoons honey**

In a blender, combine all the ingredients. Cover and process until blended. Pour into chilled glasses; serve immediately.

**PER SERVING** *141 cal., 1 g fat (trace sat. fat), 2 mg chol., 60 mg sodium, 32 g carb., 2 g fiber, 5 g pro.* **Diabetic Exchanges:** *1 starch, 1 fruit.*

HASH BROWN NESTS WITH PORTOBELLOS AND EGGS

## Goat Cheese & Ham Omelet ⒸⓂ

**START TO FINISH:** 20 MIN.
**MAKES:** 1 SERVING

- 4 egg whites
- 2 teaspoons water
- ⅛ teaspoon pepper
- 1 slice deli ham, finely chopped
- 2 tablespoons finely chopped green pepper
- 2 tablespoons finely chopped onion
- 2 tablespoons crumbled goat cheese
  Minced fresh parsley, optional

**1.** In a small bowl, whisk egg whites, water and pepper until blended; stir in ham, green pepper and onion. Heat a large nonstick skillet coated with cooking spray over medium-high heat. Pour in egg white mixture. Mixture should set immediately at edges. As egg whites set, push cooked portions toward the center, letting uncooked egg flow underneath.

**2.** When no liquid egg remains, sprinkle goat cheese on one side. Fold omelet in half; slide onto a plate. If desired, sprinkle with parsley.

**PER SERVING** *143 cal., 4 g fat (2 g sat. fat), 27 mg chol., 489 mg sodium, 5 g carb., 1 g fiber, 21 g pro.* **Diabetic Exchanges:** *3 lean meat, ½ fat.*

SUPER LOW-FAT GRANOLA CEREAL

"As a busy working mom, I need breakfast that requires minimal prep. I often combine the egg mixture in advance and refrigerate overnight. Then all I have to do in the morning is heat up my skillet. My favorite part is the goat cheese filling, which gets nice and creamy from the heat of the omelet."

—**LYNNE DIETERLE** ROCHESTER HILLS, MI

GOAT CHEESE & HAM OMELET

## Super Low-Fat Granola Cereal Ⓕ Ⓜ

Serve this delicious mix for breakfast with milk, or sprinkle it over yogurt. Also try making it with different dried fruits, such as raisins and pineapple.

—**KELLY KIRBY** WESTVILLE, NS

**PREP:** 15 MIN. • **BAKE:** 25 MIN. + COOLING
**MAKES:** 9 CUPS

- 8 cups old-fashioned oats
- 1 cup raisins
- ½ cup chopped dried apricots
- ½ cup dried cranberries
- 1½ cups packed brown sugar
- ½ cup water
- 1 teaspoon salt
- 1 teaspoon maple flavoring
- 1 teaspoon vanilla extract
  2% milk or reduced-fat plain yogurt

**1.** In a large bowl, combine the oats, raisins, apricots and cranberries; set aside. In a small saucepan, combine the brown sugar, water and salt. Cook and stir over medium heat for 3-4 minutes or until brown sugar is dissolved. Remove from the heat; stir in maple flavoring and vanilla. Pour over oat mixture; stir to coat.

**2.** Transfer to two greased 15-in. x 10-in. x 1-in. baking pans. Bake at 350° for 25-30 minutes or until crisp, stirring every 10 minutes. Cool completely on wire racks. Store in an airtight container. Serve with milk or yogurt.

**PER SERVING** *246 cal., 3 g fat (trace sat. fat), 0 chol., 143 mg sodium, 53 g carb., 4 g fiber, 6 g pro.*

ITALIAN SAUSAGE BREAKFAST WRAPS

## Italian Sausage Breakfast Wraps

My husband leaves for work at 4 a.m., and I want him to have a healthy breakfast to start the day. I usually make half a dozen of these on Sunday and keep them in the fridge so he can grab one and go.

—**DAUNA HARWOOD** UNION, MI

**START TO FINISH:** 30 MIN.
**MAKES:** 6 SERVINGS

- ¾ pound Italian turkey sausage links, casings removed
- 1 small green pepper, finely chopped
- 1 small onion, finely chopped
- 1 medium tomato, chopped
- 4 eggs
- 6 egg whites
- 1 cup chopped fresh spinach
- 6 whole wheat tortillas (8 inches)
- 1 cup (4 ounces) shredded reduced-fat cheddar cheese

**1.** In a large skillet, cook sausage, pepper, onion and tomato over medium heat until meat is no longer pink and vegetables are tender, breaking up sausage into crumbles; drain and return to pan.

**2.** In a small bowl, whisk eggs and egg whites until blended. Add egg mixture to sausage. Cook and stir until eggs are thickened and no liquid egg remains. Add spinach; cook and stir just until wilted.

**3.** Spoon ¾ cup egg mixture across center of each tortilla; top with about 2 tablespoons cheese. Fold bottom and sides of tortilla over filling and roll up.

**PER SERVING** *327 cal., 14 g fat (5 g sat. fat), 175 mg chol., 632 mg sodium, 26 g carb., 3 g fiber, 23 g pro.* **Diabetic Exchanges:** *3 lean meat, 1½ starch, 1 vegetable, 1 fat.*

 **Did you know?**

Adding a little lean protein to your morning meal will help you feel full until lunchtime. In fact, eating a healthy breakfast can reduce hunger throughout the day.

MORNING GLORY PANCAKES

## Morning Glory Pancakes M

These pancakes were inspired by the popular morning glory muffins. They are fluffy and delicious without all the oil, but they have the same great carrot, fruit and nut flavors.

—**KURT WAIT** REDWOOD CITY, CA

**START TO FINISH:** 25 MIN.
**MAKES:** 8 PANCAKES (4 SERVINGS)

- ½ cup all-purpose flour
- ½ cup whole wheat flour
- 2 tablespoons sugar
- 1 teaspoon baking powder
- ¾ teaspoon baking soda
- ¼ teaspoon salt
- 1 egg
- 1 egg white
- ¾ cup buttermilk
- 1 tablespoon canola oil
- ½ cup shredded carrots
- ½ cup unsweetened crushed pineapple, drained
- ½ cup diced peeled apple
- ¼ cup chopped walnuts, toasted

**1.** In a large bowl, whisk the first six ingredients. In another bowl, whisk egg, egg white, buttermilk and oil; stir into dry ingredients just until moistened. Stir in carrots, pineapple, apple and walnuts.

**2.** Coat a griddle with cooking spray; heat over medium heat. Pour batter by heaping ¼ cupfuls onto a hot griddle. Cook until bubbles on top begin to pop and bottoms are golden brown. Turn; cook until second side is golden brown.

**PER SERVING** *282 cal., 10 g fat (1 g sat. fat), 55 mg chol., 574 mg sodium, 40 g carb., 4 g fiber, 9 g pro.* **Diabetic Exchanges:** *2½ starch, 2 fat.*

# Southwest Breakfast Wraps M

**START TO FINISH:** 30 MIN. • **MAKES:** 4 SERVINGS

- 1 tablespoon olive oil
- 1 medium red onion, chopped
- ½ cup sliced fresh mushrooms
- 1 small green pepper, finely chopped
- 1 small sweet red pepper, finely chopped
- 1 jalapeno pepper, seeded and finely chopped
- 1 can (4 ounces) chopped green chilies
- 1 garlic clove, minced
- 8 egg whites
- ¼ cup shredded reduced-fat Mexican cheese blend
- 4 whole wheat tortillas (8 inches), warmed

**1.** In a large nonstick skillet, heat oil over medium-high heat. Add onion, mushrooms, peppers, chilies and garlic; cook and stir until peppers are crisp-tender. Remove from pan and keep warm.

**2.** In a small bowl, whisk egg whites and cheese until blended. In same skillet, add egg white mixture; cook and stir over medium heat until egg whites begin to set and no liquid egg remains.

"I always thought eating healthy wouldn't be as enjoyable as eating whatever I wanted. This recipe proved me wrong; healthy ingredients taste wonderful and are just as mouthwatering without the extra calories." —NICOLE HACKLEY CULBERTSON, MT

SOUTHWEST BREAKFAST WRAPS

PEANUT BUTTER OATMEAL

**3.** Spoon egg white mixture across center of each tortilla; top with vegetable mixture. Fold bottom and sides of tortilla over filling and roll up.

**NOTE** *Wear disposable gloves when cutting hot peppers; the oils can burn skin. Avoid touching your face.*

**PER SERVING** *254 cal., 8 g fat (1 g sat. fat), 5 mg chol., 446 mg sodium, 29 g carb., 4 g fiber, 14 g pro.* **Diabetic Exchanges:** *1½ starch, 1 lean meat, 1 vegetable, 1 fat.*

# Peanut Butter Oatmeal M

My son and I eat this every day for breakfast. It's a hearty, healthy breakfast to jump-start our day.

—**ELISABETH REITENBACH** TERRYVILLE, CT

**START TO FINISH:** 15 MIN. • **MAKES:** 2 SERVINGS

- 1¾ cups water
- ⅛ teaspoon salt
- 1 cup old-fashioned oats
- 2 tablespoons creamy peanut butter
- 2 tablespoons honey
- 2 teaspoons ground flaxseed
- 1 teaspoon ground cinnamon
  Chopped apple, optional

**1.** In a large saucepan, bring water and salt to a boil over medium heat. Stir in oats; cook 5 minutes, stirring occasionally.

**2.** Meanwhile, in a small bowl, mix peanut butter, honey, flax and cinnamon. Top servings with peanut butter mixture and apple if desired.

**PER SERVING** *323 cal., 12 g fat (2 g sat. fat), 0 chol., 226 mg sodium, 49 g carb., 6 g fiber, 11 g pro.*

## Lemon Breakfast Parfaits F S M

I serve these lively, layered parfaits as a refreshing start to the day. It's a whole new way to enjoy couscous. You can even make the couscous mixture ahead, cover and chill overnight.

—**JANELLE LEE** APPLETON, WI

**PREP:** 25 MIN. + COOLING • **MAKES:** 6 SERVINGS

- ¾ cup fat-free milk
  Dash salt
- ⅓ cup uncooked couscous
- ½ cup reduced-fat sour cream
- ½ cup lemon yogurt
- 1 tablespoon honey
- ¼ teaspoon grated lemon peel
- 1 cup sliced peeled kiwifruit
- 1 cup fresh blueberries
- 1 cup fresh raspberries
  Chopped crystallized ginger and minced fresh mint

**1.** In a small saucepan, bring milk and salt to a boil. Stir in couscous. Remove from the heat; cover and let stand for 5-10 minutes or until milk is absorbed. Fluff with a fork; cool.
**2.** In a small bowl, combine the sour cream, yogurt, honey and lemon peel. Stir in couscous.
**3.** Combine the kiwi, blueberries and raspberries; spoon ¼ cup into each of six parfait glasses. Layer with couscous mixture and remaining fruit. Garnish with ginger and mint.
**PER SERVING** *146 cal., 2 g fat (1 g sat. fat), 8 mg chol., 64 mg sodium, 27 g carb., 3 g fiber, 5 g pro.* **Diabetic Exchanges:** *1 starch, ½ fruit.*

LEMON BREAKFAST PARFAITS

RICOTTA PANCAKES WITH CINNAMON APPLES

## Ricotta Pancakes with Cinnamon Apples M

Here's a scrumptious way to start the day. My fluffy, tender pancakes are topped with sauteed cinnamon apples and a drizzle of maple syrup. Add a cup of coffee or a glass of milk and you'll be all set.

—**EVA AMUSO** CHESHIRE, MA

**START TO FINISH:** 25 MIN. • **MAKES:** 8 SERVINGS (24 PANCAKES)

- 2 medium apples, sliced
- 1 tablespoon butter
- ½ cup plus 2 tablespoons sugar, divided
- 2 teaspoons ground cinnamon
- 1¼ cups cake flour
- 3 teaspoons baking powder
- ¼ teaspoon salt
- 1 cup ricotta cheese
- 1 cup 2% milk
- 3 eggs, separated
- 1 teaspoon grated lemon peel
- 1 teaspoon lemon juice
  Maple syrup

**1.** In a large saucepan, cook apples in butter over medium heat for 6-8 minutes or until tender. Sprinkle with ½ cup sugar and cinnamon; set aside.
**2.** In a large bowl, combine the flour, baking powder and salt. In another bowl, combine the cheese, milk, egg yolks, lemon peel, juice and remaining sugar. Stir into dry ingredients just until combined. In a small bowl, beat egg whites until stiff peaks form; fold into batter.
**3.** Pour batter by ¼ cupfuls onto a greased hot griddle; turn when bubbles form on top. Cook until the second side is golden brown. Serve with apples and maple syrup.
**PER SERVING** *257 cal., 7 g fat (4 g sat. fat), 98 mg chol., 314 mg sodium, 41 g carb., 2 g fiber, 9 g pro.* **Diabetic Exchanges:** *2½ sta. ch, 1 medium-fat meat, ½ fat.*

## Mediterranean Breakfast Pitas F M

These pretty, low-fat pitas, made with egg substitute, are great for any time of day, not just breakfast. They're full of flavor and guaranteed to fill you up.
—**JOSIE-LYNN BELMONT** WOODBINE, GA

**START TO FINISH:** 25 MIN. • **MAKES:** 2 SERVINGS

- ¼ cup chopped sweet red pepper
- ¼ cup chopped onion
- 1 cup egg substitute
- ⅛ teaspoon salt
- ⅛ teaspoon pepper
- 1 small tomato, chopped
- ½ cup torn fresh baby spinach
- 1½ teaspoons minced fresh basil
- 2 whole pita breads
- 2 tablespoons crumbled feta cheese

**1.** In a small nonstick skillet coated with cooking spray, cook and stir red pepper and onion over medium heat for 3 minutes. Add the egg substitute, salt and pepper; cook and stir until set.

**2.** Combine the tomato, spinach and basil; spoon onto pitas. Top with egg mixture and sprinkle with feta cheese. Serve immediately.

**PER SERVING** *267 cal., 2 g fat (1 g sat. fat), 4 mg chol., 798 mg sodium, 41 g carb., 3 g fiber, 20 g pro.* **Diabetic Exchanges:** *2 starch, 2 lean meat, 1 vegetable.*

## Sausage & Salsa Breakfast Burritos

The best of breakfast all wrapped up in a tasty tortilla. Who could ask for anything more in a breakfast on-the-go?
—**MICHELLE BURNETT** EDEN, UT

**START TO FINISH:** 20 MIN. • **MAKES:** 6 SERVINGS

- 5 breakfast turkey sausage links
- 2 cartons (8 ounces each) egg substitute
- ½ cup salsa
- ¼ teaspoon pepper
- 6 whole wheat tortilla (8 inches), warmed
- ½ cup shredded reduced-fat cheddar cheese

**1.** Cook sausage links according to package directions. Meanwhile, in a large bowl, whisk the egg substitute, salsa and pepper. Pour into a large nonstick skillet coated with cooking spray. Cook and stir over medium heat until eggs are nearly set. Chop the sausage links. Add to egg mixture; cook and stir until completely set.

**2.** Spoon ⅓ cup egg mixture off center on each tortilla and sprinkle with 4 teaspoons cheese. Fold sides and ends over filling and roll up.

**PER SERVING** *265 cal., 10 g fat (3 g sat. fat), 25 mg chol., 602 mg sodium, 25 g carb., 2 g fiber, 18 g pro.* **Diabetic Exchanges:** *2 lean meat, 1½ starch, 1 fat.*

## Pineapple Oatmeal  M

Oatmeal for breakfast is a standard item, but I like to mix it up a bit. This version gets some natural sweetness from pineapple juice and tidbits. It is definitely worth trying!

**—MARIA REGAKIS** SOMERVILLE, MA

**START TO FINISH:** 15 MIN. • **MAKES:** 3 SERVINGS

- 1¼ cups water
- ½ cup unsweetened pineapple juice
- ¼ teaspoon salt
- 1 cup quick-cooking oats
- ¾ cup unsweetened pineapple tidbits
- ½ cup raisins
- 2 tablespoons brown sugar
- ¼ teaspoon ground cinnamon
- ¼ teaspoon vanilla extract
- ¼ cup chopped walnuts
  Fat-free milk, optional

**1.** In a large saucepan, bring water, pineapple juice and salt to a boil over medium heat. Stir in oats; cook and stir for 1-2 minutes or until thickened.

**2.** Remove from heat. Stir in pineapple, raisins, brown sugar, cinnamon and vanilla. Cover and let stand for 2-3 minutes. Sprinkle with walnuts. Serve with milk if desired.

**PER SERVING** *323 cal., 8 g fat (1 g sat. fat), 0 chol., 210 mg sodium, 61 g carb., 5 g fiber, 6 g pro.*

## Ham & Egg Pita Pockets

I made these egg pockets when my kids were running late for school one morning and I needed a quick and healthy handheld breakfast. They come together in the microwave and are ready to eat in 10 minutes.

**—SUE OLSEN** FREMONT, CA

**START TO FINISH:** 10 MIN. • **MAKES:** 1 SERVING

- 2 egg whites
- 1 egg
- ⅛ teaspoon smoked or plain paprika
- ⅛ teaspoon freshly ground pepper
- 1 slice deli ham, chopped
- 1 green onion, sliced
- 2 tablespoons shredded reduced-fat cheddar cheese
- 2 whole wheat pita pocket halves

In a microwave-safe bowl, whisk egg whites, egg, paprika and pepper until blended; stir in ham, green onion and cheese. Microwave, covered, on high for 1 minute. Stir; cook on high 30-60 seconds longer or until almost set. Serve in pitas.

**NOTE** *This recipe was tested in a 1,100-watt microwave.*
**PER SERVING** *323 cal., 10 g fat (4 g sat. fat), 231 mg chol., 769 mg sodium, 34 g carb., 5 g fiber, 27 g pro.* **Diabetic Exchanges:** *3 lean meat, 2 starch.*

GREEK BREAKFAST CASSEROLE

## Greek Breakfast Casserole C

This is a wonderful dish for a Sunday brunch, or you can cut it into six pieces and freeze for individual breakfasts throughout the week. I also like to make it with broccoli, carrots, green onions, Canadian bacon and sharp cheddar cheese; the variations are endless!

—**LAURI KNOX** PINE, CO

**PREP:** 35 MIN. • **BAKE:** 45 MIN. + STANDING
**MAKES:** 6 SERVINGS

- ½ **pound Italian turkey sausage links, casings removed**
- ½ **cup chopped green pepper**
- 1 **shallot, chopped**
- 1 **cup water-packed artichoke hearts, rinsed, drained and chopped**
- 1 **cup chopped fresh broccoli**
- ⅓ **cup sun-dried tomatoes (not packed in oil), chopped**
- 6 **eggs**
- 6 **egg whites**
- 3 **tablespoons fat-free milk**
- ½ **teaspoon Italian seasoning**
- ¼ **teaspoon garlic powder**
- ¼ **teaspoon pepper**
- ⅓ **cup crumbled feta cheese**

**1.** Preheat oven to 350°. In a large skillet, cook sausage, green pepper and shallot over medium heat 8-10 minutes or until sausage is no longer pink, breaking up sausage into crumbles; drain. Transfer mixture to an 8-in.-square baking dish coated with cooking spray. Top with artichokes, broccoli and sun-dried tomatoes.

**2.** In a large bowl, whisk eggs, egg whites, milk and seasonings until blended; pour over top. Sprinkle with feta.

**3.** Bake, uncovered, 45-50 minutes or until a knife inserted near the center comes out clean. Let stand 10 minutes before serving.

**FREEZE OPTION** *Cool baked casserole; cover and freeze. To use, partially thaw in refrigerator overnight. Remove from refrigerator 30 minutes before baking. Preheat oven to 325°. Bake casserole as directed until heated through and a thermometer inserted into center reads 165°.*

**PER SERVING** *176 cal., 9 g fat (3 g sat. fat), 229 mg chol., 495 mg sodium, 7 g carb., 1 g fiber, 17 g pro.* **Diabetic Exchanges:** *2 medium-fat meat, 1 vegetable.*

## Cardamom Sour Cream Waffles M

Sweet with just the right amount of spice, these easy waffles make it nearly impossible to skip your morning meal.

—**BARB MILLER** OAKDALE, MN

**PREP:** 15 MIN. • **COOK:** 5 MIN./BATCH
**MAKES:** 14 WAFFLES (7 SERVINGS)

- ¾ **cup all-purpose flour**
- ¾ **cup whole wheat flour**
- 1½ **teaspoons baking powder**
- 1 **teaspoon ground cardamom**
- ¾ **teaspoon baking soda**
- ½ **teaspoon ground cinnamon**
- ¼ **teaspoon salt**
- 2 **eggs**
- 1 **cup fat-free milk**
- ¾ **cup reduced-fat sour cream**
- ½ **cup packed brown sugar**
- 1 **tablespoon butter, melted**
- 1 **teaspoon vanilla extract**

**1.** In a large bowl, combine the first seven ingredients. In another bowl, whisk the eggs, milk, sour cream, brown sugar, butter and vanilla. Stir into dry ingredients just until combined.

**2.** Bake in a preheated waffle iron according to manufacturer's directions until golden brown.

**PER SERVING** *235 cal., 6 g fat (3 g sat. fat), 74 mg chol., 375 mg sodium, 39 g carb., 2 g fiber, 8 g pro.* **Diabetic Exchanges:** *2½ starch, 1 fat.*

CARDAMOM SOUR CREAM WAFFLES

"My kids love sausage and pancakes, but making them during the week was out of the question. I purchased the frozen variety on a stick but didn't like the calories, additives or price. This version of pigs-in-a-blanket is a great alternative that's much more cost effective."

—**LISA DODD** GREENVILLE, SC

PIGS IN A POOL

## Pigs in a Pool

**PREP:** 45 MIN. • **BAKE:** 20 MIN.
**MAKES:** 12 SERVINGS

- 1 **pound reduced-fat bulk pork sausage**
- 2 **cups all-purpose flour**
- ¼ **cup sugar**
- 1 **tablespoon baking powder**
- 1 **teaspoon salt**
- ½ **teaspoon ground cinnamon**
- ¼ **teaspoon ground nutmeg**
- 1 **egg, lightly beaten**
- 2 **cups fat-free milk**
- 2 **tablespoons canola oil**
- 2 **tablespoons honey**
  **Maple syrup, optional**

**1.** Preheat oven to 350°. Coat mini-muffin cups with cooking spray. Shape sausage into forty-eight ¾-in. balls. Place meatballs on a rack coated with cooking spray in a shallow baking pan.

Bake 15-20 minutes or until cooked through. Drain on paper towels. In a large bowl, whisk flour, sugar, baking powder, salt and spices. In another bowl, whisk egg, milk, oil and honey until blended. Add to flour mixture; stir just until moistened.

**2.** Place a sausage ball in each muffin cup; cover with batter. Bake 20-25 minutes or until lightly browned. Cool 5 minutes before removing from pans to wire racks. Serve warm with syrup if desired.

**FREEZE OPTION** *Freeze cooled muffins in resealable plastic freezer bags. To use, microwave each muffin on high for 20-30 seconds or until heated through.*

**PER SERVING** *234 cal., 10 g fat (3 g sat. fat), 45 mg chol., 560 mg sodium, 26 g carb., 1 g fiber, 10 g pro.* **Diabetic Exchanges:** *1½ starch, 1 medium-fat meat, ½ fat.*

## Herb Breakfast Frittata C M

I came up with this recipe by using what I had in the fridge. Yukon Gold potatoes give this frittata a yummy bottom crust.
—**KATHERINE HANSEN** BRUNSWICK, ME

**START TO FINISH:** 30 MIN.
**MAKES:** 4 SERVINGS

- ¼ **cup thinly sliced red onion**
- 1 **tablespoon olive oil**
- 1 **large Yukon Gold potato, peeled and thinly sliced**
- 6 **eggs**
- 1 **teaspoon minced fresh rosemary or ¼ teaspoon dried rosemary, crushed**
- 1 **teaspoon minced fresh thyme or ¼ teaspoon dried thyme**
- ¼ **teaspoon salt**
- ⅛ **teaspoon crushed red pepper flakes**
- ⅛ **teaspoon pepper**
- 2 **tablespoons shredded cheddar cheese**

**1.** In an 8-in. ovenproof skillet, saute onion in oil until tender. Using a slotted spoon, remove onion and keep warm. Arrange potato in a single layer over bottom of pan.

**2.** In a small bowl, whisk the eggs, seasonings and onion; pour over potatoes. Cover and cook for 4-6 minutes or until nearly set.

**3.** Uncover skillet. Broil 3-4 in. from the heat for 2-3 minutes or until eggs are completely set. Sprinkle with cheese. Let stand for 5 minutes. Cut into wedges.

**PER SERVING** *204 cal., 12 g fat (4 g sat. fat), 321 mg chol., 277 mg sodium, 13 g carb., 1 g fiber, 11 g pro.* **Diabetic Exchanges:** *1 starch, 1 medium-fat meat, 1 fat.*

top tip

## Blueberries on the Side

Round out your breakfast with a side of blueberries. Studies have found that the tiny purple berries are loaded with valuable antioxidants that can slow brain aging and protect your memory.

93

96

100

# Ready in 30

**"** With only five ingredients, which can easily be doubled, these mouthwatering kabobs are a favorite to make and eat. To prevent wooden skewers from burning, soak them in water for 30 minutes before threading on the meat.**"**

**—CAROLE FRASER** TORONTO, ON
*about her recipe, Balsamic-Glazed Beef Skewers, on page 99*

## Confetti Tilapia Packets F C

This idea came to me after watching a friend grill fish in foil. You can use flounder, cod or tilapia; the flavors are fantastic!
—BARBARA SCHINDLER NAPOLEON, OH

**START TO FINISH:** 30 MIN.
**MAKES:** 4 SERVINGS

- 1 medium green pepper, cut into ¾-inch pieces
- 4 green onions, sliced
- 3 bacon strips, chopped
- 1 celery rib, chopped
- 1 large tomato, chopped
- ½ teaspoon salt
- ⅛ teaspoon pepper
- 4 tilapia fillets (4 ounces each)
- 4 teaspoons lemon juice

**1.** In a large skillet, saute the green pepper, onions, bacon and celery until vegetables are tender and bacon is crisp; drain. Add the tomato, salt and pepper; heat through.

**2.** Place each fillet on a double thickness of heavy-duty foil (about 12 in. square). Drizzle fillets with lemon juice. Top with vegetable mixture. Fold foil around fish and seal tightly.

**3.** Grill, covered, over medium-hot heat for 15-20 minutes or until fish flakes easily with a fork. Open foil carefully to allow steam to escape.
**PER SERVING** *141 cal., 3 g fat (1 g sat. fat), 60 mg chol., 459 mg sodium, 5 g carb., 2 g fiber, 24 g pro.* **Diabetic Exchanges:** *3 lean meat, 1 vegetable.*

MEDITERRANEAN CHICKEN STIR-FRY

CONFETTI TILAPIA PACKETS

## Mediterranean Chicken Stir-Fry

Barley is a chewier and more flavorful alternative to white rice. Try making the switch in this quick and colorful garden-fresh stir-fry.
—TASTE OF HOME TEST KITCHEN

**START TO FINISH:** 30 MIN.
**MAKES:** 4 SERVINGS

- 2 cups water
- 1 cup quick-cooking barley
- 1 pound boneless skinless chicken breasts, cubed
- 3 teaspoons olive oil, divided
- 1 medium onion, chopped
- 2 medium zucchini, chopped
- 2 garlic cloves, minced
- 1 teaspoon dried oregano
- ½ teaspoon dried basil
- ¼ teaspoon salt
- ¼ teaspoon pepper
  Dash crushed red pepper flakes
- 2 plum tomatoes, chopped
- ½ cup pitted Greek olives, chopped
- 1 tablespoon minced fresh parsley

**1.** In a small saucepan, bring water to a boil. Stir in barley. Reduce heat; cover and simmer for 10-12 minutes or until barley is tender. Remove from the heat; let stand for 5 minutes.

**2.** Meanwhile, in a large skillet or wok, stir-fry chicken in 2 teaspoons oil until no longer pink. Remove and keep warm.

**3.** Stir-fry onion in remaining oil for 3 minutes. Add the zucchini, garlic, oregano, basil, salt, pepper and pepper flakes; stir-fry 2-4 minutes longer or until vegetables are crisp-tender. Add the chicken, tomatoes, olives and parsley. Serve with barley.
**PER SERVING** *403 cal., 12 g fat (2 g sat. fat), 63 mg chol., 498 mg sodium, 44 g carb., 11 g fiber, 31 g pro.* **Diabetic Exchanges:** *3 lean meat, 2 starch, 2 fat, 1 vegetable.*

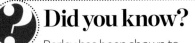 **Did you know?**
Barley has been shown to lower LDL "bad" cholesterol and may help reduce the risk of heart diease. Of all the whole grains, it's the highest in fiber, with about 17 percent fiber compared with 10 percent in oats and 3.5 percent in brown rice.

## Caribbean Chicken Stir-Fry

**START TO FINISH:** 25 MIN.
**MAKES:** 4 SERVINGS

- 2 teaspoons cornstarch
- ¼ cup water
- 1 pound boneless skinless chicken breasts, cut into ½-inch strips
- 2 teaspoons Caribbean jerk seasoning
- 1 can (15 ounces) mixed tropical fruit, drained and coarsely chopped
- 2 packages (8.8 ounces each) ready-to-serve brown rice

1. In a small bowl, mix cornstarch and water until smooth.
2. Coat a large skillet with cooking spray; heat over medium-high heat. Add chicken; sprinkle with jerk seasoning. Stir-fry 3-5 minutes or until no longer pink. Stir cornstarch mixture and add to pan with fruit. Bring to a boil; cook and stir 1-2 minutes or until sauce is thickened.
3. Meanwhile, cook brown rice according to package directions. Serve with chicken.

**PER SERVING** *432 cal., 5 g fat (1 g sat. fat), 63 mg chol., 210 mg sodium, 60 g carb., 3 g fiber, 28 g pro.*

MEXICAN FIESTA STEAK STIR-FRY

"Fruit cocktail in stir-fry? You might be surprised by how good this dish is. It's a promising option when time is tight."

—**JEANNE HOLT** MENDOTA HEIGHTS, MN

CARIBBEAN CHICKEN STIR-FRY

## Mexican Fiesta Steak Stir-Fry Ⓒ

The best part of throwing a weeknight party is being able to enjoy time with family. With this flavorful stir-fry on the menu, you'll be out of the kitchen with time to spare!

—**PATRICIA SWART** GALLOWAY, NJ

**START TO FINISH:** 30 MIN.
**MAKES:** 4 SERVINGS

- 1 pound boneless beef top loin steak, trimmed and cut into thin strips
- 3 garlic cloves, minced
- 1 to 2 tablespoons canola oil
- 1 package (14 ounces) frozen pepper strips, thawed
- 1⅓ cups chopped sweet onion
- 2 plum tomatoes, chopped
- 1 can (4 ounces) chopped green chilies
- ½ teaspoon salt
- ½ teaspoon dried oregano
- ¼ teaspoon pepper
  Hot cooked rice

1. In a large skillet or wok, stir-fry beef and garlic in oil until meat is no longer pink. Remove and keep warm.
2. Add peppers and onion to pan; stir-fry until tender. Stir in the tomatoes, chilies, salt, oregano, pepper and beef; heat through. Serve with rice.

**PER SERVING** *247 cal., 9 g fat (2 g sat. fat), 50 mg chol., 473 mg sodium, 13 g carb., 3 g fiber, 26 g pro.* **Diabetic Exchanges:** *3 lean meat, 2 vegetable, 1 fat.*

## Parmesan Pork Medallions ⓒ

I was so happy to find this recipe. I have served it countless times for family and friends. It takes very little prep time and adapts easily to serve any number.
—ANGELA CIOCCA SALTSBURG, PA

**START TO FINISH:** 20 MIN. • **MAKES:** 2 SERVINGS

- ½ pound pork tenderloin
- 2 tablespoons seasoned bread crumbs
- 1 tablespoon grated Parmesan cheese
- ¼ teaspoon salt
  Dash pepper
- 2 teaspoons canola oil
- ¼ cup chopped onion
- 1 garlic clove, minced

**1.** Cut pork into four slices; flatten to ¼-in. thickness. In a large resealable plastic bag, combine the bread crumbs, cheese, salt and pepper. Add pork, one slice at a time, and shake to coat.

**2.** In a large skillet over medium heat, cook pork in oil for 2-3 minutes on each side or until meat is no longer pink. Remove and keep warm.

**3.** Add onion to the pan; cook and stir until tender. Add garlic, cook 1 minute longer. Serve with pork.

**PER SERVING** 220 cal., 9 g fat (2 g sat. fat), 65 mg chol., 487 mg sodium, 8 g carb., 1 g fiber, 25 g pro. **Diabetic Exchanges:** 3 lean meat, 1 fat, ½ starch.

## Tenderloin Steaks with Cherry Sauce ⓒ

This recipe stars a delectable sauce made with wine and plump cherries, and the steak is portioned just right.
—JACOB KITZMAN SEATTLE, WA

**START TO FINISH:** 25 MIN. • **MAKES:** 4 SERVINGS

- ⅓ cup dried tart cherries
- ¾ cup port wine
- 2 teaspoons butter
- ¾ teaspoon salt, divided
- ⅛ teaspoon plus ¼ teaspoon coarsely ground pepper
- 4 beef tenderloin steaks (4 ounces each)
- 1 green onion, chopped

**1.** Place cherries and wine in a large saucepan. Bring to a boil; cook for 5 minutes or until liquid is reduced to ¼ cup. Stir in the butter, ¼ teaspoon salt and ⅛ teaspoon pepper.

**2.** Sprinkle steaks with remaining salt and pepper. Broil 4 in. from the heat for 4-6 minutes on each side or until meat reaches desired doneness (for medium-rare, a thermometer should read 145°; medium, 160°; well-done, 170°).

**3.** Serve steaks with cherry sauce and sprinkle with green onion.

**PER SERVING** 291 cal., 9 g fat (4 g sat. fat), 55 mg chol., 461 mg sodium, 15 g carb., 1 g fiber, 25 g pro. **Diabetic Exchanges:** 3 lean meat, 1 starch, ½ fat.

## Blueberry-Dijon Chicken

Blueberries and chicken may seem like a strange combination, but prepare to be pleasantly surprised. I add a sprinkling of minced fresh basil as the finishing touch.

**—SUSAN MARSHALL** COLORADO SPRINGS, CO

**START TO FINISH:** 30 MIN. • **MAKES:** 4 SERVINGS

- 4 **boneless skinless chicken breast halves (6 ounces each)**
- ¼ **teaspoon salt**
- ¼ **teaspoon pepper**
- 1 **tablespoon butter**
- ½ **cup blueberry preserves**
- ⅓ **cup raspberry vinegar**
- ¼ **cup fresh or frozen blueberries**
- 3 **tablespoons Dijon mustard**
  **Minced fresh basil or tarragon, optional**

**1.** Sprinkle chicken with salt and pepper. In a large skillet, cook chicken in butter over medium heat for 6-8 minutes on each side or until a thermometer reads 170°. Remove and keep warm.

**2.** In the same skillet, combine the preserves, vinegar, blueberries and mustard, stirring to loosen browned bits from pan. Bring to a boil; cook and stir until thickened. Serve with chicken. Sprinkle with basil if desired.

**PER SERVING** *331 cal., 7 g fat (3 g sat. fat), 102 mg chol., 520 mg sodium, 31 g carb., trace fiber, 34 g pro.* **Diabetic Exchanges:** *5 lean meat, 1½ starch, ½ fat.*

## Cherry-Glazed Chicken with Toasted Pecans

What started out as a way to use up some leftover preserves and cheese turned out to be a super-simple family dinner that I make all the time now.

**—KERI COTTON** LAKEVILLE, MN

**START TO FINISH:** 30 MIN. • **MAKES:** 4 SERVINGS

- 4 **boneless skinless chicken breast halves (4 ounces each)**
- ¾ **cup cherry preserves**
- 1 **teaspoon onion powder**
- 2 **ounces fontina cheese, thinly sliced**
- 2 **tablespoons chopped pecans, toasted**

**1.** Preheat oven to 375°. Place chicken in an ungreased 11-in. x 7-in. baking dish. Top with preserves; sprinkle with onion powder. Bake, uncovered, 18-22 minutes or until a thermometer reads 165°.

**2.** Top with cheese; bake 5 minutes longer or until cheese is melted. Sprinkle with pecans.

**NOTE** *To toast nuts, spread in a 15-in. x 10-in. x 1-in. baking pan. Bake at 350° for 5-10 minutes or until lightly browned, stirring occasionally. Or, spread in a dry nonstick skillet and heat over low heat until lightly browned, stirring occasionally.*

**PER SERVING** *354 cal., 10 g fat (4 g sat. fat), 79 mg chol., 168 mg sodium, 40 g carb., trace fiber, 27 g pro.*

GLAZED SHRIMP & ASPARAGUS

## Glazed Shrimp & Asparagus

With its spicy Asian flavor, this shrimp and asparagus combo is excellent for a special occasion or a quick-fix weeknight dinner.

—**JOAN DUCKWORTH** LEE'S SUMMIT, MO

**START TO FINISH:** 30 MIN.
**MAKES:** 4 SERVINGS

- 8 ounces uncooked whole wheat angel hair pasta
- 1 tablespoon cornstarch
- ¾ cup water
- 1 tablespoon soy sauce
- 1 tablespoon honey
- 1 pound uncooked large shrimp, peeled and deveined
- 3 teaspoons peanut oil, divided
- 1 teaspoon sesame oil
- 1 pound fresh asparagus, trimmed and cut into 2- to 3-inch lengths
- 1 tablespoon minced fresh gingerroot
- 2 garlic cloves, minced
- ¼ teaspoon crushed red pepper flakes
- 1 tablespoon sesame seeds

**1.** Cook pasta according to package directions. In a small bowl, combine the cornstarch, water, soy sauce and honey until smooth; set aside.
**2.** In a large skillet or wok, stir-fry shrimp in 1 teaspoon peanut oil and the sesame oil until shrimp turn pink. Remove and keep warm.
**3.** Stir-fry asparagus in remaining peanut oil for 2 minutes. Add the ginger, garlic, pepper flakes and sesame seeds; stir-fry 2 minutes longer or until asparagus is crisp-tender.
**4.** Stir cornstarch mixture and add to the pan. Bring to a boil; cook and stir for 2 minutes or until thickened. Add shrimp; heat through. Drain pasta; serve with shrimp mixture.
**PER SERVING** *386 cal., 8 g fat (1 g sat. fat), 138 mg chol., 376 mg sodium, 53 g carb., 8 g fiber, 29 g pro.*

### top tip
## One Shrimp, Two Shrimp

Shrimp are generally sold by the count number, rather than the size. The count is the number of shrimp it takes to make one pound. This means the lower the number, the bigger the shrimp. For large shrimp, look for a count between 31 and 35.

## Peppered Sole C

My daughter loves this recipe—it's the only way she'll eat fish. I'm just happy it's so healthy for us.

—**JEANNETTE BAYE** AGASSIZ, BC

**START TO FINISH:** 25 MIN.
**MAKES:** 4 SERVINGS

- 2 cups sliced fresh mushrooms
- 2 tablespoons butter
- 2 garlic cloves, minced
- 4 sole fillets (4 ounces each)
- ¼ teaspoon lemon-pepper seasoning
- ¼ teaspoon paprika
- ⅛ teaspoon cayenne pepper
- 1 medium tomato, chopped
- 2 green onions, thinly sliced

**1.** In a large skillet, saute mushrooms in butter until tender. Add garlic; saute 1 minute longer. Place fillets over mushrooms. Sprinkle with lemon pepper, paprika and cayenne.
**2.** Cover and cook over medium heat for 5-10 minutes or until fish flakes easily with a fork. Sprinkle with tomato and onions.
**PER SERVING** *174 cal., 7 g fat (4 g sat. fat), 69 mg chol., 166 mg sodium, 4 g carb., 1 g fiber, 23 g pro.* **Diabetic Exchanges:** *3 lean meat, 1½ fat, 1 vegetable.*

PEPPERED SOLE

"Homemade salsa adds zip to these mouthwatering bean cakes. Serve on a bun for a scrumptious veggie burger." —**ROXANNE CHAN** ALBANY, CA

BLACK BEAN CAKES WITH MOLE SALSA

## Grilled Halibut Steaks **C**

No one would guess you use everyday ingredients like brown sugar, soy sauce and lemon juice in this simple recipe. I always get compliments.

—**MARY ANN DELL** PHOENIXVILLE, PA

**START TO FINISH:** 25 MIN.
**MAKES:** 4 SERVINGS

- 2 tablespoons brown sugar
- 2 tablespoons butter
- 1 tablespoon lemon juice
- 2 teaspoons soy sauce
- 1 teaspoon minced garlic
- ½ teaspoon pepper
- 4 halibut steaks (5 ounces each)

**1.** In a small saucepan, combine the first six ingredients. Cook and stir until butter is melted. Remove from the heat; set aside.
**2.** Moisten a paper towel with cooking oil; using long-handled tongs, rub on grill rack to coat lightly. Grill halibut, covered, over medium-hot heat or broil 4 in. from the heat for 4-5 minutes on each side or until fish flakes easily with a fork, basting frequently with butter mixture.
**PER SERVING** *236 cal., 9 g fat (4 g sat. fat), 60 mg chol., 273 mg sodium, 7 g carb., trace fiber, 30 g pro.* **Diabetic Exchanges:** *4 lean meat, 1½ fat, ½ starch.*

## Black Bean Cakes with Mole Salsa **M**

**START TO FINISH:** 30 MIN.
**MAKES:** 6 SERVINGS (1¼ CUPS SALSA)

- 1 can (15 ounces) black beans, rinsed and drained
- 1 egg, beaten
- 1 cup shredded zucchini
- ½ cup dry bread crumbs
- ¼ cup shredded Mexican cheese blend
- 2 tablespoons chili powder
- ¼ teaspoon salt
- ¼ teaspoon baking powder
- ¼ teaspoon ground cumin
- 2 tablespoons olive oil

**SALSA**
- 2 medium tomatoes, chopped
- 1 small green pepper, chopped
- 3 tablespoons grated chocolate
- 1 green onion, thinly sliced
- 2 tablespoons minced fresh cilantro
- 1 tablespoon lime juice
- 1 to 2 teaspoons minced chipotle pepper in adobo sauce
- 1 teaspoon honey

**1.** In a small bowl, mash beans. Add the egg, zucchini, bread crumbs, cheese, chili powder, salt, baking powder and cumin; mix well. Shape into six patties; brush both sides with oil. Place on a baking sheet.
**2.** Broil 3-4 in. from the heat for 3-4 minutes on each side or until a thermometer reads 160°.
**3.** Meanwhile, in a small bowl, combine the salsa ingredients. Serve with black bean cakes.
**PER SERVING** *206 cal., 10 g fat (3 g sat. fat), 39 mg chol., 397 mg sodium, 23 g carb., 6 g fiber, 8 g pro.* **Diabetic Exchanges:** *2 fat, 1½ starch, 1 lean meat.*

GRILLED HALIBUT STEAKS

## Peach Chicken

This sweet and savory entree will appeal to the whole family. The chicken's bread crumb coating makes it especially homey.

**—TASTE OF HOME TEST KITCHEN**

**START TO FINISH:** 30 MIN.
**MAKES:** 4 SERVINGS

- 1 can (15 ounces) sliced peaches in extra-light syrup
- 2 teaspoons cornstarch
- ¼ cup peach preserves
- 1 tablespoon white wine or chicken broth
- ¼ cup seasoned bread crumbs
- 1 tablespoon grated Parmesan cheese
- ¼ teaspoon salt
- ¼ teaspoon pepper
- 4 boneless skinless chicken breast halves (6 ounces each)
- 2 tablespoons butter, divided
- 2 green onions, chopped
  Hot cooked pasta

**1.** Drain peaches, reserving juice. In a small bowl, combine cornstarch and reserved juice until smooth. Add preserves and wine; set aside.

**2.** In a large resealable plastic bag, combine the bread crumbs, cheese, salt and pepper. Add chicken, one piece at a time, and shake to coat. In a large skillet, cook chicken in 1 tablespoon butter over medium heat for 4-6 minutes on each side or until chicken juices run clear. Remove and keep warm.

**3.** In the same skillet, melt remaining butter. Stir cornstarch mixture and add to pan. Bring to a boil; cook and stir for 2 minutes or until thickened. Add chicken and peaches; heat through. Sprinkle with onions; serve with pasta.

**PER SERVING** *359 cal., 10 g fat (5 g sat. fat), 109 mg chol., 278 mg sodium, 31 g carb., 1 g fiber, 35 g pro.* **Diabetic Exchanges:** *5 lean meat, 1½ fat, 1 starch, 1 fruit.*

## Turkey Sausage with Pasta

Love Italian food? You'll be craving what's good for you when this turkey dish is on the menu. It balances meat, pasta and the best of the garden's bounty.

**—MARY TALLMAN** ARBOR VITAE, WI

**START TO FINISH:** 30 MIN.
**MAKES:** 6 SERVINGS

- 1 pound Italian turkey sausage links, casings removed
- 1 large onion, chopped
- 1 large green pepper, chopped
- 1¼ cups sliced fresh mushrooms
- 2 garlic cloves, minced
- 2 cans (14½ ounces each) diced tomatoes, undrained
- 1 teaspoon Italian seasoning
- 1 teaspoon chili powder
- 6 cups uncooked spiral pasta
- ½ cup shredded part-skim mozzarella cheese

**1.** Crumble sausage into a large nonstick skillet. Add the onion, green pepper and mushrooms. Cook over medium heat until meat is no longer pink. Add garlic; cook 1 minute longer. Drain.

**2.** Stir in the tomatoes, Italian seasoning and chili powder. Bring to a boil. Reduce heat; simmer, uncovered, for 10 minutes.

**3.** Meanwhile, cook pasta according to package directions; drain. Serve sausage mixture over pasta; sprinkle with cheese.

**PER SERVING** *396 cal., 10 g fat (3 g sat. fat), 51 mg chol., 679 mg sodium, 54 g carb., 5 g fiber, 24 g pro.*

PEACH CHICKEN

 **top tip**

### For a More Filling Meal

Next time you make pasta, try using 100 percent whole grain pasta. Not only is it richer in nutrients than the refined white stuff, it's full of fiber, which keeps you feeling full for longer.

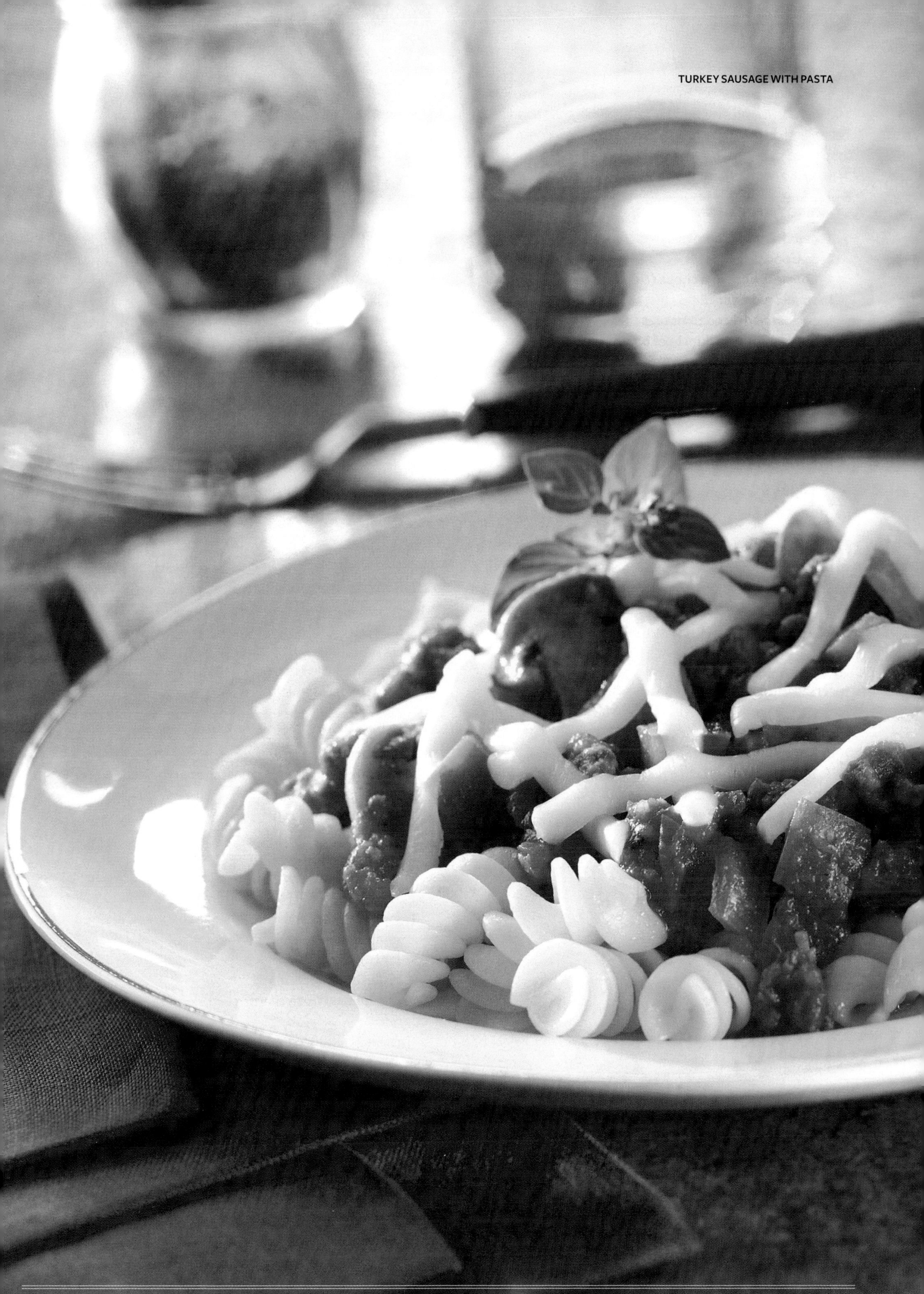

## Saucy Pork Chop Skillet

I like this skillet dinner because it's quick, but mostly because it's really good. Served over brown rice or whole grain noodles, it's healthier than most comfort food dinners, and it doesn't cost a lot to feed six people.

**—DONNA ROBERTS** MANHATTAN, KS

**START TO FINISH:** 30 MIN. • **MAKES:** 6 SERVINGS

- 3 **cups instant brown rice**
- 2 **teaspoons canola oil**
- 6 **boneless pork loin chops (6 ounces each)**
- 1 **small onion, sliced**
- 1 **cup canned diced tomatoes**
- 1 **cup reduced-sodium beef broth**
- 1 **tablespoon dried parsley flakes**
- ½ **teaspoon salt**
- ¼ **teaspoon pepper**
- ⅛ **teaspoon dried basil**
- ⅛ **teaspoon dried oregano**
- 2 **tablespoons all-purpose flour**
- ½ **cup water**

**1.** Cook rice according to package directions. Meanwhile, in a large nonstick skillet coated with cooking spray, heat oil over medium-high heat. Brown pork chops on both sides. Remove from the pan.

**2.** Cook and stir onion in drippings over medium-high heat until tender. Stir in the tomatoes, broth, parsley and seasonings. Bring to a boil. Return pork. Reduce heat; simmer, covered, for 6-8 minutes or until a thermometer inserted into pork reads 145°.

**3.** Remove pork to a serving plate. Mix flour and water until smooth; stir into pan. Bring to a boil; cook and stir for 2 minutes or until thickened. Pour over pork; serve with rice.

**PER SERVING** *436 cal., 13 g fat (4 g sat. fat), 83 mg chol., 382 mg sodium, 39 g carb., 3 g fiber, 38 g pro.* **Diabetic Exchanges:** *5 lean meat, 2½ starch.*

SAUCY PORK CHOP SKILLET

MEXICAN SKILLET RICE

## Mexican Skillet Rice

I never come home with leftovers when I take this dish to potlucks and parties. But I do bring back quite a few compliments.

**—MARY ANN DELL** PHOENIXVILLE, PA

**START TO FINISH:** 30 MIN. • **MAKES:** 6 SERVINGS

- 1 **egg, beaten**
- 1 **pound chicken tenderloins, chopped**
- 1 **small onion, chopped**
- 1 **tablespoon olive oil**
- 2 **garlic cloves, minced**
- 2 **cups cooked jasmine or long grain rice**
- 1 **can (15 ounces) black beans, rinsed and drained**
- 1 **can (11 ounces) Mexicorn, drained**
- 1 **jar (7 ounces) roasted sweet red peppers, drained and sliced**
- 1 **jar (8 ounces) taco sauce**
- 2 **green onions, chopped**
- ¼ **cup minced fresh cilantro**

**1.** In a large skillet coated with cooking spray, cook and stir egg over medium-high heat until set. Remove and set aside.

**2.** In the same skillet, stir-fry chicken and onion in oil until chicken is no longer pink. Add garlic; cook 1 minute longer. Stir in the rice, beans, Mexicorn, peppers, taco sauce and green onions; heat through. Stir in reserved egg. Sprinkle rice with cilantro.

**PER SERVING** *302 cal., 4 g fat (1 g sat. fat), 80 mg chol., 793 mg sodium, 40 g carb., 5 g fiber, 25 g pro.* **Diabetic Exchanges:** *3 lean meat, 2 starch, ½ fat.*

## Balsamic-Glazed Beef Skewers ▣

With only five ingredients, which can easily be doubled, these mouthwatering kabobs are a favorite to make and eat. To prevent wooden skewers from burning, soak them in water for 30 minutes before threading on the meat.

**—CAROLE FRASER** TORONTO, ON

**START TO FINISH:** 25 MIN. • **MAKES:** 4 SERVINGS

- ¼ cup balsamic vinaigrette
- ¼ cup barbecue sauce
- 1 teaspoon Dijon mustard
- 1 beef top sirloin steak (1 pound), cut into 1-inch cubes
- 2 cups cherry tomatoes

**1.** In a large bowl, whisk vinaigrette, barbecue sauce and mustard until blended. Reserve ¼ cup marinade for basting. Add beef to remaining marinade; toss to coat.

**2.** Alternately thread beef and tomatoes on four metal or soaked wooden skewers. Moisten a paper towel with cooking oil; using long-handled tongs, rub on grill rack to coat lightly.

**3.** Grill skewers, covered, over medium heat or broil 4 in. from heat 6-9 minutes or until beef reaches desired doneness, turning occasionally and basting frequently with reserved marinade during the last 3 minutes.

**PER SERVING** *194 cal., 7 g fat (2 g sat. fat), 46 mg chol., 288 mg sodium, 7 g carb., 1 g fiber, 25 g pro.* **Diabetic Exchanges:** *3 lean meat, 1½ fat, ½ starch.*

"This pasta dish is a wonderful blend of tender, crisp, colorful vegetables and a creamy Parmesan cheese sauce."

**—DARLENE BRENDEN** SALEM, OR

CREAMY PASTA PRIMAVERA

BALSAMIC-GLAZED BEEF SKEWERS

## Creamy Pasta Primavera Ⓜ

**START TO FINISH:** 30 MIN. • **MAKES:** 6 SERVINGS

- 2 cups uncooked gemelli or spiral pasta
- 1 pound fresh asparagus, trimmed and cut into 2-inch pieces
- 3 medium carrots, cut into strips
- 2 teaspoons canola oil
- 2 cups cherry tomatoes, halved
- 1 garlic clove, minced
- ½ cup grated Parmesan cheese
- ½ cup heavy whipping cream
- ¼ teaspoon pepper

**1.** Cook pasta according to package directions. In a large skillet, saute asparagus and carrots in oil until crisp-tender. Add tomatoes and garlic; cook 1 minute longer.

**2.** Stir in the cheese, cream and pepper. Drain pasta; toss with asparagus mixture.

**PER SERVING** *275 cal., 12 g fat (6 g sat. fat), 33 mg chol., 141 mg sodium, 35 g carb., 3 g fiber, 10 g pro.* **Diabetic Exchanges:** *2 starch, 2 fat, 1 vegetable.*

TILAPIA WITH CITRUS SAUCE

## Ham & Zucchini Italiano c

I strongly believe dinner should be three things: healthy, delicious and simple. With fresh zucchini, ham and marinara sauce baked with mozzarella, you can accomplish all three in the time it takes to describe the dish to a grateful family.

—MADISON MAYBERRY AMES, IA

**START TO FINISH:** 30 MIN.
**MAKES:** 4 SERVINGS

- 3 medium zucchini, cut diagonally into ¼-inch slices
- 1 tablespoon olive oil
- 1 teaspoon dried basil
- ½ teaspoon salt
- ¼ teaspoon pepper
- ½ pound smoked deli ham, cut into strips
- 1 cup marinara or spaghetti sauce
- ¾ cup shredded part-skim mozzarella cheese

**1.** In a large skillet, saute zucchini in oil until crisp-tender. Sprinkle with basil, salt and pepper.
**2.** With a slotted spoon, transfer half of the zucchini to a greased 8-in. baking dish; spread evenly. Layer with half of the ham, marinara sauce and cheese. Repeat layers.
**3.** Bake, uncovered, at 450° for 10-12 minutes or until heated through and cheese is melted. Serve with a slotted spoon.
**PER SERVING** *196 cal., 8 g fat (3 g sat. fat), 36 mg chol., 1,013 mg sodium, 14 g carb., 3 g fiber, 17 g pro.*

HAM & ZUCCHINI ITALIANO

## Tilapia with Citrus Sauce c

The lemon, lime and orange sauce adds zest to this flaky, delicately flavored fish.

—FRANCIS GARLAND ANNISTON, AL

**START TO FINISH:** 30 MIN.
**MAKES:** 4 SERVINGS

- ½ cup 2% milk
- ½ cup all-purpose flour
- ½ teaspoon salt
- ½ teaspoon pepper
- 4 tilapia fillets (4 ounces each)
  Olive oil-flavored cooking spray
- 3 garlic cloves, minced
- 1 tablespoon butter
- 2 teaspoons olive oil
- ½ small lemon, sliced
- ½ medium lime, sliced
- ½ small navel orange, sliced
- 3 tablespoons lemon juice
- 3 tablespoons lime juice
- 2 tablespoons orange juice
- 2 green onions, finely chopped

**1.** Place milk in a shallow bowl. In another shallow bowl, combine the flour, salt and pepper. Dip fish into milk, then coat with flour mixture.
**2.** Spray fillets with cooking spray. In a large nonstick skillet coated with cooking spray, cook fish over medium-high heat for 3-4 minutes on each side or until fish flakes easily with a fork. Remove and keep warm.
**3.** In the same pan, saute garlic in butter and oil for 1 minute. Add the lemon, lime and orange slices, juices and onions; cook 1 minute longer. Serve with fish.
**PER SERVING** *197 cal., 8 g fat (3 g sat. fat), 63 mg chol., 142 mg sodium, 11 g carb., 1 g fiber, 22 g pro.* **Diabetic Exchanges:** *3 lean meat, 1 fat, ½ fruit.*

OPEN-FACED TURKEY TACOS

## Pork with Curried Apple & Couscous

The aroma of this delicious dinner will really whet your appetite. Curry brings earthy flavor while raisins and apples lend a touch of sweetness.
—TASTE OF HOME TEST KITCHEN

**START TO FINISH:** 30 MIN.
**MAKES:** 2 SERVINGS

- ¾ **pound pork tenderloin**
- ¼ **teaspoon salt**
- ⅛ **teaspoon pepper**
- 3 **teaspoons reduced-fat butter, divided**
- 1 **green onion, thinly sliced**
- 1 **garlic clove, minced**
- 1 **small apple, peeled and sliced**
- 1 **tablespoon raisins**
- 1 **teaspoon cornstarch**
- 1 **teaspoon curry powder**
- ⅓ **cup reduced-sodium chicken broth**
- 1½ **cups hot cooked couscous**

**1.** Sprinkle pork with salt and pepper. In a large skillet, brown pork in 2 teaspoons butter. Reduce heat to low; cover and cook for 15-20 minutes or until a thermometer reaches 160°, turning occasionally. Remove pork and keep warm.

**2.** In the same skillet, saute onion and garlic in remaining butter until tender. Add apple and raisins; saute 2 minutes longer. Combine the cornstarch, curry powder and broth until smooth; stir into apple mixture. Bring to a boil; cook and stir for 1-2 minutes or until thickened. Serve with pork and couscous.

**PER SERVING** *406 cal., 9 g fat (4 g sat. fat), 102 mg chol., 513 mg sodium, 41 g carb., 3 g fiber, 39 g pro.* **Diabetic Exchanges:** *5 lean meat, 2 starch, 1 fat, ½ fruit.*

## Open-Faced Turkey Tacos

I like to serve this filling open-faced tortilla with a side of cold applesauce. If you like things spicy, use a medium or hot salsa.
—DALE JENNE MARENGO, IL

**START TO FINISH:** 20 MIN.
**MAKES:** 10 SERVINGS

- 1 **pound lean ground turkey**
- 1 **medium onion, chopped**
- 1 **can (16 ounces) fat-free refried beans**
- 1 **jar (16 ounces) salsa**
- 10 **flour tortillas (6 inches), warmed**
- 2 **cups shredded lettuce**
- 2 **medium tomatoes, chopped**
- 2 **medium green peppers, chopped**
- 2 **medium sweet red peppers, chopped**
- 10 **tablespoons fat-free sour cream**

In a large skillet, cook turkey and onion over medium heat until meat is no longer pink; drain. Add beans and salsa; cook and stir until heated through. Spread ½ cup turkey mixture over each tortilla. Top with lettuce, tomatoes, peppers and sour cream.
**PER SERVING** *265 cal., 7 g fat (1 g sat. fat), 38 mg chol., 674 mg sodium, 32 g carb., 6 g fiber, 16 g pro.* **Diabetic Exchanges:** *2 starch, 2 lean meat, 1 vegetable.*

### Did you know?

Salsa, meaning sauce, comes in many varieties. Salsa verde is made with tomatillos or green tomatoes. Salsa negra is made with dried chilies, oil and garlic; and salsa taquera (taco sauce) is made with tomato paste.

# Beef Entrees

104 108 113

66A friend gave this recipe to me when I got married. The ingredients looked so strange that I was scared to try it. But once I did, it became one of our favorite quick dinners.99

**—SHANNON KOENE** BLACKSBURG, VA
*about her recipe, Curried Beef Pitas with Cucumber Sauce, on page 109*

## Spud-Stuffed Peppers

We don't care for rice, so I created a yummy stuffed-pepper recipe that uses fresh potatoes from my garden.

—JOYCE JANDERA HANOVER, KS

**PREP:** 25 MIN. • **BAKE:** 40 MIN.
**MAKES:** 2 SERVINGS

> 2 medium green peppers
> ½ pound lean ground beef (90% lean)
> 1 medium potato, peeled and grated
> 1½ teaspoons chili powder
> ¼ teaspoon salt
>   Dash coarsely ground pepper
> ¼ cup shredded reduced-fat cheddar cheese

**1.** Cut tops off peppers and remove seeds. In a large saucepan, cook peppers in boiling water for 4-5 minutes. Drain and rinse in cold water; invert on paper towels.

**2.** In a nonstick skillet, cook beef and potato over medium heat until meat is no longer pink; drain. Stir in the chili powder, salt and pepper. Spoon into peppers.

**3.** Place in a small baking pan coated with cooking spray. Cover and bake at 350° for 35 minutes. Sprinkle with cheese. Bake, uncovered, 5-10 minutes longer or until cheese is melted.

**PER SERVING** *332 cal., 12 g fat (6 g sat. fat), 66 mg chol., 487 mg sodium, 28 g carb., 5 g fiber, 29 g pro.* **Diabetic Exchanges:** *3 lean meat, 2 vegetable, 1 starch, 1 fat.*

SPUD-STUFFED PEPPERS

PRESTO PIZZA PATTIES

## Presto Pizza Patties

Craving both beef and pizza? These patties feature both in an open-faced sandwich. They're great for a weeknight meal since they take only 30 minutes to make.

—BARBARA SCHINDLER NAPOLEON, OH

**START TO FINISH:** 30 MIN.
**MAKES:** 6 SERVINGS

> 2 egg whites
> ½ cup seasoned bread crumbs
> ½ cup finely chopped green pepper
> 1 can (8 ounces) pizza sauce, divided
> ¼ cup finely chopped onion
> 1 garlic clove, minced
> 1 pound lean ground beef (90% lean)
> 6 slices Italian bread (½ inch thick)
> 2 teaspoons olive oil
> 1½ teaspoons Italian seasoning
> ½ cup shredded part-skim mozzarella cheese

**1.** In a large bowl, combine the egg whites, bread crumbs, green pepper, ⅓ cup pizza sauce, onion and garlic. Crumble beef over mixture and mix well. Shape into six oval patties.

**2.** In a large nonstick skillet, cook patties over medium heat for 4-5 minutes on each side or until a meat thermometer reads 160° and juices run clear.

**3.** Meanwhile, place bread on an ungreased baking sheet. Brush tops with oil; sprinkle with Italian seasoning. Broil 4 in. from the heat for 2-3 minutes or until lightly toasted.

**4.** Microwave remaining pizza sauce, covered, on high for 10-20 seconds or until heated through. Place patties on toast; top with cheese and sauce.

**PER SERVING** *299 cal., 11 g fat (4 g sat. fat), 53 mg chol., 527 mg sodium, 26 g carb., 2 g fiber, 23 g pro.* **Diabetic Exchanges:** *3 lean meat, 1½ starch.*

## Zesty Horseradish Meat Loaf [C]

**PREP:** 15 MIN. • **BAKE:** 45 MIN. + STANDING
**MAKES:** 8 SERVINGS

- 4 slices whole wheat bread, crumbled
- ¼ cup fat-free milk
- ½ cup finely chopped celery
- ¼ cup finely chopped onion
- ¼ cup prepared horseradish
- 2 tablespoons Dijon mustard
- 2 tablespoons chili sauce
- 1 egg, lightly beaten
- 1½ teaspoons Worcestershire sauce
- ½ teaspoon salt
- ¼ teaspoon pepper
- 1½ pounds lean ground beef (90% lean)
- ½ cup ketchup

**1.** In a large bowl, soak bread in milk for 5 minutes. Drain and discard milk. Stir in the celery, onion, horseradish, mustard, chili sauce, egg, Worcestershire sauce, salt and pepper. Crumble beef over mixture and mix well.

**2.** Shape into a loaf in an 11-in. x 7-in. baking dish coated with cooking spray. Spread top with ketchup. Bake at 350° for 45-55 minutes or until no pink remains and a thermometer reads 160°. Let stand for 10 minutes before cutting.

**3.** Serve immediately, or before spreading with ketchup and baking, freeze meat loaf in a freezer container for up to 3 months.

**TO USE FROZEN MEAT LOAF** *Thaw in the refrigerator overnight. Spread top with ketchup. Bake as directed.*

**PER SERVING** *207 cal., 8 g fat (3 g sat. fat), 79 mg chol., 640 mg sodium, 14 g carb., 1 g fiber, 19 g pro.* **Diabetic Exchanges:** *2 lean meat, 1 starch.*

BEEFY TOMATO RICE SKILLET

"You'll love the bit of heat this tasty meat loaf has. Make sandwiches out of the leftovers to get double duty from this delicious meal with a kick."
—NANCY ZIMMERMAN CAPE MAY COURT HOUSE, NJ

ZESTY HORSERADISH MEAT LOAF

## Beefy Tomato Rice Skillet

For an easy home-style dinner that is truly filling, it's tough to beat a one-dish skillet. Especially when you can feed six people in less than 30 minutes.
—ELLYN GRAEBERT YUMA, AZ

**START TO FINISH:** 25 MIN.
**MAKES:** 6 SERVINGS

- 1 pound lean ground beef (90% lean)
- 1 cup chopped celery
- ⅔ cup chopped onion
- ½ cup chopped green pepper
- 1 can (11 ounces) whole kernel corn, drained
- 1 can (10¾ ounces) reduced-sodium condensed tomato soup, undiluted
- 1 cup water
- 1 teaspoon Italian seasoning
- 1 cup uncooked instant rice

**1.** In a large skillet over medium heat, cook the beef, celery, onion and pepper until meat is no longer pink and vegetables are tender; drain.

**2.** Add the corn, soup, water and Italian seasoning; bring to a boil. Stir in rice; cover and remove from the heat. Let stand for 10 minutes or until rice is tender.

**PER SERVING** *261 cal., 7 g fat (3 g sat. fat), 37 mg chol., 397 mg sodium, 29 g carb., 2 g fiber, 18 g pro.* **Diabetic Exchanges:** *2 starch, 2 lean meat.*

TEXAS TACOS

## Texas Tacos

With my kids' food likes and dislikes in mind, I created this recipe by combining a bunch of ingredients I know they like. The tacos are perfect for making ahead, and I often keep the beefy mixture in a slow cooker on warm so the kids can simply stuff it into taco shells after an afternoon of soccer practice.

**—SUSAN SCULLY** MASON, OH

**START TO FINISH:** 30 MIN.
**MAKES:** 10 SERVINGS

- 1½ **pounds lean ground beef (90% lean)**
- 1 **medium sweet red pepper, chopped**
- 1 **small onion, chopped**
- 1 **can (14½ ounces) diced tomatoes, drained**
- 1⅓ **cups frozen corn, thawed**
- 1 **can (8 ounces) tomato sauce**
- 2 **tablespoons chili powder**
- ½ **teaspoon salt**
- 1 **package (8.8 ounces) ready-to-serve brown rice**
- 20 **taco shells**
  **Optional toppings: shredded lettuce, chopped fresh tomatoes and reduced-fat sour cream**

**1.** In a Dutch oven, cook beef, red pepper and onion over medium heat 8-10 minutes or until beef is no longer pink and vegetables are tender, breaking up beef into crumbles. Drain.
**2.** Stir in tomatoes, corn, tomato sauce, chili powder and salt; bring to a boil. Add rice; heat through. Serve in taco shells with toppings of your choice.
**PER SERVING** *294 cal., 11 g fat (4 g sat. fat), 42 mg chol., 420 mg sodium, 30 g carb., 3 g fiber, 17 g pro. **Diabetic Exchanges:** 2 starch, 2 lean meat.*

 **Did you know?**
What do canned tomatoes have that fresh tomatoes don't? Heat involved in the canning process of tomatoes releases lycopene, a carotenoid that can lower the risk of heart disease as well as prostate and breast cancer.

GINGER STEAK FRIED RICE

## Ginger Steak Fried Rice

For a perfect end-of-the-week meal, combine all the ingredients in one pan and serve with rice. I learned a great tip for the steak recently: Partially freeze, and it becomes so much easier to slice.

**—SIMONE GARZA** EVANSVILLE, IN

**START TO FINISH:** 30 MIN.
**MAKES:** 4 SERVINGS

- 2 **eggs, lightly beaten**
- 2 **teaspoons olive oil**
- 1 **beef top sirloin steak (¾ pound), cut into thin strips**
- 4 **tablespoons reduced-sodium soy sauce, divided**
- 1 **package (12 ounces) broccoli coleslaw mix**
- 1 **cup frozen peas**
- 2 **tablespoons grated fresh gingerroot**
- 3 **garlic cloves, minced**
- 2 **cups cold cooked brown rice**
- 4 **green onions, sliced**

**1.** In a large nonstick skillet coated with cooking spray, cook and stir eggs over medium heat until no liquid remains, breaking up eggs into small pieces. Remove from pan; wipe skillet clean if necessary.
**2.** In the same pan, heat oil over medium-high heat. Add beef; stir-fry 1-2 minutes or until no longer pink. Stir in 1 tablespoon soy sauce; remove from pan.
**3.** Add coleslaw mix, peas, ginger and garlic to same pan; cook and stir until coleslaw mix is crisp-tender. Add rice and remaining soy sauce; tossing to combine rice with vegetable mixture and heat through. Stir in cooked eggs, beef and green onions; heat through.
**PER SERVING** *346 cal., 9 g fat (3 g sat. fat), 140 mg chol., 732 mg sodium, 36 g carb., 6 g fiber, 29 g pro. **Diabetic Exchanges:** 3 lean meat, 2 starch, 1 vegetable, ½ fat.*

SLOW COOKED PEPPER STEAK

## Slow Cooked Pepper Steak

Pepper steak is one of my favorite dishes, but I'm always disappointed when the beef is too tough. This recipe solves that problem! The slow cooker keeps things simple and makes the meat very tender. I've stored leftovers in one big resealable bag and also in individual portions for quick lunches.

—JULIE RHINE ZELIENOPLE, PA

**PREP:** 30 MIN. • **COOK:** 6 HOURS • **MAKES:** 12 SERVINGS

- 1  beef top round roast (3 pounds)
- 1  large onion, sliced
- 1  large green pepper, sliced
- 1  large sweet red pepper, sliced
- 4  garlic cloves, minced
- 1  cup water
- ⅓  cup cornstarch
- ½  cup reduced-sodium soy sauce
- 2  teaspoons sugar
- 2  teaspoons ground ginger
- 8  cups hot cooked brown rice

1. In a 5-qt. slow cooker, combine the first six ingredients. Cook, covered, on low 6-8 hours or until meat is tender.
2. Remove roast and vegetables to a serving platter using a slotted spoon; tent with foil. Pour cooking juices into a large saucepan; skim fat. Bring to a boil. In a small bowl, mix cornstarch, soy sauce, sugar and ginger until smooth; stir into saucepan. Return to a boil, stirring constantly; cook and stir 1-2 minutes or until thickened. Serve with roast, vegetables and rice.
**PER SERVING** *322 cal., 5 g fat (1 g sat. fat), 64 mg chol., 444 mg sodium, 38 g carb., 3 g fiber, 30 g pro.* **Diabetic Exchanges:** *3 lean meat, 2 starch.*

## Baked Spaghetti

It takes a little longer to make baked spaghetti, but the difference in taste, texture and richness is well worth the time. I serve this family-style dish with a tossed green salad and breadsticks for a hearty yet healthy meal.

—BETTY RABE MAHTOMEDI, MN

**PREP:** 20 MIN. • **BAKE:** 30 MIN. + STANDING • **MAKES:** 6 SERVINGS

- 8  ounces uncooked spaghetti, broken into thirds
- 1  egg
- ½  cup fat-free milk
- ½  pound lean ground beef (90% lean)
- ½  pound Italian turkey sausage links, casings removed
- 1  small onion, chopped
- ¼  cup chopped green pepper
- 1  jar (14 ounces) meatless spaghetti sauce
- 1  can (8 ounces) no-salt-added tomato sauce
- ½  cup shredded part-skim mozzarella cheese

1. Cook spaghetti according to package directions; drain. In a large bowl, beat egg and milk. Add spaghetti; toss to coat. Transfer to a 13-in. x 9-in. baking dish coated with cooking spray.
2. In a large skillet, cook the beef, sausage, onion and green pepper over medium heat until meat is no longer pink; drain. Stir in spaghetti sauce and tomato sauce. Spoon over the spaghetti mixture.
3. Bake, uncovered, at 350° for 20 minutes. Sprinkle with the cheese. Bake 10 minutes longer or until cheese is melted. Let stand for 10 minutes before cutting.
**PER SERVING** *343 cal., 10 g fat (3 g sat. fat), 87 mg chol., 616 mg sodium, 39 g carb., 3 g fiber, 23 g pro.* **Diabetic Exchanges:** *2 starch, 2 medium-fat meat, 1 vegetable.*

BAKED SPAGHETTI

> "A friend gave this recipe to me when I got married. The ingredients looked so strange that I was scared to try it. But once I did, it became one of our favorite quick dinners." —**SHANNON KOENE** BLACKSBURG, VA

CURRIED BEEF PITAS WITH CUCUMBER SAUCE

## Curried Beef Pitas with Cucumber Sauce

**START TO FINISH:** 25 MIN. • **MAKES:** 4 SERVINGS (1½ CUPS SAUCE)

- 1 cup fat-free plain Greek yogurt
- 1 cup finely chopped peeled cucumber
- 1 tablespoon minced fresh mint
- 2 garlic cloves, minced
- 2 teaspoons snipped fresh dill
- 2 teaspoons lemon juice
- ¼ teaspoon salt

PITAS

- 1 pound lean ground beef (90% lean)
- 1 small onion, chopped
- 1 medium Golden Delicious apple, finely chopped
- ¼ cup raisins
- 2 teaspoons curry powder
- ¼ teaspoon salt
- 8 whole wheat pita pocket halves

**1.** In a small bowl, mix the first seven ingredients. Refrigerate until serving.

**2.** In a large skillet, cook beef and onion over medium heat 6-8 minutes or until beef is no longer pink, breaking up beef into crumbles; drain. Add apple, raisins, curry powder and salt; cook until apples are tender, stirring occasionally. Serve in pita halves with sauce.

**PER SERVING** *429 cal., 11 g fat (4 g sat. fat), 71 mg chol., 686 mg sodium, 50 g carb., 6 g fiber, 36 g pro.*

## Beef-Stuffed Cabbage Rolls

My family loves this recipe, it's quick to put together and it really satisfies without being too fattening. This dish stands alone as a great, light meal.

—**LYNN BOWEN** GERALDINE, AL

**PREP:** 20 MIN. • **COOK:** 6 HOURS • **MAKES:** 6 SERVINGS

- 12 cabbage leaves
- 1 cup cooked brown rice
- ¼ cup finely chopped onion
- 1 egg, lightly beaten
- ¼ cup fat-free milk
- ½ teaspoon salt
- ¼ teaspoon pepper
- 1 pound lean ground beef (90% lean)

SAUCE

- 1 can (8 ounces) tomato sauce
- 1 tablespoon brown sugar
- 1 tablespoon lemon juice
- 1 teaspoon Worcestershire sauce

**1.** In batches, cook the cabbage in boiling water 3-5 minutes or until crisp-tender. Drain; cool slightly. Trim the thick vein from the bottom of each cabbage leaf, making a V-shaped cut.

**2.** In a large bowl, combine rice, onion, egg, milk, salt and pepper. Add beef; mix lightly but thoroughly. Place about ¼ cup beef mixture on each cabbage leaf. Pull together cut edges of leaf to overlap; fold over filling. Fold in sides and roll up.

**3.** Place six rolls in a 4- or 5-qt. slow cooker, seam side down. In a bowl, mix sauce ingredients; pour half of the sauce over cabbage rolls. Top with remaining rolls and sauce. Cook, covered, on low 6-8 hours or until a thermometer inserted into beef reads 160° and cabbage is tender.

**PER SERVING** *204 cal., 7 g fat (3 g sat. fat), 83 mg chol., 446 mg sodium, 16 g carb., 2 g fiber, 18 g pro.* **Diabetic Exchanges:** *2 lean meat, 1 starch.*

BEEF-STUFFED CABBAGE ROLLS

## Grilled Sirloin Kabobs with Peach Salsa

FInding a new way to cook with salsa is just one of the perks of this quick and easy dish. Peaches, peach preserves and peach salsa star in these beef kabobs with a blend of hot and sweet flavors.

—**BETH ROYALS** RICHMOND, VA

**START TO FINISH:** 25 MIN. • **MAKES:** 6 SERVINGS

   3  **tablespoons peach preserves**
   1  **tablespoon finely chopped seeded jalapeno pepper**
   1  **beef top sirloin steak (1½ pounds), cut into 1-inch cubes**
   ½  **teaspoon salt**
   ¼  **teaspoon pepper**
   3  **medium peaches, cut into sixths**
   1½ **cups peach salsa**

**1.** In a small bowl, mix preserves and jalapeno. Season beef with salt and pepper. Alternately thread beef and peaches onto six metal or soaked wooden skewers.
**2.** Moisten a paper towel with cooking oil; using long-handled tongs, rub on grill rack to coat lightly. Grill kabobs, covered, over medium heat or broil 4 in. from heat 6-8 minutes or until beef reaches desired doneness, turning occasionally. Remove from grill; brush with preserves mixture. Serve with salsa.
**PER SERVING** *219 cal., 5 g fat (2 g sat. fat), 46 mg chol., 427 mg sodium, 17 g carb., 3 g fiber, 25 g pro.* **Diabetic Exchanges:** *3 lean meat, ½ starch, ½ fruit.*

## Cheeseburger Macaroni Skillet

Here's the ultimate simple and filling dinner that uses items I typically have right in my own pantry. It's so easy to prepare and cooks in one skillet, which makes cleanup a snap.

—**JULI MEYERS** HINESVILLE, GA

**START TO FINISH:** 30 MIN. • **MAKES:** 6 SERVINGS

   1  **pound lean ground beef (90% lean)**
   8  **ounces uncooked whole wheat elbow macaroni**
   3  **cups reduced-sodium beef broth**
   ¾  **cup fat-free milk**
   3  **tablespoons ketchup**
   2  **teaspoons Montreal steak seasoning**
   1  **teaspoon prepared mustard**
   ¼  **teaspoon onion powder**
   1  **cup (4 ounces) shredded reduced-fat cheddar cheese**
      **Minced chives**

**1.** In a large skillet, cook beef over medium heat for 6-8 minutes or until no longer pink, breaking into crumbles; drain.
**2.** Stir in macaroni, broth, milk, ketchup, steak seasoning, mustard and onion powder; bring to a boil. Reduce heat; simmer, uncovered, 10-15 minutes or until pasta is tender. Stir in cheese until melted. Sprinkle with chives.
**PER SERVING** *338 cal., 11 g fat (5 g sat. fat), 64 mg chol., 611 mg sodium, 32 g carb., 4 g fiber, 27 g pro.*

## Ozark Sloppy Joes

Years ago, my family operated a snack boat on Missouri's Lake of the Ozarks. These popular sloppy joes were a hit with all the hungry boaters.

—**MICHELE DELANTY** CAMDENTON, MO

**START TO FINISH:** 25 MIN. • **MAKES:** 8 SERVINGS

- 1½ **pounds lean ground beef (90% lean)**
- 1 **medium green pepper, chopped**
- 1 **small onion, chopped**
- 2 **teaspoons sugar**
- 1½ **teaspoons all-purpose flour**
- 1½ **teaspoons Italian seasoning**
- ½ **teaspoon chili powder**
- ¼ **teaspoon salt**
- ¼ **teaspoon garlic powder**
- ⅛ **teaspoon cayenne pepper**
- 1 **can (8 ounces) tomato sauce**
- 1½ **teaspoons Worcestershire sauce**
- 8 **hamburger buns, split**

**1.** In a large skillet, cook the beef, green pepper and onion over medium heat until meat is no longer pink; drain.
**2.** Stir in the sugar, flour, seasonings, tomato sauce and Worcestershire sauce. Cover and simmer for 10-15 minutes, stirring occasionally. Spoon ½ cup onto each bun.
**PER SERVING** *268 cal., 8 g fat (3 g sat. fat), 42 mg chol., 478 mg sodium, 26 g carb., 2 g fiber, 21 g pro.* **Diabetic Exchanges:** *2 starch, 2 lean meat.*

## Grilled Flank Steak

Friends shared this three-ingredient marinade years ago, and it's been a favorite since. Serve this steak with salad and grilled potatoes for a quick meal.

—**BEVERLY DIETZ** SURPRISE, AZ

**PREP:** 5 MIN. + MARINATING • **GRILL:** 15 MIN. + STANDING
**MAKES:** 8 SERVINGS

- 1 **cup barbecue sauce**
- ½ **cup burgundy wine or beef broth**
- ¼ **cup lemon juice**
- 1 **beef flank steak (2 pounds)**

**1.** In a bowl, combine the barbecue sauce, wine and lemon juice. Pour 1 cup marinade into a large resealable plastic bag; add the steak. Seal bag and turn to coat; refrigerate for 4 hours or overnight. Cover and refrigerate remaining marinade.
**2.** Drain meat and discard marinade. Grill steak, covered, over medium heat 6-8 minutes on each side or until meat reaches desired doneness (for medium-rare, a thermometer should read 145°; medium, 160°; well-done, 170°). Let stand for 10 minutes before slicing. To serve, thinly slice across the grain. Serve with reserved marinade.
**PER SERVING** *195 cal., 9 g fat (4 g sat. fat), 54 mg chol., 271 mg sodium, 4 g carb., trace fiber, 22 g pro.* **Diabetic Exchanges:** *3 lean meat, 1 fat.*

## Hearty Beef & Cabbage Pockets

**PREP: 1 HOUR + RISING • BAKE: 15 MIN.
MAKES: 2 DOZEN**

- 24 **frozen dough Texas-size whole wheat dinner rolls, thawed**
- 1½ **pounds lean ground beef (90% lean)**
- ½ **pound reduced-fat bulk pork sausage**
- 1 **large onion, chopped**
- 1 **pound carrots, grated**
- 2 **cans (4 ounces each) chopped green chilies**
- 2 **tablespoons prepared mustard**
- ½ **teaspoon salt**
- ½ **teaspoon pepper**
- 1 **small head cabbage, shredded**
- 2 **egg whites**
- 2 **teaspoons water
  Caraway seeds**

**1.** Let dough stand at room temperature 30-40 minutes or until softened. In a Dutch oven, cook beef, sausage and onion over medium heat 12-15 minutes or until meat is no longer pink, breaking meat into crumbles; drain. Stir in carrots, chilies, mustard, salt and pepper. Add cabbage in batches; cook and stir until tender.

**2.** On a lightly floured surface, press or roll each dinner roll into a 5-in. circle. Top with a heaping ⅓ cup filling; bring edges of dough up over filling and pinch to seal.

**3.** Place on baking sheets coated with cooking spray, seam side down. Cover with kitchen towels; let rise in a warm place until almost doubled, about 45 minutes. Preheat oven to 350°.

**4.** Whisk egg whites and water; brush over tops. Sprinkle with caraway seeds. Bake 15-20 minutes or until golden brown.

**PER SERVING** *239 cal., 7 g fat (2 g sat. fat), 24 mg chol., 379 mg sodium, 33 g carb., 2 g fiber, 12 g pro.* **Diabetic Exchanges:** *2 starch, 1 lean meat.*

"I found this recipe many years ago, and the only ingredients listed were hamburger, cabbage, onion, salt and pepper. After a bit of experimenting, I decided this is one for the books. If you have time, use a homemade dough. Or use a 48-ounce package of frozen whole wheat bread dough if you can't find frozen rolls. Just cut the bread into 24 pieces."
—**ELAINE CLARK** WELLINGTON, KS

**HEARTY BEEF & CABBAGE POCKETS**

**GREEK-STYLE SUPPER**

## Greek-Style Supper

An all-in-one meal like this is great for busy weeknights. I add a pinch of cinnamon to make the dish shine. There's minimal prep work and cleanup is just as easy!
—**ALICE BOWER** ROANOKE, IL

**START TO FINISH:** 30 MIN.
**MAKES:** 4 SERVINGS

- ½ **pound lean ground beef (90% lean)**
- ½ **cup chopped onion**
- 1 **can (14½ ounces) reduced-sodium beef broth**
- 1 **can (14½ ounces) diced tomatoes, undrained**
- 1½ **cups uncooked penne pasta**
- 1½ **cups frozen cut green beans, thawed**
- 2 **tablespoons tomato paste**
- 2 **teaspoons dried oregano**
- ½ **teaspoon garlic powder**
- ¼ **teaspoon ground cinnamon**
- ¾ **cup crumbled feta cheese**

**1.** In a large skillet, cook beef and onion over medium heat until meat is no longer pink. Meanwhile, in a large saucepan, bring broth and tomatoes to a boil; add pasta. Reduce heat; simmer, uncovered, for 15-20 minutes or until pasta is tender, stirring occasionally.

**2.** Drain beef mixture; add to pasta. Stir in the green beans, tomato paste, oregano, garlic powder and cinnamon; heat through. Sprinkle with cheese.

**PER SERVING** *294 cal., 8 g fat (4 g sat. fat), 41 mg chol., 621 mg sodium, 33 g carb., 6 g fiber, 21 g pro.* **Diabetic Exchanges:** *2 starch, 2 lean meat, 1 vegetable.*

## Tenderloin with Cremini-Apricot Stuffing C

A simple-to-make dinner-party meal is an accurate description of this dish. The cooking juices leave the beef very tender, and the sweet and savory stuffing complements it well. Your guests will be giving you kudos.

—MARIE RIZZIO INTERLOCHEN, MI

**PREP:** 35 MIN. • **BAKE:** 35 MIN. + STANDING
**MAKES:** 10 SERVINGS

- 1 **cup sliced baby portobello (cremini) mushrooms**
- ⅓ **cup chopped onion**
- ⅓ **cup chopped celery**
- 2 **tablespoons butter**
- ½ **cup chopped dried apricots**
- 1 **tablespoon minced fresh rosemary**
- 1 **beef tenderloin roast (2½ pounds)**
- 1 **tablespoon olive oil**
- 3 **garlic cloves, minced**
- ½ **teaspoon salt**
- ¼ **teaspoon pepper**

1. In a large skillet, saute the mushrooms, onion and celery in butter until tender. Transfer to a small bowl; stir in apricots and rosemary. Cool slightly.
2. Cut a lengthwise slit down the center of the tenderloin to within ½ in. of bottom. Open tenderloin so it lies flat. On each half, make another lengthwise slit down the center to within ½ in. of bottom; open roast and cover with plastic wrap. Flatten to ½-in. thickness. Remove plastic.
3. Spread mushroom mixture over meat. Roll up jelly-roll style, starting with a long side. Tie at 1½-in. to 2-in. intervals with kitchen string.
4. Combine the oil, garlic, salt and pepper; rub over roast. In a large ovenproof skillet, brown roast on all sides.
5. Bake at 425° for 35-50 minutes or until meat reaches desired doneness (for medium-rare, a thermometer should read 145°; medium, 160°; well-done, 170°). Let stand for 10 minutes before slicing. Place slices on a platter and spoon pan juices over the top.

**PER SERVING** *219 cal., 10 g fat (4 g sat. fat), 56 mg chol., 143 mg sodium, 6 g carb., 1 g fiber, 25 g pro.* **Diabetic Exchanges:** *3 lean meat, 1 fat, ½ starch.*

## Southwest Burgers

There's a food stand I frequent for a burger with a Southwestern flair. This is my lightened-up version of their cheese-stuffed gourmet Southwest burger. Mine is just as good but better for the waistline.

—DEBORAH FORBES FORT WORTH, TX

**PREP:** 25 MIN. + CHILLING • **GRILL:** 15 MIN.
**MAKES:** 8 SERVINGS

- 1 **can (15 ounces) black beans, rinsed and drained**
- 1 **small red onion, finely chopped**
- ½ **cup frozen corn, thawed**
- ¼ **cup dry bread crumbs**

SOUTHWEST BURGERS

- 1 **can (4 ounces) chopped green chilies**
- 2 **tablespoons Worcestershire sauce**
- 1 **teaspoon garlic powder**
- ½ **teaspoon ground cumin**
- ¼ **teaspoon pepper**
- ½ **pound lean ground beef (90% lean)**
- ½ **pound extra-lean ground turkey**
- ½ **cup fat-free mayonnaise**
- ¼ **cup salsa**
- 8 **slices pepper jack cheese (½ ounce each)**
- 8 **whole wheat hamburger buns, split**

OPTIONAL TOPPINGS
   **Lettuce leaves, tomato slices and red onion rings**

1. In a large bowl, coarsely mash beans. Stir in the onion, corn, bread crumbs, chilies, Worcestershire sauce and seasonings. Crumble beef and turkey over mixture and mix well. Shape into eight patties. Refrigerate for 1 hour. Combine mayonnaise and salsa; refrigerate until serving.
2. Moisten a paper towel with cooking oil; using long-handled tongs, lightly coat the grill rack. Grill burgers, covered, over medium heat or broil 4 in. from the heat for 5-7 minutes on each side or until a thermometer reads 165° and juices run clear.
3. Top with cheese; cover and grill 1-2 minutes longer or until cheese is melted. Serve on buns with toppings if desired.

**PER SERVING** *341 cal., 10 g fat (4 g sat. fat), 45 mg chol., 698 mg sodium, 42 g carb., 7 g fiber, 24 g pro.* **Diabetic Exchanges:** *3 starch, 2 lean meat.*

TENDERLOIN WITH
CREMINI-APRICOT STUFFING

117

119

124

# Chicken Favorites

❝Curry and mustard complement the sweet fruit and crunchy nuts in this guilt-free salad. I also like it on whole wheat toast or scooped up with apple slices.❞

**—JOANNA PERDOMO** CHICAGO, IL
*about her recipe, Curried Chicken Salad, on page 123*

SPINACH-STUFFED
CHICKEN PARMESAN

## Spinach-Stuffed Chicken Parmesan C

Every time I buy a loaf of bread, I use the heels to make bread crumbs. Just pop them into the toaster, crush and store in a labeled baggie. That way I always have crumbs on hand for quick recipes like this.

—**KELLIE FOGLIO** SALEM, WI

**PREP:** 25 MIN. • **BAKE:** 30 MIN. • **MAKES:** 4 SERVINGS

- 4 **cups fresh spinach**
- 2 **garlic cloves, minced**
- 2 **teaspoons olive oil**
- 2 **tablespoons grated Parmesan cheese, divided**
- ¼ **teaspoon salt**
- ¼ **teaspoon pepper**
- 4 **boneless skinless chicken breast halves (4 ounces each)**
- ½ **cup dry whole wheat bread crumbs**
- 1 **egg, lightly beaten**
- 2 **cans (8 ounces each) no-salt-added tomato sauce**
- 1 **teaspoon dried basil**
- 1 **teaspoon dried oregano**
- ¾ **cup shredded part-skim mozzarella cheese**

1. Preheat oven to 375°. In a large skillet, cook and stir spinach and garlic in oil just until wilted. Drain. Stir in 1 tablespoon Parmesan cheese, salt and pepper.

2. Pound chicken breasts with a meat mallet to ⅛-in. thickness. Spread each with 1 tablespoon spinach mixture. Fold chicken in half enclosing filling; secure with toothpicks.

3. Place bread crumbs and egg in separate shallow bowls. Dip chicken in egg, then roll in crumbs to coat. Place seam side down in an 8-in.-square baking dish coated with cooking spray. Bake, uncovered, 20 minutes.

4. Meanwhile, in a large bowl, combine tomato sauce, basil and oregano. Pour over chicken. Sprinkle with mozzarella cheese and remaining Parmesan cheese. Bake, uncovered, 10-15 minutes longer or until a thermometer reads 165°. Discard toothpicks before serving.

**PER SERVING** *281 cal., 10 g fat (4 g sat. fat), 104 mg chol., 432 mg sodium, 14 g carb., 2 g fiber, 31 g pro.* **Diabetic Exchanges:** *4 lean meat, 1 starch, ½ fat.*

## Chicken Continental

Mushroom lovers rejoice! This juicy chicken perfectly combines garlic and mushrooms into a flavorful entree.

—**REBECCA BAIRD** SALT LAKE CITY, UT

**PREP:** 30 MIN. • **COOK:** 40 MIN. • **MAKES:** 4 SERVINGS

- ⅔ **cup uncooked brown rice**
- 2 **tablespoons plus 2 teaspoons cornstarch, divided**
- ¼ **teaspoon garlic-herb seasoning blend**
- 4 **boneless skinless chicken breast halves (5 ounces each)**
- 1 **tablespoon olive oil**
- ¾ **pound sliced fresh mushrooms**
- 6 **green onions, thinly sliced**
- ¼ **cup balsamic vinegar**
- 2 **garlic cloves, minced**
- 1 **tablespoon capers, drained**
- ¾ **cup reduced-sodium chicken broth**
- 1 **bay leaf**
- 1 **teaspoon minced fresh thyme or ¼ teaspoon dried thyme**
- 2 **teaspoons cold water**

1. Cook rice according to package directions. In a small bowl, combine 2 tablespoons cornstarch and the seasoning blend; sprinkle over chicken on both sides.

2. In a large skillet over medium heat, brown chicken in oil. Remove and keep warm. Add mushrooms and onions to the pan; cook and stir for 3 minutes. Add the vinegar, garlic and capers; cook and stir 2 minutes longer.

3. Return chicken to the pan; carefully add the broth, bay leaf and thyme. Bring to a boil. Reduce heat; cover and simmer for 10 minutes or until a thermometer reads 170°.

4. Combine the remaining cornstarch with the water until smooth; stir into the pan. Bring to a boil; cook and stir for 2 minutes or until thickened. Discard bay leaf. Serve chicken and mushrooms with rice.

**PER SERVING** *354 cal., 8 g fat (2 g sat. fat), 78 mg chol., 265 mg sodium, 35 g carb., 4 g fiber, 35 g pro.* **Diabetic Exchanges:** *4 lean meat, 2 starch, 1 vegetable, ½ fat.*

CHICKEN CONTINENTAL

GRILLED CHICKEN WITH
BLACK BEAN SALSA

## Grilled Chicken with Black Bean Salsa

Black bean salsa with mango gives this dish a Mexican taste without too much heat. I like to slice the chicken and serve it over wild rice or brown rice.
—**TERRI CLOUSE** CONNOQUENESSING, PA

**PREP:** 15 MIN. + MARINATING • **GRILL:** 10 MIN. • **MAKES:** 5 SERVINGS

- 1　cup lime juice
- 2　tablespoons olive oil
- 2　teaspoons ground cumin
- 1　teaspoon salt
- 1　teaspoon dried oregano
- ½　teaspoon pepper
- 5　boneless skinless chicken breast halves (4 ounces each)

**BLACK BEAN SALSA**
- 1　can (15 ounces) black beans, rinsed and drained
- 1　mango, peeled and cubed
- ¼　cup minced fresh cilantro
- 3　tablespoons lime juice
- 1　tablespoon olive oil
- 2　teaspoons brown sugar
- 1　teaspoon minced jalapeno pepper

**1.** In a small bowl, whisk the first six ingredients. Pour ⅔ cup marinade into a large resealable plastic bag. Add chicken; seal bag and turn to coat. Refrigerate 1-2 hours. Reserve remaining marinade for basting. In a small bowl, combine salsa ingredients; toss to combine.

**2.** Drain chicken, discarding marinade. Grill chicken, covered, over medium heat or broil 4 in. from heat 5-6 minutes on each side or until a thermometer reads 165°, basting occasionally with reserved marinade during the last 4 minutes. Serve with salsa.

**NOTE** *Wear disposable gloves when cutting hot peppers; the oils can burn skin. Avoid touching your face.*

**PER SERVING** *266 cal., 7 g fat (1 g sat. fat), 63 mg chol., 339 mg sodium, 23 g carb., 4 g fiber, 27 g pro.* **Diabetic Exchanges:** *3 lean meat, 1½ starch, 1 fat.*

## Citrus-Spiced Roast Chicken ⬛

I am the designated Thanksgiving host in my family because of my chipotle citrus roast turkey. Even finicky eaters love it. That's why I use the same recipe for chicken, so we can enjoy it year-round.
—**ROBIN HAAS** CRANSTON, RI

**PREP:** 20 MIN. • **BAKE:** 1 HOUR + STANDING • **MAKES:** 6 SERVINGS

- 3　tablespoons orange marmalade
- 4½　teaspoons chopped chipotle peppers in adobo sauce
- 3　garlic cloves, minced
- ¾　teaspoon salt, divided
- ½　teaspoon ground cumin
- 1　broiler/fryer chicken (4 pounds)

**1.** Preheat oven to 350°. Mix marmalade, chipotle peppers, garlic, ½ teaspoon salt and cumin. With fingers, carefully loosen skin from chicken; rub mixture under the skin.

**2.** Place chicken on a rack in a shallow roasting pan, breast side up. Tuck wings under chicken; tie drumsticks together. Rub skin with remaining salt.

**3.** Roast 1 to 1¼ hours or until a thermometer inserted into thigh reads 180°. Baste occasionally with pan drippings. (Cover loosely with foil if chicken browns too quickly.)

**4.** Remove chicken from oven; tent with foil. Let stand 15 minutes before carving. Remove and discard skin before serving. If desired, skim fat and thicken pan drippings for gravy. Serve with chicken.

**PER SERVING** *239 cal., 8 g fat (2 g sat. fat), 98 mg chol., 409 mg sodium, 8 g carb., trace fiber, 32 g pro.* **Diabetic Exchange:** *4 lean meat.*

CITRUS-SPICED ROAST CHICKEN

## Blackberry Chicken C

My family and I like to go blackberry picking together. Then we make jams and pies and freeze the leftover berries to make this chicken dish all year long.

—**LAURA VAN NESS** CLEARLAKE OAKS, CA

**PREP:** 20 MIN. • **BAKE:** 20 MIN.
**MAKES:** 6 SERVINGS

- 2 **tablespoons plus ½ cup fresh blackberries, divided**
- ½ **cup reduced-sodium chicken broth, divided**
- 2 **tablespoons brown sugar**
- 2 **tablespoons white wine vinegar**
- 1 **teaspoon olive oil**
- 2 **garlic cloves, minced**
- ¾ **teaspoon paprika, divided**
- ¼ **teaspoon ground cumin**
- 6 **boneless skinless chicken breast halves (5 ounces each)**
- 4½ **teaspoons minced fresh thyme**
- ½ **teaspoon salt**
- ¼ **teaspoon pepper**
- 2 **teaspoons cornstarch**

**1.** In a small bowl, mash 2 tablespoons berries. Add ¼ cup broth, brown sugar, vinegar, oil, garlic, ¼ teaspoon paprika and cumin.

**2.** Place chicken in an 11-in. x 7-in. baking dish coated with cooking spray; pour broth mixture over the top. Sprinkle with thyme, salt, pepper and remaining paprika.

**3.** Bake, uncovered, at 375° for 20-25 minutes or until a thermometer reads 170°, basting occasionally with pan juices. Remove chicken and keep warm.

**4.** Skim fat from pan drippings. In a small saucepan, combine cornstarch and remaining broth until smooth. Gradually stir in drippings. Bring to a boil; cook and stir for 1-2 minutes or until thickened. Serve with chicken; sprinkle with remaining blackberries.

**PER SERVING** *192 cal., 4 g fat (1 g sat. fat), 78 mg chol., 315 mg sodium, 8 g carb., 1 g fiber, 29 g pro.* **Diabetic Exchanges:** *4 lean meat, ½ starch.*

GREEK CHICKEN DINNER

## Greek Chicken Dinner

Feta cheese takes this chicken and potato dinner over the top. Serve with a side salad tossed with pepperoncinis, black olives and low-fat vinaigrette for a fresh and healthy meal.

—**TASTE OF HOME TEST KITCHEN**

**PREP:** 15 MIN. • **BAKE:** 50 MIN.
**MAKES:** 6 SERVINGS

- 7 **medium red potatoes, cut into 1-inch cubes**
- 6 **boneless skinless chicken thighs (about 1½ pounds)**
- ½ **cup reduced-fat sun-dried tomato salad dressing**
- 2 **teaspoons Greek seasoning**
- 1 **teaspoon dried basil**
- ½ **cup crumbled reduced-fat feta cheese**

**1.** In a large bowl, combine the first five ingredients. Transfer to a 13-in. x 9-in. baking dish coated with cooking spray.

**2.** Cover and bake at 400° for 40 minutes. Sprinkle with cheese. Bake, uncovered, 10-15 minutes longer or until chicken juices run clear and potatoes are tender.

**PER SERVING** *316 cal., 12 g fat (3 g sat. fat), 79 mg chol., 767 mg sodium, 25 g carb., 2 g fiber, 26 g pro.* **Diabetic Exchanges:** *3 lean meat, 1½ starch, 1 fat.*

BLACKBERRY CHICKEN

## Chicken Creole C

I ladle this vegetable-packed chicken dish over jasmine rice. It's a long-grain rice that's not as sticky as most, but any cooked rice, including brown, will work.
—VIRGINIA CROWELL LYONS, OR

**PREP:** 20 MIN. • **COOK:** 30 MIN.
**MAKES:** 8 SERVINGS

- 2 medium green peppers, chopped
- 1 large onion, thinly sliced
- 2 celery ribs, chopped
- 4 garlic cloves, minced
- 4 teaspoons canola oil, divided
- ½ pound fresh mushrooms, sliced
- 2 cans (14½ ounces each) diced tomatoes, undrained
- ½ cup chicken broth
- 2 tablespoons minced fresh oregano or 2 teaspoons dried oregano
- 2 tablespoons lemon juice
- 1 tablespoon minced fresh basil or 1 teaspoon dried basil
- ½ teaspoon salt
- ½ teaspoon pepper
- ½ teaspoon crushed red pepper flakes
- 2 pounds boneless skinless chicken breasts, cubed
  Hot cooked rice
  Minced fresh parsley, optional

**1.** In a large saucepan, saute the green peppers, onion, celery and garlic in 2 teaspoons oil until tender. Add mushrooms; cook until liquid has evaporated. Stir in the tomatoes, broth, oregano, lemon juice, basil and spices. Bring to a boil. Reduce heat; cover and simmer 5-10 minutes or until slightly thickened and flavors are blended.

**2.** Meanwhile, in a Dutch oven, saute chicken in remaining oil in batches until no longer pink. Return chicken to pan; stir in sauce. Heat through, stirring to loosen browned bits from pan. Serve over rice; garnish with parsley if desired.

**FREEZE OPTION** *Freeze cooled chicken and sauce mixture in freezer containers. To use, partially thaw in refrigerator overnight. Heat through in a covered saucepan, gently stirring and adding a little broth or water if necessary.*

**PER SERVING** *189 cal., 5 g fat (1 g sat. fat), 63 mg chol., 380 mg sodium, 10 g carb., 3 g fiber, 25 g pro.* **Diabetic Exchanges:** *3 lean meat, 2 vegetable, ½ fat.*

PINEAPPLE-MANGO CHICKEN

## Pineapple-Mango Chicken

Combining pineapple, mango and spices makes a sauce for chicken that is such a unique recipe and a favorite of ours.
—KIM WAITES RUTHERFORDTON, NC

**START TO FINISH:** 30 MIN.
**MAKES:** 4 SERVINGS

- 1½ cups undrained crushed pineapple
- ½ cup golden raisins
- ¼ teaspoon ground cinnamon
- ¼ teaspoon ground cloves
- ⅛ teaspoon ground nutmeg
- 2 medium mangoes, peeled and chopped
- 4 boneless skinless chicken breast halves (5 ounces each)
- ½ teaspoon salt
- ⅛ teaspoon pepper
  Hot cooked rice

**1.** In a small saucepan, combine the first five ingredients; bring to a boil over medium heat. Reduce heat; simmer, uncovered, for 4-6 minutes or until sauce is thickened and raisins are plumped, stirring occasionally. Stir in mangoes; heat through. Set aside.

**2.** Moisten a paper towel with cooking oil; using long-handled tongs, lightly coat the grill rack. Sprinkle chicken with salt and pepper. Grill chicken, covered, over medium heat or broil 4 in. from the heat for 5-8 minutes on each side or until a thermometer reads 170°. Serve with sauce and rice.

**PER SERVING** *350 cal., 4 g fat (1 g sat. fat), 78 mg chol., 369 mg sodium, 52 g carb., 4 g fiber, 30 g pro.*

CHICKEN CREOLE

CHICKEN BREASTS WITH VEGGIES

## Chicken Breasts with Veggies

This is my own spin-off of a favorite family recipe. I think the vegetables are delicious baked with the chicken because they pick up the marinade flavor.

—**TONY LENTINI** ROGUE RIVER, OR

**PREP:** 20 MIN. + MARINATING
**BAKE:** 40 MIN • **MAKES:** 2 SERVINGS

- 1 tablespoon olive oil
- 1 tablespoon balsamic vinegar
- 1 tablespoon Worcestershire sauce
- 1 tablespoon reduced-sodium teriyaki sauce
- 1½ teaspoons reduced-sodium soy sauce
- 2 boneless skinless chicken breast halves (5 ounces each)
- 1 small potato, peeled and cut into ½-inch cubes
- 2 large fresh mushrooms, sliced
- 1 large carrot, sliced
- 1 small green pepper, chopped
- 7 pitted ripe olives, halved
- ⅓ cup chopped onion
- 1 tablespoon grated Parmesan cheese
- ½ teaspoon Italian seasoning

**1.** In a small bowl, combine the first five ingredients. Pour 2 tablespoons marinade into a large resealable plastic bag; add the chicken. Seal bag and turn to coat; refrigerate for up to 4 hours. Cover and refrigerate remaining marinade.

**2.** Drain chicken and discard marinade. Place chicken in an 11-in. x 7-in. baking dish coated with cooking spray. Arrange the potato, mushrooms, carrot, green pepper, olives and onion around chicken. Drizzle with reserved marinade. Sprinkle with cheese and Italian seasoning.

**3.** Cover and bake at 375° for 40-45 minutes or until a thermometer reads 170°.

**PER SERVING** *337 cal., 11 g fat (2 g sat. fat), 81 mg chol., 576 mg sodium, 26 g carb., 4 g fiber, 33 g pro. Diabetic Exchanges: 4 lean meat, 1½ fat, 1 starch, 1 vegetable.*

"Use a fresh orange for the zest and juice in this tasty recipe that combines citrus with maple syrup and balsamic vinegar."

—**LILY JULOW** LAWRENCEVILLE, GA

ORANGE-MAPLE GLAZED CHICKEN

## Orange-Maple Glazed Chicken C

**PREP:** 25 MIN. • **GRILL:** 10 MIN.
**MAKES:** 6 SERVINGS

- ⅓ cup orange juice
- ⅓ cup maple syrup
- 2 tablespoons balsamic vinegar
- 1½ teaspoons Dijon mustard
- 1 teaspoon salt, divided
- ¾ teaspoon pepper, divided
- 1 tablespoon minced fresh basil or 1 teaspoon dried basil
- ½ teaspoon grated orange peel
- 6 boneless skinless chicken breast halves (6 ounces each)

**1.** In a small saucepan, combine the orange juice, syrup, vinegar, mustard, ½ teaspoon salt and ¼ teaspoon pepper. Bring to a boil; cook until liquid is reduced to ½ cup, about 5 minutes. Stir in basil and orange peel. Remove from the heat; set aside.

**2.** Sprinkle chicken with remaining salt and pepper. Grill chicken, covered, over medium heat for 5-7 minutes on each side or until a thermometer reads 165°, basting frequently with orange juice mixture.

**PER SERVING** *240 cal., 4 g fat (1 g sat. fat), 94 mg chol., 508 mg sodium, 15 g carb., trace fiber, 34 g pro. Diabetic Exchanges: 5 lean meat, 1 starch.*

## Did you know?

Pure maple syrup contains minerals such as calcium, potassium, magnesium, manganese, phosphorus and iron.

## Grilled Honey-Lime Chicken C

Make-ahead marinade is your best friend when feeding a crowd. You can have several bags made up, but grill only what you need for the moment; then grill more when the group is ready for another round.

**—MARYBETH WRIGHT** MAITLAND, FL

**PREP:** 10 MIN. + MARINATING • **GRILL:** 10 MIN. • **MAKES:** 8 SERVINGS

- ¾ cup oil and vinegar salad dressing
- ½ cup honey
- 3 tablespoons lime juice
- ½ teaspoon salt
- ½ teaspoon pepper
- 8 boneless skinless chicken breast halves (6 ounces each)

**1.** In a small bowl, combine the first five ingredients. Pour 1 cup marinade into a large resealable plastic bag; add the chicken. Seal bag and turn to coat; refrigerate for 2 hours. Cover and refrigerate remaining marinade.

**2.** Drain chicken and discard marinade. Moisten a paper towel with cooking oil; using long-handled tongs, lightly coat the grill rack. Grill chicken, covered, over medium heat or broil 4 in. from the heat for 4-5 minutes on each side, or until a thermometer reads 170°, basting occasionally with reserved marinade.

**PER SERVING** *286 cal., 9 g fat (1 g sat. fat), 94 mg chol., 476 mg sodium, 15 g carb., trace fiber, 34 g pro.* **Diabetic Exchanges:** *5 lean meat, 1 starch, 1 fat.*

## Salsa Orange Chicken Skillet

I think this is a fun dish to make for guests because it's not your average chicken dinner, and everyone thinks it took a lot of time to make.

**—NANCY DAUGHERTY** CORTLAND, OH

**START TO FINISH:** 25 MIN. • **MAKES:** 4 SERVINGS

- 2 cups uncooked instant brown rice
- 1 pound boneless skinless chicken breasts, cut into 1-inch cubes
- 2 teaspoons canola oil
- 1 cup chunky salsa
- ¼ cup orange marmalade
- 2 tablespoons lime juice
- 1 tablespoon brown sugar
- ¼ teaspoon ground allspice
- 2 tablespoons minced fresh cilantro

**1.** Cook rice according to package directions. Meanwhile, in a large nonstick skillet coated with cooking spray, cook chicken in oil over medium heat for 5 minutes or until no longer pink.

**2.** Stir in the salsa, marmalade, lime juice, brown sugar and allspice. Bring to a boil. Reduce heat; simmer, uncovered, for 2 minutes. Sprinkle with cilantro. Serve with rice.

**PER SERVING** *397 cal., 6 g fat (1 g sat. fat), 63 mg chol., 357 mg sodium, 53 g carb., 4 g fiber, 27 g pro.*

## Curried Chicken Salad

Curry and mustard complement the sweet fruit and crunchy nuts in this guilt-free salad. I also like it on whole wheat toast or scooped up with apple slices.

**—JOANNA PERDOMO** CHICAGO, IL

**START TO FINISH:** 15 MIN. • **MAKES:** 4 SERVINGS

- 3 **cups cubed cooked chicken breast**
- 1 **medium apple, finely chopped**
- ¼ **cup slivered almonds, toasted**
- 2 **tablespoons golden raisins**
- 2 **tablespoons dried cranberries**
- ½ **cup fat-free plain Greek yogurt**
- ¼ **cup apricot preserves**
- 2 **tablespoons curry powder**
- 1 **tablespoon Dijon mustard**
- ½ **teaspoon salt**
- ¼ **to ½ teaspoon pepper**
  **Lettuce leaves**

In a small bowl, combine the first five ingredients. In a small bowl, whisk the yogurt, preserves, curry, mustard, salt and pepper; pour over chicken mixture and toss to coat. Serve on lettuce leaves.

**PER SERVING** *323 cal., 7 g fat (1 g sat. fat), 81 mg chol., 477 mg sodium, 30 g carb., 3 g fiber, 36 g pro.* **Diabetic Exchanges:** *4 lean meat, 1 starch, ½ fruit, ½ fat.*

## Tuscan Chicken C

I started making this dinner after a trip to Tuscany. It's juicy and delicious and always brings back wonderful memories. It's nice to serve with pasta or even stuffing.

**—DEBRA LEGRAND** PORT ORCHARD, WA

**START TO FINISH:** 15 MIN. • **MAKES:** 4 SERVINGS

- 4 **boneless skinless chicken breast halves (5 ounces each)**
- ½ **teaspoon salt**
- ½ **teaspoon pepper**
- 2 **garlic cloves, sliced**
- 2 **teaspoons dried rosemary, crushed**
- ½ **teaspoon rubbed sage**
- ½ **teaspoon dried thyme**
- 2 **tablespoons olive oil**

**1.** Flatten chicken to ½-in. thickness; sprinkle with salt and pepper.
**2.** In a large skillet over medium heat, cook and stir the garlic, rosemary, sage and thyme in oil for 1 minute. Add chicken; cook for 5-6 minutes on each side or until chicken juices run clear.
**PER SERVING** *217 cal., 10 g fat (2 g sat. fat), 78 mg chol., 364 mg sodium, 1 g carb., 1 g fiber, 29 g pro.* **Diabetic Exchanges:** *4 lean meat, 1½ fat.*

## Chipotle-Apple Chicken Breasts

The sweetness of the apple, the smokiness of the bacon and the heat from the chipotle pepper blend so well together in this delicious entree. It's my husband's favorite.

—SHANNON ABDOLLMOHAMMADI WOODINVILLE, WA

**PREP:** 25 MIN. • **BAKE:** 15 MIN. • **MAKES:** 2 SERVINGS

- 2 **bacon strips, diced**
- 1 **small tart apple, peeled and coarsely chopped**
- 2 **tablespoons dried minced onion**
- 2 **tablespoons unsweetened applesauce**
- ½ **to 1 teaspoon chipotle peppers in adobo sauce, chopped**
- 2 **boneless skinless chicken breast halves (6 ounces each)**
- 2 **teaspoons olive oil**
- 1 **teaspoon all-purpose flour**
- ½ **cup unsweetened apple juice**
- ¼ **teaspoon salt**
- ⅛ **teaspoon pepper**

**1.** In a small skillet, cook bacon over medium heat until crisp. Using a slotted spoon, remove to paper towels; drain, reserving 1 teaspoon drippings. Saute apple in drippings until tender. Add the onion, applesauce, chipotle peppers and bacon; saute 2 minutes longer.

**2.** Cut a pocket in each chicken breast half; stuff with apple mixture. In a small skillet, brown chicken in oil on both sides.

**3.** Transfer to an ungreased 8-in. square baking dish. Bake, uncovered, at 425° for 12-15 minutes or until a thermometer reads 170°.

**4.** Meanwhile, add the flour, apple juice, salt and pepper to the skillet; stir to loosen browned bits. Bring to a boil; cook and stir for 2 minutes or until thickened. Serve with chicken.

**PER SERVING** *335 cal., 12 g fat (3 g sat. fat), 99 mg chol., 489 mg sodium, 19 g carb., 1 g fiber, 37 g pro.* **Diabetic Exchanges:** *5 lean meat, 1½ fat, 1 fruit.*

CHIPOTLE-APPLE CHICKEN BREASTS

GARDEN VEGETABLE & CHICKEN SKILLET

## Garden Vegetable & Chicken Skillet

Who doesn't love a dinner that comes together in one skillet? Especially one that tastes this fresh and delicious. A hint of lemon and thyme comes through in every forkful.

—TASTE OF HOME TEST KITCHEN

**PREP:** 20 MIN. • **COOK:** 20 MIN. • **MAKES:** 4 SERVINGS

- 1½ **pounds boneless skinless chicken breasts, cut into ½-inch cubes**
- 1 **medium yellow summer squash, chopped**
- 1 **medium onion, chopped**
- 1 **medium carrot, chopped**
- 2 **tablespoons butter**
- 3 **cups fresh baby spinach**
- 1 **garlic clove, minced**
- ½ **teaspoon salt**
- ½ **teaspoon dried thyme**
- ¼ **teaspoon pepper**
- 1 **cup uncooked instant brown rice**
- 1¼ **cups water**
- 1 **tablespoon lemon juice**

**1.** In a large skillet, saute the chicken, squash, onion and carrot in butter for 5-6 minutes or until chicken is no longer pink; drain. Add the spinach, garlic, salt, thyme and pepper; cook 2 minutes longer.

**2.** Stir in rice and water. Bring to a boil. Reduce heat; cover and simmer for 10-15 minutes or until rice is tender. Stir in lemon juice.

**PER SERVING** *355 cal., 11 g fat (5 g sat. fat), 109 mg chol., 453 mg sodium, 25 g carb., 3 g fiber, 38 g pro.* **Diabetic Exchanges:** *5 lean meat, 1 starch, 1 vegetable, 1 fat.*

### ? Did you know?

Artichokes are loaded with folate, fiber and vitamins C and K, and they're ranked No. 7 on the USDA's top 20 list of antioxidant-rich foods.

## Chicken with Basil Artichoke Sauce ☐

Lemon-flavored chicken and a basil-artichoke sauce make this an elegant entree for a special occasion dinner. It's delicious served over hot cooked pasta or rice.

—**ANDREA METZLER** MOSCOW, ID

**PREP:** 20 MIN. • **BAKE:** 20 MIN. • **MAKES:** 4 SERVINGS

- 4 boneless skinless chicken breast halves (4 ounces each)
- ¼ teaspoon salt
- ¼ teaspoon pepper
- 1 tablespoon canola oil
- 2 tablespoons lemon juice

**SAUCE**

- 3½ teaspoons cornstarch
- 1½ cups milk
- 1 can (14 ounces) water-packed artichoke hearts, rinsed, drained and quartered
- 3 tablespoons grated Parmesan cheese
- 2 tablespoons minced fresh basil
- 2 tablespoons white wine or chicken broth
- 2 teaspoons lemon juice
- ¼ teaspoon salt
- ¼ teaspoon pepper

**1.** Rub chicken with salt and pepper. In a large skillet, brown chicken in oil on both sides. Transfer to a greased 13-in. x 9-in. baking dish. Drizzle with lemon juice. Bake, uncovered, at 375° for 20-25 minutes or until chicken juices run clear.

**2.** Meanwhile, in a small heavy saucepan, whisk cornstarch and milk until smooth. Bring to a boil; cook and stir for 2 minutes or until thickened. Stir in the remaining ingredients; heat through. Serve sauce with chicken.

**PER SERVING** *282 cal., 10 g fat (3 g sat. fat), 75 mg chol., 692 mg sodium, 15 g carb., trace fiber, 30 g pro. Diabetic Exchanges: 3 lean meat, 1½ fat, 1 starch.*

BASIL-MINT CHICKEN THIGHS

CHICKEN WITH BASIL ARTICHOKE SAUCE

## Basil-Mint Chicken Thighs ☐

Fresh basil and mint come through in every bite of these marinated and grilled chicken thighs. Make extras for an extraordinary taco salad the next day.

—**KAREN NAIHE** EWA BEACH, HI

**PREP:** 15 MIN. + MARINATING • **GRILL:** 10 MIN. • **MAKES:** 6 SERVINGS

- 6 boneless skinless chicken thighs (4 ounces each)
- 4½ teaspoons lemon juice
- 4½ teaspoons olive oil
- 1 tablespoon reduced-sodium soy sauce
- 1 teaspoon chili powder
- ½ teaspoon salt
- ½ teaspoon pepper
- ½ cup fresh mint leaves
- ¼ cup fresh basil leaves
- 4 garlic cloves, minced
- 1 tablespoon fresh cilantro leaves

**1.** Place chicken thighs in large resealable plastic bag. In a blender, combine the remaining ingredients. Cover and process until pureed. Add to bag. Seal and turn to coat. Refrigerate overnight.

**2.** Moisten a paper towel with cooking oil; using long-handled tongs, lightly coat the grill rack. Grill chicken, covered, over medium heat or broil 4-6 inches from the heat for 3-4 minutes on each side or until a thermometer reads 180°.

**PER SERVING** *202 cal., 11 g fat (3 g sat. fat), 76 mg chol., 346 mg sodium, 2 g carb., 1 g fiber, 22 g pro. Diabetic Exchanges: 3 lean meat, ½ fat.*

## Chicken Florentine Meatballs

**PREP:** 40 MIN. • **COOK:** 20 MIN.
**MAKES:** 6 SERVINGS

- 2 eggs, lightly beaten
- 1 package (10 ounces) frozen chopped spinach, thawed and squeezed dry
- ½ cup dry bread crumbs
- ¼ cup grated Parmesan cheese
- 1 tablespoon dried minced onion
- 1 garlic clove, minced
- ¼ teaspoon salt
- ⅛ teaspoon pepper
- 1 pound ground chicken
- 1 medium spaghetti squash

**SAUCE**

- ½ pound sliced fresh mushrooms
- 2 teaspoons olive oil
- 1 can (14½ ounces) diced tomatoes, undrained
- 1 can (8 ounces) tomato sauce
- 2 tablespoons minced fresh parsley
- 1 garlic clove, minced
- 1 teaspoon dried oregano
- 1 teaspoon dried basil

**1.** In a large bowl, combine the first eight ingredients. Crumble chicken over mixture and mix well. Shape into 1½-in. balls.

**2.** Place meatballs on a rack in a shallow baking pan. Bake, uncovered, at 400° for 20-25 minutes or until no longer pink. Meanwhile, cut squash in half lengthwise; discard seeds. Place squash cut side down on a microwave-safe plate. Microwave, uncovered, on high for 15-18 minutes or until tender.

**3.** For sauce, in a large nonstick skillet, saute mushrooms in oil until tender. Stir in the remaining ingredients. Bring to a boil. Reduce heat; simmer, uncovered, for 8-10 minutes or until slightly thickened. Add meatballs and heat through.

**4.** When squash is cool enough to handle, use a fork to separate strands. Serve with meatballs and sauce.

**NOTE** *This recipe was tested in a 1,100-watt microwave.*

**PER SERVING** *303 cal., 12 g fat (3 g sat. fat), 123 mg chol., 617 mg sodium, 31 g carb., 7 g fiber, 22 g pro.* **Diabetic Exchanges:** *3 lean meat, 2 starch, ½ fat.*

"These baked meatballs come out juicy and tender every time. They're equally delicious served over pasta or in a sub, but I prefer them with spaghetti squash."
—**DIANE NEMITZ** LUDINGTON, MI

CHICKEN FLORENTINE MEATBALLS

## Italian Chicken Sausage and Orzo

Light, quick and tasty are my kind of recipes. This one has a nice blend of Italian seasoning and a hint of heat from the crushed red pepper. If you like it milder, use less, or if you like to bring on the heat, use more.

—**DEBRA PAQUETTE** UPTON, MA

**START TO FINISH:** 30 MIN.
**MAKES:** 5 SERVINGS

- 1 cup uncooked orzo pasta
- 1 package (12 ounces) fully cooked Italian chicken sausage links, cut into ¾-inch slices
- 3 teaspoons olive oil, divided
- 1 cup chopped onion
- 3 garlic cloves, minced
- ¼ cup white wine or chicken broth
- 1 can (28 ounces) whole tomatoes, drained and chopped
- 2 tablespoons minced fresh parsley
- 1 tablespoon capers, drained
- ½ teaspoon dried oregano
- ½ teaspoon dried basil
- ¼ teaspoon crushed red pepper flakes
- ¼ teaspoon pepper
- ½ cup crumbled feta cheese

**1.** Cook pasta according to package directions.

**2.** Meanwhile, brown the sausages in 2 teaspoons oil in a large skillet. Remove and keep warm. In the same pan, saute onion in remaining oil until tender. Add garlic and wine; cook 1 minute longer, stirring to loosen browned bits from pan.

**3.** Stir in the tomatoes, parsley, capers, oregano, basil, pepper flakes and pepper. Bring to a boil. Reduce heat; simmer, uncovered, for 5 minutes. Stir in orzo and sausage; heat through. Sprinkle with cheese.

**PER SERVING** *363 cal., 11 g fat (3 g sat. fat), 58 mg chol., 838 mg sodium, 42 g carb., 3 g fiber, 21 g pro.* **Diabetic Exchanges:** *2 starch, 2 lean meat, 2 vegetable, 1 fat.*

133

135

139

# Turkey Specialties

❝After a long day at school, I want something that is healthy but also quick to prepare. A little splash of wine or chicken broth on this turkey dish really brings all the flavors together.❞

—**CATHY RAU** NEWPORT, OR
*about her recipe, Weeknight Pasta Supper, on page 137*

## Turkey Picadillo

I serve this over short cut pasta or egg noodles and garnish it with sour cream and a sprinkling of chopped scallions. The leftovers reheat wonderfully and make a tasty lunch.

—**ANITA PINNEY** SANTA ROSA, CA

**START TO FINISH:** 30 MIN. • **MAKES:** 4 SERVINGS

- 5⅓ cups uncooked whole wheat egg noodles
- 1 pound lean ground turkey
- 1 medium green pepper, chopped
- 1 small onion, chopped
- 2 garlic cloves, minced
- 2 teaspoons chili powder
- ¼ teaspoon pepper
- 1 can (14½ ounces) Italian diced tomatoes, undrained
- ½ cup golden raisins
  Reduced-fat sour cream and chopped green onions, optional

**1.** Cook noodles according to package directions.

**2.** Meanwhile, in a large nonstick skillet, cook the turkey, green pepper and onion over medium heat until turkey is no longer pink; drain. Add the garlic, chili powder and pepper; cook 1 minute longer. Stir in tomatoes and raisins; heat through. Drain noodles; serve with turkey mixture. Garnish with sour cream and green onions if desired.

**PER SERVING** *463 cal., 11 g fat (3 g sat. fat), 90 mg chol., 535 mg sodium, 69 g carb., 9 g fiber, 30 g pro.*

## Creamed Turkey on Mashed Potatoes

This meal is true comfort food. The creamy turkey mixture blends perfectly with tasty mashed potatoes.

—**TASTE OF HOME TEST KITCHEN**

**START TO FINISH:** 20 MIN. • **MAKES:** 4 SERVINGS

- ½ cup chopped onion
- 2 tablespoons butter
- 2 tablespoons all-purpose flour
- ¼ teaspoon salt
- ⅛ teaspoon white pepper
- 2 cups fat-free milk
- 2 cups cubed cooked turkey breast
- 1 cup frozen mixed vegetables
- 2 cups mashed potatoes (with added milk and butter)

**1.** In a large saucepan, saute the onion in butter until tender. Sprinkle with the flour, salt and pepper. Stir in the milk until blended.

**2.** Bring to a boil; cook and stir for 2 minutes or until thickened and bubbly. Add the turkey and vegetables; cover and simmer until heated through. Serve over mashed potatoes.

**PER SERVING** *358 cal., 11 g fat (6 g sat. fat), 89 mg chol., 628 mg sodium, 35 g carb., 4 g fiber, 29 g pro.* **Diabetic Exchanges:** *3 lean meat, 2 starch, 1½ fat, ½ fat-free milk.*

## Turkey Tenderloins with Raspberry BBQ Sauce

Sweet and tangy raspberry sauce is a perfect complement to versatile turkey tenderloins. In fact, the sauce is so good, you'll be tempted to eat it with a spoon.

**—DEIRDRE DEE COX** KANSAS CITY, KS

**START TO FINISH:** 30 MIN. • **MAKES:** 2 SERVINGS

  2   turkey breast tenderloins (5 ounces each)
  ⅛   teaspoon salt
  ⅛   teaspoon pepper
  2   teaspoons olive oil
  1   teaspoon cornstarch
  ¼   cup cranberry-raspberry juice
  2   tablespoons Heinz 57 steak sauce
  2   tablespoons red raspberry preserves
  ½   teaspoon lemon juice

**1.** Sprinkle turkey with salt and pepper. In a large nonstick skillet over medium heat, brown turkey in oil on all sides. Cover and cook for 10-12 minutes or until a thermometer reads 170°. Remove and keep warm.
**2.** Combine cornstarch and juice until smooth; add to the pan. Stir in the steak sauce, preserves and lemon juice. Bring to a boil; cook and stir for 1 minute or until thickened. Slice turkey; serve with sauce.
**PER SERVING** *275 cal., 6 g fat (1 g sat. fat), 69 mg chol., 425 mg sodium, 22 g carb., trace fiber, 33 g pro.*

## Peanut Turkey Satay 🄲

I found this recipe years ago and immediately served it for a company dinner. It's easy and fun and takes only minutes to cook, but it makes a fancy entree for special occasions. The peanut butter and soy sauce lend a nice Asian flavor.

**—LISA MAHON FLUEGEMAN** CINCINNATI, OH

**START TO FINISH:** 15 MIN. • **MAKES:** 2 SERVINGS

  4½   teaspoons red wine vinegar
  4½   teaspoons reduced-sodium soy sauce
  1   tablespoon sugar
  1   tablespoon creamy peanut butter
  ¼   teaspoon ground ginger
  ½   pound turkey breast tenderloins

**1.** In a small bowl, whisk the first five ingredients; set aside 1 tablespoon for basting. Cut turkey into long strips (about 1½ in. wide x ¼ in. thick). Add to soy sauce mixture in bowl; toss to coat.
**2.** Weave turkey strips accordion-style onto two metal or soaked wooden skewers. Broil 3-4 in. from the heat for 2-3 minutes on each side or until turkey is no longer pink, basting with reserved soy sauce mixture.
**PER SERVING** *202 cal., 6 g fat (1 g sat. fat), 56 mg chol., 552 mg sodium, 9 g carb., 1 g fiber, 29 g pro.* **Diabetic Exchanges:** *3 lean meat, ½ fruit.*

## Makeover Sausage-Stuffed Peppers

**PREP:** 45 MIN. • **BAKE:** 40 MIN.
**MAKES:** 4 SERVINGS

- 2 **cups instant brown rice**
- 4 **medium green peppers**
- ¾ **pound Italian turkey sausage links, casings removed**
- 1 **medium onion, chopped**
- 1 **celery rib, chopped**
- 1 **shallot, chopped**
- 1 **tablespoon reduced-sodium soy sauce**
- 1½ **teaspoons chili powder**
- ½ **teaspoon garlic powder**
- ½ **teaspoon cayenne pepper**
- ½ **cup shredded cheddar cheese**

**1.** Cook rice according to package directions. Meanwhile, cut tops from peppers; chop tops, discarding stems, and set aside. Remove seeds from peppers.

**2.** In a Dutch oven, cook peppers in boiling water for 3-5 minutes. Drain and rinse in cold water; set aside.

**3.** In a large skillet, cook the sausage, onion, celery, shallot and chopped green pepper over medium heat until meat is no longer pink and vegetables are tender; drain. Stir in the rice, soy sauce, chili powder, garlic powder and cayenne. Spoon into peppers. Place in an 8-in. square baking dish coated with cooking spray.

**4.** Cover and bake at 350° for 35-40 minutes or until peppers are tender. Sprinkle with cheese; bake 5 minutes longer or until cheese is melted.

**PER SERVING** *359 cal., 11 g fat (4 g sat. fat), 46 mg chol., 621 mg sodium, 47 g carb., 5 g fiber, 18 g pro.* **Diabetic Exchanges:** *2 starch, 2 medium-fat meat, 2 vegetable.*

TURKEY PEAR SKILLET

## Turkey Pear Skillet

Cooking turkey tenderloins in a sweet wine and cranberry broth keeps them tender and juicy. Also try this with chicken.
—**TASTE OF HOME TEST KITCHEN**

**PREP:** 10 MIN. • **COOK:** 25 MIN.
**MAKES:** 6 SERVINGS

- 2 **tablespoons cornstarch**
- 1 **cup chicken broth**
- ½ **cup sweet white wine**
- ½ **cup cranberry juice**
- 1 **teaspoon rubbed sage**
- ¼ **teaspoon salt**
- 1 **package (20 ounces) turkey breast tenderloins, cut into thin strips**
- 1 **cup thinly sliced onion**
- 2 **tablespoons olive oil**
- 3 **medium pears, peeled and sliced**
- ½ **cup chopped walnuts**
- ½ **cup dried cranberries**
- 2 **tablespoons minced fresh parsley**
  **Hot cooked long grain and wild rice mix, optional**

**1.** In a small bowl, combine the cornstarch, broth, wine, cranberry juice, sage and salt until blended; set aside. In a large skillet, saute turkey and onion in oil for 10-12 minutes or until meat is no longer pink.

**2.** Stir broth mixture and add to skillet. Bring to a boil; cook and stir for 2 minutes or until thickened. Add the pears, walnuts, cranberries and parsley; cover and cook for 3 minutes or until heated through. Serve with rice if desired.

**PER SERVING** *328 cal., 12 g fat (1 g sat. fat), 46 mg chol., 307 mg sodium, 30 g carb., 3 g fiber, 25 g pro.*

"When I tried this makeover version of stuffed peppers, I was surprised how much I enjoyed it. I don't usually like them, but my husband loves them. We preferred them with yellow and red bell peppers instead of green."
—**TAMI KUEHL** LOUP CITY, NE

MAKEOVER SAUSAGE-STUFFED PEPPERS

## Asian Turkey Lettuce Cups

Lettuce cups are such a cool idea for a light lunch or even an appetizer! When I want to make it easier for my kids to eat, I mix everything up with shredded lettuce and serve it in a bowl.

—DIANA RIOS LYTLE, TX

**START TO FINISH:** 30 MIN.
**MAKES:** 4 SERVINGS

- 3 tablespoons reduced-sodium soy sauce
- 2 teaspoons sugar
- 2 teaspoons sesame oil
- 1 teaspoon Thai chili sauce, optional
- 1 pound lean ground turkey
- 1 celery rib, chopped
- 1 tablespoon minced fresh gingerroot
- 1 garlic clove, minced
- 1 can (8 ounces) whole water chestnuts, drained and chopped
- 1 medium carrot, shredded
- 2 cups cooked brown rice
- 8 Bibb or Boston lettuce leaves

**1.** In a small bowl, whisk soy sauce, sugar, sesame oil and, if desired, chili sauce until blended. In a large skillet, cook turkey and celery 6-9 minutes or until turkey is no longer pink, breaking up turkey into crumbles; drain.
**2.** Add ginger and garlic to turkey; cook 2 minutes. Stir in soy sauce mixture, water chestnuts and carrot; cook 2 minutes longer. Stir in rice; heat through. Serve in lettuce leaves.

**PER SERVING** *353 cal., 13 g fat (3 g sat. fat), 90 mg chol., 589 mg sodium, 35 g carb., 4 g fiber, 24 g pro.* **Diabetic Exchanges:** *3 lean meat, 2 starch, 1 vegetable, ½ fat.*

ASIAN TURKEY LETTUCE CUPS

TURKEY CURRY

## Turkey Curry C

I'm always looking for new and interesting ways to use leftover turkey, especially around the holidays. This is a zesty entree you can make as spicy as you like by varying the amount of curry powder.

—MARTHA BALSER CINCINNATI, OH

**START TO FINISH:** 20 MIN.
**MAKES:** 4 SERVINGS

- 1 cup sliced celery
- ½ cup sliced carrots
- 1 cup fat-free milk, divided
- 2 tablespoons cornstarch
- ¾ cup reduced-sodium chicken broth
- 2 cups diced cooked turkey or chicken
- 2 tablespoons dried minced onion
- ½ teaspoon garlic powder
- 1 to 4 teaspoons curry powder
  Hot cooked rice, optional

**1.** Lightly coat a skillet with cooking spray; saute celery and carrots until tender. In a bowl, mix ¼ cup milk and cornstarch until smooth. Add broth and remaining milk; mix until smooth.
**2.** Pour over vegetables. Bring to a boil; cook and stir for 2 minutes or until thickened. Add the turkey, onion, garlic powder and curry powder; cook until heated through, stirring occasionally. Serve with rice if desired.

**PER SERVING** *232 cal., 6 g fat (0 sat. fat), 37 mg chol., 206 mg sodium, 15 g carb., 0 fiber, 29 g pro.* **Diabetic Exchanges:** *3 lean meat, 1 starch.*

MEXICALI CASSEROLE

## Mexicali Casserole

Kids will love this hearty yet mild-tasting Mexican-style supper. It's also popular at potluck dinners.

—**GERTRUDIS MILLER** EVANSVILLE, IN

**PREP:** 15 MIN. • **BAKE:** 55 MIN.
**MAKES:** 6 SERVINGS

- 1 **pound lean ground turkey**
- 1½ **cups chopped onions**
- ½ **cup chopped green pepper**
- 1 **garlic clove, minced**
- 1 **teaspoon chili powder**
- ½ **teaspoon salt**
- 1 **can (16 ounces) kidney beans, rinsed and drained**
- 1 **can (14½ ounces) diced tomatoes, undrained**
- 1 **cup water**
- ⅔ **cup uncooked long grain rice**
- ⅓ **cup sliced ripe olives**
- ½ **cup shredded reduced-fat cheddar cheese**

**1.** Preheat oven to 375°. In a large skillet coated with cooking spray, cook turkey, onions and green pepper over medium heat until meat is no longer pink and vegetables are tender. Add garlic; cook 1 minute. Drain. Sprinkle with chili powder and salt. Stir in beans, tomatoes, water, rice and olives.
**2.** Transfer to a 2½-qt. baking dish coated with cooking spray. Cover and bake 50-55 minutes or until rice is tender. Uncover; sprinkle with cheese. Bake 5 minutes or until cheese is melted.
**PER SERVING** *348 cal., 10 g fat (3 g sat. fat), 66 mg chol., 508 mg sodium, 41 g carb., 9 g fiber, 24 g pro.* **Diabetic Exchanges:** *3 lean meat, 2 starch, 2 vegetable.*

## Plan for Leftovers

When shopping for a big holiday feast, have a recipe ready for using up the leftovers. That way you can make sure you have all the ingredients on hand for making Turkey Potpies or Turkey Curry, p. 133.

TURKEY POTPIES

## Turkey Potpies

I always use the leftovers from our big holiday turkey to prepare this recipe. I think my family enjoys the potpies more than the original feast!

—**LILY JULOW** LAWRENCEVILLE, GA

**PREP:** 40 MIN. • **BAKE:** 20 MIN.
**MAKES:** 8 SERVINGS

- 4⅓ **cups sliced baby portobello mushrooms**
- 1 **large onion, chopped**
- 1 **tablespoon olive oil**
- 2½ **cups cubed cooked turkey**
- 1 **package (16 ounces) frozen peas and carrots**
- ¼ **teaspoon salt**
- ¼ **teaspoon pepper**
- ¼ **cup cornstarch**
- 2½ **cups chicken broth**
- ¼ **cup sour cream**

**TOPPING**
- 1½ **cups all-purpose flour**
- 2 **teaspoons sugar**
- 1½ **teaspoons baking powder**
- 1 **teaspoon dried thyme**
- ¼ **teaspoon baking soda**
- ¼ **teaspoon salt**
- 2 **tablespoons cold butter**
- 1 **cup buttermilk**
- 1 **tablespoon canola oil**

**1.** In a Dutch oven, saute mushrooms and onion in oil until tender. Stir in the turkey, peas and carrots, salt and pepper. Combine cornstarch and broth until smooth; gradually stir into the pan. Bring to a boil. Reduce heat; cook and stir for 2 minutes or until thickened. Stir in sour cream. Transfer to eight greased 8-oz. ramekins.
**2.** In a large bowl, combine the flour, sugar, baking powder, thyme, baking soda and salt. Cut in butter until mixture resembles coarse crumbs. In a small bowl, combine buttermilk and oil; stir into dry ingredients just until moistened. Drop by heaping teaspoonfuls over filling.
**3.** Bake, uncovered, at 400° for 20-25 minutes or until topping is golden brown and filling is bubbly. Let stand 5 minutes before serving.
**PER SERVING** *314 cal., 11 g fat (4 g sat. fat), 49 mg chol., 701 mg sodium, 34 g carb., 3 g fiber, 20 g pro.* **Diabetic Exchanges:** *2 starch, 2 lean meat, 1½ fat.*

SPANISH TURKEY TENDERLOINS

## Spanish Turkey Tenderloins

If you're hungry for warm-weather fare, try this. The grilled turkey and the bright, sunny colors of the relish look and taste like summer.

**—ROXANNE CHAN** ALBANY, CA

**PREP:** 20 MIN. • **GRILL:** 15 MIN. • **MAKES:** 6 SERVINGS

- 1  package (20 ounces) turkey breast tenderloins
- 1  tablespoon olive oil
- ½  teaspoon salt
- ½  teaspoon pepper
- ¼  teaspoon paprika

**RELISH**
- 1  plum tomato, chopped
- 1  large navel orange, peeled, sectioned and chopped
- ¼  cup sliced pimiento-stuffed olives
- 1  green onion, finely chopped
- 2  tablespoons minced fresh oregano or 2 teaspoons dried oregano
- 2  tablespoons sliced almonds
- 2  tablespoons minced fresh parsley
- 1  large garlic clove, minced
- 1  tablespoon capers, drained
- 1  teaspoon lemon juice
- ½  teaspoon grated lemon peel
- ¼  teaspoon salt

**1.** Rub the turkey with oil; sprinkle with salt, pepper and paprika.

**2.** Grill, covered, over medium heat or broil 4 in. from the heat for 15-20 minutes or until a thermometer reads 170°, turning occasionally. Let stand for 5 minutes before slicing.

**3.** Meanwhile, in a small bowl, combine the relish ingredients. Serve with turkey.

**PER SERVING** 163 cal., 6 g fat (1 g sat. fat), 46 mg chol., 510 mg sodium, 6 g carb., 1 g fiber, 23 g pro. **Diabetic Exchanges:** 3 lean meat, ½ starch, ½ fat.

## Turkey Sausage Pizza

If pizza night is a must in your house, double this recipe and freeze one for later. Then you can have a hot homemade pizza ready in less than 30 minutes.

**—MELISSA JELINEK** MENOMONEE FALLS, WI

**PREP:** 20 MIN. • **BAKE:** 15 MIN. • **MAKES:** 8 SLICES

- 1  loaf (1 pound) frozen bread dough, thawed
- ¾  pound Italian turkey sausage links, casings removed
- ½  cup sliced onion
- ½  cup sliced fresh mushrooms
- ½  cup chopped green pepper
- ½  cup pizza sauce
- 2  cups (8 ounces) shredded part-skim mozzarella cheese

**1.** With greased fingers, press dough onto a 12-in. pizza pan coated with cooking spray. Prick dough thoroughly with a fork. Bake at 400° for 10-12 minutes or until lightly browned.

**2.** Meanwhile, in a large skillet, cook the sausage, onion, mushrooms and green pepper over medium heat for 6-8 minutes or until sausage is no longer pink, breaking up sausage into crumbles; drain.

**3.** Spread crust with pizza sauce. Top with sausage mixture; sprinkle with cheese. Bake 12-15 minutes longer or until crust is golden brown and cheese is melted.

**FREEZE OPTION** *Wrap and freeze cooled pizza. To use, thaw overnight in the refrigerator. Unwrap; bake on a pizza pan at 400° for 18-22 minutes or until heated through.*

**PER SERVING** 283 cal., 9 g fat (4 g sat. fat), 32 mg chol., 668 mg sodium, 30 g carb., 3 g fiber, 18 g pro. **Diabetic Exchanges:** 2 starch, 2 lean meat, ½ fat.

TURKEY SAUSAGE PIZZA

WEEKNIGHT PASTA SUPPER

## Weeknight Pasta Supper

**PREP:** 20 MIN. • **COOK:** 20 MIN. • **MAKES:** 4 SERVINGS

- 3 cups uncooked bow tie pasta
- 10 ounces lean ground turkey
- 8 ounces sliced baby portobello mushrooms
- 2 garlic cloves, minced
- 2 teaspoons olive oil
- 1 can (14½ ounces) fire-roasted diced tomatoes, undrained
- ¼ cup dry red wine or chicken broth
- 5 pitted Greek olives, chopped
- 1 teaspoon dried basil
- 1 teaspoon dried oregano
- 1 teaspoon dried parsley flakes
- ½ teaspoon salt
- ⅛ teaspoon coarsely ground pepper
- 2 cups fresh baby spinach, chopped
- 1 tablespoon grated Parmesan cheese

**1.** Cook pasta according to package directions.
**2.** Meanwhile, in a large nonstick skillet, cook turkey until no longer pink; drain. Remove meat; set aside and keep warm.
**3.** In the same skillet, cook mushrooms and garlic in oil until tender. Stir in the tomatoes, wine, olives, seasonings and turkey. Bring to a boil. Reduce heat; simmer, uncovered, for 10 minutes.
**4.** Drain pasta. Stir into turkey mixture. Stir in spinach; cook 1-2 minutes longer or until spinach is wilted. Sprinkle with cheese.
**PER SERVING** *411 cal., 11 g fat (3 g sat. fat), 57 mg chol., 751 mg sodium, 52 g carb., 4 g fiber, 24 g pro.*

## Golden Apricot-Glazed Turkey Breast S C

Basted with a simple glaze, this wonderfully tender turkey bakes to a lovely golden brown. Make it the centerpiece of your holiday table; guests will be glad you did.
—**GREG FONTENOT** THE WOODLANDS, TX

**PREP:** 10 MIN. • **BAKE:** 1½ HOURS + STANDING
**MAKES:** 15 SERVINGS

- ½ cup apricot preserves
- ¼ cup balsamic vinegar
- ¼ teaspoon pepper
  Dash salt
- 1 bone-in turkey breast (5 pounds)

**1.** Preheat oven to 325°. Combine preserves, vinegar, pepper and salt. Place turkey breast on a rack in a large shallow roasting pan.
**2.** Bake, uncovered, 1½ to 2 hours or until a thermometer reads 170°, basting every 30 minutes with apricot mixture. (Cover loosely with foil if turkey browns too quickly.) Cover and let stand 15 minutes before slicing.
**PER SERVING** *236 cal., 8 g fat (2 g sat. fat), 81 mg chol., 84 mg sodium, 8 g carb., trace fiber, 32 g pro.* **Diabetic Exchanges:** *4 lean meat, ½ starch*

GOLDEN APRICOT-GLAZED TURKEY BREAST

## Tangy Turkey Saute

Convenient turkey breast cutlets are topped with a rich Marsala wine sauce for this simple and tasty main dish.

—AMY WENGER SEVERANCE, CO

**START TO FINISH:** 30 MIN.
**MAKES:** 4 SERVINGS

- ¼ cup all-purpose flour
- 8 turkey breast cutlets (2 ounces each)
- 3 tablespoons olive oil, divided
- 2 cups sliced fresh mushrooms
- ½ cup thinly sliced green onions
- 1 garlic clove, minced
- ½ cup chicken broth
- 1 cup Marsala wine or additional chicken broth
- ½ teaspoon salt
- ¼ teaspoon dried thyme
- 1 tablespoon minced fresh parsley

**1.** Place flour in a large resealable plastic bag. Add turkey, a few pieces at a time, and shake to coat. In a large skillet, saute turkey in 2 tablespoons oil in batches for 2 minutes on each side or until no longer pink; drain. Remove and keep warm.

**2.** In same skillet, saute mushrooms and onions in remaining oil for 3 minutes or until crisp-tender. Add garlic; cook 1 minute longer. Stir in the broth, wine, salt and thyme. Bring to a boil; cook and stir for 3 minutes or until slightly thickened. Stir in parsley. Serve with turkey.

**PER SERVING** *240 cal., 11 g fat (1 g sat. fat), 9 mg chol., 428 mg sodium, 16 g carb., 1 g fiber, 6 g pro.*

BROCCOLI SAUSAGE SIMMER

TANGY TURKEY SAUTE

## Broccoli Sausage Simmer

A dinner that all comes together in one skillet is always a winner. This one also happens to be ready in 30 minutes.

—LISA MONTGOMERY ELMIRA, ON

**START TO FINISH:** 30 MIN.
**MAKES:** 4 SERVINGS

- 1 pound Italian turkey sausage links, cut into ¼-inch slices
- 1 medium bunch broccoli, cut into florets
- ½ cup sliced red onion
- 1 can (14½ ounces) no-salt-added diced tomatoes
- 1 tablespoon minced fresh basil or 1 teaspoon dried basil
- 1 tablespoon minced fresh parsley or 1 teaspoon dried parsley flakes
- 1 teaspoon sugar
- 3 cups cooked spiral pasta

In a large skillet, saute the sausage, broccoli and onion for 5-6 minutes or until broccoli is crisp-tender. Add the tomatoes, basil, parsley and sugar. Cover and simmer for 10 minutes. Add pasta and heat through.

**PER SERVING** *384 cal., 12 g fat (2 g sat. fat), 68 mg chol., 760 mg sodium, 44 g carb., 8 g fiber, 28 g pro.* **Diabetic Exchanges:** *3 medium-fat meat, 2 starch, 2 vegetable.*

## Turkey 'n' Squash Lasagna

I came up with this lasagna recipe when spaghetti squash was on sale at the supermarket, and it was a hit with all my friends. I used ground turkey because I'm trying to cook healthier.

—**NANCY BEALL** COLORADO SPRINGS, CO

**PREP:** 70 MIN. • **BAKE:** 50 MIN. + STANDING
**MAKES:** 12 SERVINGS

- 1 **medium spaghetti squash (2 to 2½ pounds)**
- 1 **pound lean ground turkey**
- 1 **large onion, chopped**
- 1 **tablespoon olive oil, divided**
- 2 **garlic cloves, minced**
- 2 **cans (28 ounces each) crushed tomatoes**
- 1 **can (6 ounces) tomato paste**
- ⅓ **cup minced fresh parsley**
- 1 **teaspoon sugar**
- 1 **teaspoon dried basil**
- 1 **teaspoon dried oregano**
- ½ **teaspoon salt**
- ¼ **teaspoon pepper**
- 1 **egg, lightly beaten**
- 1 **carton (15 ounces) reduced-fat ricotta cheese**
- ¾ **cup plus 2 tablespoons grated Parmesan cheese, divided**
- 2 **medium zucchini, sliced**
- 6 **lasagna noodles, cooked and drained**
- 2 **cups (8 ounces) shredded part-skim mozzarella cheese, divided**

**1.** With a sharp knife, pierce spaghetti squash 10 times. Place on a microwave-safe plate; microwave on high for 5-6 minutes. Turn; cook 4-5 minutes longer or until fork-tender. Cover and let stand for 15 minutes. Cut squash in half lengthwise; discard seeds. Scoop out squash, separating strands with a fork; set aside.

**2.** In a large saucepan, cook turkey and onion in 1½ teaspoons oil over medium heat until meat is no longer pink. Add garlic; cook 1 minute longer. Drain. Stir in the tomatoes, tomato paste, parsley, sugar and seasonings. Bring to a boil. Reduce heat; cover and simmer for 30 minutes.

**3.** In a small bowl, combine the egg, ricotta and ¾ cup Parmesan until blended. In a small skillet, saute zucchini in remaining oil until crisp-tender.

**4.** Spread 1½ cups meat sauce into a 13-in. x 9-in. baking dish coated with cooking spray. Layer with three noodles and half of the zucchini, spaghetti squash and ricotta mixture. Sprinkle with 1½ cups mozzarella and half of remaining sauce. Top with the remaining noodles, zucchini, spaghetti squash, ricotta mixture and sauce (dish will be full).

**5.** Place dish on a baking sheet. Bake, uncovered, at 350° for 45-55 minutes or until edges are bubbly. Sprinkle with remaining mozzarella and Parmesan cheeses. Bake 5 minutes longer or until cheese is melted. Let stand for 10 minutes before cutting.
**NOTE** *This recipe was tested in a 1,100-watt microwave.*
**PER SERVING** *311 cal., 12 g fat (5 g sat. fat), 72 mg chol., 548 mg sodium, 31 g carb., 5 g fiber, 22 g pro.* **Diabetic Exchanges:** *2 starch, 2 lean meat, 1 fat.*

## Did you know?

When cooked, the flesh of a spaghetti squash can be scraped with a fork into long spaghetti-shaped strands. With fewer than 50 calories per cup, it's an excellent substitution for pasta.

TURKEY 'N' SQUASH LASAGNA

# Italian Turkey Meat Loaf

**PREP:** 15 MIN. • **BAKE:** 40 MIN.
**MAKES:** 6 SERVINGS

- 6 garlic cloves, halved
- 2 medium carrots, cut into chunks
- 1 small onion, cut into wedges
- 1 can (15 ounces) black beans, rinsed and drained
- 1 cup quick-cooking oats
- ½ cup fat-free milk
- 1 can (6 ounces) tomato paste, divided
- 3 teaspoons Italian seasoning, divided
- 1 teaspoon seasoned salt
- 1 package (20 ounces) lean ground turkey
- 1 tablespoon water

**1.** Preheat oven to 350°. Place garlic, carrots and onion in a food processor; pulse until finely chopped. Add beans; process until blended. In a large bowl, combine oats, milk, half of the tomato paste; 1½ teaspoons Italian seasoning, seasoned salt and black bean mixture. Add turkey; mix lightly but thoroughly.

**2.** Shape into a loaf and place in an 11-in. x 7-in. baking dish coated with cooking spray. Bake, uncovered, for 30 minutes.

**3.** Combine water and remaining tomato paste and Italian seasoning; spread over meat loaf. Bake 10-15 minutes longer or until a thermometer reads 165°. Let stand 10 minutes before slicing.

**PER SERVING** *298 cal., 9 g fat (2 g sat. fat), 75 mg chol., 517 mg sodium, 30 g carb., 6 g fiber, 25 g pro.* **Diabetic Exchanges:** *3 lean meat, 2 starch.*

"It's easy to whip up this turkey and bean meat loaf on weeknights, and it makes fantastic sandwiches the next day. It's a little softer than most meat loaves, but it slices perfectly and holds its shape while serving." —**LAURIE BOCK** LYNDEN, WA

ITALIAN TURKEY MEAT LOAF

## Italian Sausage-Stuffed Zucchini

I've always had to be creative when getting my family to eat vegetables, so I decided to make stuffed zucchini using the pizza flavors that everyone loves. It worked! We like to include sausage for a main dish, but this could be a meatless side dish too.

**—DONNA MARIE RYAN** TOPSFIELD, MA

**PREP:** 35 MIN. • **BAKE:** 20 MIN.
**MAKES:** 6 SERVINGS

- 6 medium zucchini (about 8 ounces each)
- 1 pound Italian turkey sausage links, casings removed
- 2 medium tomatoes, seeded and chopped
- 1 cup panko (Japanese) bread crumbs
- ⅓ cup grated Parmesan cheese
- ⅓ cup minced fresh parsley
- 2 tablespoons minced fresh oregano or 2 teaspoons dried oregano
- 2 tablespoons minced fresh basil or 2 teaspoons dried basil
- ¼ teaspoon pepper
- ¾ cup shredded part-skim mozzarella cheese

**1.** Preheat oven to 350°. Cut each zucchini lengthwise in half. Scoop out pulp, leaving a ¼-in. shell; chop pulp. Place zucchini shells in a large microwave-safe dish. In batches, microwave, covered, on high 2-3 minutes or until crisp-tender.

**2.** In a large skillet, cook sausage and zucchini pulp over medium heat 6-8 minutes or until sausage is no longer pink, breaking sausage into crumbles; drain. Stir in tomatoes, bread crumbs, Parmesan cheese, herbs and pepper. Spoon into zucchini shells.

**3.** Place in two ungreased 13-in. x 9-in. baking dishes. Bake, covered, 15-20 minutes or until zucchini is tender. Sprinkle with mozzarella cheese. Bake, uncovered, 5-8 minutes longer or until cheese is melted.

**PER SERVING** *206 cal., 9 g fat (3 g sat. fat), 39 mg chol., 485 mg sodium, 16 g carb., 3 g fiber, 17 g pro.* **Diabetic Exchanges:** *2 lean meat, 2 vegetable, ½ starch.*

## Tasty Turkey and Mushrooms ⓒ

Sliced mushrooms star in this tender turkey recipe. It takes just minimal preparation and makes a great main dish for my husband and me.

**—NANCY ZIMMERMAN**
CAPE MAY COURT HOUSE, NJ

**START TO FINISH:** 15 MIN.
**MAKES:** 2 SERVINGS

- 1 garlic clove, minced
- 1 tablespoon butter
- ½ pound boneless skinless turkey breast, cut into 2-inch strips
- ¾ cup reduced-sodium beef broth
- 1 tablespoon tomato paste
- 2 cups sliced fresh mushrooms
- ⅛ teaspoon salt

In a large nonstick skillet, saute garlic in butter until tender. Add turkey; cook until juices run clear. Remove and keep warm. Add the broth, tomato paste, mushrooms and salt to skillet; cook for 3-5 minutes or until mushrooms are tender, stirring occasionally. Return turkey to the pan and heat through.

**PER SERVING** *209 cal., 7 g fat (4 g sat. fat), 88 mg chol., 435 mg sodium, 5 g carb., 1 g fiber, 31 g pro.* **Diabetic Exchanges:** *4 lean meat, 1 vegetable, 1½ fat.*

146

144

160

# Pork, Ham & More

**❝**I had a pork tenderloin and ripe peaches that begged to be put together. The results couldn't have been more irresistible! Here's a fresh entree that tastes like summer.**❞**

—**JULIA GOSLIGA** ADDISON, VT
*about her recipe, Just Peachy Pork Tenderloin, on page 154*

PORK CHOPS WITH CABBAGE 'N' TOMATO

# Pork Chops with Cabbage 'n' Tomato C

You won't believe the great flavor in this dish. Tomato and sweet red pepper make it a feast for your eyes and your stomach!
—**WILLIAM BABRICK** WASHINGTON, IN

**START TO FINISH:** 25 MIN.
**MAKES:** 2 SERVINGS

- 2 **boneless pork loin chops (4 ounces each)**
- ¼ **teaspoon olive oil**
- 1 **medium onion, chopped**
- ½ **cup chopped sweet red pepper**
- 1 **cup shredded cabbage**
- 1 **small tomato, chopped**
- ⅓ **cup reduced-sodium chicken broth**
- ⅛ **to ¼ teaspoon pepper**
- ⅛ **teaspoon salt**
- ⅛ **teaspoon paprika**

**1.** In a large nonstick skillet coated with cooking spray, brown pork chops. Remove and keep warm. In the same skillet, add the oil, onion and red pepper. Cook for 3-5 minutes or until vegetables are tender. Stir in the cabbage, tomato, broth, pepper, salt and paprika.

**2.** Return chops to the pan. Reduce heat; cover and simmer for 8-10 minutes or until a thermometer reads 160° and vegetables are tender.
**PER SERVING** *202 cal., 7 g fat (2 g sat. fat), 55 mg chol., 286 mg sodium, 10 g carb., 3 g fiber, 24 g pro.* **Diabetic Exchanges:** *3 lean meat, 2 vegetable.*

# Grilled Lamb Chops with Wine Sauce C

A rich sauce and grilled tomatoes and garlic make this dish a keeper.
—**KAREN GORMAN** GUNNISON, CO

**PREP:** 25 MIN. • **GRILL:** 30 MIN.
**MAKES:** 4 SERVINGS

- 2 **tablespoons finely chopped sweet onion**
- 3 **teaspoons olive oil, divided**
- 1 **cup dry red wine**
- 1 **teaspoon butter**
- 1 **teaspoon minced fresh thyme or ¼ teaspoon dried thyme**
- 1 **cup cherry tomatoes**
- 6 **whole unpeeled garlic cloves**
- 2 **garlic cloves, minced**
- ¼ **teaspoon salt**
- ¼ **teaspoon pepper**
- 4 **lamb rib or loin chops (6 ounces each)**

**1.** In a small saucepan, saute onion in 1 teaspoon oil until tender; add the wine. Bring to a boil; cook until liquid is reduced to 2 tablespoons. Stir in butter and thyme. Remove from the heat; keep warm.

**2.** Place tomatoes on a double thickness of heavy-duty foil. Drizzle with 1 teaspoon oil. Fold foil around tomatoes and seal tightly; set aside. Repeat with whole garlic cloves and remaining oil. Grill garlic, covered, over medium heat for 30 minutes.

**3.** Meanwhile, combine the minced garlic, salt and pepper; rub over chops. Grill lamb and tomato packet, covered, over medium heat for 6-8 minutes on each side or until lamb reaches desired doneness (for medium-rare, a thermometer should read 145°; medium, 160°; well-done, 170°).

**4.** Open tomato packet carefully to allow steam to escape; place tomatoes in a small bowl. When garlic is cool enough to handle, squeeze softened garlic over tomatoes; toss to coat. Serve lamb with tomatoes and sauce.
**PER SERVING** *262 cal., 11 g fat (4 g sat. fat), 70 mg chol., 221 mg sodium, 6 g carb., 1 g fiber, 22 g pro.* **Diabetic Exchanges:** *3 lean meat, ½ starch, ½ fat.*

GRILLED LAMB CHOPS WITH WINE SAUCE

PINEAPPLE-GLAZED PORK ROAST

## Lemon-Mustard Pork Chops ⓒ

**START TO FINISH:** 20 MIN.
**MAKES:** 4 SERVINGS

- 4   boneless pork loin chops (1-inch thick and 6 ounces each)
- 2   tablespoons lemon juice
- 2   tablespoons minced fresh parsley
- 2   tablespoons Dijon mustard
- 1   garlic clove, minced
- 1   teaspoon grated lemon peel
- ½   teaspoon dried rosemary, crushed
- ¼   teaspoon salt
    Lemon wedges

**1.** Drizzle pork chops with lemon juice. Combine the parsley, mustard, garlic, lemon peel, rosemary and salt; brush over both sides of chops.

**2.** Place pork on a greased broiler pan. Broil 4-5 in. from the heat for 4-5 minutes on each side or until a thermometer reads 145°. Let meat stand for 5 minutes before serving. Serve with lemon wedges.

**PER SERVING** *239 cal., 10 g fat (4 g sat. fat), 82 mg chol., 376 mg sodium, 3 g carb., trace fiber, 33 g pro.* **Diabetic Exchange:** *5 lean meat.*

## Pineapple-Glazed Pork Roast ⓒ

Some dinners are so simple and tasty they work for everyday family meals as well as for entertaining company. This is the one that always gets me oohs and aahs.
—**NANCY WHITFORD** EDWARDS, NY

**PREP:** 10 MIN. • **BAKE:** 50 MIN. + STANDING
**MAKES:** 10 SERVINGS

- 1   boneless pork loin roast (2½ pounds)
- ¾   teaspoon salt
- ¼   teaspoon pepper
- ⅓   cup pineapple preserves
- 2   tablespoons stone-ground mustard
- ¼   teaspoon dried basil
- 1   can (20 ounces) unsweetened pineapple tidbits, drained

**1.** Preheat oven to 350°. Place roast on a rack in a shallow roasting pan, fat side up. Sprinkle with salt and pepper. Roast 25 minutes.

**2.** Meanwhile, for glaze, in a small bowl, whisk preserves, mustard and basil; brush half of mixture over roast. Add pineapple to roasting pan. Roast 25-35 minutes longer or until a thermometer reads 145°.

**3.** Remove roast from oven and brush with remaining glaze; tent loosely with foil. Let stand 10 minutes before slicing. Using a slotted spoon, serve pineapple with pork.

**PER SERVING** *195 cal., 5 g fat (2 g sat. fat), 56 mg chol., 271 mg sodium, 14 g carb., 1 g fiber, 22 g pro.* **Diabetic Exchanges:** *3 lean meat, ½ starch.*

"This recipe is lip-smackin' good! These tangy chops combine colorful, flavorful ingredients for a delightful main course."
—**KATHLEEN SPECHT** CLINTON, MT

LEMON-MUSTARD PORK CHOPS

## Pork 'n' Pea Pod Stir-Fry

Once the pork tenderloin is marinated, I can have a sweet-hot stir-fry ready for dinner in less than half an hour. We like this dish extra spicy, so I use a tablespoon of red pepper flakes.

—JANE SHAPTON IRVINE, CA

**PREP:** 10 MIN. + MARINATING
**COOK:** 15 MIN. • **MAKES:** 3 SERVINGS

- 2 tablespoons reduced-sodium soy sauce
- 2 tablespoons honey
- 1½ teaspoons minced fresh gingerroot
- ½ to 1 teaspoon crushed red pepper flakes
- ¾ pound pork tenderloin, cut into 2-inch strips
- 1 tablespoon cornstarch
- ⅓ cup orange juice
- 2 tablespoons cider vinegar
- 2 teaspoons canola oil
- 1 pound fresh snow peas
- 2 teaspoons minced garlic
- 1 teaspoon grated orange peel

**1.** In a small bowl, combine the soy sauce, honey, ginger and pepper flakes. Place 3 tablespoons in a large resealable plastic bag; add the pork. Seal bag and turn to coat; refrigerate for 1 hour. Cover and refrigerate remaining marinade.

**2.** Combine the cornstarch, orange juice, vinegar and reserved marinade; stir until blended and set aside. Drain and discard marinade from pork. In a large nonstick skillet or wok, stir-fry pork in oil for 4-5 minutes or until no longer pink. Remove pork and keep warm.

**3.** In the same pan, stir-fry snow peas for 2-3 minutes or until crisp-tender. Stir in garlic and orange peel. Stir cornstarch mixture and stir into pan. Bring to a boil; cook and stir for 1-2 minutes or until thickened. Return pork to the pan; heat through.

**PER SERVING** *286 cal., 7 g fat (2 g sat. fat), 63 mg chol., 354 mg sodium, 26 g carb., 4 g fiber, 28 g pro.* **Diabetic Exchanges:** *3 lean meat, 2 vegetable, 1 starch, ½ fat.*

CRANBERRY-STUFFED PORK CHOPS

## Cranberry-Stuffed Pork Chops

A savory corn bread-cranberry stuffing suits these tender chops. The recipe can easily be doubled for four.

—LOREE REININGER POLK CITY, FL

**PREP:** 15 MIN. • **BAKE:** 25 MIN.
**MAKES:** 2 SERVINGS

- 3 tablespoons chopped onion
- 1 tablespoon chopped pecans
- 1 small garlic clove, minced
- ½ teaspoon butter
- ¼ cup corn bread stuffing mix
- 3 tablespoons dried cranberries
- 2 tablespoons hot water
- 2 boneless pork loin chops (5 ounces each)
- 4 teaspoons red currant jelly, warmed

**1.** In a small nonstick skillet coated with cooking spray, saute the onion, pecans and garlic in butter until onion is tender. Stir in the stuffing mix, cranberries and water. Remove from the heat.

**2.** Carefully cut a pocket in each pork chop; stuff with cranberry mixture. Place on a baking sheet coated with cooking spray. Bake at 350° for 22-28 minutes or until a thermometer reads 160°. Brush with jelly.

**PER SERVING** *326 cal., 12 g fat (4 g sat. fat), 71 mg chol., 177 mg sodium, 26 g carb., 1 g fiber, 29 g pro.* **Diabetic Exchanges:** *4 lean meat, 1½ starch.*

PORK 'N' PEA POD STIR-FRY

## Pork Tenderloin Medallions with Strawberry Sauce C

Pork tenderloin paired with strawberries is a heavenly match. It's made even more special with a tangy feta garnish. Serve with roasted spring vegetables.
—**KATIE WOLLGAST** FLORISSANT, MO

**PREP:** 15 MIN. • **COOK:** 20 MIN.
**MAKES:** 8 SERVINGS

- 1½ cups reduced-sodium beef broth
- 2 cups chopped fresh strawberries, divided
- ½ cup white wine vinegar
- ¼ cup packed brown sugar
- ¼ cup reduced-sodium soy sauce
- 3 garlic cloves, minced
- 2 pork tenderloins (1 pound each), cut into ½-inch slices
- 1 teaspoon garlic powder
- ½ teaspoon salt
- ½ teaspoon pepper
- 2 tablespoons canola oil
- 2 tablespoons cornstarch
- 2 tablespoons cold water
- ½ cup crumbled feta cheese
- ½ cup chopped green onions

**1.** In a large saucepan, combine broth, 1 cup strawberries, vinegar, brown sugar, soy sauce and garlic; bring to a boil. Reduce heat; simmer, uncovered, 15 minutes or until slightly thickened. Strain mixture and set aside liquid, discarding solids.
**2.** Sprinkle pork with garlic powder, salt and pepper. In a large skillet, heat oil over medium heat. Brown pork on both sides. Remove and keep warm.
**3.** Add broth mixture to the same skillet; bring to a boil. Combine cornstarch and water until smooth and gradually stir into skillet.
**4.** Return pork to skillet. Bring to a boil. Reduce heat; cook and stir 2 minutes or until sauce is thickened and pork is tender. Serve pork with sauce. Top with feta cheese, onions and remaining strawberries.
**PER SERVING** *244 cal., 9 g fat (2 g sat. fat), 68 mg chol., 649 mg sodium, 15 g carb., 1 g fiber, 25 g pro.* **Diabetic Exchanges:** *3 lean meat, 1 starch, ½ fat.*

APPLE-GLAZED HOLIDAY HAM

## Apple-Glazed Holiday Ham

Each Christmas, I'm asked to prepare this entree. I'm happy to oblige because it's easy to assemble, bakes for a few hours unattended and is simply delicious.
—**EMORY DOTY** JASPER, GA

**PREP:** 10 MIN. • **BAKE:** 2½ HOURS
**MAKES:** 15 SERVINGS

- 1 spiral-sliced fully cooked bone-in ham (7 to 9 pounds)
- ½ cup packed brown sugar
- ½ cup unsweetened applesauce
- ½ cup unsweetened apple juice
- ¼ cup maple syrup
- ¼ cup molasses
- 1 tablespoon Dijon mustard
  Dash ground ginger
  Dash ground cinnamon

**1.** Place ham on a rack in a shallow roasting pan. Bake, uncovered, at 325° for 2 hours.
**2.** In a small saucepan, combine the remaining ingredients. Cook and stir over medium heat until heated through. Brush ham with some of the glaze; bake 30-60 minutes longer or until a thermometer reads 140°, brushing occasionally with the remaining glaze.
**PER SERVING** *242 cal., 6 g fat (2 g sat. fat), 93 mg chol., 1,138 mg sodium, 17 g carb., trace fiber, 31 g pro.*

PORK TENDERLOIN MEDALLIONS
WITH STRAWBERRY SAUCE

### ? Did you know?

Strawberries are rich in nitrate, which can increase the flow of blood and oxygen to your muscles. This prevents muscle fatigue and makes exercising easier.

WARM FAJITA SALAD

## Warm Fajita Salad

When I didn't have tortillas in the house to wrap up the meat in this recipe, I made it into a hearty salad instead. It was delicious!

—**BOBBIE JO YOKLEY** FRANKLIN, KY

**PREP:** 10 MIN. + MARINATING • **COOK:** 10 MIN.
**MAKES:** 4 SERVINGS

- 1 cup lime juice
- ¼ cup reduced-sodium chicken broth
- ¼ cup reduced-sodium soy sauce
- 2 garlic cloves, minced
- 1 tablespoon canola oil
- 1 teaspoon sugar
- 1 teaspoon liquid smoke, optional
- ¾ teaspoon ground cumin
- ½ teaspoon dried oregano
- ¼ teaspoon ground ginger
- ¼ teaspoon hot pepper sauce
- 1 pound boneless pork loin, trimmed and cut into thin strips
- 1 large onion, sliced
- 1 medium green pepper, cut into strips
- 1 medium sweet yellow pepper, cut into strips
- 1 tablespoon lemon juice
- 6 cups torn romaine
- 12 cherry tomatoes, quartered

**1.** In a large resealable plastic bag, combine the lime juice, broth, soy sauce, garlic, oil, sugar and seasonings. Set aside 2 tablespoons; cover and refrigerate. Add pork to remaining marinade; toss to coat. Cover and refrigerate for 30 minutes to 3 hours, turning occasionally.
**2.** Drain pork, discarding marinade. Heat reserved marinade in a large skillet over medium-high heat. Add the pork, onion and peppers; stir-fry for 3-4 minutes or until pork is no longer pink. Drizzle with lemon juice. Remove from the heat.
**3.** Arrange lettuce on four individual plates; top with meat mixture and tomatoes.
**PER SERVING** *280 cal., 11 g fat (3 g sat. fat), 67 mg chol., 707 mg sodium, 21 g carb., 4 g fiber, 27 g pro.* **Diabetic Exchanges:** *3 lean meat, 2 vegetable, 1 fat, ½ starch.*

## Sweet & Sour Pork

My grandmother made this for me on Valentine's Day when I was a child. Now I make it for my children on Valentine's. I usually make brown rice or rice noodles and add thinly sliced bok choy to increase the vegetable intake. I've never had leftovers.

—**BARBARA HINTERBERGER** BUFFALO, NY

**PREP:** 20 MIN. • **COOK:** 15 MIN. • **MAKES:** 4 SERVINGS

- 1 can (20 ounces) unsweetened pineapple chunks
- ⅓ cup water
- ⅓ cup cider vinegar
- 3 tablespoons brown sugar
- 2 tablespoons cornstarch
- 1 tablespoon reduced-sodium soy sauce
- 1 teaspoon Worcestershire sauce
- ½ teaspoon salt
- 1 pound pork tenderloin, cut into ½-inch pieces
- 1 teaspoon paprika
- 1 tablespoon canola oil
- 1 medium green pepper, thinly sliced
- 1 small onion, thinly sliced
- 2 cups hot cooked brown rice

**1.** Drain pineapple, reserving ⅔ cup juice; set pineapple aside. In a small bowl, mix water, vinegar, brown sugar, cornstarch, soy sauce, Worcestershire sauce, salt and reserved pineapple juice until smooth; set aside.
**2.** Sprinkle pork with paprika. In a large nonstick skillet coated with cooking spray, brown pork in oil.
**3.** Stir cornstarch mixture and add to pan. Bring to a boil; cook and stir 1 minute or until thickened. Add green pepper, onion and pineapple. Reduce heat; simmer, covered, 6-8 minutes or until pork is tender. Serve with rice.
**PER SERVING** *428 cal., 9 g fat (2 g sat. fat), 63 mg chol., 519 mg sodium, 61 g carb., 4 g fiber, 26 g pro.*

SWEET & SOUR PORK

HONEY-MUSTARD
PORK TENDERLOIN

## Pork Tenderloin with Mango Relish c

Colorful mango relish is a refreshing counterpoint to the heat in the meat rub I use to pep up a number of pork dishes. These roasted tenderloins are sure to turn out nice and juicy.

—**GLORIA BRADLEY** NAPERVILLE, IL

**PREP:** 15 MIN. • **BAKE:** 45 MIN. • **MAKES:** 6 SERVINGS

1½ teaspoons ground coriander
 1 teaspoon ground cumin
 ½ teaspoon salt
 ½ teaspoon sugar
 ½ teaspoon ground chipotle pepper
 ½ teaspoon smoked Spanish paprika
 2 pork tenderloins (¾ pound each)
**MANGO RELISH**
 1 medium mango, peeled and chopped
 2 plum tomatoes, seeded and chopped
 ⅓ cup chopped onion
 ⅓ cup chopped seeded peeled cucumber
 ¼ cup minced fresh cilantro
 1 jalapeno pepper, seeded and chopped
 3 tablespoons lime juice

**1.** In a small bowl, combine the first six ingredients. Set aside ½ teaspoon for relish; rub remaining spice mixture over tenderloins. Place in a lightly greased 13-in. x 9-in. baking pan. Bake, uncovered, at 350° for 45-50 minutes or until a thermometer reads 160°. Let stand for 5 minutes.
**2.** Meanwhile, in a small bowl, combine mango, tomatoes, onion, cucumber, cilantro and jalapeno. Combine lime juice and reserved spice mixture; add to mango mixture and toss to coat. Slice pork; serve with relish.
**NOTE** *Wear disposable gloves when cutting hot peppers; the oils can burn skin. Avoid touching your face.*
**PER SERVING** *171 cal., 4 g fat (1 g sat. fat), 63 mg chol., 245 mg sodium, 9 g carb., 2 g fiber, 23 g pro.* **Diabetic Exchanges:** *3 lean meat, ½ starch.*

"This meal is quick, easy and so good. I usually have all the ingredients on hand and everyone enjoys the honey-mustard flavor." —**JOYCE MOYNIHAN** LAKEVILLE, MN

## Honey-Mustard Pork Tenderloin

**START TO FINISH:** 30 MIN. • **MAKES:** 4 SERVINGS

 1 pork tenderloin (1 pound)
**GLAZE**
 ¼ cup honey
 2 tablespoons brown sugar
 2 tablespoons cider vinegar
 1 tablespoon prepared mustard
 ½ teaspoon salt
 ¼ teaspoon pepper

**1.** Place pork on a greased rack in a 15-in. x 10-in. x 1-in. baking pan lined with foil. In a small bowl, combine glaze ingredients; set aside 3 tablespoons glaze for basting. Spoon remaining glaze over pork.
**2.** Bake, uncovered, at 400° for 24-28 minutes or until a thermometer reads 145°, basting occasionally with reserved glaze. Let stand for 5 minutes before slicing.
**PER SERVING** *226 cal., 4 g fat (1 g sat. fat), 63 mg chol., 386 mg sodium, 25 g carb., trace fiber, 23 g pro.* **Diabetic Exchanges:** *3 lean meat, 1½ starch.*

PORK TENDERLOIN WITH MANGO RELISH

TUSCAN PORK STEW

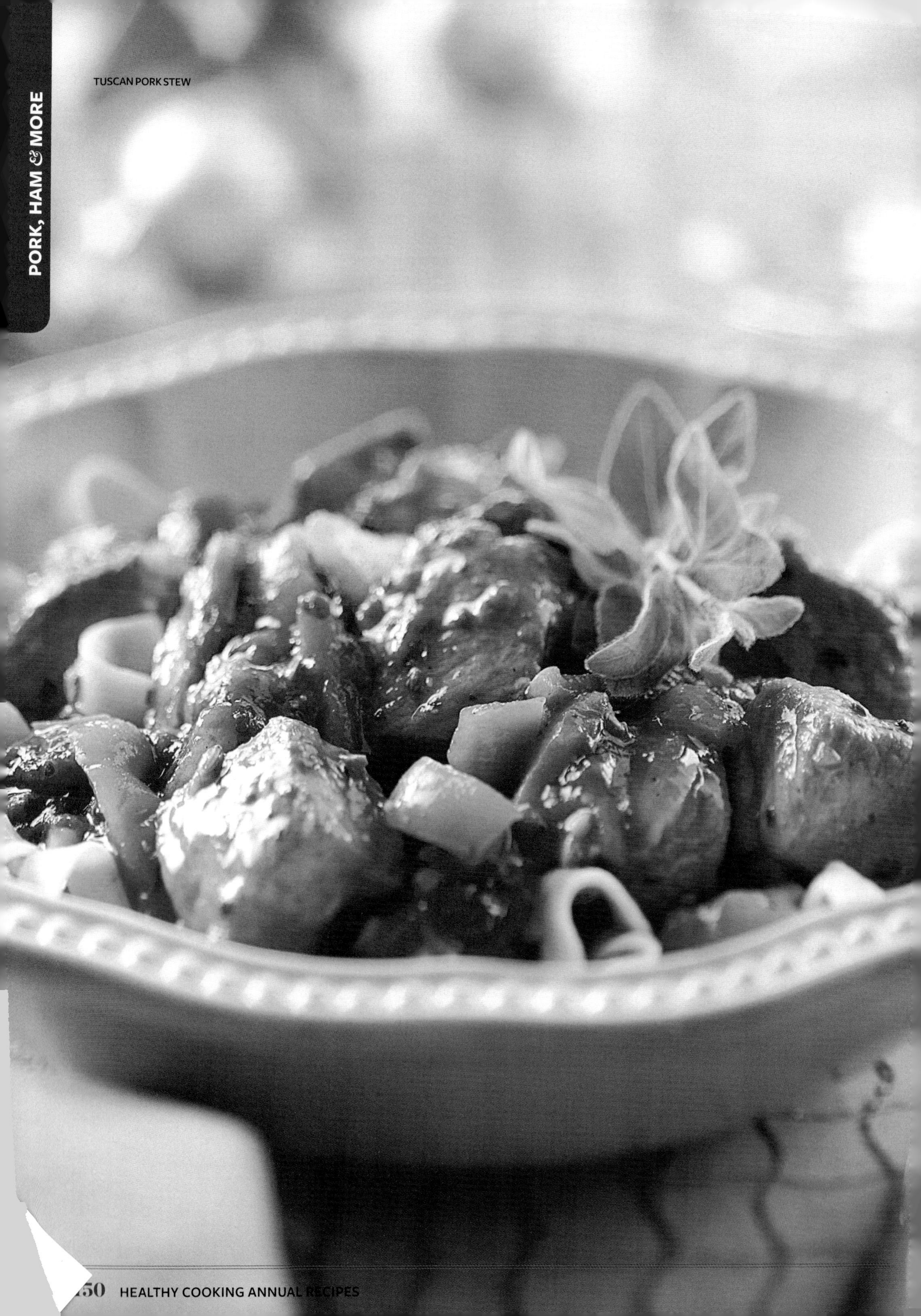

# Tuscan Pork Stew

Tender chunks of pork slowly cook in a nicely seasoned wine-infused sauce. Add some crushed red pepper flakes for a little more kick.

**—PENNY HAWKINS** MEBANE, NC

**PREP:** 15 MIN. • **COOK:** 8½ HOURS
**MAKES:** 8 SERVINGS

- 1½ **pounds boneless pork loin roast, cut into 1-inch cubes**
- 2 **tablespoons olive oil**
- 2 **cans (14½ ounces each) Italian diced tomatoes, undrained**
- 2 **cups reduced-sodium chicken broth**
- 2 **cups frozen pepper stir-fry vegetable blend, thawed**
- ½ **cup dry red wine or additional reduced-sodium chicken broth**
- ¼ **cup orange marmalade**
- 2 **garlic cloves, minced**
- 1 **teaspoon dried oregano**
- ½ **teaspoon fennel seed**
- ½ **teaspoon pepper**
- ⅛ **teaspoon crushed red pepper flakes, optional**
- 2 **tablespoons cornstarch**
- 2 **tablespoons cold water**
  **Hot cooked fettuccine, optional**

**1.** In a large skillet, brown pork in oil; drain. Transfer to a 5-qt. slow cooker.
**2.** Stir in the tomatoes, broth, vegetable blend, wine, marmalade, garlic, oregano, fennel seed, pepper and pepper flakes if desired. Cover and cook on low for 8-10 hours or until meat is tender.
**3.** Combine cornstarch and water until smooth; gradually stir into stew. Cover and cook on high for 30 minutes or until thickened. Serve with fettuccine if desired.
**PER SERVING** *232 cal., 7 g fat (2 g sat. fat), 42 mg chol., 614 mg sodium, 19 g carb., 1 g fiber, 19 g pro.* **Diabetic Exchanges:** *2 lean meat, 1 starch, 1 vegetable, ½ fat.*

 **Did you know?**
In general, Tuscan cooking is characterized by simple food not smothered in heavy sauces. Olive oil is used generously in soups and to pour over bread or salad.

CARIBBEAN CHUTNEY-CRUSTED CHOPS

# Caribbean Chutney-Crusted Chops

I like to impress dinner guests with delicious meals, and these lamb chops are one of my best. It all started with a jar of chutney I received in a gift basket. Folks think these sophisticated chops take a lot of work, but they're done in 30 minutes!

**—JOSEPHINE PIRO** EASTON, PA

**START TO FINISH:** 30 MIN.
**MAKES:** 4 SERVINGS

- 1 **cup soft bread crumbs**
- 1½ **teaspoons Caribbean jerk seasoning**
- ¼ **cup mango chutney**
- ½ **teaspoon salt**
- ½ **teaspoon pepper**
- 4 **lamb loin chops (2 inches thick and 8 ounces each)**

**1.** Preheat oven to 450°. In a shallow bowl, combine bread crumbs and jerk seasoning; set aside. Combine the chutney, salt and pepper; spread over both sides of lamb chops. Coat with crumb mixture.
**2.** Place the lamb chops on a rack coated with cooking spray in a shallow baking pan. Bake 20-25 minutes or until meat reaches desired doneness (for medium-rare, a thermometer should read 145°; medium 160°; well-done 170°).
**PER SERVING** *296 cal., 10 g fat (3 g sat. fat), 91 mg chol., 711 mg sodium, 20 g carb., trace fiber, 30 g pro.* **Diabetic Exchanges:** *4 lean meat, 1 starch.*

# Curried Lamb Stir-Fry

Apple lends a little sweetness to this mildly seasoned stir-fry. Tender strips of lamb contrast nicely with the crunchy snow peas and water chestnuts.

—**PRISCILLA ROOT** ENGLEWOOD, CO

**START TO FINISH:** 15 MIN.
**MAKES:** 4 SERVINGS

- 1 teaspoon cornstarch
- ¼ teaspoon curry powder
- ¼ cup chicken broth
- 1 tablespoon soy sauce
- ¾ pound boneless lamb, cut into ⅛-inch strips
- 1 small onion, chopped
- 2 tablespoons canola oil, divided
- 2 garlic cloves, minced
- 1 small red apple, chopped
- ½ cup chopped green pepper
- ½ cup sliced celery
- 1 can (8 ounces) sliced water chestnuts, drained
- 6 ounces fresh or frozen snow peas
- ¼ teaspoon ground ginger
  Hot cooked rice

**1.** In a small bowl, combine cornstarch and curry powder. Stir in broth and soy sauce until smooth; set aside.

**2.** In a large skillet or wok, saute the lamb and onion in 1 tablespoon oil until meat is browned. Add garlic; cook 1 minute longer. Remove and keep warm.

**3.** In the same skillet, stir-fry the apple, green pepper, celery, water chestnuts, peas and ginger in remaining oil until crisp-tender. Add lamb mixture.

**4.** Stir broth mixture and add to skillet. Bring to a boil; cook and stir for 2 minutes or until thickened. Serve with rice.

**SPICY CURRIED LAMB STIR-FRY**
*Substitute 1 to 1½ teaspoons minced fresh gingerroot for the ground ginger. Add ¼ teaspoon cayenne pepper to the apple mixture. Proceed as directed.*
**PER SERVING** *250 cal., 12 g fat (3 g sat. fat), 47 mg chol., 345 mg sodium, 19 g carb., 4 g fiber, 18 g pro.* **Diabetic Exchanges:** *2 lean meat, 1½ fat, 1 starch, 1 vegetable.*

JAVA-SPICE RUB FOR PORK

# Java-Spice Rub for Pork ⓒ

Ground coffee is the secret ingredient in this special rub, which could also be used on beef steaks.

—**MARK MORGAN** WATERFORD, WI

**START TO FINISH:** 10 MIN.
**MAKES:** 12 BATCHES

- 1 tablespoon finely ground coffee
- 1 teaspoon kosher salt
- 1 teaspoon brown sugar
- 1 teaspoon chili powder
- ½ teaspoon ground cumin
- ½ teaspoon ground cinnamon
- ½ teaspoon pepper
- ¼ teaspoon garlic powder

**ADDITIONAL INGREDIENTS (FOR EACH BATCH)**
- 1 pork tenderloin (1 pound)
- 1 tablespoon canola oil

In a small bowl, combine the first eight ingredients. Transfer to a small spice jar. Store in a cool, dry place for up to 2 months.

**TO PREPARE PORK TENDERLOIN**
*Brush pork with oil; rub with 1 tablespoon seasoning mix. Cover and refrigerate at least 2 hours or overnight.*

**TO PREPARE GRILL FOR INDIRECT HEAT** *Grill pork, covered, over indirect medium-hot heat for 25-30 minutes or until a thermometer reads 160°. Let stand for 5 minutes before slicing.*
**PER SERVING** *166 cal., 7 g fat (2 g sat. fat), 63 mg chol., 204 mg sodium, 1 g carb., trace fiber, 23 g pro.* **Diabetic Exchanges:** *3 lean meat, 1 fat.*

CURRIED LAMB STIR-FRY

# Pork Medallions with Squash & Greens

The colors of the dish remind me of autumn, my favorite season. Butternut squash is nutritious as well as colorful. This is an example of cooking it a way other than mashed and sweetened. The pork tenderloin medallions are mildly seasoned with rosemary and are very tender.

—**LOUISE NOWAK** COLUMBIA, CT

**PREP:** 35 MIN. • **COOK:** 10 MIN.
**MAKES:** 8 SERVINGS

- 2 quarts water
- 4 cups chopped mustard greens
- 1 medium butternut squash, peeled and cut into ½-inch cubes
- 3 medium leeks (white portion only), halved and sliced
- 3 tablespoons olive oil
- 2 garlic cloves, minced
- ⅛ teaspoon crushed red pepper flakes
- 1½ cups reduced-sodium chicken broth
- ½ teaspoon salt

**PORK MEDALLIONS**

- 2 pork tenderloins (¾ pound each), cut into eight slices
- ⅓ cup all-purpose flour
- ½ teaspoon salt
- ¼ teaspoon pepper
- ¼ teaspoon dried rosemary, crushed
- 1 teaspoon cornstarch
- ½ cup apple cider or juice
- ⅓ cup reduced-sodium chicken broth
- 1 tablespoon olive oil
- 1 tablespoon butter
- 1 medium tart apple, peeled and chopped

**1.** In a large saucepan, bring water to a boil. Add mustard greens; cook, uncovered, for 3-5 minutes or until tender.

**2.** Meanwhile, in a Dutch oven, saute squash and leeks in oil until tender. Add garlic and pepper flakes; saute 1 minute longer. Stir in broth and salt. Bring to a boil. Reduce heat; simmer, uncovered, for 8 minutes or until liquid has almost evaporated. Drain greens and add to squash mixture; set aside and keep warm.

**3.** Cover pork with plastic wrap. Flatten to ¼-in. thickness. Remove plastic. In a large resealable plastic bag, combine the flour, salt, pepper and rosemary. Add pork, a few pieces at a time, and shake to coat.

**4.** In a small bowl, whisk the cornstarch, apple cider and broth until smooth; set aside.

**5.** In a large skillet, cook pork in oil and butter until meat juices run clear. Remove and keep warm. Add apple to the pan; cook and stir for 2-4 minutes or until crisp-tender.

**6.** Stir cornstarch mixture; add to the pan. Bring to a boil; cook and stir for 2 minutes or until thickened. Add pork; heat through. Top with apple mixture; serve with squash mixture.

**PER SERVING** *272 cal., 11 g fat (3 g sat. fat), 51 mg chol., 669 mg sodium, 24 g carb., 5 g fiber, 20 g pro.* **Diabetic Exchanges:** *2 lean meat, 1½ starch, 1½ fat.*

PORK MEDALLIONS WITH SQUASH & GREENS

## Just Peachy Pork Tenderloin

I had a pork tenderloin and ripe peaches that begged to be put together. The results couldn't have been more irresistible! Here's a fresh entree that tastes like summer.

—JULIA GOSLIGA ADDISON, VT

**START TO FINISH:** 20 MIN. • **MAKES:** 4 SERVINGS

- 1 pork tenderloin (1 pound), cut into 12 slices
- ½ teaspoon salt
- ¼ teaspoon pepper
- 2 teaspoons olive oil
- 4 medium peaches, peeled and sliced
- 1 tablespoon lemon juice
- ¼ cup peach preserves

**1.** Flatten each tenderloin slice to ¼-in. thickness. Sprinkle with salt and pepper. In a large nonstick skillet over medium heat, cook pork in oil until juices run clear. Remove and keep warm.

**2.** Add peaches and lemon juice, stirring to loosen browned bits. Cook and stir over medium heat for 3-4 minutes or until peaches are tender. Stir in the pork and preserves; heat through.

**PER SERVING** *241 cal., 6 g fat (2 g sat. fat), 63 mg chol., 340 mg sodium, 23 g carb., 2 g fiber, 23 g pro.* **Diabetic Exchanges:** *3 lean meat, 1 fruit, ½ starch, ½ fat.*

## Peppered Pork Pitas

The combination of tender pork and sweet red peppers in these sandwiches will appeal to the whole family. Sometimes I add caramelized onions—they're especially good with garlic mayo. It's fun to experiment with your own variations.

—KATHERINE WHITE CLEMMONS, NC

**START TO FINISH:** 20 MIN. • **MAKES:** 4 SERVINGS

- 1 pound boneless pork loin chops, cut into thin strips
- 1 tablespoon olive oil
- 2 teaspoons coarsely ground pepper
- 2 garlic cloves, minced
- 1 jar (12 ounces) roasted sweet red peppers, drained and julienned
- 4 whole pita breads, warmed

In a small bowl, combine the pork, oil, pepper and garlic; toss to coat. In a large skillet, saute pork mixture until no longer pink. Add red peppers; heat through. Serve with pita breads.

**PER SERVING** *380 cal., 11 g fat (3 g sat. fat), 55 mg chol., 665 mg sodium, 37 g carb., 2 g fiber, 27 g pro.* **Diabetic Exchanges:** *3 lean meat, 2 starch, 1 fat.*

## Herb-Rubbed Pork Loin 🄲

A savory herb rub—and a mere 15 minutes prep time—turns plain pork roast into an easy, elegant entree.

**—ROBIN SCHLOESSER** CHESTER, NJ

**PREP:** 15 MIN. • **BAKE:** 1 HOUR + STANDING • **MAKES:** 12 SERVINGS

- 1 **tablespoon olive oil**
- 2 **teaspoons each minced fresh marjoram, rosemary, sage and thyme**
- 1 **teaspoon salt**
- ½ **teaspoon pepper**
- 1 **boneless whole pork loin roast (4 pounds)**
- 1 **cup water**

**1.** In a small bowl, combine the oil, herbs, salt and pepper; rub over pork. Place roast on a rack in a large shallow roasting pan. Pour water into pan.

**2.** Bake, uncovered, at 350° for 1 to 1½ hours or until a thermometer reads 160°. Transfer to a serving platter. Let stand for 10 minutes before slicing.

**PER SERVING** *198 cal., 8 g fat (3 g sat. fat), 75 mg chol., 240 mg sodium, trace carb., trace fiber, 29 g pro.* **Diabetic Exchange:** *4 lean meat.*

## Chipotle-Raspberry Pork Chops

My husband and I love this dinner because it's easy to throw together after a long day of work. Plus, we appreciate that it's tasty and healthy.

**—JENNIFER RAY** PONCHA SPRINGS, CO

**START TO FINISH:** 20 MIN. • **MAKES:** 4 SERVINGS (¼ CUP SAUCE)

- ½ **cup seedless raspberry preserves**
- 1 **chipotle pepper in adobo sauce, finely chopped**
- ½ **teaspoon salt**
- 4 **bone-in pork loin chops (7 ounces each)**

**1.** In a small saucepan, cook and stir preserves and chipotle pepper over medium heat until heated through. Reserve ¼ cup for serving. Sprinkle pork with salt; brush with remaining raspberry sauce.

**2.** Lightly grease a grill or broiler pan rack. Grill chops, covered, over medium heat or broil 4 in. from heat 4-5 minutes on each side or until a thermometer reads 145°. Let stand 5 minutes before serving. Serve with reserved sauce.

**PER SERVING** *308 cal., 9 g fat (3 g sat. fat), 86 mg chol., 395 mg sodium, 27 g carb., trace fiber, 30 g pro.*

PORK CHOPS IN ORANGE SAUCE

## Pork Chops with Onions C

My mother-in-law shared this simple main dish recipe with me, and it's always well-received.

—JILL VAN NUIS MARIETTA, GA

**PREP:** 20 MIN. • **BAKE:** 40 MIN.
**MAKES:** 6 SERVINGS

- 6 **bone-in pork loin chops (7 ounces each)**
- 1 **tablespoon canola oil**
- ¾ **teaspoon salt**
- ½ **teaspoon pepper**
- 2 **medium sweet onions, sliced and separated into rings**
- 1 **cup reduced-sodium beef broth**
- 1 **tablespoon cornstarch**
- 2 **tablespoons cold water**

**1.** In a large nonstick skillet, brown pork chops in oil over medium heat. Sprinkle with salt and pepper. Transfer to an ungreased baking dish.
**2.** Saute onions in drippings until tender. Spoon over chops; add broth. Cover and bake at 325° for 10-15 minutes or until a thermometer reads 145°. Remove pork chops and onions; keep warm. Let meat stand for 5 minutes before serving.
**3.** In a small saucepan, combine cornstarch and water until smooth; stir in pan juices. Bring to a boil; cook and stir for 1-2 minutes or until thickened. Serve with pork and onions.
**PER SERVING** *252 cal., 11 g fat (3 g sat. fat), 87 mg chol., 433 mg sodium, 6 g carb., 1 g fiber, 31 g pro.* **Diabetic Exchanges:** *5 lean meat, 1 vegetable, 1 fat.*

PORK CHOPS WITH ONIONS

## Pork Chops in Orange Sauce S C

These luscious pork chops prove that meals don't have to be complicated to be special. The easy orange sauce with cloves dresses up everyday chops in no time, but your family will think you went all out.

—BILLIE MOSS WALNUT CREEK, CA

**PREP:** 20 MIN. • **COOK:** 20 MIN.
**MAKES:** 4 SERVINGS

- ¼ **teaspoon paprika**
- ¼ **teaspoon pepper**
- 4 **boneless pork loin chops (6 ounces each)**
- ¾ **cup orange juice**
- 2 **tablespoons sugar**
- 6 **whole cloves**
- ½ **teaspoon grated orange peel**
- 2 **tablespoons all-purpose flour**
- ¼ **cup cold water**

**1.** Combine paprika and pepper; rub over both sides of pork chops. Brown chops in a large nonstick skillet coated with cooking spray.
**2.** Combine the orange juice, sugar, cloves and orange peel; pour over pork. Cover and simmer for 4-5 minutes or until a thermometer reads 145°. Remove chops and keep warm.
**3.** In a small bowl, combine flour and water until smooth; stir into cooking juices. Bring to a boil; cook and stir for 2 minutes or until thickened. Discard cloves. Serve sauce with pork chops.
**PER SERVING** *288 cal., 10 g fat (4 g sat. fat), 82 mg chol., 47 mg sodium, 14 g carb., trace fiber, 33 g pro.* **Diabetic Exchanges:** *5 lean meat, 1 starch.*

CAROLINA MARINATED PORK TENDERLOIN

## Carolina Marinated Pork Tenderloin S C

Three bold ingredients will change your grilled pork tenderloin for life. This is exactly the kind of rich, savory, easy-to-prepare recipe I like to serve to company.
—**SHARISSE DUNN** ROCKY POINT, NC

**PREP:** 10 MIN. + MARINATING
**GRILL:** 20 MIN. • **MAKES:** 4 SERVINGS

- ¼ cup molasses
- 2 tablespoons spicy brown mustard
- 1 tablespoon cider vinegar
- 1 pork tenderloin (1 pound)

**1.** In a large resealable plastic bag, combine the molasses, mustard and vinegar; add pork. Seal bag and turn to coat; refrigerate for 8 hours or overnight.
**2.** Prepare grill for indirect heat, using a drip pan. Drain and discard marinade. Moisten a paper towel with cooking oil; using long-handled tongs, rub the grill rack to lightly coat.
**3.** Place pork over drip pan and grill, covered, over indirect medium-hot heat for 20-27 minutes or until a thermometer reads 145°, turning occasionally. Let stand for 5 minutes before slicing.
**PER SERVING** *160 cal., 4 g fat (1 g sat. fat), 63 mg chol., 90 mg sodium, 7 g carb., 0 fiber, 22 g pro.* **Diabetic Exchanges:** *3 lean meat, ½ starch.*

## Apricot Pork Medallions S

**START TO FINISH:** 20 MIN.
**MAKES:** 4 SERVINGS

- 1 pork tenderloin (1 pound), cut into eight slices
- 1 tablespoon plus 1 teaspoon butter, divided
- ½ cup apricot preserves
- 2 green onions, sliced
- 1 tablespoon cider vinegar
- ¼ teaspoon ground mustard

**1.** Pound pork slices with a meat mallet to ½-in. thickness. In a large skillet, heat 1 tablespoon butter over medium heat. Brown pork on each side. Remove pork from pan, reserving drippings.
**2.** Add preserves, green onions, vinegar, mustard and remaining butter to pan; bring just to a boil, stirring to loosen browned bits from pan. Reduce heat; simmer, covered, 3-4 minutes to allow flavors to blend.
**3.** Return pork to pan; cook until pork is tender. Let stand 5 minutes before serving.
**PER SERVING** *266 cal., 8 g fat (4 g sat. fat), 73 mg chol., 89 mg sodium, 26 g carb., trace fiber, 23 g pro.*

"There's nothing we love more than a great pork dish for supper in our house, and this recipe is up there with the best of them. I find that apricot preserves give the pork just the right amount of sweetness without being overwhelming."
—**CRYSTAL BRUNS** ILIFF, CO

APRICOT PORK MEDALLIONS

## Fruity Pork Roast ☐

I like using the slow cooker because it gives me time for other preparations and frees the oven. Plus, it usually doesn't matter if you serve the food later than planned. This pork roast, which I created by adapting other recipes, gets a special flavor from the fruit.

—MARY JEPPESEN-DAVIS ST. CLOUD, MN

**PREP:** 25 MIN.
**COOK:** 8 HOURS + STANDING
**MAKES:** 8 SERVINGS

- ½ medium lemon, sliced
- ½ cup dried cranberries
- ⅓ cup golden raisins
- ⅓ cup unsweetened apple juice
- 3 tablespoons sherry or additional unsweetened apple juice
- 1 teaspoon minced garlic
- ½ teaspoon ground mustard
- 1 boneless pork loin roast (3 pounds)
- ½ teaspoon salt
- ¼ teaspoon pepper
- ⅛ to ¼ teaspoon ground ginger
- 1 medium apple, peeled and sliced
- ½ cup packed fresh parsley sprigs

**1.** In a small bowl, combine the first seven ingredients; set aside. Cut roast in half; sprinkle with salt, pepper and ginger.

**2.** Transfer to a 3-qt. slow cooker. Pour fruit mixture over roast. Place apple and parsley around roast. Cover and cook on low for 8-10 hours or until meat is tender.

**3.** Transfer meat to a serving platter. Let stand for 10-15 minutes before slicing.

**PER SERVING** *272 cal., 8 g fat (3 g sat. fat), 85 mg chol., 200 mg sodium, 15 g carb., 1 g fiber, 33 g pro.* **Diabetic Exchanges:** *5 lean meat, 1 fruit.*

## Down-Home Pork Chops ☐

Zippy sauce made of brown sugar, crushed red pepper flakes and soy sauce adds personality to this otherwise straightforward main dish.

—DENISE HRUZ GERMANTOWN, WI

**START TO FINISH:** 25 MIN.
**MAKES:** 4 SERVINGS

- 4 boneless pork loin chops (4 ounces each)
- 1 tablespoon canola oil
- 1 garlic clove, minced
- ½ cup beef broth
- 2 tablespoons brown sugar
- 1 tablespoon soy sauce
- ¼ teaspoon crushed red pepper flakes
- 2 teaspoons cornstarch
- 2 tablespoons cold water

**1.** In a large skillet over medium-high heat, brown pork chops on both sides in oil; remove and set aside. Add garlic to the pan; saute for 1 minute. Stir in the broth, brown sugar, soy sauce and pepper flakes. Return chops to the pan; cover and simmer for 8-10 minutes or until thermometer reads 160°.

**2.** Remove chops and keep warm. Combine cornstarch and water until smooth; stir into broth mixture. Bring to a boil; cook and stir for 1 minute or until thickened. Serve with chops.

**PER SERVING** *219 cal., 10 g fat (3 g sat. fat), 55 mg chol., 376 mg sodium, 8 g carb., trace fiber, 23 g pro.* **Diabetic Exchanges:** *3 lean meat, 1 fat, ½ starch.*

## Slow Cooking

You can place ingredients in the slow cooker the night before and store it in the refrigerator overnight. When cooking the next day, remember that starting to cook with cold stoneware and cold food will affect the time it takes to cook the meat. Be sure to use an instant read thermometer to make sure your food is done.

FRUITY PORK ROAST

DOWN-HOME PORK CHOPS

PLUM-GOOD PORK CHOPS

## Cider-Molasses Pork Tenderloin with Pears

**PREP:** 25 MIN. • **BAKE:** 25 MIN. • **MAKES:** 6 SERVINGS

- 2 **pork tenderloins (1 pound each)**
- 3 **tablespoons olive oil**
- 4 **teaspoons minced fresh rosemary or 1 teaspoon dried rosemary, crushed**
- 1 **teaspoon salt**
- 1 **teaspoon pepper**
- 6 **medium pears, peeled, halved and cored**
- 1 **cup apple cider or juice**
- ½ **cup molasses**
- ¼ **cup balsamic vinegar**

**1.** Place pork on a rack in a shallow roasting pan. Combine the oil, rosemary, salt and pepper; rub over pork. Arrange pears around pork. In a small bowl, combine the remaining ingredients; pour over the top.

**2.** Bake at 425° for 25-30 minutes or until a thermometer reads 160°, basting occasionally with pan juices. Let stand for 5 minutes before slicing.

**PER SERVING** *437 cal., 12 g fat (3 g sat. fat), 84 mg chol., 472 mg sodium, 53 g carb., 5 g fiber, 31 g pro.*

"I think this is the perfect dinner for entertaining. Drizzling the pork tenderloin with a robust molasses sauce and serving it with tender, sweet baked pears will have everyone asking for more." **—LISA RENSHAW** KANSAS CITY, MO

## Plum-Good Pork Chops

Ginger and plum sauce add Asian flavor that makes this dish a standout. A side of crunchy coleslaw is the perfect partner.

**—TASTE OF HOME TEST KITCHEN**

**START TO FINISH:** 30 MIN. • **MAKES:** 4 SERVINGS

- 4 **bone-in pork loin chops (7 ounces each)**
- 2 **teaspoons canola oil**
- ¾ **cup plum sauce**
- ¼ **cup orange juice**
- 5 **teaspoons reduced-sodium soy sauce**
- 2 **garlic cloves, minced**
- 2 **teaspoons Dijon mustard**
- 1 **teaspoon minced fresh gingerroot**
- ¼ **teaspoon pepper**
- 1 **package (12 ounces) broccoli coleslaw mix**
- 1 **medium carrot, grated**
- 2 **green onions, chopped**
- 2 **teaspoons sesame seeds, toasted**

**1.** In a large skillet, brown chops in oil. Combine the plum sauce, orange juice, soy sauce, garlic, mustard, ginger and pepper; pour over chops. Bring to a boil. Reduce heat; cover and simmer for 15-20 minutes or until tender. Remove pork chops and keep warm. Set aside ½ cup sauce mixture.

**2.** In the same skillet, cook the coleslaw mix, carrot and onions over medium heat until crisp-tender. Serve with pork chops; drizzle with reserved sauce and sprinkle with sesame seeds.

**PER SERVING** *373 cal., 11 g fat (3 g sat. fat), 86 mg chol., 685 mg sodium, 30 g carb., 3 g fiber, 33 g pro.* **Diabetic Exchanges:** *4 lean meat, 1½ starch, 1 vegetable, ½ fat.*

CIDER-MOLASSES PORK TENDERLOIN WITH PEARS

GLAZED ROSEMARY PORK ROAST

## Glazed Rosemary Pork Roast

For a change of pace, I'll serve this special pork roast at holiday gatherings. It's a welcome break from traditional turkey or ham, and when dressed with an herb-infused glaze featuring rosemary, thyme and sage, its flavor is unbeatable.

—JOYCE MANIER BEECH GROVE, IN

**PREP:** 20 MIN. • **COOK:** 4 HOURS • **MAKES:** 8 SERVINGS

- 1 boneless whole pork loin roast (3 pounds)
- 1 tablespoon butter
- 1 teaspoon olive oil
- 1 large onion, sliced
- 1 tablespoon brown sugar
- 1 tablespoon minced fresh rosemary
- 1 teaspoon dried thyme
- 1 teaspoon rubbed sage
- 1 teaspoon grated orange peel
- ½ teaspoon pepper
- ¼ teaspoon salt
- ⅔ cup apricot jam
- ½ cup orange juice
- 1 bay leaf

**1.** Cut roast in half. In a large skillet, brown roast in butter and oil on all sides. Transfer to a 4- or 5-qt. slow cooker.

**2.** Add onion to the same skillet; cook and stir until tender. Stir in the brown sugar, herbs, orange peel, pepper and salt. Spread over pork. Combine jam and orange juice; pour over top. Add bay leaf.

**3.** Cover and cook on low for 4 hours or until a meat thermometer reads 160°. Discard bay leaf.

**PER SERVING** *314 cal., 10 g fat (4 g sat. fat), 88 mg chol., 145 mg sodium, 22 g carb., 1 g fiber, 33 g pro.*

## Pork Roast Dinner

I am single and love to cook, so I often cook for friends who either don't cook or who work nights. They love new recipes, and this was one of their favorites. The leftover meat makes great barbecue pork sandwiches the next day.

—LISA CHAMBERLAIN ST. CHARLES, IL

**PREP:** 30 MIN. + MARINATING • **COOK:** 8 HOURS
**MAKES:** 8 SERVINGS

- 2 teaspoons minced garlic
- 2 teaspoons fennel seed, crushed
- 1½ teaspoons dried rosemary, crushed
- 1 teaspoon dried oregano
- 1 teaspoon paprika
- ¾ teaspoon salt
- ¼ teaspoon pepper
- 1 boneless whole pork loin roast (3 to 4 pounds)
- 1½ pounds medium potatoes, peeled and cut into chunks
- 1½ pounds large sweet potatoes, peeled and cut into chunks
- 2 large sweet onions, cut into eighths
- ½ cup chicken broth

**1.** Combine the garlic, fennel, rosemary, oregano, paprika, salt and pepper; rub over pork. Cover and refrigerate for 8 hours.

**2.** Place potatoes and onions in a 5-qt. slow cooker. Top with pork. Pour broth over meat. Cover and cook on low for 8-10 hours or until meat and vegetables are tender.

**3.** Let meat stand 10-15 minutes before slicing.

**PER SERVING** *369 cal., 9 g fat (3 g sat. fat), 99 mg chol., 349 mg sodium, 29 g carb., 3 g fiber, 41 g pro.* **Diabetic Exchanges:** *5 lean meat, 2 starch.*

PORK ROAST DINNER

174

170

174

# Fish & Seafood

❝My husband and I like to eat seafood at least once a week. Oranges and lemon juice give scallops a refreshing burst of flavor.❞

**—CHERI HAWTHORNE** NORTH CANTON, OH
*about her recipe, Citrus Scallops, on page 168*

## Shrimp and Scallop Couscous c

Served over couscous or rice, this is a simple and filling dish full of flavor, especially when garnished with fresh basil.

—MARVIN MEUSER JR. PRINCETON, IN

**START TO FINISH:** 30 MIN.
**MAKES:** 4 SERVINGS

- 2 medium zucchini, julienned
- 1 medium green pepper, julienned
- 2 tablespoons olive oil
- 3 plum tomatoes, chopped
- 4 green onions, chopped
- 1 tablespoon minced fresh basil or 1 teaspoon dried basil
- 3 teaspoons chili powder
- 1 garlic clove, minced
- ½ teaspoon dried oregano
- ½ pound uncooked medium shrimp, peeled and deveined
- ½ pound bay scallops
- ¼ teaspoon salt
- ⅛ teaspoon pepper
  Hot cooked couscous or rice
  Thinly sliced fresh basil leaves, optional

**1.** In a large skillet, saute zucchini and green pepper in oil until tender. Add the tomatoes, onions, basil, chili powder, garlic and oregano. Bring to a boil. Reduce heat; simmer, uncovered, for 5 minutes.

**2.** Stir in the shrimp, scallops, salt and pepper. Return to a boil. Reduce heat; simmer, uncovered, for 5 minutes or until shrimp turn pink and scallops are opaque. Serve with couscous. Garnish with sliced basil if desired.

**PER SERVING** *201 cal., 9 g fat (1 g sat. fat), 88 mg chol., 342 mg sodium, 11 g carb., 3 g fiber, 21 g pro.* **Diabetic Exchanges:** *3 lean meat, 1½ fat, 1 vegetable.*

CRAB-TOPPED COD

## Crab-Topped Cod c

Richly flavored crab dresses up mild and flaky cod in this incredibly low-fat dish. In summer, try individually wrapping the fillets in foil and grilling them over indirect heat.

—CHERYL WOODSON LIBERTY, MO

**START TO FINISH:** 30 MIN.
**MAKES:** 4 SERVINGS

- 1 can (6 ounces) lump crabmeat, drained
- 1 plum tomato, seeded and diced
- ½ cup grated Parmesan cheese
- 2 tablespoons drained capers
- 2 tablespoons sherry or chicken broth
- ½ teaspoon coarsely ground pepper
- 4 cod fillets (5 ounces each)
- ¼ teaspoon salt
  Snipped fresh dill

**1.** In a small bowl, combine the first six ingredients. Sprinkle cod with salt and place in a greased 13-in. x 9-in. baking dish. Top fillets with crab mixture.

**2.** Bake, uncovered, at 350° for 20-25 minutes or until cod flakes easily with a fork. Garnish with fresh dill.

**PER SERVING** *198 cal., 4 g fat (2 g sat. fat), 100 mg chol., 647 mg sodium, 2 g carb., trace fiber, 35 g pro.* **Diabetic Exchange:** *4 lean meat.*

SHRIMP AND SCALLOP COUSCOUS

## Honey-Pecan Baked Cod C

One night at dinner, while vacationing in the Blue Ridge Mountains, we tried a pecan-encrusted trout, which we enjoyed so much that we re-created it when we got home. Now we enjoy this tasty version with fresh or frozen cod.
—LANA GERMAN LENOIR, NC

**START TO FINISH:** 30 MIN.
**MAKES:** 6 SERVINGS

- 3 tablespoons honey
- 2 tablespoons butter, melted
- 1 tablespoon reduced-sodium soy sauce
- 1½ teaspoons lemon-pepper seasoning
- ½ teaspoon garlic powder
- ½ teaspoon paprika
- ¼ teaspoon seasoned salt
- 1½ cups finely chopped pecans
- 6 cod fillets (6 ounces each)

**1.** Preheat oven to 400°. In a shallow bowl, combine first seven ingredients. Place pecans in another shallow bowl. Dip fillets in honey mixture, then coat with pecans.

**2.** Place in a greased 13-in. x 9-in. dish. Bake, uncovered, 15-20 minutes or until fish flakes easily with a fork.

**PER SERVING** *330 cal., 19 g fat (4 g sat. fat), 75 mg chol., 398 mg sodium, 12 g carb., 2 g fiber, 29 g pro.* **Diabetic Exchanges:** *4 lean meat, 3 fat, ½ starch.*

HONEY-PECAN BAKED COD

SHRIMP & BROCCOLI BROWN RICE PAELLA

"Years ago my husband and I were vacationing in France and came across an open market where a fellow from Spain was making paella in a skillet; we've been hooked ever since. I love to whip this up for a large group, but if the gathering is small, I know I can easily freeze leftovers for another time."
—JONI HILTON ROCKLIN, CA

## Shrimp & Broccoli Brown Rice Paella

**PREP:** 45 MIN. • **COOK:** 50 MIN.
**MAKES:** 8 SERVINGS

- 1 tablespoon olive oil
- 1 medium onion, chopped
- 1 medium sweet red pepper, chopped
- 1 cup sliced fresh mushrooms
- 2 cups uncooked long grain brown rice
- 2 garlic cloves, minced
- 2 teaspoons paprika
- ½ teaspoon salt
- ½ teaspoon cayenne pepper
- ¼ teaspoon saffron threads
- 6 cups chicken stock
- 2 pounds uncooked large shrimp, peeled and deveined
- 1½ cups fresh broccoli florets
- 1 cup frozen peas

**1.** In a Dutch oven, heat oil over medium-high heat. Add onion, red pepper and mushrooms; cook and stir 6-8 minutes or until tender. Stir in rice, garlic and seasonings; cook 1-2 minutes longer.

**2.** Stir in stock; bring to a boil. Reduce heat; simmer, covered, 40-45 minutes or until liquid is absorbed and rice is tender. Add shrimp and broccoli; cook 8-10 minutes longer or until shrimp turn pink. Stir in peas; heat through.

**FREEZE OPTION** *Place cooled paella in freezer containers. To use, partially thaw in refrigerator overnight. Microwave, covered, on high in a microwave-safe dish until heated through, stirring gently and adding a little stock or water if necessary.*

**PER SERVING** *331 cal., 5 g fat (1 g sat. fat), 138 mg chol., 693 mg sodium, 44 g carb., 4 g fiber, 27 g pro.* **Diabetic Exchanges:** *3 lean meat, 2½ starch.*

## Grilled Salmon with Avocado Salsa C

I'm not usually a seafood fan, but I ordered a similar salmon dish at a restaurant, and I couldn't stop eating it. My homemade version has become a favorite with family and friends.
—**RENEE MCILHERAN** LOCKPORT, IL

**START TO FINISH:** 25 MIN. • **MAKES:** 4 SERVINGS

- 1 large tomato, seeded and chopped
- 1 medium ripe avocado, peeled and chopped
- 1 small onion, chopped
- ½ cup minced fresh cilantro
- 1½ teaspoons olive oil
- 1 garlic clove, minced
- 2 tablespoons plus 2 teaspoons balsamic vinaigrette, divided
- 4 salmon fillets (4 ounces each)
- ¼ teaspoon salt
- ¼ teaspoon pepper

**1.** In a small bowl, combine the tomato, avocado, onion, cilantro, oil, garlic and 2 tablespoons vinaigrette. Chill until serving.

**2.** Moisten a paper towel with cooking oil; using long-handled tongs, lightly rub the grill rack to coat. Sprinkle salmon with salt and pepper. Place salmon skin side down on grill rack. Grill, covered, over medium heat for 7-9 minutes or until the salmon flakes easily with a fork. Brush with remaining vinaigrette. Serve with salsa.

**PER SERVING** *301 cal., 21 g fat (3 g sat. fat), 57 mg chol., 295 mg sodium, 9 g carb., 4 g fiber, 21 g pro.* ***Diabetic Exchanges:*** *3 lean meat, 2 fat.*

## Cajun Shrimp C

There's plenty of sauce with these savory shrimp. You can serve them over grits or linguine. Or if you'd like something heartier, serve with beans and rice. I always have some bread on the side to soak up anything extra.
—**MARK OPPE** NORTH POLE, AK

**START TO FINISH:** 25 MIN. • **MAKES:** 4 SERVINGS

- 3 tablespoons butter
- 2 garlic cloves, minced
- ½ cup amber beer or beef broth
- 1 teaspoon Worcestershire sauce
- 1 teaspoon pepper
- ½ teaspoon salt
- ½ teaspoon dried thyme
- ½ teaspoon dried rosemary, crushed
- ½ teaspoon crushed red pepper flakes
- ¼ teaspoon cayenne pepper
- ⅛ teaspoon dried oregano
- 1 pound uncooked large shrimp, peeled and deveined
  Hot cooked grits, optional

In a large skillet, heat butter over medium-high heat. Add garlic; cook and stir 1 minute. Stir in beer, Worcestershire sauce and seasonings; bring to a boil. Add shrimp; cook 3-4 minutes or until shrimp turn pink, stirring occasionally. If desired, serve over grits.

**PER SERVING** *191 cal., 10 g fat (6 g sat. fat), 160 mg chol., 505 mg sodium, 3 g carb., trace fiber, 19 g pro.* ***Diabetic Exchanges:*** *3 lean meat, 2 fat.*

## Pan-Fried Scallops with White Wine Reduction ☐

I learned the simple art of reduction from a cooking class, and I think the flavor is fabulous! Despite the fancy title, this special-occasion entree is easy to prepare.
—**KATHERINE ROBINSON** GLENWOOD SPRINGS, CO

**START TO FINISH:** 30 MIN. • **MAKES:** 8 SERVINGS

- 2 **pounds sea scallops**
- 1 **teaspoon salt**
- ¼ **teaspoon pepper**
- 2 **tablespoons olive oil**

**WHITE WINE REDUCTION**
- ½ **cup white wine or chicken broth**
- ⅓ **cup orange juice**
- ¼ **cup finely chopped onion**
- 1 **teaspoon dried oregano**
- 1 **teaspoon Dijon mustard**
- 1 **garlic clove, minced**
- 3 **tablespoons cold butter, cubed**

**1.** Sprinkle scallops with salt and pepper. In a large skillet, saute scallops in oil until firm and opaque. Remove and keep warm.

**2.** Add wine to the skillet, stirring to loosen browned bits from pan. Stir in the orange juice, onion, oregano, mustard and garlic. Bring to a boil; cook and stir for 2-3 minutes or until reduced by half. Remove from the heat; stir in butter until melted. Serve with scallops.

**PER SERVING** *181 cal., 9 g fat (3 g sat. fat), 49 mg chol., 524 mg sodium, 5 g carb., trace fiber, 19 g pro.* **Diabetic Exchanges:** *3 lean meat, 2 fat.*

## Grilled Tilapia with Pineapple Salsa ☐☐

I found this recipe in a seafood cookbook years ago, and it's been one of my favorites. The fresh, slightly spicy salsa is a delightful complement to the fish.
—**BETH FLEMING** DOWNERS GROVE, IL

**START TO FINISH:** 25 MIN. • **MAKES:** 8 SERVINGS (2 CUPS SALSA)

- 2 **cups cubed fresh pineapple**
- 2 **green onions, chopped**
- ¼ **cup finely chopped green pepper**
- ¼ **cup minced fresh cilantro**
- 4 **teaspoons plus 2 tablespoons lime juice, divided**
- ⅛ **teaspoon plus ¼ teaspoon salt, divided**
  **Dash cayenne pepper**
- 1 **tablespoon canola oil**
- 8 **tilapia fillets (4 ounces each)**
- ⅛ **teaspoon pepper**

**1.** In a small bowl, combine the pineapple, onions, green pepper, cilantro, 4 teaspoons lime juice, ⅛ teaspoon salt and cayenne. Chill until serving.

**2.** Combine oil and remaining lime juice; drizzle over fillets. Sprinkle with pepper and remaining salt.

**3.** Moisten a paper towel with cooking oil; using long-handled tongs, lightly rub the grill rack to coat. Grill fish, covered, over medium heat or broil 4 in. from the heat for 3-4 minutes on each side or until fish flakes easily with a fork. Serve with salsa.

**PER SERVING** *131 cal., 3 g fat (1 g sat. fat), 55 mg chol., 152 mg sodium, 6 g carb., 1 g fiber, 21 g pro.* **Diabetic Exchanges:** *3 lean meat, ½ fruit.*

SOUTHWEST-STYLE COD

## Southwest-Style Cod c

Make tonight Fish Night! This festive recipe with a little zip will guarantee dinner is anything but boring.

**—TASTE OF HOME TEST KITCHEN**

**START TO FINISH:** 30 MIN.
**MAKES:** 4 SERVINGS

- 1 **small onion, chopped**
- 1 **small green pepper, chopped**
- 2 **teaspoons olive oil**
- 2 **garlic cloves, minced**
- 1 **can (15 ounces) tomato sauce**
- 2 **medium tomatoes, chopped**
- 1 **can (2¼ ounces) sliced ripe olives, drained**
- ½ **teaspoon ground cumin**
- ¼ **teaspoon hot pepper sauce**
- ⅛ **teaspoon pepper**
- 4 **cod fillets (6 ounces each)**

**1.** In a large skillet, saute onion and green pepper in oil until tender. Add garlic; saute 1 minute longer. Stir in the tomato sauce, tomatoes, olives, cumin, pepper sauce and pepper. Bring to a boil. Reduce heat; simmer, uncovered, for 5 minutes.

**2.** Add fillets. Cover and cook over medium heat for 10-14 minutes or until fish flakes easily with a fork, turning once.
**PER SERVING** *226 cal., 6 g fat (1 g sat. fat), 65 mg chol., 734 mg sodium, 12 g carb., 3 g fiber, 30 g pro.* **Diabetic Exchanges:** *4 lean meat, 2 vegetable, 1 fat.*

## Citrus Scallops

My husband and I like to eat seafood at least once a week. Oranges and lemon juice give scallops a refreshing burst of zesty flavor.

**—CHERI HAWTHORNE** NORTH CANTON, OH

**START TO FINISH:** 15 MIN.
**MAKES:** 4 SERVINGS

- 1 **medium green or sweet red pepper, julienned**
- 4 **green onions, chopped**
- 1 **garlic clove, minced**
- 2 **tablespoons olive oil**
- 1 **pound sea scallops**
- ½ **teaspoon salt**
- ¼ **teaspoon crushed red pepper flakes**
- 2 **tablespoons lime juice**
- ½ **teaspoon grated lime peel**
- 4 **medium navel oranges, peeled and sectioned**
- 2 **teaspoons minced fresh cilantro Hot cooked rice or pasta**

In a large skillet, saute the pepper, onions and garlic in oil for 1 minute. Add scallops, salt and pepper flakes; cook for 4 minutes. Add lime juice and peel; cook for 1 minute. Reduce heat. Add orange sections and cilantro; cook 2 minutes longer or until scallops are opaque. Serve with rice or pasta.
**PER SERVING** *240 cal., 8 g fat (1 g sat. fat), 37 mg chol., 482 mg sodium, 23 g carb., 4 g fiber, 21 g pro.* **Diabetic Exchanges:** *3 lean meat, 1½ fat, 1 frui*

## ? Did you know?

Scallops swim by opening and closing their shells using a powerful muscle called the adductor. This is the fleshy "scallop" that you eat. In addition to being an excellent source of protein, scallops are high in vitamin B12, a key nutrient for DNA production.

CITRUS SCALLOPS

ASPARAGUS SALAD WITH GRILLED SALMON

## Asparagus Salad with Grilled Salmon

This salad's a little sweet, a little savory and very refreshing. Healthy asparagus boasts anti-inflammatory nutrients and vitamins A, B and C. It's fabulous grilled; you'll want to fix this again and again.

**—JENNE DELKUS** DES PERES, MO

**START TO FINISH:** 30 MIN.
**MAKES:** 4 SERVINGS

- ⅓ **cup maple syrup**
- 2 **tablespoons Dijon mustard**
- 1 **tablespoon olive oil**
- 1 **teaspoon snipped fresh dill**
- 4 **salmon fillets (4 ounces each)**
- 1 **pound fresh asparagus, trimmed**
- 4 **cups spring mix salad greens**
- 1 **cup shredded carrots**
- 1 **hard-cooked egg, cut into eight wedges**
  **Coarsely ground pepper**

**1.** In a small bowl, whisk the syrup, mustard, oil and dill; set aside.

**2.** Place salmon skin side down on grill rack. Grill, covered, over medium heat for 5 minutes. Meanwhile, in a shallow bowl, drizzle asparagus with 1 tablespoon dressing; toss to coat. Arrange asparagus on a grilling grid; place on the grill rack with salmon. Spoon 1 tablespoon dressing over salmon.

**3.** Grill salmon and asparagus, covered, for 4-6 minutes or until salmon flakes easily with a fork and asparagus is crisp-tender, turning asparagus once.

**4.** Divide salad greens among four plates and sprinkle with carrots. Remove skin from salmon. Arrange the egg wedges, asparagus and salmon over salads. Drizzle with remaining dressing; sprinkle with pepper.

**NOTE** *If you do not have a grilling grid, use a disposable foil pan. Poke holes in the bottom of the pan with a meat fork to allow liquid to drain.*

**PER SERVING** *336 cal., 16 g fat (3 g sat. fat), 110 mg chol., 294 mg sodium, 26 g carb., 3 g fiber, 23 g pro.* **Diabetic Exchanges:** *3 lean meat, 2 vegetable, 1 starch, 1 fat.*

## Balsamic-Glazed Tuna Steaks F C

Thanks to a delicious balsamic glaze, the tuna steaks have a slight sweetness. Ready in minutes, they're perfect for hectic days.

**—LAURA MCDOWELL** LAKE VILLA, IL

**START TO FINISH:** 15 MIN.
**MAKES:** 4 SERVINGS

- 4 **tuna steaks (¾ inch thick and 6 ounces each)**
- 1¼ **teaspoons pepper**
- ¼ **teaspoon salt**
- 4 **teaspoons dark brown sugar**
- ½ **teaspoon cornstarch**
- ¼ **cup chicken broth**
- 1 **tablespoon balsamic vinegar**
- 1 **tablespoon soy sauce**

**1.** Sprinkle tuna with pepper and salt. Moisten a paper towel with cooking oil; using long-handled tongs, lightly rub the grill rack to coat. Grill fish, covered, over medium heat or broil 4 in. from the heat for 3-5 minutes on each side for medium-rare or until slightly pink in the center.

**2.** Meanwhile, in a small saucepan, combine the remaining ingredients until smooth. Bring to a boil; cook and stir for 1 minute or until thickened. Serve with fish.

**PER SERVING** *210 cal., 2 g fat (trace sat. fat), 77 mg chol., 505 mg sodium, 6 g carb., trace fiber, 40 g pro.* **Diabetic Exchanges:** *5 lean meat, ½ starch.*

BALSAMIC-GLAZED TUNA STEAKS

## Baked Cod Piccata with Asparagus C

It takes longer for the oven to preheat than it does to prepare this delicious dish. While it's baking, I throw together a quick salad.

—**BARBARA LENTO** HOUSTON, PA

**START TO FINISH:** 30 MIN.
**MAKES:** 4 SERVINGS

- 1 **pound fresh asparagus, trimmed**
- ¼ **cup water**
- 1 **pound cod fillet, cut into four pieces**
- 2 **tablespoons lemon juice**
- 1 **teaspoon salt-free lemon-pepper seasoning**
- ½ **teaspoon garlic powder**
- 2 **tablespoons butter, cubed**
- 2 **teaspoons capers**
  **Minced fresh parsley, optional**

**1.** Place asparagus in an ungreased 11-in. x 7-in. baking dish; add water. Arrange cod over asparagus. Sprinkle with lemon juice, lemon pepper and garlic powder. Dot with butter; sprinkle with capers.
**2.** Bake, uncovered, at 400° for 12-15 minutes or until fish flakes easily with a fork and asparagus is tender. If desired, sprinkle with parsley.
**PER SERVING** *150 cal., 7 g fat (4 g sat. fat), 58 mg chol., 265 mg sodium, 3 g carb., 1 g fiber, 20 g pro.* **Diabetic Exchanges:** *3 lean meat, 1 fat.*

## Tuna with Tuscan White Bean Salad

Once the tuna hits the grill, do not move it around or it may tear. This recipe is for tuna that is still pink in the middle (medium rare). Increase the cooking time for tuna that is more cooked through.

—**VANCE WERNER JR.** FRANKLIN, WI

**START TO FINISH:** 30 MIN.
**MAKES:** 4 SERVINGS

- 1 **can (15 ounces) white kidney or cannellini beans, rinsed and drained**
- 3 **celery ribs, finely chopped**
- 1 **medium sweet red pepper, finely chopped**
- 1 **plum tomato, seeded and finely chopped**
- ½ **cup fresh basil leaves, thinly sliced**
- ¼ **cup finely chopped red onion**
- 3 **tablespoons olive oil**
- 2 **tablespoons red wine vinegar**
- 1 **tablespoon lemon juice**
- ¼ **teaspoon salt**
- ¼ **teaspoon pepper**

**TUNA**
- 4 **tuna steaks (6 ounces each)**
- 1 **tablespoon olive oil**
- ¼ **teaspoon salt**
- ¼ **teaspoon pepper**

**1.** In a large bowl, combine the first six ingredients. In a small bowl, whisk the oil, vinegar, lemon juice, salt and pepper. Pour over bean mixture; toss to coat. Refrigerate until serving.
**2.** Brush tuna with oil. Sprinkle with salt and pepper. Moisten a paper towel with cooking oil; using long-handled tongs, lightly rub the grill rack to coat. Grill tuna, covered, over high heat or broil 3-4 in. from the heat for 3-4 minutes on each side for medium-rare or until slightly pink in the center. Serve with salad.
**PER SERVING** *409 cal., 16 g fat (2 g sat. fat), 77 mg chol., 517 mg sodium, 20 g carb., 6 g fiber, 45 g pro.* **Diabetic Exchanges:** *5 lean meat, 3 fat, 1 starch, 1 vegetable.*

BAKED COD PICCATA WITH ASPARAGUS

TUNA WITH TUSCAN WHITE BEAN SALAD

## Shrimp Pad Thai

You can make this yummy Thai classic in no time. Find fish sauce and chili garlic sauce in the Asian foods aisle of your grocery store. This homemade version is way better than takeout.

—**ELISE RAY** SHAWNEE, KS

**START TO FINISH:** 30 MIN. • **MAKES:** 4 SERVINGS

- 4 ounces uncooked thick rice noodles
- ½ pound uncooked small shrimp, peeled and deveined
- 2 teaspoons canola oil
- 1 large onion, chopped
- 1 garlic clove, minced
- 1 egg, lightly beaten
- 3 cups coleslaw mix
- 4 green onions, thinly sliced
- ⅓ cup rice vinegar
- ¼ cup sugar
- 3 tablespoons reduced-sodium soy sauce
- 2 tablespoons fish sauce or additional reduced-sodium soy sauce
- 2 to 3 teaspoons chili garlic sauce
- 2 tablespoons chopped salted peanuts
  Chopped fresh cilantro leaves

**1.** Cook noodles according to package directions.
**2.** In a large nonstick skillet or wok, stir-fry shrimp in oil until shrimp turn pink; remove and set aside. Add onion and garlic to the pan. Make a well in the center of the onion mixture; add egg. Stir-fry for 2-3 minutes or until egg is completely set. Add the coleslaw mix, green onions, vinegar, sugar, soy sauce, fish sauce, chili garlic sauce and peanuts; heat through. Return shrimp to the pan and heat through. Drain noodles; toss with shrimp mixture. Garnish with cilantro.
**PER SERVING** *306 cal., 7 g fat (1 g sat. fat), 122 mg chol., 649 mg sodium, 45 g carb., 3 g fiber, 15 g pro.*

PECAN-ORANGE SALMON

"This baked salmon recipe is definitely a keeper—from the zesty taste of orange and mustard to the crunchy pecan topping. Simple yet elegant, it can serve as the healthy centerpiece of any meal."
—**KARI CAVEN** COEUR D'ALENE, ID

## Pecan-Orange Salmon ▣

**START TO FINISH:** 25 MIN. • **MAKES:** 4 SERVINGS

- ⅓ cup orange juice
- 1 tablespoon grated orange peel
- 1 tablespoon Dijon mustard
- 1 tablespoon honey
- 2 teaspoons olive oil
- ½ teaspoon salt
- ¼ teaspoon pepper
- 4 salmon fillets (5 ounces each)
- 2 tablespoons finely chopped pecans

**1.** In a small bowl, combine the first seven ingredients. Place salmon in a greased 11-in. x 7-in. baking dish. Pour orange juice mixture over salmon; sprinkle with pecans.
**2.** Bake, uncovered, at 425° for 15-18 minutes or until fish flakes easily with a fork.
**PER SERVING** *297 cal., 18 g fat (3 g sat. fat), 71 mg chol., 456 mg sodium, 8 g carb., 1 g fiber, 24 g pro.* **Diabetic Exchanges:** *4 lean meat, 1½ fat, ½ starch.*

SHRIMP PAD THAI

## Broccoli Tuna Casserole

When I was in the Navy, a co-worker's wife shared this recipe with me. I've tweaked it over the years, but it still brings back memories of my Navy "family" away from home.

—YVONNE COOK HASKINS, OH

**PREP:** 35 MIN. • **BAKE:** 1 HOUR • **MAKES:** 8 SERVINGS

- 5 cups uncooked whole wheat egg noodles
- 1 teaspoon butter
- ¼ cup chopped onion
- ¼ cup cornstarch
- 2 cups fat-free milk
- 1 teaspoon dried basil
- 1 teaspoon dried thyme
- ¾ teaspoon salt
- ½ teaspoon pepper
- 1 cup reduced-sodium chicken broth
- 1 cup (4 ounces) shredded Monterey Jack cheese, divided
- 4 cups frozen broccoli florets, thawed
- 2 pouches (6.4 ounces each) albacore white tuna in water
- ⅓ cup panko (Japanese) bread crumbs
- 1 tablespoon butter, melted

**1.** Preheat oven to 350°. Cook noodles according to package directions; drain. Transfer to a shallow 3-qt. or 13-in. x 9-in. baking dish coated with cooking spray.
**2.** Meanwhile, in a large nonstick skillet coated with cooking spray, heat butter over medium-high heat. Add onion; cook and stir until tender. In a small bowl, whisk cornstarch, milk and seasonings until smooth; stir into pan. Stir in broth. Bring to a boil; cook and stir 2 minutes or until thickened. Stir in ¾ cup cheese until melted; stir in broccoli and tuna.
**3.** Spoon over noodles; mix well. Sprinkle with remaining cheese. Toss bread crumbs with melted butter; sprinkle over casserole. Bake, covered, 45 minutes. Bake, uncovered, 15-20 minutes longer or until cheese is melted.
**PER SERVING** *271 cal., 8 g fat (4 g sat. fat), 38 mg chol., 601 mg sodium, 30 g carb., 4 g fiber, 22 g pro.* **Diabetic Exchanges:** *2 starch, 2 lean meat, ½ fat.*

BROCCOLI TUNA CASSEROLE

COD & VEGETABLE SKILLET

## Cod & Vegetable Skillet C

This one-dish meal combines lean protein with a colorful vegetable medley. A well-flavored sauce pulls it all together, creating a lovely weeknight dinner.

—TASTE OF HOME TEST KITCHEN

**START TO FINISH:** 30 MIN. • **MAKES:** 4 SERVINGS

- ½ pound fresh green beans, trimmed
- 1 cup fresh baby carrots, cut in half lengthwise
- 1 medium onion, halved and sliced
- 3 tablespoons butter
- 1 tablespoon all-purpose flour
- ½ teaspoon dried thyme
- ½ teaspoon salt
- ¼ teaspoon pepper
- 1 cup reduced-sodium chicken broth
- ¼ cup white wine or reduced-sodium chicken broth
- 4 cod or haddock fillets (4 ounces each)

**1.** In a large skillet, saute the beans, carrots and onion in butter for 2 minutes. Stir in flour and seasonings until blended; gradually add broth and wine. Bring to a boil; cook and stir for 2 minutes or until thickened.
**2.** Add fillets to the pan. Reduce heat; cover and simmer for 10-12 minutes or until fish flakes easily with a fork.
**PER SERVING** *229 cal., 9 g fat (6 g sat. fat), 88 mg chol., 621 mg sodium, 12 g carb., 3 g fiber, 24 g pro.* **Diabetic Exchanges:** *3 lean meat, 2 vegetable, 2 fat.*

### ? Did you know?

Cod is a low-fat, flaky fish that is a good source of protein, phosphorus, niacin and vitamin B12. A 3-ounce cooked portion of cod has less than 90 calories and one gram of fat, and 15 to 20 grams of protein. Good substitutions include halibut, haddock, tilapia and grouper.

BAKED CRAB CAKES

## Baked Crab Cakes 🄲

Reel in a breezy taste of the seashore with these baked, rather than fried, crab cakes. For a heftier "burger," make two larger patties and serve on buns.

—**AMELIA SUNDERLAND** NASHVILLE, TN

**PREP:** 15 MIN. + CHILLING • **BAKE:** 25 MIN.
**MAKES:** 2 SERVINGS

- 1 **can (6 ounces) crabmeat, drained, flaked and cartilage removed**
- ½ **cup soft bread crumbs**
- ¼ **cup shredded carrot**
- 1 **egg, lightly beaten**
- 1 **tablespoon butter, melted**
- 1 **teaspoon minced fresh parsley**
- 1 **teaspoon mayonnaise**
- ¾ **teaspoon Worcestershire sauce**
- ¼ **teaspoon ground mustard**
- ⅛ **teaspoon salt**
- ⅛ **teaspoon pepper**
  **Tartar sauce, optional**

**1.** In a large bowl, combine the first 11 ingredients. Shape into four patties; cover and refrigerate for at least 30 minutes.

**2.** Place crab cakes on a baking sheet coated with cooking spray. Bake at 350° for 25 minutes or until golden brown. Serve with tartar sauce if desired.

**PER SERVING** *228 cal., 12 g fat (5 g sat. fat), 198 mg chol., 619 mg sodium, 8 g carb., 1 g fiber, 22 g pro.* **Diabetic Exchanges:** *3 lean meat, 1½ fat, ½ starch.*

## Shrimp Skewers with Asian Quinoa

Quinoa is a more complete protein than most other grains. Once you serve this, you'll be hearing requests for the flavorful Asian-inspired dish.

—**TASTE OF HOME TEST KITCHEN**

**START TO FINISH:** 30 MIN.
**MAKES:** 4 SERVINGS

- ¼ **cup rice vinegar**
- 3 **tablespoons apricot preserves**
- 2 **tablespoons olive oil**
- 2 **garlic cloves, minced**
- ½ **teaspoon reduced-sodium soy sauce**
- ¼ **teaspoon salt**
- ¼ **teaspoon ground ginger**
- ¼ **teaspoon pepper**
- 1 **cup water**
- ⅔ **cup quinoa, rinsed**
- 1¾ **cups frozen broccoli, carrots and water chestnuts, thawed and coarsely chopped**
- 1¼ **pounds uncooked jumbo shrimp, peeled and deveined**

**1.** In a small bowl, combine the first eight ingredients. In a small saucepan, combine the water, quinoa and ⅓ cup vinegar mixture. Bring to a boil. Reduce heat; cover and simmer for 12-15 minutes or until liquid is absorbed. Remove from the heat. Stir in vegetables. Cover and let stand for 10 minutes.

**2.** Meanwhile, thread shrimp on four metal or soaked wooden skewers. If grilling the shrimp, moisten a paper towel with cooking oil; using long-handled tongs, lightly rub the grill rack to coat.

**3.** Grill shrimp, covered, over medium heat or broil 4 in. from the heat for 6-8 minutes or until shrimp turn pink, basting frequently with remaining vinegar mixture and turning once. Serve with quinoa.

**NOTE** *Look for quinoa in the cereal, rice or organic food aisle.*

**PER SERVING** *348 cal., 10 g fat (1 g sat. fat), 172 mg chol., 365 mg sodium, 36 g carb., 3 g fiber, 28 g pro.* **Diabetic Exchanges:** *3 lean meat, 2 starch, 1½ fat.*

SHRIMP SKEWERS WITH ASIAN QUINOA

CRAB-STUFFED FLOUNDER
WITH HERBED AIOLI

## Crab-Stuffed Flounder with Herbed Aioli [c]

If you like seafood, you'll love this scrumptious flounder. The light and creamy aioli sauce tops it off with fresh tones of chives and garlic.

—BEVERLY OFERRALL LINKWOOD, MD

**PREP:** 20 MIN. • **BAKE:** 20 MIN.
**MAKES:** 6 SERVINGS

- ¼ cup egg substitute
- 2 tablespoons fat-free milk
- 1 tablespoon minced chives
- 1 tablespoon reduced-fat mayonnaise
- 1 tablespoon Dijon mustard
  Dash hot pepper sauce
- 1 pound lump crabmeat
- 6 flounder fillets (6 ounces each)
  Paprika

**AIOLI**
- ⅓ cup reduced-fat mayonnaise
- 2 teaspoons minced chives
- 2 teaspoons minced fresh parsley
- 2 teaspoons lemon juice
- 1 garlic clove, minced

**1.** In a small bowl, combine the first six ingredients; gently fold in crab. Cut fillets in half widthwise; place six halves in a 15-in. x 10-in. x 1-in. baking pan coated with cooking spray. Spoon crab mixture over fillets; top with remaining fish. Sprinkle with paprika.
**2.** Bake at 400° for 20-24 minutes or until fish flakes easily with a fork. Meanwhile, combine the aioli ingredients. Serve with fish.
**PER SERVING** *276 cal., 8 g fat (1 g sat. fat), 153 mg chol., 585 mg sodium, 3 g carb., trace fiber, 45 g pro.* **Diabetic Exchanges:** *5 lean meat, 1 fat.*

## Tilapia with Sauteed Spinach [c]

You'll love this delicious restaurant-quality meal fit for guests. Since it's all cooked in the same skillet, cleanup won't be a chore at all.

—TASTE OF HOME TEST KITCHEN

**PREP:** 20 MIN. • **COOK:** 15 MIN.
**MAKES:** 4 SERVINGS

- 1 egg, lightly beaten
- ½ cup dry bread crumbs
- 1 teaspoon Italian seasoning
- ¾ teaspoon salt, divided
- ¼ teaspoon garlic powder
- ¼ teaspoon paprika
- 4 tilapia fillets (6 ounces each)
- 4 tablespoons olive oil, divided
- 1 small onion, chopped
- 1 garlic clove, minced
- 5 cups fresh baby spinach
- ⅛ teaspoon crushed red pepper flakes
- ⅛ teaspoon pepper
- ¼ cup chopped walnuts, toasted

**1.** Place egg in a shallow bowl. In another shallow bowl, combine the bread crumbs, Italian seasoning, ½ teaspoon salt, garlic powder and paprika. Dip fillets in egg, then bread crumb mixture.

**2.** In a large skillet, cook fillets in 3 tablespoons oil over medium heat for 4-5 minutes on each side or until golden brown and fish flakes easily with a fork. Remove and keep warm.
**3.** In the same skillet, saute onion in remaining oil until tender. Add garlic; cook 1 minute longer. Stir in the spinach, pepper flakes, pepper and remaining salt. Cook and stir for 3-4 minutes or until spinach is wilted. Serve with fillets; sprinkle with walnuts.
**PER SERVING** *362 cal., 21 g fat (3 g sat. fat), 115 mg chol., 446 mg sodium, 9 g carb., 2 g fiber, 37 g pro.*

**Best Choice**

When shopping for fish, U.S.-farmed tilapia is ranked as a "Best Choice" by Monterey Bay Aquarium's Seafood Watch Program. Central and South American-farm-raised tilapia are good alternatives. Try to avoid farm-raised tilapia from Asia, where pollution is often a problem.

TILAPIA WITH SAUTEED SPINACH

180

183

187

# Meatless Mains

66 I am always looking for recipes that will encourage students to eat vegetables, and this vegetarian quesadilla has been a huge success. You can use other vegetables, such as mushrooms, eggplant, asparagus and broccoli. Just remember to roast the vegetables first. 99

—**KATHY CARLAN** CANTON, GA
*about her recipe, Roasted Vegetable Quesadillas, on page 182*

## California Quinoa M

**START TO FINISH:** 30 MIN.
**MAKES:** 4 SERVINGS

- 1 **tablespoon olive oil**
- 1 **cup quinoa, rinsed and well drained**
- 2 **garlic cloves, minced**
- 1 **medium zucchini, chopped**
- 2 **cups water**
- ¾ **cup garbanzo beans or chickpeas, rinsed and drained**
- 1 **medium tomato, finely chopped**
- ½ **cup crumbled feta cheese**
- ¼ **cup finely chopped Greek olives**
- 2 **tablespoons minced fresh basil**
- ¼ **teaspoon pepper**

In a large saucepan, heat oil over medium-high heat. Add quinoa and garlic; cook and stir 2-3 minutes or until quinoa is lightly browned. Stir in zucchini and water; bring to a boil. Reduce heat; simmer, covered, 12-15 minutes or until liquid is absorbed. Stir in remaining ingredients; heat through.

**PER SERVING** *310 cal., 11 g fat (3 g sat. fat), 8 mg chol., 353 mg sodium, 42 g carb., 6 g fiber, 11 g pro.* **Diabetic Exchanges:** *2 starch, 1½ fat, 1 lean meat, 1 vegetable.*

"I'm always changing this salad up. Here I used tomato, zucchini and olives for a Greek-inspired salad. Try adding a few more favorite fresh veggies you know your whole family will love."
—**ELIZABETH LUBIN** HUNTINGTON BEACH, CA

CALIFORNIA QUINOA

BLACK BEAN-SWEET
POTATO SKILLET

## Black Bean-Sweet Potato Skillet F M

My fiance loves sweet potatoes. By adding black beans, I came up with a nutritionally complete main dish. Its bright orange and black color makes it fun for Halloween.
—**APRIL STREVELL** RED BANK, NJ

**PREP:** 15 MIN. • **COOK:** 40 MIN.
**MAKES:** 5 SERVINGS

- 1 **medium onion, chopped**
- 1 **tablespoon olive oil**
- 2 **cans (15 ounces each) black beans, rinsed and drained**
- 2 **medium sweet potatoes, peeled and finely chopped**
- 1 **can (14½ ounces) vegetable broth**
- 1 **teaspoon minced chipotle pepper in adobo sauce**
- ¼ **teaspoon pepper**
- ¼ **teaspoon ground cinnamon**
- 1¼ **cups uncooked couscous**

1. In a large skillet, saute onion in oil until tender. Add the beans, sweet potatoes, broth, chipotle, pepper and cinnamon.
2. Bring to a boil. Reduce heat; cover and simmer for 25 minutes. Uncover and simmer 5-10 minutes longer or until potatoes are very tender and mixture is thickened, stirring occasionally.
3. Meanwhile, cook couscous according to package directions. Serve with black bean mixture.

**PER SERVING** *294 cal., 3 g fat (trace sat. fat), 0 chol., 727 mg sodium, 54 g carb., 10 g fiber, 12 g pro.*

## Roasted Vegetable Penne Bake M

For a twist, grill the veggies, which also gives them great flavor. Toss the veggies with seasoning and oil. Poke holes in a disposable foil-lined pan, add vegetables and grill covered over medium heat, 4-5 minutes per side or until crisp-tender.

**—ROBYN CAVALLARO** EASTON, PA

**PREP:** 30 MIN. • **BAKE:** 20 MIN.
**MAKES:** 6 SERVINGS

- 2 large zucchini, cut into 1-inch pieces
- 1 medium sweet red pepper, cut into 1-inch pieces
- ½ pound medium fresh mushrooms, halved
- 1 small onion, cut into 1-inch pieces
- 2 tablespoons olive oil
- 1½ teaspoons Italian seasoning
- 2 cups uncooked penne pasta
- 1 can (15 ounces) crushed tomatoes, undrained
- 2 ounces provolone cheese, shredded
- ¾ cup frozen peas, thawed
- ¼ cup shredded part-skim mozzarella cheese
- ¼ cup plus 2 tablespoons grated Parmesan cheese, divided
- ½ teaspoon salt
- ½ teaspoon pepper
- 1 tablespoon butter, cubed

1. In a large bowl, combine the zucchini, red pepper, mushrooms, onion, oil and Italian seasoning; toss to coat. Arrange in a single layer in an ungreased 15-in. x 10-in. x 1-in. baking pan. Bake, uncovered, at 425° for 20-25 minutes or until tender.

2. Meanwhile, cook pasta according to package directions; drain. In a large bowl, combine the pasta, roasted vegetables, tomatoes, provolone cheese, peas, mozzarella cheese, ¼ cup Parmesan cheese, salt and pepper.

3. Transfer to a greased 11-in. x 7-in. baking dish. Sprinkle with remaining Parmesan cheese; dot with butter. Cover and bake at 350° for 10 minutes. Uncover; bake 10-15 minutes longer or until bubbly.

**PER SERVING** *283 cal., 12 g fat (5 g sat. fat), 19 mg chol., 520 mg sodium, 33 g carb., 5 g fiber, 14 g pro.* **Diabetic Exchanges:** *2 vegetable, 1½ starch, 1 lean meat, ½ fat.*

## Skinny Eggplant Parmesan M

You save a lot of calories when you bake the eggplant patties instead of frying in oil. I like to add some strips of sweet red pepper while sauteing the mushrooms for a pop of color.

**—MARY BANNISTER** ALBION, NY

**PREP:** 45 MIN. • **BAKE:** 30 MIN. + STANDING
**MAKES:** 4 SERVINGS

- ½ cup fat-free milk
- 1 cup dry bread crumbs
- 2 teaspoons Italian seasoning, divided
- 1 large eggplant, peeled and cut into ½-inch slices
- ½ pound sliced fresh mushrooms
- 1 cup chopped sweet onion
- 2 teaspoons olive oil
- 2 garlic cloves, minced
- 8 fresh basil leaves, thinly sliced
- 1 jar (24 ounces) marinara sauce
- ¼ cup dry red wine or vegetable broth
- ¾ cup shredded part-skim mozzarella cheese
- ¾ cup part-skim ricotta cheese
- ¼ cup shredded Parmesan cheese

1. Place milk in a shallow bowl. In another shallow bowl, combine bread crumbs and 1 teaspoon Italian seasoning. Dip eggplant in milk, then bread crumb mixture. Place on a baking sheet coated with cooking spray. Bake at 350° for 30-40 minutes or until tender.

2. Meanwhile, in a large skillet, saute mushrooms and onion in oil until tender. Add garlic; cook 1 minute longer. Remove from the heat. Stir in basil and remaining Italian seasoning.

3. Spread ½ cup marinara sauce into a 2-qt. baking dish coated with cooking spray. In a small bowl, combine wine and remaining marinara sauce. Layer with half of the eggplant, mushroom mixture, mozzarella cheese, ricotta cheese and ¾ cup sauce mixture. Repeat layers. Top with remaining sauce; sprinkle with Parmesan cheese.

4. Bake, uncovered, at 350° for 30-35 minutes or until heated through and cheese is melted. Let stand for 10 minutes before cutting.

**PER SERVING** *342 cal., 11 g fat (6 g sat. fat), 31 mg chol., 560 mg sodium, 42 g carb., 10 g fiber, 20 g pro.* **Diabetic Exchanges:** *2 lean meat, 2 vegetable, 1½ starch, ½ fat.*

ROASTED VEGETABLE PENNE BAKE

## Did you know?

Ever wonder how eggplant got its name? During the Middle Ages, traders introduced a certain variety of eggplant to Europe that was white and shaped like an egg.

ROASTED BUTTERNUT LINGUINE

## Roasted Butternut Linguine M

Squash is one of our favorite vegetables, and this is my husband's preferred fall dish. He looks forward to it all year.

**—KIM CAPUTO** CANNON FALLS, MN

**PREP:** 15 MIN. • **BAKE:** 45 MIN. • **MAKES:** 4 SERVINGS

- 4 cups cubed peeled butternut squash
- 1 medium red onion, chopped
- 3 tablespoons olive oil
- ¼ teaspoon crushed red pepper flakes
- ½ pound uncooked linguine
- 2 cups julienned Swiss chard
- 1 tablespoon minced fresh sage
- ½ teaspoon salt
- ¼ teaspoon pepper

**1.** Preheat oven to 350°. Place the squash and onion in a 15-in. x 10-in. x 1-in. baking pan coated with cooking spray. Combine the oil and pepper flakes; drizzle over the vegetables and toss to coat.

**2.** Bake, uncovered, 45-50 minutes or until tender, stirring occasionally.

**3.** Meanwhile, cook pasta according to package directions; drain and place in a large bowl. Add squash mixture, Swiss chard, sage, salt and pepper; toss to combine.

**PER SERVING** *384 cal., 12 g fat (2 g sat. fat), 0 chol., 344 mg sodium, 64 g carb., 6 g fiber, 10 g pro.*

## Portobellos with Ratatouille M

These veggie-stuffed mushrooms are so hearty, meat eaters in the house won't feel left out. An appealing entree, it's bursting with color, taste and texture.

**—MARIE RIZZIO** INTERLOCHEN, MI

**PREP:** 30 MIN. • **BAKE:** 25 MIN. • **MAKES:** 4 SERVINGS

- 1 large onion, chopped
- 1 tablespoon plus 1 teaspoon olive oil, divided
- 5 garlic cloves, minced, divided
- 1 small eggplant, peeled and cubed
- 2 medium zucchini, cubed
- 1 medium sweet red pepper, chopped
- ¼ cup tomato paste
- 2 teaspoons red wine vinegar
- 1 teaspoon minced fresh thyme or ¼ teaspoon dried thyme
- ½ teaspoon salt
- ⅛ teaspoon pepper
  Dash cayenne pepper
- 2 medium tomatoes, chopped
- 4 large portobello mushrooms (4 to 4½ inches)
- 2 packages (6 ounces each) fresh baby spinach
  Minced fresh parsley and shaved Parmesan cheese

**1.** In a large skillet, saute onion in 1 tablespoon oil until tender. Add 3 garlic cloves; cook 1 minute longer. Stir in the eggplant, zucchini, red pepper, tomato paste, vinegar and seasonings.

**2.** Transfer to a 15-in. x 10-in. x 1-in. baking pan coated with cooking spray. Bake at 400° for 10 minutes. Stir in tomatoes; bake 15-20 minutes longer or until vegetables are tender.

**3.** Meanwhile, remove and discard stems and gills from mushrooms. Place mushrooms, stem side up, on a baking sheet coated with cooking spray; drizzle with remaining oil and sprinkle with remaining garlic. Bake at 400° for 20-25 minutes or until tender, turning once.

**4.** Place spinach in a large nonstick skillet coated with cooking spray; cook and stir for 4-5 minutes or until wilted.

**5.** Divide spinach among four plates; top with mushrooms. Fill mushrooms with ratatouille; sprinkle with parsley and cheese.

**PER SERVING** *184 cal., 6 g fat (1 g sat. fat), 0 chol., 397 mg sodium, 29 g carb., 9 g fiber, 9 g pro.* ***Diabetic Exchanges:*** *2 starch, 1 fat.*

PORTOBELLOS WITH RATATOUILLE

MAD ABOUT "MEAT" LOAF

## Mad About "Meat" Loaf C M

Meat loaf gets all the fixings with spinach, carrots, zucchini and whole grains. But remember, when grinding the nuts in a food processor, be sure to add a little flour so you don't end up with nut butter.

—**SUSAN PRESTON** EAGLE CREEK, OR

**PREP:** 30 MIN. • **BAKE:** 50 MIN. • **MAKES:** 6 SERVINGS

- 1 package (6 ounces) fresh baby spinach
- 1 cup (4 ounces) shredded cheddar cheese, divided
- ⅔ cup mashed cooked carrots
- 1 slice whole wheat bread, torn into pieces
- 2 eggs, lightly beaten
- ½ cup grated zucchini
- ½ cup tomato sauce, divided
- ⅓ cup grated Parmesan cheese
- ¼ cup finely chopped onion
- 3 tablespoons ground flaxseed
- 3 tablespoons ground walnuts
- 1 tablespoon olive oil
- 1 garlic clove, minced
- 1 teaspoon Italian seasoning
- ½ teaspoon dried sage leaves
- ¼ teaspoon salt
- ⅛ teaspoon pepper

**1.** In a large saucepan, bring ½ in. of water to a boil. Add spinach; cover and boil for 3-4 minutes or until wilted. Drain and squeeze dry.

**2.** In a large bowl, combine ¾ cup cheddar cheese, carrots, bread, eggs, zucchini, ¼ cup tomato sauce, Parmesan cheese, onion, flaxseed, walnuts, oil, garlic, seasonings and spinach. Pat into a greased 8-in. x 4-in. loaf pan; top with remaining tomato sauce.

**3.** Bake, uncovered, at 325° for 45 minutes. Sprinkle with remaining cheddar cheese. Bake 4-7 minutes longer or until heated through and cheese is melted. Let stand for 5 minutes before slicing.

**PER SERVING** *198 cal., 14 g fat (6 g sat. fat), 94 mg chol., 451 mg sodium, 9 g carb., 3 g fiber, 11 g pro.*

## Pesto Veggie Pizza M

A thoughtful granddaughter gave me the recipe for this wonderful pizza. It's delicious down to its whole wheat crust. One bite and I'm in veggie heaven!

—**AGNES WARD** STRATFORD, ON

**PREP:** 25 MIN. • **BAKE:** 10 MIN. • **MAKES:** 6 SLICES

- 2 cups sliced fresh mushrooms
- 1 cup fresh broccoli florets, chopped
- ¾ cup thinly sliced zucchini
- ½ cup julienned sweet yellow pepper
- ½ cup julienned sweet red pepper
- 1 small red onion, thinly sliced and separated into rings
- 1 tablespoon prepared pesto
- 1 prebaked 12-inch thin whole wheat pizza crust
- ⅓ cup pizza sauce
- 2 tablespoons grated Romano or Parmesan cheese
- ¼ cup sliced ripe olives
- ½ cup crumbled reduced-fat feta cheese
- ½ cup shredded part-skim mozzarella cheese

**1.** In a large nonstick skillet coated with cooking spray, saute the mushrooms, broccoli, zucchini, peppers and onion until tender. Remove from the heat; stir in pesto.

**2.** Place crust on a 12-in. pizza pan; spread with pizza sauce. Sprinkle with Romano cheese; top with vegetable mixture and olives. Sprinkle with feta and mozzarella.

**3.** Bake at 450° for 8-12 minutes or until crust is lightly browned and mozzarella is melted.

**PER SERVING** *220 cal., 8 g fat (4 g sat. fat), 12 mg chol., 570 mg sodium, 29 g carb., 5 g fiber, 13 g pro.* **Diabetic Exchanges:** *1½ starch, 1 lean meat, 1 vegetable, 1 fat.*

PESTO VEGGIE PIZZA

## Roasted Vegetable Quesadillas M

I am always looking for recipes that will encourage students to eat vegetables, and this vegetarian quesadilla has been a huge success. You can use other vegetables, such as mushrooms, eggplant, asparagus and broccoli. Just remember to roast the vegetables first.
—**KATHY CARLAN** CANTON, GA

**PREP:** 40 MIN. • **COOK:** 5 MIN./BATCH • **MAKES:** 8 SERVINGS

- 2 medium red potatoes, quartered and sliced
- 1 medium zucchini, quartered and sliced
- 1 medium sweet red pepper, sliced
- 1 small onion, chopped
- 2 tablespoons olive oil
- 1 garlic clove, minced
- ½ teaspoon salt
- ½ teaspoon dried oregano
- ¼ teaspoon pepper
- 1 cup (4 ounces) shredded part-skim mozzarella cheese
- 1 cup (4 ounces) shredded reduced-fat cheddar cheese
- 8 whole wheat tortillas (8 inches)

**1.** In a large bowl, combine the first nine ingredients. Transfer to a 15-in. x 10-in. x 1-in. baking pan. Bake at 425° for 24-28 minutes or until potatoes are tender.
**2.** In a small bowl, combine cheeses. Place tortillas on a griddle coated with cooking spray. Spread ⅓ cup vegetable mixture over half of each tortilla. Sprinkle with ¼ cup cheese. Fold over and cook over low heat for 1-2 minutes on each side or until cheese is melted.
**PER SERVING** 279 cal., 12 g fat (4 g sat. fat), 18 mg chol., 479 mg sodium, 30 g carb., 3 g fiber, 12 g pro. **Diabetic Exchanges:** 2 starch, 1½ fat, 1 lean meat.

## Calico Pepper Frittata C M

My garden-fresh frittata has all-day appeal. I serve it for breakfast, brunch, lunch and even dinner. It's made in a skillet, so there's no need to heat up the oven.
—**LORETTA KELCINSKI** KUNKLETOWN, PA

**START TO FINISH:** 30 MIN. • **MAKES:** 4 SERVINGS

- 1 medium green pepper, chopped
- 1 medium sweet red pepper, chopped
- 1 jalapeno pepper, seeded and chopped
- 1 medium onion, chopped
- 1 garlic clove, minced
- 1 tablespoon olive oil
- 5 eggs
- 1¼ cups egg substitute
- 1 tablespoon grated Romano cheese
- ½ teaspoon salt
- ⅛ teaspoon pepper

**1.** In a large nonstick skillet, saute peppers, onion and garlic in oil until crisp-tender. In a large bowl, whisk eggs and egg substitute. Pour into the skillet. Sprinkle with cheese, salt and pepper.
**2.** As the eggs set, lift edges, letting uncooked portion flow underneath. Cook until eggs are completely set, about 8-10 minutes. Cut into wedges.
**NOTE** Wear disposable gloves when cutting hot peppers; the oils can burn skin. Avoid touching your face.
**PER SERVING** 201 cal., 10 g fat (3 g sat. fat), 268 mg chol., 559 mg sodium, 10 g carb., 2 g fiber, 17 g pro. **Diabetic Exchanges:** 2 lean meat, 2 vegetable, 1 fat.

## Tuscan Portobello Stew M

This is a heart-healthy, one-skillet meal that is quick and easy to prepare yet elegant enough for company. I take this to my school's potlucks, where it is devoured by vegetarian teachers and students alike.
—**JANE SIEMON** VIROQUA, WI

**PREP:** 20 MIN. • **COOK:** 20 MIN. • **MAKES:** 4 SERVINGS

- 2 **large portobello mushrooms, coarsely chopped**
- 1 **medium onion, chopped**
- 3 **garlic cloves, minced**
- 2 **tablespoons olive oil**
- ½ **cup white wine or vegetable broth**
- 1 **can (28 ounces) diced tomatoes, undrained**
- 2 **cups chopped fresh kale**
- 1 **bay leaf**
- 1 **teaspoon dried thyme**
- ½ **teaspoon dried basil**
- ½ **teaspoon dried rosemary, crushed**
- ¼ **teaspoon salt**
- ¼ **teaspoon pepper**
- 2 **cans (15 ounces each) white kidney or cannellini beans, rinsed and drained**

**1.** In a large skillet, saute the mushrooms, onion and garlic in oil until tender. Add the wine. Bring to a boil; cook until liquid is reduced by half. Stir in the tomatoes, kale and seasonings. Bring to a boil. Reduce heat; cover and simmer for 8-10 minutes.

**2.** Add beans; heat through. Discard bay leaf.

**PER SERVING** *309 cal., 8 g fat (1 g sat. fat), 0 chol., 672 mg sodium, 46 g carb., 13 g fiber, 12 g pro.* **Diabetic Exchanges:** *2 starch, 2 vegetable, 1½ fat, 1 lean meat.*

## Pronto Vegetarian Peppers M

In the summer I love to serve these peppers with salad and a roll. At the end of summer, I freeze them for cold months when produce costs are high. For a hot meal on a cold day, I serve them with a side of warm pasta tossed in olive oil.
—**RENEE HOLLOBAUGH** ALTOONA, PA

**START TO FINISH:** 25 MIN. • **MAKES:** 2 SERVINGS

- 2 **large sweet red peppers**
- 1 **cup canned stewed tomatoes**
- ⅓ **cup instant brown rice**
- 2 **tablespoons hot water**
- ¾ **cup canned kidney beans, rinsed and drained**
- ½ **cup frozen corn, thawed**
- 2 **green onions, thinly sliced**
- ⅛ **teaspoon crushed red pepper flakes**
- ½ **cup shredded part-skim mozzarella cheese**
- 1 **tablespoon grated Parmesan cheese**

**1.** Cut peppers in half lengthwise; remove seeds. Place peppers in an ungreased shallow microwave-safe dish. Cover and microwave on high for 3-4 minutes or until tender.

**2.** Combine the tomatoes, rice and water in a small microwave-safe bowl. Cover and microwave on high for 5-6 minutes or until rice is tender. Stir in the beans, corn, onions and pepper flakes; spoon into peppers.

**3.** Sprinkle with cheeses. Microwave, uncovered, for 3-4 minutes or until heated through.

**NOTE** *This recipe was tested in a 1,100-watt microwave.*

**PER SERVING** *341 cal., 7 g fat (3 g sat. fat), 19 mg chol., 556 mg sodium, 56 g carb., 11 g fiber, 19 g pro.*

FIVE-CHEESE JUMBO SHELLS

## Five-Cheese Jumbo Shells M

Using five cheeses in one recipe doesn't usually translate to a dish that's considered light, but this meatless meal is proof that it can be done with great success. And the shells freeze beautifully.

—LISA RENSHAW KANSAS CITY, MO

**PREP:** 45 MIN. • **BAKE:** 50 MIN. + STANDING
**MAKES:** 8 SERVINGS

- 24 uncooked jumbo pasta shells
- 1 tablespoon olive oil
- 1 medium zucchini, shredded and squeezed dry
- ½ pound baby portobello mushrooms, chopped
- 1 medium onion, finely chopped
- 2 cups reduced-fat ricotta cheese
- ½ cup shredded part-skim mozzarella cheese
- ½ cup shredded provolone cheese
- ½ cup grated Romano cheese
- 1 egg, lightly beaten
- 1 teaspoon Italian seasoning
- ½ teaspoon crushed red pepper flakes
- 1 jar (24 ounces) meatless spaghetti sauce
- ¼ cup grated Parmesan cheese

1. Preheat oven to 350°. Cook shells according to package directions for al dente; drain.
2. In a large skillet, heat oil over medium-high heat. Add vegetables; cook and stir until tender. Remove from heat. In a bowl, combine ricotta, mozzarella, provolone and Romano cheeses; stir in egg, seasonings and vegetables.
3. Spread 1 cup sauce into a 13-in. x 9-in. baking dish coated with cooking spray. Fill pasta shells with cheese mixture; place in baking dish. Top with remaining sauce. Sprinkle with Parmesan cheese.

### ⊘ Did you know?

One cup of black beans offers 15 grams of fiber. Add beans to four dishes a week and you could cut your risk of heart disease by 22 percent according to researchers at Tulane University.

4. Bake, covered, 40 minutes. Uncover; bake 10 minutes longer or until cheese is melted. Let stand 10 minutes before serving.
**PER SERVING** *298 cal., 9 g fat (5 g sat. fat), 55 mg chol., 642 mg sodium, 36 g carb., 3 g fiber, 18 g pro.* **Diabetic Exchanges:** *2 starch, 2 lean meat, ½ fat.*

## Mexican Black Bean Burgers M

**PREP:** 20 MIN.+ CHILLING • **BAKE:** 20 MIN.
**MAKES:** 4 SERVINGS

- 1 can (4 ounces) chopped green chilies
- ½ medium onion, cut into wedges
- ½ medium sweet red pepper, chopped
- 4 garlic cloves, halved
- 1 can (15 ounces) black beans, rinsed and drained
- 1 egg
- 1 tablespoon chili powder
- ¾ teaspoon ground cumin
- ¾ cup dry whole wheat bread crumbs
- 4 whole wheat hamburger buns, split
- 4 tablespoons reduced-fat sour cream
- 4 tablespoons salsa

1. Preheat oven to 375°. Place chilies, onion, pepper and garlic in a food processor; pulse until finely chopped. Drain and set aside. In a large bowl, mash beans. Add the onion mixture, egg, chili powder, cumin and bread crumbs; mix well.
2. Shape into four patties; transfer to a 15-in. x 10-in. x 1-in. baking pan coated with cooking spray. Refrigerate for 30 minutes. Bake 8-10 minutes on each side or until heated through. Serve on buns with sour cream and salsa.
**PER SERVING** *354 cal., 6 g fat (2 g sat. fat), 58 mg chol., 751 mg sodium, 64 g carb., 12 g fiber, 15 g pro.*

"My husband's a vegetarian so I love finding meatless recipes we all like. These burgers are not only easy to make, but they freeze well. We sometimes top them with chipotle mayo for a more smoky flavor. They're good with hot sauce, too." —ELLEN FINGER LANCASTER, PA

MEXICAN BLACK BEAN BURGERS

## Veggie Lasagna

This is my daughter-in-law's recipe. It's tasty and a little different from usual lasagna recipes...even meatless ones!

—ALYCE WYMAN PEMBINA, ND

**PREP:** 30 MIN. • **BAKE:** 40 MIN. + STANDING
**MAKES:** 2 CASSEROLES (9 SERVINGS EACH)

- 18 uncooked lasagna noodles
- 2 eggs, lightly beaten
- 2 egg whites
- 2 cartons (15 ounces each) reduced-fat ricotta cheese
- 4 teaspoons dried parsley flakes
- 2 teaspoons dried basil
- 2 teaspoons dried oregano
- 1 teaspoon pepper
- 8 cups garden-style spaghetti sauce
- 4 cups (16 ounces) shredded part-skim mozzarella cheese
- 2 packages (16 ounces each) frozen cut green beans or 8 cups cut fresh green beans
- ⅔ cup grated Parmesan cheese

**1.** Cook noodles according to package directions. Meanwhile, in a small bowl, whisk the eggs, egg whites, ricotta cheese, parsley, basil, oregano and pepper; set aside.

**2.** In each of two 13-in. x 9-in. baking dishes coated with cooking spray, spread 1 cup spaghetti sauce. Drain noodles; place three noodles over spaghetti sauce in each dish.

**3.** Layer each with a quarter of the ricotta mixture, 1 cup spaghetti sauce, 1 cup mozzarella cheese, three lasagna noodles and half of green beans. Top each with the remaining ricotta mixture, 1 cup spaghetti sauce, remaining lasagna noodles, spaghetti sauce and mozzarella cheese. Sprinkle Parmesan cheese over each.

**4.** Cover and freeze one casserole for up to 3 months. Bake remaining lasagna, uncovered, at 375° for 40-45 minutes or until bubbly and edges are lightly browned. Let stand for 10 minutes before serving.

**TO USE FROZEN LASAGNA** *Thaw in the refrigerator overnight. Remove from the refrigerator 30 minutes before baking. Cover and bake at 375° for 1¼ to 1½ hours or until bubbly. Let stand for 10 minutes before serving.*
**PER SERVING** *320 cal., 10 g fat (5 g sat. fat), 56 mg chol., 713 mg sodium, 38 g carb., 5 g fiber, 18 g pro.* **Diabetic Exchanges:** *2 starch, 2 lean meat, 2 vegetable.*

### top tip — Sodium Smarts

When choosing spaghetti or marinara sauce, look for brands with the fewest ingredients and with less than 400 mg sodium per serving.

VEGGIE LASAGNA

1 can (14½ ounces) diced tomatoes, undrained
1 can (8 ounces) tomato sauce
½ teaspoon Italian seasoning
¼ teaspoon salt
¼ teaspoon crushed red pepper flakes
⅛ teaspoon fennel seed, crushed
1 cup uncooked long grain rice
1 can (16 ounces) butter beans, rinsed and drained
1 can (16 ounces) red beans, rinsed and drained

1. In a Dutch oven, heat oil over medium-high heat. Add the green pepper, onion and celery; cook and stir until tender. Add garlic, cook 1 minute longer.
2. Add the water, tomatoes, tomato sauce and seasonings. Bring to a boil; stir in rice. Reduce heat; cover and simmer for 15-18 minutes or until liquid is absorbed and rice is tender. Stir in beans; heat through.
**PER SERVING** *281 cal., 3 g fat (trace sat. fat), 0 chol., 796 mg sodium, 56 g carb., 9 g fiber, 11 g pro.*

VEG JAMBALAYA

## Bean & Bulgur Chili F M

A steaming bowl of this zesty three-bean chili will warm you throughout the year. Bulgur adds great texture and heartiness, so you won't miss the meat.
—**TARI AMBLER** SHOREWOOD, IL

**PREP:** 25 MIN. • **COOK:** 40 MIN.
**MAKES:** 10 SERVINGS (3½ QUARTS)

2 large onions, chopped
2 celery ribs, chopped
1 large green pepper, chopped
4 teaspoons olive oil
4 garlic cloves, minced
1 large carrot, shredded
2 tablespoons chili powder
1 teaspoon dried oregano
½ teaspoon coarsely ground pepper
½ teaspoon ground cumin
⅛ teaspoon ground cinnamon
⅛ teaspoon ground allspice
2 cans (14½ ounces each) no-salt-added diced tomatoes, undrained
1 can (14½ ounces) fire-roasted diced tomatoes, undrained
1 can (16 ounces) kidney beans, rinsed and drained
1 can (15 ounces) pinto beans, rinsed and drained
1 can (15 ounces) black beans, rinsed and drained
1 can (14 ounces) vegetable broth
⅓ cup tomato paste
1 cup bulgur
Reduced-fat sour cream, optional

1. In a Dutch oven over medium heat, cook the onions, celery and green pepper in oil until tender. Add garlic; cook 1 minute longer. Stir in carrot and seasonings; cook and stir 1 minute longer.
2. Stir in the tomatoes, beans, broth and tomato paste. Bring to a boil. Reduce heat; cover and simmer for 30 minutes.
3. Meanwhile, cook bulgur according to package directions. Stir into chili; heat through. Garnish each serving with sour cream if desired.
**PER SERVING** *240 cal., 3 g fat (trace sat. fat), 0 chol., 578 mg sodium, 45 g carb., 12 g fiber, 11 g pro.* **Diabetic Exchanges:** *2 starch, 2 vegetable, 1 lean meat.*

## Veg Jambalaya F M

This rice dish is great when you crave Creole but don't have chicken or sausage on hand. Plus it's full of fiber and will keep you feeling full.
—**CRYSTAL BRUNS** ILIFF, CO

**PREP:** 10 MIN. • **COOK:** 30 MIN.
**MAKES:** 6 SERVINGS

1 tablespoon canola oil
1 medium green pepper, chopped
1 medium onion, chopped
1 celery rib, chopped
3 garlic cloves, minced
2 cups water

"Raita, an Indian condiment made with yogurt, elevates this vegetarian dish into a satisfying gourmet wrap. I sometimes substitute diced mango or cucumber for the pineapple and add fresh herbs like cilantro or mint."
—**JENNIFER BECKMAN** FALLS CHURCH, VA

INDIAN SPICED CHICKPEA WRAPS

## Indian Spiced Chickpea Wraps M

**START TO FINISH:** 30 MIN.
**MAKES:** 4 SERVINGS (1⅓ CUPS SAUCE)

**RAITA**
- 1 cup (8 ounces) reduced-fat plain yogurt
- ½ cup drained unsweetened pineapple tidbits
- ¼ teaspoon salt
- ¼ teaspoon ground cumin

**WRAPS**
- 2 teaspoons canola oil
- 1 small onion, chopped
- 1 tablespoon minced fresh gingerroot
- 2 garlic cloves, minced
- ½ teaspoon curry powder
- ¼ teaspoon each salt, ground cumin and ground coriander
- ¼ teaspoon cayenne pepper, optional
- 1 can (15 ounces) chickpeas or garbanzo beans, rinsed and drained

- 1 cup canned crushed tomatoes
- 4 whole wheat tortillas (8 inches), warmed
- 3 cups fresh baby spinach

**1.** In a small bowl, mix raita ingredients; set aside.
**2.** For wraps, in a nonstick skillet coated with cooking spray, heat oil over medium-high heat. Add onion; cook and stir until tender. Add ginger, garlic and seasonings; cook and stir 1 minute longer.
**3.** Stir in chickpeas and tomatoes. Bring to a boil. Reduce heat; simmer, uncovered, for 5-8 minutes or until slightly thickened, stirring occasionally.
**4.** Near the center of each tortilla, arrange spinach and chickpea mixture; top with raita. Roll up tightly; serve immediately.
**PER SERVING** *355 cal., 9 g fat (1 g sat. fat), 3 mg chol., 745 mg sodium, 56 g carb., 9 g fiber, 13 g pro.*

## Vegetarian Enchilada Bake M

I've had this budget-friendly vegetarian recipe for years. The Tex-Mex flavors are so tasty, you won't even miss the meat.
—**BARBARA STELLUTO** DEVON, PA

**PREP:** 20 MIN. • **BAKE:** 20 MIN. + STANDING
**MAKES:** 3 SERVINGS

- 1 cup shredded zucchini
- 1 tablespoon finely chopped sweet red pepper
- 1 teaspoon olive oil
- 1 garlic clove, minced
- ¾ cup frozen corn
- ¾ cup black beans, rinsed and drained
- ⅛ teaspoon salt
- ⅛ teaspoon ground cumin
- ¾ cup salsa
- 2 tablespoons minced fresh cilantro
- 3 corn tortillas (6 inches)
- ¾ cup shredded cheddar cheese
  Sour cream, optional

**1.** In a large skillet, saute zucchini and pepper in oil until pepper is crisp-tender. Add garlic; cook 1 minute longer. Add the corn, beans, salt and cumin; saute 2-3 minutes longer. Stir in salsa and cilantro.
**2.** Place a tortilla in the bottom of a 1½-qt. round baking dish coated with cooking spray. Spread with ⅔ cup vegetable mixture; sprinkle with ¼ cup cheese. Repeat layers twice.
**3.** Bake, uncovered, at 350° for 20-25 minutes or until heated through and cheese is melted. Let stand for 10 minutes before serving. Serve with sour cream if desired.
**PER SERVING** *286 cal., 11 g fat (6 g sat. fat), 30 mg chol., 676 mg sodium, 37 g carb., 5 g fiber, 12 g pro.* **Diabetic Exchanges:** *2 starch, 2 fat, 1 lean meat.*

**Did you know?**

Fiber-rich foods such as chickpeas lower the risk of heart disease, cancer and type 2 diabetes. Fiber is also important for weight control because it's filling and is found in foods that are low in calories.

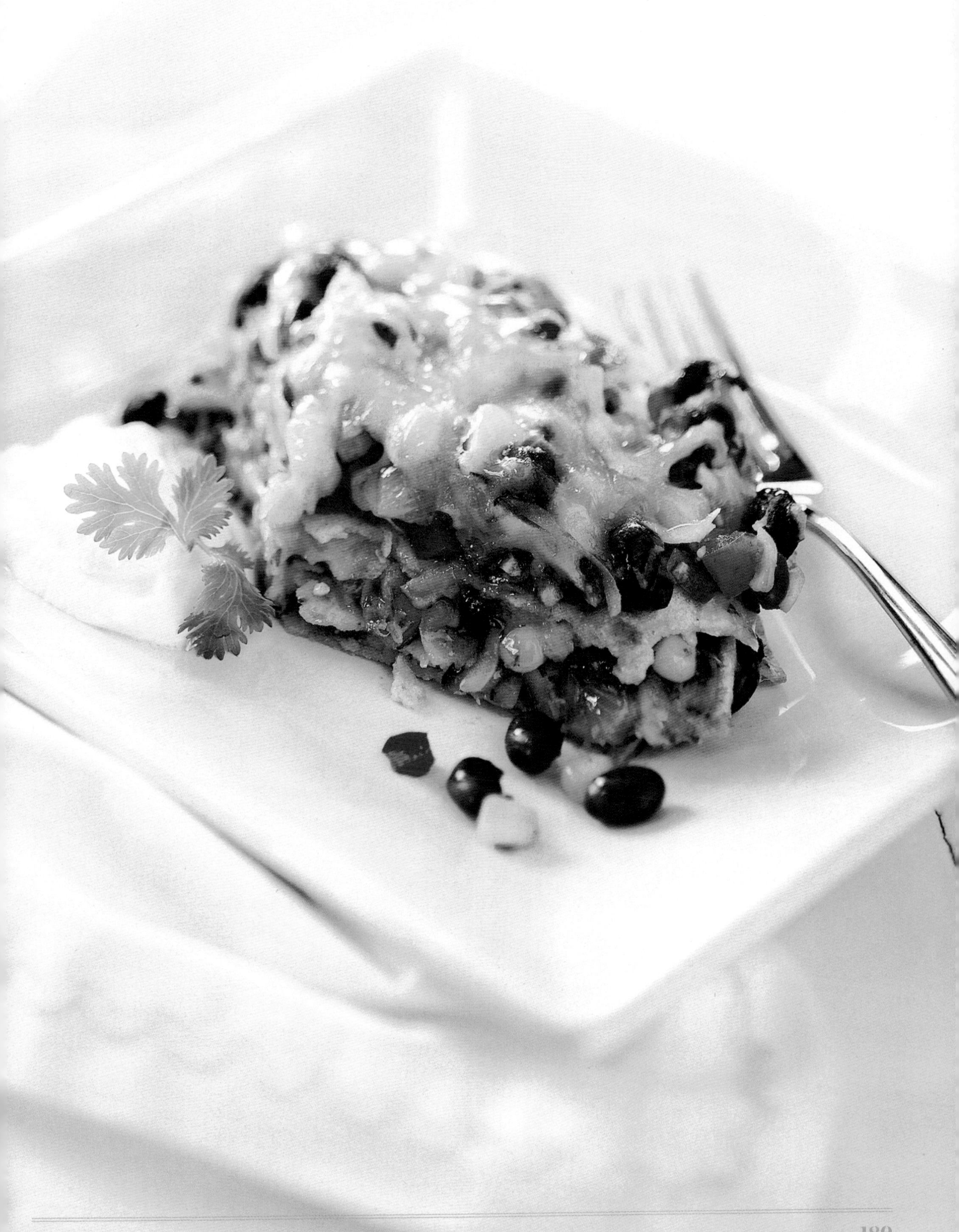

193

196

201

# The Bread Basket

66 As a toddler, my son loved bananas, so we always had them in the house. When we didn't eat them all before they were too ripe, we experimented beyond basic banana bread. That's how we came up with Elvis Banana Bread! 99

**—LIZ SOMPPI** GREENFIELD, WI
*about her recipe, Elvis Banana Bread, on page 194*

## Apple Walnut Bran Muffins M

My mom taught me how to make these soft, tasty muffins. The recipe makes a big batch, so you can freeze the extras or share with co-workers, family or friends.

—**KELLY KIRBY** WESTVILLE, NS

**PREP:** 25 MIN. • **BAKE:** 20 MIN. + COOLING • **MAKES:** 2 DOZEN

- 3 cups all-purpose flour
- 2 teaspoons baking powder
- 2 teaspoons ground cinnamon
- 1 teaspoon salt
- ½ teaspoon baking soda
- ¼ teaspoon ground nutmeg
- 1½ cups 2% milk
- 4 eggs
- ⅔ cup packed brown sugar
- ½ cup canola oil
- 2 teaspoons vanilla extract
- 3 cups All-Bran
- 2 cups shredded peeled tart apples
- 1 cup chopped walnuts
- 1 cup raisins

**1.** In a large bowl, combine the first six ingredients. In another bowl, combine the milk, eggs, brown sugar, oil and vanilla. Stir into dry ingredients just until moistened. Fold in remaining ingredients.

**2.** Fill greased or paper-lined muffin cups three-fourths full. Bake at 350° for 18-22 minutes or until a toothpick inserted into muffin comes out clean. Cool for 5 minutes before removing from pans to wire racks.

**PER SERVING** *220 cal., 9 g fat (1 g sat. fat), 36 mg chol., 200 mg sodium, 32 g carb., 4 g fiber, 6 g pro.*

# Flour Substitution

top tip

Looking to add more whole grains to your baked goods? Try using whole wheat pastry flour, which is lower in gluten than regular whole wheat flour. Start by replacing one-third of the all-purpose flour with the pastry flour, but remember to minimize mixing once liquids are added, as stirring will develop the gluten and toughen the baked goods.

## Sunflower Oatmeal Loaves F M

With oats, wheat germ and sunflower kernels, a thin slice of this dense bread goes a long way. Brushing the top with egg and sprinkling it with seeds gives it a glossy, textured finish.

—**COURTNEY TAGLAUER** FAIRFIELD, IA

**PREP:** 45 MIN. + RISING • **BAKE:** 20 MIN. + COOLING
**MAKES:** 4 LOAVES (8 SLICES EACH)

- 1 cup old-fashioned oats
- 1¼ cups boiling water
- ½ cup honey
- 2 tablespoons butter
- 3 to 4 cups all-purpose flour, divided
- 1 cup whole wheat flour
- ½ cup toasted wheat germ
- 2 packages (¼ ounce each) active dry yeast
- 2 teaspoons salt
- ½ cup sunflower kernels
- 1 egg yolk
- ¼ teaspoon cold water
- 4 teaspoons sesame seeds

**1.** Place oats in a small bowl; add boiling water, honey and butter. Let stand until mixture cools to 120°-130°, stirring occasionally.

**2.** In a large bowl, combine 2 cups all-purpose flour, whole wheat flour, wheat germ, yeast and salt. Beat in oat mixture until blended. Stir in sunflower kernels and enough remaining flour to form a stiff dough (dough will be sticky).

**3.** Turn onto a lightly floured surface; knead until smooth and elastic, about 6-8 minutes. Place in a greased bowl, turning once to grease the top. Cover and let rise in a warm place until doubled, about 1 hour.

**4.** Punch dough down; turn onto a lightly floured surface. Divide into four portions; shape into 8-in. x 2-in. loaves. Place on greased baking sheets. Cover and let rise until doubled, about 30 minutes.

**5.** Beat egg yolk and cold water; brush over loaves. Sprinkle with sesame seeds. With a sharp knife, cut slits in tops of loaves.

**6.** Bake at 350° for 20-25 minutes or until golden brown. Remove from pans to wire racks to cool.

**PER SERVING** *110 cal., 3 g fat (1 g sat. fat), 8 mg chol., 164 mg sodium, 19 g carb., 2 g fiber, 3 g pro.* **Diabetic Exchanges:** *1 starch, ½ fat.*

APPLE WALNUT BRAN MUFFINS

## Chewy Soft Pretzels ▣ Ⓜ

These homemade pretzels never last long around our house. My kids love to make them, and eat them! I serve them to company with a variety of dips, such as pizza sauce, ranch dressing, spinach dip or hot mustard.

—ELVIRA MARTENS ALDERGROVE, BC

**PREP:** 1 HOUR + RISING • **BAKE:** 15 MIN. • **MAKES:** 1 DOZEN

- 1 package (¼ ounce) active dry yeast
- 1½ cups warm water (110° to 115°)
- 1 tablespoon sugar
- 2 teaspoons salt
- 4 to 4¼ cups all-purpose flour
- 8 cups water
- ½ cup baking soda
- 1 egg, lightly beaten
  Kosher salt, sesame seeds, poppy seeds or grated Parmesan cheese

**1.** In a large bowl, dissolve yeast in warm water. Add the sugar, salt and 2 cups flour; beat until smooth. Stir in enough remaining flour to form a stiff dough.

**2.** Turn onto a floured surface; knead until smooth and elastic, about 5 minutes. Place in a greased bowl, turning once to grease top. Cover and let rise in a warm place until doubled, about 1 hour.

**3.** Punch dough down; divide into 12 portions. Roll each into an 18-in. rope; twist into a pretzel shape.

**4.** In a large saucepan, bring water and baking soda to a boil. Place pretzels into boiling water, one at a time, for 30 seconds. Remove with a slotted spoon; drain on paper towels.

**5.** Place on greased baking sheets. Brush with egg; sprinkle with desired topping.

**6.** Bake at 425° for 12-14 minutes or until golden brown. Remove from pans to wire racks. Serve warm.

**PER SERVING** *163 cal., 1 g fat (trace sat. fat), 18 mg chol., 400 mg sodium, 33 g carb., 1 g fiber, 5 g pro.*

AUTHENTIC BOSTON BROWN BREAD

## Authentic Boston Brown Bread ▣ Ⓜ

Made with rye flour, molasses and brown sugar, the rustic, old-fashioned flavor of this hearty bread is out of this world!

—SHARON DELANEY-CHRONIS SOUTH MILWAUKEE, WI

**PREP:** 20 MIN. • **COOK:** 50 MIN. + STANDING
**MAKES:** 1 LOAF (12 SLICES)

- ½ cup cornmeal
- ½ cup whole wheat flour
- ½ cup rye flour
- ½ teaspoon baking powder
- ½ teaspoon baking soda
- ¼ teaspoon salt
- 1 cup buttermilk
- ⅓ cup molasses
- 2 tablespoons brown sugar
- 1 tablespoon canola oil
- 3 tablespoons chopped walnuts, toasted
- 3 tablespoons raisins
  Cream cheese, softened, optional

**1.** In a large bowl, combine the first six ingredients. In another bowl, whisk the buttermilk, molasses, brown sugar and oil. Stir into dry ingredients just until moistened. Fold in walnuts and raisins. Transfer to a greased 8-in. x 4-in. loaf pan; cover with foil.

**2.** Place pan on a rack in a boiling-water canner or other large, deep pot; add 1 in. of hot water to kettle. Bring to a gentle boil; cover and steam for 45-50 minutes or until a toothpick inserted near the center comes out clean, adding more water to the kettle as needed.

**3.** Remove pan from the kettle; let stand for 10 minutes before removing bread from pan to a wire rack. Serve with cream cheese if desired.

**PER SERVING** *124 cal., 3 g fat (trace sat. fat), 1 mg chol., 145 mg sodium, 23 g carb., 2 g fiber, 3 g pro.* **Diabetic Exchanges:** *1½ starch, ½ fat.*

CHEWY SOFT PRETZELS

"As a toddler, my son loved bananas, so we always had them in the house. When we didn't eat them all before they were too ripe, we experimented beyond basic banana bread. That's how we came up with Elvis Banana Bread!"

**—LIZ SOMPPI** GREENFIELD, WI

ELVIS BANANA BREAD

## Elvis Banana Bread M

**PREP:** 30 MIN. • **BAKE:** 45 MIN. + COOLING
**MAKES:** 3 MINI LOAVES (6 SLICES EACH)

- 2 **cups all-purpose flour**
- 1 **cup sugar**
- 1 **teaspoon baking powder**
- 1 **teaspoon baking soda**
- 1 **teaspoon salt**
- 1 **teaspoon pumpkin pie spice**
- 4 **medium ripe bananas, mashed**
- 2 **eggs**
- ½ **cup creamy peanut butter**
- ¼ **cup unsweetened applesauce**
- ¼ **cup canola oil**
- 2 **teaspoons vanilla extract**
- ⅔ **cup semisweet chocolate chips**

**1.** Preheat oven to 350°. In a large bowl, whisk the first six ingredients. In another bowl, whisk bananas, eggs, peanut butter, applesauce, oil and vanilla until blended. Add to flour mixture; stir just until moistened. Fold in chocolate chips.

**2.** Transfer to three 5¾-in. x 3-in. x 2-in. loaf pans coated with cooking spray. Bake 45-50 minutes or until a toothpick inserted into center comes out clean. Cool in pans 10 minutes before removing to a wire rack to cool.

**FREEZE OPTION** *Freeze cooled loaves in resealable plastic freezer bags. To use, thaw at room temperature or, if desired, microwave each loaf on high for 60-75 seconds or until heated through.*

**PER SERVING** *227 cal., 9 g fat (2 g sat. fat), 24 mg chol., 266 mg sodium, 34 g carb., 2 g fiber, 4 g pro.*

## Pumpkin Cranberry Muffins M

Spicy pumpkin perks up these muffins, and cranberries lend a sweet-and-sour tang. With all the flavors of fall, they're great to bring to a holiday brunch.
**—LYNNE PARRISH** PHOENIX, AZ

**PREP:** 20 MIN. • **BAKE:** 15 MIN.
**MAKES:** 1 DOZEN

- 1¼ **cups whole wheat flour**
- ¾ **cup sugar**
- ¼ **cup oat bran**
- 1½ **teaspoons ground cinnamon**
- 1 **teaspoon baking powder**
- 1 **teaspoon baking soda**
- ½ **teaspoon salt**
- 2 **eggs, beaten**
- 1 **cup canned pumpkin**
- ⅔ **cup plain yogurt**
- ¼ **cup canola oil**
- ¾ **cup dried cranberries**

**1.** In a large bowl, combine the first seven ingredients. In another bowl, combine the eggs, pumpkin, yogurt and oil. Stir into dry ingredients just until moistened. Fold in cranberries. Coat muffin cups with cooking spray or use paper liners; fill three-fourths full with batter.

**2.** Bake at 400° for 15-20 minutes or until a toothpick comes out clean. Cool for 5 minutes before removing from pan to a wire rack.

**PER SERVING** *188 cal., 6 g fat (1 g sat. fat), 37 mg chol., 255 mg sodium, 32 g carb., 3 g fiber, 4 g pro.* **Diabetic Exchanges:** *2 starch, 1 fat.*

PUMPKIN CRANBERRY MUFFINS

SUN-DRIED TOMATO FOCACCIA

## Sun-Dried Tomato Focaccia F M

Think this bread looks inviting? Well, it tastes even better than it looks. The sun-dried tomatoes and red onions give it a style and flavor that no one will be able to resist.

—**KATHY KATZ** OCALA, FL

**PREP:** 1 HOUR 40 MIN. + RISING
**BAKE:** 20 MIN.
**MAKES:** 2 LOAVES (8 SERVINGS EACH)

- ¼ cup chopped sun-dried tomatoes (not packed in oil)
- ½ cup boiling water
- 1¼ cups warm V8 juice (70° to 80°)
- 2 tablespoons olive oil
- ¼ cup grated Parmesan cheese
- 1 tablespoon dried parsley flakes
- 2 teaspoons sugar
- 1 teaspoon salt
- 1 teaspoon dried basil
- ½ teaspoon garlic powder
- 2 cups whole wheat flour
- 1½ cups all-purpose flour
- 2 teaspoons active dry yeast

**TOPPING**
- 2 tablespoons slivered sun-dried tomatoes (not packed in oil)
- ¼ cup boiling water
- 12 thin slices red onion, halved
- 1 tablespoon olive oil

**1.** In a small bowl, combine chopped sun-dried tomatoes and boiling water. Let stand for 5 minutes; drain.

**2.** In bread machine pan, place the V8 juice, oil, softened tomatoes, cheese, parsley, sugar, salt, basil, garlic powder, flours and yeast in order suggested by manufacturer. Select dough setting (check dough after 5 minutes of mixing; add 1 to 2 tablespoons of water or flour if needed).

**3.** In a small bowl, combine slivered tomatoes and boiling water. Let stand for 5 minutes; drain and pat dry with paper towels.

**4.** When cycle is completed, turn dough onto a lightly floured surface. Punch down. Divide in half; roll each portion into a 9-in. circle. Transfer to two greased 9-in. round baking pans.

**5.** Using the end of a wooden spoon handle, make ¼-in. indentations in dough. Arrange tomato slivers and onion slices over dough; press down lightly. Cover and let rise in a warm place until doubled, about 30 minutes. Brush with oil. Bake at 375° for 20-25 minutes or until golden brown. Remove to wire racks.

**PER SERVING** *135 cal., 3 g fat (1 g sat. fat), 1 mg chol., 247 mg sodium, 23 g carb., 3 g fiber, 4 g pro.* **Diabetic Exchanges:** *1½ starch, ½ fat.*

## Cinnamon Zucchini Bread M

The only way Mom could get me to eat veggies was to bake this zucchini bread. When I grew up, I lightened her original recipe, so it's even better for me.

**—KATHIE MEYER** ROUND ROCK, TX

**PREP:** 25 MIN. • **BAKE:** 50 MIN. + COOLING
**MAKES:** 1 LOAF (12 SLICES)

 ¾ cup sugar
 ¼ cup unsweetened applesauce
 ¼ cup canola oil
 2 egg whites
 1 teaspoon vanilla extract
 1½ cups all-purpose flour
 1½ teaspoons ground cinnamon
 1 teaspoon baking powder
 ½ teaspoon salt
 ½ teaspoon ground nutmeg
 ¼ teaspoon baking soda
 1¼ cups shredded peeled zucchini
 ½ cup raisins

**1.** In a small bowl, beat the sugar, applesauce, oil, egg whites and vanilla until well blended. Combine the flour, cinnamon, baking powder, salt, nutmeg and baking soda; gradually beat into sugar mixture. Fold in zucchini and raisins.
**2.** Transfer to an 8-in. x 4-in. loaf pan coated with cooking spray. Bake at 350° for 50-60 minutes or until a toothpick inserted near the center comes out clean. Cool for 10 minutes before removing from pan to a wire rack to cool completely.
**PER SERVING** *174 cal., 5 g fat (trace sat. fat), 0 chol., 170 mg sodium, 31 g carb., 1 g fiber, 3 g pro.* **Diabetic Exchanges:** *2 starch, 1 fat.*

## Blackberry Whole Wheat Coffee Cake S M

This low-fat coffee cake is studded with luscious blackberries. Wonderfully soft and tender, it's also good made with fresh or frozen blueberries or raspberries.

**—CAROL FORCUM** MARION, IL

**PREP:** 20 MIN. • **BAKE:** 35 MIN. + COOLING • **MAKES:** 20 SERVINGS

 1½ cups all-purpose flour
 1⅓ cups packed brown sugar
 1 cup whole wheat flour
 2 teaspoons baking powder
 ½ teaspoon baking soda
  Dash salt
 1 egg
 1 cup buttermilk
 ⅓ cup canola oil
 ⅓ cup unsweetened applesauce
 2 teaspoons vanilla extract
 2 cups fresh or frozen blackberries

**1.** In a large bowl, combine the first six ingredients. In a small bowl, combine the egg, buttermilk, oil, applesauce and vanilla. Stir into dry ingredients just until moistened. Fold in blackberries.
**2.** Transfer to a 13-in. x 9-in. baking pan coated with cooking spray. Bake at 375° for 35-40 minutes or until a toothpick inserted near the center comes out clean. Cool on a wire rack.
**PER SERVING** *160 cal., 4 g fat (trace sat. fat), 11 mg chol., 102 mg sodium, 28 g carb., 2 g fiber, 3 g pro.* **Diabetic Exchanges:** *2 starch, 1 fat.*

## Corn Muffins with Honey Butter

I turn classic corn bread muffins into something special by serving them with a delicious honey butter.

**—SUZANNE MCKINLEY** LYONS, GA

**PREP:** 20 MIN. • **BAKE:** 20 MIN.
**MAKES:** 16 MUFFINS (⅓ CUP HONEY BUTTER)

- ¼ cup butter, softened
- ¼ cup reduced-fat cream cheese
- ½ cup sugar
- 2 eggs
- 1½ cups fat-free milk
- 1½ cups all-purpose flour
- 1½ cups yellow cornmeal
- 4 teaspoons baking powder
- ¾ teaspoon salt

**HONEY BUTTER**
- ¼ cup butter, softened
- 2 tablespoons honey

**1.** In a large bowl, cream the butter, cream cheese and sugar until light and fluffy. Add eggs, one at a time, beating well after each addition. Stir in the milk. Combine the flour, cornmeal, baking powder and salt; add to creamed mixture just until moistened.

**2.** Coat muffin cups with cooking spray; fill three-fourths full with batter. Bake at 400° for 18-22 minutes or until a toothpick inserted near the center comes out clean. Cool for 5 minutes before removing from pans to wire racks. Beat butter and honey until blended; serve with warm muffins.

**PER SERVING** *198 cal., 7 g fat (4 g sat. fat), 45 mg chol., 285 mg sodium, 29 g carb., 1 g fiber, 4 g pro.* **Diabetic Exchanges:** *2 starch, 1½ fat.*

## Orange-Berry Yogurt Muffins

These are my husband's favorite muffins, so I love to keep them on hand. They freeze and reheat beautifully. Just warm them in the oven for 30 seconds and you're ready to go!

**—AMBER CUMMINGS** INDIANAPOLIS, IN

**PREP:** 15 MIN. • **BAKE:** 25 MIN. • **MAKES:** 15 MUFFINS

- 1 cup all-purpose flour
- 1 cup whole wheat flour
- ¾ cup sugar
- 3 teaspoons baking powder
- ¼ teaspoon salt
- 1 cup fat-free plain Greek yogurt
- ½ cup orange juice
- ⅓ cup unsweetened applesauce
- 2 egg whites
- 1 egg
- 4 teaspoons grated orange peel
- 1 cup fresh blueberries or frozen unsweetened blueberries, unthawed

**1.** Preheat oven to 350°. In a large bowl, whisk flours, sugar, baking powder and salt. In another bowl, whisk yogurt, orange juice, applesauce, egg whites, egg and orange peel until blended. Add to flour mixture; stir just until moistened. Fold in blueberries.

**2.** Coat muffin cups with cooking spray; fill three-fourths full with batter. Bake 24-26 minutes or until a toothpick inserted into center comes out clean. Cool 5 minutes before removing from pans to wire racks. Serve warm.

**PER SERVING** *126 cal., 1 g fat (trace sat. fat), 14 mg chol., 140 mg sodium, 26 g carb., 2 g fiber, 5 g pro.* **Diabetic Exchange:** *1½ starch.*

## Glazed Coconut-Banana Bread M

Give your celebration a tropical flair with this exotic variation of banana bread. It's quick to prepare, giving you plenty of time to focus on other holiday details.

—**KATHERINE L. NELSON** CENTERVILLE, UT

**PREP:** 20 MIN. • **BAKE:** 50 MIN.
**MAKES:** 1 LOAF (16 SLICES)

- ¼ cup butter, softened
- 1 cup sugar
- 2 eggs
- 1½ cups mashed ripe bananas (2 to 3 medium)
- ¼ cup reduced-fat plain yogurt
- 3 tablespoons unsweetened apple juice
- ½ teaspoon vanilla extract
- 2 cups all-purpose flour
- ¾ teaspoon baking soda
- ½ teaspoon salt
- ½ cup plus 1 tablespoon flaked coconut, divided
- ½ cup confectioners' sugar
- 1 tablespoon lime juice

**1.** In a large bowl, cream butter and sugar until crumbly. Add eggs, one at a time, beating well after each addition. Stir in the bananas, yogurt, apple juice and vanilla. Combine the flour, baking soda and salt; add to creamed mixture. Stir in ½ cup coconut.

**2.** Transfer to a greased 9-in. x 5-in. loaf pan. Sprinkle with remaining coconut. Bake at 350° for 50-55 minutes or until a toothpick inserted near the center comes out clean. Cool for 10 minutes before removing from pan to a wire rack.

**3.** Combine confectioners' sugar and lime juice; drizzle over warm bread.

**PER SERVING** *193 cal., 5 g fat (3 g sat. fat), 34 mg chol., 174 mg sodium, 35 g carb., 1 g fiber, 3 g pro.* **Diabetic Exchanges:** *2 starch, 1 fat.*

## Bran-ana Bread M

Light, scrumptious and easy on the wallet, this soft chocolate-chip banana bread is made with nutritious bran and flax.

—**JANET AND GRETA PODLESKI**
KITCHENER, ON

**PREP:** 20 MIN. • **BAKE:** 50 MIN. + COOLING
**MAKES:** 1 LOAF (16 SLICES)

- 1½ cups all-purpose flour
- ½ cup wheat bran
- ⅓ cup granulated sugar
- ¼ cup ground flaxseed
- 1 teaspoon each baking soda and baking powder
- ½ teaspoon cinnamon
- ¼ teaspoon salt
- 1½ cups mashed ripe bananas
- ¾ cup plain yogurt (2%)
- 2 eggs
- 2 tablespoons butter, melted
- 1 teaspoon vanilla
- ½ cup finely chopped walnuts
- ⅓ cup miniature semisweet chocolate chips

**1.** In a large bowl, combine the flour, wheat bran, sugar, ground flaxseed, baking soda, baking powder, cinnamon and salt.

**2.** In a small bowl, whisk the bananas, yogurt, eggs, butter and vanilla. Add wet ingredients to dry ingredients and stir just until moistened. Fold in nuts and chocolate chips.

**3.** Spoon batter into a greased 9-in. x 5-in. pan. Bake for about 50 minutes, or until a toothpick inserted near the center comes out clean. Cool for 10 minutes before removing from pan to wire rack. Serve warm.

**PER SERVING** *161 cal., 7 g fat (2 g sat. fat), 32 mg chol., 141 mg sodium, 23 g carb., 3 g fiber, 5 g pro.* **Diabetic Exchanges:** *1½ starch, 1½ fat.*

GLAZED COCONUT-BANANA BREAD

### Did you know?

The scientific name for banana is *Musa sapientum*, which means "fruit of the wise men." With more than 96% of American households buying them at least once a month, bananas seem to be a wise choice for many consumers.

GINGER PEAR MUFFINS

## Applesauce Spice Bread F S M

This bread is wonderful toasted and will make your house smell like there's an apple pie in the oven. Try it with apple butter and enjoy!

—**ROGER BROWN** ASSARIA, KS

**PREP:** 15 MIN. • **BAKE:** 3 HOURS
**MAKES:** 1 LOAF (1½ POUNDS, 16 SLICES)

- ¾ cup water (70° to 80°)
- ½ cup sweetened applesauce (70° to 80°)
- 2 tablespoons brown sugar
- 1 tablespoon canola oil
- 1½ teaspoons apple pie spice
- ¾ teaspoon salt
- 3 cups bread flour
- ⅓ cup quick-cooking oats
- 2 tablespoons nonfat dry milk powder
- 2¼ teaspoons active dry yeast

**1.** In bread machine pan, place all ingredients in order suggested by manufacturer. Select basic bread setting. Choose crust color and loaf size if available.

**2.** Check dough after 5 minutes of mixing; add 1 to 2 tablespoons of water or flour if needed. Bake according to bread machine directions.

**PER SERVING** *107 cal., 1 g fat (trace sat. fat), trace chol., 117 mg sodium, 22 g carb., 1 g fiber, 4 g pro.* **Diabetic Exchange:** *1½ starch.*

APPLESAUCE SPICE BREAD

## Ginger Pear Muffins M

**PREP:** 25 MIN. • **BAKE:** 20 MIN.
**MAKES:** 1½ DOZEN

- ¾ cup packed brown sugar
- ⅓ cup canola oil
- 1 egg
- 1 cup buttermilk
- 2½ cups all-purpose flour
- 1 teaspoon baking soda
- 1 teaspoon ground ginger
- ½ teaspoon salt
- ½ teaspoon ground cinnamon
- 2 cups chopped peeled fresh pears

**TOPPING**
- ⅓ cup packed brown sugar
- ¼ teaspoon ground ginger
- 2 teaspoons butter, melted

**1.** In a small bowl, beat the brown sugar, oil and egg until well blended. Beat in buttermilk. In a small bowl, combine the flour, baking soda, ginger, salt and cinnamon; gradually beat into buttermilk mixture until blended. Stir in pears. Fill paper-lined muffin cups two-thirds full.

**2.** For topping, combine brown sugar and ginger. Stir in butter until crumbly. Sprinkle over batter.

**3.** Bake at 350° for 18-22 minutes or until a toothpick inserted near the center comes out clean. Cool for 5 minutes before removing from pans to wire racks. Serve warm.

**PER SERVING** *174 cal., 5 g fat (1 g sat. fat), 13 mg chol., 162 mg sodium, 30 g carb., 1 g fiber, 3 g pro.* **Diabetic Exchanges:** *2 starch, 1 fat.*

BLUEBERRY COFFEE CAKE

## Blueberry Coffee Cake M

Every time I have company for dinner or go to someone's house for a meal, I'm asked to make this cake.
—**LESLIE PALMER** SWAMPSCOTT, MA

**PREP:** 20 MIN. • **BAKE:** 40 MIN. • **MAKES:** 14 SERVINGS

⅓ cup butter, softened
¾ cup sugar
1 egg
¼ cup egg substitute
1 teaspoon vanilla extract
2 cups all-purpose flour
1 teaspoon baking powder
1 teaspoon baking soda
¼ teaspoon salt
1 cup (8 ounces) reduced-fat sour cream
1 cup fresh or frozen blueberries

**TOPPING**
3 tablespoons sugar
2 teaspoons ground cinnamon
2 teaspoons confectioners' sugar

**1.** In a large bowl, beat the butter and sugar until crumbly, about 2 minutes. Beat in the egg, egg substitute and vanilla. Combine the flour, baking powder, baking soda and salt; add to the egg mixture alternately with the sour cream. Fold in the blueberries.
**2.** Coat a 10-in. fluted tube pan with cooking spray and dust with flour. Spoon half of the batter into prepared pan. Combine sugar and cinnamon; sprinkle half over batter. Repeat layers.
**3.** Bake at 350° for 40-50 minutes or until a toothpick inserted near the center comes out clean. Cool for 10 minutes before removing from pan to a wire rack to cool completely. Dust with confectioners' sugar.
**NOTE** *If using frozen blueberries, do not thaw before adding to batter.*
**PER SERVING** *191 cal., 7 g fat (4 g sat. fat), 32 mg chol., 218 mg sodium, 30 g carb., 1 g fiber, 4 g pro. Diabetic Exchanges: 2 starch, 1½ fat.*

## Whole Wheat Rolls F M

Even though these are whole wheat rolls, they have a light texture and are soft and tender. This recipe reminds me of many happy times with my family.
—**WILMA ORLANO** CARROLL, IA

**PREP:** 40 MIN. + RISING • **BAKE:** 10 MIN. • **MAKES:** 2 DOZEN

1½ cups boiling water
⅓ cup wheat bran
3 tablespoons ground flaxseed
1½ teaspoons salt
1 teaspoon ground cinnamon
⅓ cup honey
¼ cup canola oil
2 packages (¼ ounce each) active dry yeast
¼ cup warm water (110° to 115°)
2 teaspoons sugar
1½ cups whole wheat flour
2½ to 3 cups bread flour

**1.** In a small bowl, pour boiling water over the wheat bran, flaxseed, salt and cinnamon. Add the honey and oil. Let stand until mixture cools to 110°-115°, stirring occasionally.
**2.** In a large bowl, dissolve yeast in warm water. Add the sugar, whole wheat flour and wheat bran mixture. Beat on medium speed for 3 minutes. Stir in enough bread flour to form a firm dough.
**3.** Turn onto a floured surface; knead until smooth and elastic, about 6-8 minutes. Place in a greased bowl, turning once to grease the top. Cover and let rise in a warm place until doubled, about 1 hour. Punch dough down.
**4.** Turn onto a lightly floured surface; divide into 24 pieces. Shape each into a roll. Place 2 in. apart on greased baking sheets. Cover and let rise until doubled, about 30 minutes.
**5.** Bake at 375° for 10-15 minutes or until golden brown. Remove from pans to wire racks.
**PER SERVING** *120 cal., 3 g fat (trace sat. fat), 0 chol., 149 mg sodium, 22 g carb., 2 g fiber, 4 g pro. Diabetic Exchanges: 1½ starch, ½ fat.*

WHOLE WHEAT ROLLS

## Java Muffins M

These muffins sure do get me going in the morning, especially with a hot cup of coffee.

—**ZAINAB AHMED** MOUNTLAKE TERRACE, WA

**START TO FINISH:** 30 MIN. • **MAKES:** 1 DOZEN

- ¼ cup butter, softened
- 1 cup packed brown sugar
- 2 eggs
- ¼ cup unsweetened applesauce
- ½ cup buttermilk
- ½ cup strong brewed coffee
- 1 tablespoon instant coffee granules
- ½ teaspoon vanilla extract
- 1 cup all-purpose flour
- ¾ cup whole wheat flour
- 1½ teaspoons baking powder
- ½ teaspoon baking soda
- ½ teaspoon ground cinnamon
- ¼ teaspoon salt
- ½ cup finely chopped pecans, divided

**1.** Preheat oven to 375°. In a large bowl, beat butter and brown sugar until crumbly, about 2 minutes. Add eggs; mix well. Beat in applesauce. In a small bowl, whisk buttermilk, coffee, coffee granules and vanilla until granules are dissolved; gradually add to butter mixture.

**2.** In another bowl, whisk flours, baking powder, baking soda, cinnamon and salt. Add to butter mixture; stir just until moistened. Fold in ¼ cup pecans.

**3.** Coat muffin cups with cooking spray or use paper liners; fill three-fourths full. Sprinkle with remaining pecans. Bake 15-20 minutes or until a toothpick inserted into center comes out clean. Cool 5 minutes before removing from pan to a wire rack. Serve warm.

**PER SERVING** *220 cal., 9 g fat (3 g sat. fat), 46 mg chol., 209 mg sodium, 33 g carb., 2 g fiber, 4 g pro.* **Diabetic Exchanges:** *2 starch, 1½ fat.*

## Vermont Honey-Wheat Bread F S M

You don't have to be a health nut to enjoy this hearty loaf. Made with whole wheat flour, oats and wheat germ, this bread gets its pleasant sweetness from the honey and maple syrup.

—**RODERICK CRANDALL** HARTLAND, VT

**PREP:** 30 MIN. + RISING • **BAKE:** 30 MIN. + COOLING
**MAKES:** 2 LOAVES (16 SLICES EACH)

- 2 packages (¼ ounce each) active dry yeast
- ¾ cup warm water (110° to 115°)
- 1 cup old-fashioned oats
- 1 cup warm buttermilk (110° to 115°)
- ½ cup maple syrup
- ½ cup honey
- 2 eggs, lightly beaten
- ⅓ cup butter, softened
- ⅓ cup toasted wheat germ
- 1 teaspoon salt
- 1½ cups whole wheat flour
- 3 to 4 cups all-purpose flour

**TOPPING**

- 1 egg white
- 1 tablespoon water
- ¼ cup old-fashioned oats

**1.** In a large bowl, dissolve yeast in warm water. Add the oats, buttermilk, syrup, honey, eggs, butter, wheat germ, salt and whole wheat flour. Beat on medium speed for 3 minutes. Stir in enough all-purpose flour to form a firm dough.

**2.** Turn onto a floured surface; knead until smooth and elastic, about 6-8 minutes. Place in a bowl coated with cooking spray, turning once to coat top. Cover and let rise in a warm place until doubled, about 1 hour.

**3.** Punch the dough down. Shape into two loaves; place each in a 9-in. x 5-in. loaf pan coated with cooking spray. Cover and let rise in a warm place until doubled, about 45 minutes.

**4.** Beat egg white and water; brush over loaves. Sprinkle with oats. Bake at 375° for 30-35 minutes or until golden brown. Remove from pans to wire racks to cool.

**PER SERVING** *133 cal., 3 g fat (1 g sat. fat), 19 mg chol., 108 mg sodium, 24 g carb., 2 g fiber, 4 g pro.* **Diabetic Exchanges:** *1½ starch, ½ fat.*

VERMONT HONEY-WHEAT BREAD

SEEDED BUTTERNUT SQUASH BRAID

"Crunchy, green-hulled pumpkin seeds (better known as pepitas) add a slightly nutty taste to this rich and chewy bread. Because of their high oil content, pepitas can spoil quickly. Make sure you store them in the freezer to keep them fresh."

—**CHERYL PERRY** HERTFORD, NC

## Seeded Butternut Squash Braid M

**PREP:** 45 MIN.+ RISING • **BAKE:** 20 MIN.
**MAKES:** 1 LOAF (18 SLICES)

- 2¾ cups uncooked cubed peeled butternut squash
- 1 package (¼ ounce) active dry yeast
- ⅓ cup warm 2% milk (110° to 115°)
- 2 tablespoons warm water (110° to 115°)
- ½ cup pepitas or sunflower kernels
- ¼ cup butter, softened
- 1 egg
- 3 tablespoons brown sugar
- ½ teaspoon salt
- 3½ to 4 cups all-purpose flour

**TOPPING**
- 1 egg
- 1 tablespoon water
- ¼ cup pepitas or sunflower kernels

1. Place squash in a large saucepan and cover with water. Bring to a boil. Reduce heat; cover and cook for 15-20 minutes or until tender. Drain and mash squash (you will need 2 cups); cool to 110°-115°.

2. In a small bowl, dissolve yeast in warm milk and water. In a large bowl, combine the pepitas, butter, egg, brown sugar, salt, cooked squash, yeast mixture and 2 cups flour; beat on medium speed for 3 minutes. Stir in enough remaining flour to form a soft dough (dough will be sticky).

3. Turn onto a floured surface; knead until smooth and elastic, about 6-8 minutes. Place in a greased bowl, turning once to grease the top. Cover with plastic wrap and let rise in a warm place until doubled, about 1 hour.

4. Punch dough down. Turn onto a lightly floured surface; divide into thirds. Shape each into a 26-in. rope; braid ropes. Transfer to a greased baking sheet; form into a circle, pinching ends together to seal. Cover with a clean kitchen towel; let rise in a warm place until doubled, about 45 minutes.

5. For topping, beat egg and water; brush over braid. Sprinkle with pepitas. Bake at 350° for 18-23 minutes or until golden brown. Remove from pan to wire rack.

**PER SERVING** *192 cal., 7 g fat (3 g sat. fat), 31 mg chol., 150 mg sodium, 25 g carb., 2 g fiber, 7 g pro.* **Diabetic Exchanges:** *1½ starch, 1 fat.*

## Spiced Pear Bread F S M

My mom and I put up our own pears, so I always have plenty on hand when I want to make this wonderful bread.

—**RACHEL BAREFOOT** LINDEN, MI

**PREP:** 15 MIN. • **BAKE:** 50 MIN. + COOLING
**MAKES:** 4 MINI LOAVES (6 SLICES EACH)

- 3¾ cups all-purpose flour
- 1 cup sugar
- 3 teaspoons ground cinnamon
- 1 teaspoon baking soda
- 1 teaspoon baking powder
- 1 teaspoon ground cloves
- ½ teaspoon salt
- 3 eggs
- 3 cans (15¼ ounces each) sliced pears, drained and mashed
- ¼ cup unsweetened applesauce
- ¼ cup canola oil

1. In a large bowl, combine the first seven ingredients. In a small bowl, whisk the eggs, pears, applesauce and oil. Stir into dry ingredients just until moistened.

2. Pour into four 5¾-in. x 3-in. x 2-in. loaf pans coated with cooking spray. Bake at 350° for 50-60 minutes or until a toothpick inserted near the center comes out clean. Cool for 10 minutes before removing from pans to wire racks.

**PER SERVING** *160 cal., 3 g fat (trace sat. fat), 27 mg chol., 131 mg sodium, 30 g carb., 1 g fiber, 3 g pro.* **Diabetic Exchanges:** *2 starch, ½ fat.*

## Did you know?

Pears ripen best when off the tree. That might explain why the ones you find in the grocery store are hard and green. To help them ripen faster, place them in a paper bag and store at room temperature until ripe.

SPICED PEAR BREAD

## Asiago Bagels M

These thick and chewy bagels feature a mild cheese flavor that makes them ideal for brunch.

**—TAMI KUEHL** LOUP CITY, NE

**PREP:** 30 MIN. + STANDING
**BAKE:** 15 MIN. + COOLING
**MAKES:** 1 DOZEN

- 1 cup water (70° to 80°)
- 2 eggs
- ¼ cup plus 1 tablespoon olive oil
- 2 tablespoons honey
- ¾ cup shredded Asiago cheese, divided
- ⅓ cup nonfat dry milk powder
- 1½ teaspoons salt
- 1 teaspoon dried basil
- 2 cups whole wheat flour
- 1½ cups plus 2 tablespoons all-purpose flour
- 4 teaspoons active dry yeast
- 1 egg white
- 1 tablespoon water

**1.** In bread machine pan, place the water, eggs, oil, honey, ½ cup cheese, milk powder, salt, basil, flours and yeast in order suggested by manufacturer. Select dough setting (check dough after 5 minutes of mixing; add 1 to 2 tablespoons of water or flour if needed).

**2.** When cycle is completed, turn dough onto a lightly floured surface. Shape into 12 balls. Push thumb through centers to form a 1½-in. hole. Stretch and shape dough to form an even ring. Cover and let rest for 10 minutes; flatten bagels slightly.

**3.** Fill a Dutch oven two-thirds full with water; bring to a boil. Drop bagels, two at a time, into boiling water. Cook for 45 seconds; turn and cook 45 seconds longer. Remove with a slotted spoon; drain well on paper towels.

**4.** In a small bowl, combine egg white and water; brush over bagels. Sprinkle with remaining cheese. Place 2 in. apart on greased baking sheets. Bake at 400° for 15-20 minutes or until golden brown. Remove to wire racks to cool.

**PER SERVING** *239 cal., 9 g fat (2 g sat. fat), 42 mg chol., 342 mg sodium, 32 g carb., 3 g fiber, 9 g pro.* **Diabetic Exchanges:** *2 starch, 1½ fat.*

CRANBERRY-PECAN QUICK BREAD

## Cranberry-Pecan Quick Bread S M

With whole wheat flour, flaxseed, oats, cranberries and pecans, a slice of this quick bread is a satisfying start to your day.

**—WENDY MAROTTA** WILSON, NY

**PREP:** 20 MIN. • **BAKE:** 35 MIN. + COOLING
**MAKES:** 2 LOAVES (12 SLICES EACH)

- 1¾ cups all-purpose flour
- ¾ cup whole wheat flour
- ¾ cup sugar
- ¼ cup quick-cooking oats
- ¼ cup ground almonds
- 2 tablespoons ground flaxseed
- 1 teaspoon baking powder
- ¾ teaspoon salt
- ½ teaspoon baking soda
- 2 eggs
- 1¼ cups orange juice
- ¼ cup butter, melted
- ¼ cup unsweetened applesauce
- 1 cup dried cranberries
- ¼ cup chopped pecans

**1.** In a large bowl, combine the first nine ingredients. In a small bowl, whisk the eggs, orange juice, butter and applesauce. Stir into dry ingredients just until moistened. Fold in cranberries and pecans.

**2.** Transfer to two greased 8-in. x 4-in. loaf pans. Bake at 350° for 35-40 minutes or until a toothpick inserted near the center comes out clean. Cool for 10 minutes before removing from pans to wire racks.

**PER SERVING** *135 cal., 4 g fat (1 g sat. fat), 23 mg chol., 137 mg sodium, 23 g carb., 1 g fiber, 3 g pro.* **Diabetic Exchanges:** *1½ starch, 1 fat.*

ASIAGO BAGELS

## Favorite Maple Oatmeal Bread 🄵 🄼

This is one of my favorite recipes, especially since it features maple syrup from my home state.

—**MARIAN TOBIN** UNDERHILL, VT

**PREP:** 20 MIN. + RISING • **BAKE:** 40 MIN.
**MAKES:** 2 LOAVES (16 SLICES EACH)

- ¾ cup boiling water
- 1 cup old-fashioned oats
- 1 cup hot brewed coffee
- ½ cup maple syrup
- ⅓ cup canola oil
- 2 teaspoons salt
- 2 packages (¼ ounce each) active dry yeast
- ¼ cup warm water (110° to 115°)
- 2 eggs, lightly beaten
- ½ cup sugar
- 5½ to 6 cups bread flour

**1.** In a large bowl, pour boiling water over oats. Add the coffee, syrup, oil and salt. Let stand until mixture cools to 110°-115°, stirring occasionally.
**2.** In a large bowl, dissolve yeast in warm water. Add the oat mixture, eggs, sugar and 2 cups flour. Beat until smooth. Stir in enough remaining flour to form a soft dough.
**3.** Turn onto a floured surface; knead until smooth and elastic, about 6-8 minutes. Place in a greased bowl, turning once to grease top. Cover and let rise in a warm place until doubled, about 1 hour.
**4.** Punch dough down. Turn onto a lightly floured surface; divide in half. Shape into loaves. Place in two greased 9-in. x 5-in. loaf pans. Cover and let rise until doubled, about 30 minutes.
**5.** Bake at 350° for 40-45 minutes or until golden brown. Remove from pans to wire racks to cool.
**PER SERVING** *129 cal., 3 g fat (trace sat. fat), 13 mg chol., 152 mg sodium, 23 g carb., 1 g fiber, 4 g pro.* **Diabetic Exchanges:** *1½ starch, ½ fat.*

## Blackberry Lemon Muffins 🄼

These tender muffins are bursting with flavor, and they remind me of spring. Garnish them with grated lemon peel for added color and an extra puckery punch.

—**VICKY PALMER** ALBUQUERQUE, NM

**PREP:** 20 MIN. • **BAKE:** 15 MIN.
**MAKES:** 1 DOZEN

- 2 cups all-purpose flour
- ½ cup sugar
- 2 teaspoons baking powder
- ½ teaspoon salt
- ¼ teaspoon baking soda
- 2 eggs

BLACKBERRY LEMON MUFFINS

- 1 cup fat-free milk
- ⅓ cup butter, melted
- ⅓ cup lemon juice
- 1 cup fresh blackberries

**GLAZE**

- 1 cup confectioners' sugar
- 1 tablespoon butter, melted
- 1 to 2 tablespoons lemon juice
  Grated lemon peel, optional

**1.** Preheat oven to 375°. In a large bowl, whisk the first five ingredients. In another bowl, whisk eggs, milk, melted butter and lemon juice until blended. Add to flour mixture; stir just until moistened. Fold in blackberries.
**2.** Fill greased or foil-lined muffin cups three-fourths full. Bake 15-18 minutes or until a toothpick inserted into center comes out clean. Cool 5 minutes before removing from pan to a wire rack.
**3.** In a small bowl, mix confectioners' sugar, melted butter and enough lemon juice to reach desired consistency. Drizzle over warm muffins. If desired, sprinkle with lemon peel.
**PER SERVING** *226 cal., 7 g fat (4 g sat. fat), 52 mg chol., 255 mg sodium, 37 g carb., 1 g fiber, 4 g pro.*

FAVORITE MAPLE OATMEAL BREAD

208

209

218

# Table for 2

66 Mushrooms are the key to making these comforting Philly 'steak' sandwiches into a nice meatless meal option that's tangy and tasty. 99

**—VERONICA VICHIT-VADAKAN** PORTLAND, OR
*about her recipe, Philly Cheese Fakes for Two, on page 219*

# Apple Pork Chops for Two [C]

Sweet-tart apple, onion, thyme and Dijon give these chops delightful flavor.

—**DEBORAH WILLIAMS** PEORIA, AZ

**START TO FINISH:** 25 MIN.
**MAKES:** 2 SERVINGS

- 1 teaspoon cornstarch
- ⅓ cup chicken broth
- 2 boneless pork loin chops (4 ounces each)
- 1 teaspoon canola oil
- 1 small apple, peeled and thinly sliced
- ¼ cup finely chopped onion
- 3 tablespoons unsweetened apple juice
- 1 teaspoon Dijon mustard
- ⅛ teaspoon dried thyme

**1.** In a small bowl, combine cornstarch and broth; set aside. In a large skillet, brown pork chops in oil. Remove and keep warm.

**2.** In the same skillet, saute apple and onion until apple is crisp-tender. Stir in the broth mixture, apple juice, mustard and thyme; bring to a boil. Add pork chops. Reduce heat; cover and simmer for 8-10 minutes or until a thermometer reads 160°.

**PER SERVING** *224 cal., 9 g fat (3 g sat. fat), 55 mg chol., 256 mg sodium, 13 g carb., 1 g fiber, 22 g pro.* **Diabetic Exchanges:** *3 lean meat, 1 starch, ½ fat.*

BLT SKILLET

APPLE PORK CHOPS FOR TWO

# BLT Skillet

This weeknight meal is fast and reminiscent of a BLT, with its chunks of bacon and tomato. The whole wheat linguine gives the skillet dish extra flavor and texture.

—**EDRIE O'BRIEN** DENVER, CO

**START TO FINISH:** 25 MIN.
**MAKES:** 2 SERVINGS

- 4 ounces uncooked whole wheat linguine
- 4 bacon strips, cut into 1½-inch pieces
- 1 plum tomato, cut into 1-inch pieces
- 1 garlic clove, minced
- 1½ teaspoons lemon juice
- ¼ teaspoon salt
- ¼ teaspoon pepper
- 2 tablespoons grated Parmesan cheese
- 1 tablespoon minced fresh parsley

**1.** Cook linguine according to package directions. Meanwhile, in a large skillet, cook bacon over medium heat until crisp. Remove to paper towels; drain, reserving 1 teaspoon drippings.

**2.** In the drippings, saute tomato and garlic for 1-2 minutes or until heated through. Stir in the bacon, lemon juice, salt and pepper.

**3.** Drain linguine; add to the skillet. Sprinkle with cheese and parsley; toss to coat.

**PER SERVING** *302 cal., 10 g fat (3 g sat. fat), 20 mg chol., 670 mg sodium, 45 g carb., 7 g fiber, 13 g pro.*

# Oven-Fried Parmesan Potatoes M

I found this recipe in a newspaper and adjusted it somewhat by adding additional Parmesan cheese. This is a wonderful side dish, and since the potatoes are cooked with the skin on, they are nutritious as well as delicious.

—JANE HARLOW PANAMA CITY, FL

**PREP:** 10 MIN. • **BAKE:** 25 MIN.
**MAKES:** 2 SERVINGS

- 2 medium potatoes, sliced
- 1 tablespoon canola oil
- 3 tablespoons grated Parmesan cheese
- ½ teaspoon garlic powder
- ½ teaspoon paprika
- ¼ teaspoon salt
- ⅛ teaspoon pepper

**1.** Place potatoes in a large bowl. Drizzle with oil. Sprinkle with cheese, garlic powder, paprika, salt and pepper; toss to coat. Transfer to a greased 15-in. x 10-in. x 1-in. baking pan.
**2.** Bake, uncovered, at 450° for 25-30 minutes or until golden brown, stirring once.
**PER SERVING** *267 cal., 9 g fat (2 g sat. fat), 7 mg chol., 423 mg sodium, 39 g carb., 4 g fiber, 8 g pro.*

OVEN-FRIED PARMESAN POTATOES

CREAMY BERRY SMOOTHIES

"No one can tell there's tofu in these silky smoothies. For me, the blend of berries and pomegranate juice is a welcome delight."
—SONYA LABBE WEST HOLLYWOOD, CA

# Creamy Berry Smoothies F S M

**START TO FINISH:** 10 MIN.
**MAKES:** 2 SERVINGS

- ½ cup pomegranate juice
- 1 tablespoon agave syrup or honey
- 3 ounces silken firm tofu (about ½ cup)
- 1 cup frozen unsweetened mixed berries
- 1 cup frozen unsweetened strawberries

Place all ingredients in a blender; cover and process until blended. Serve immediately.
**PER SERVING** *157 cal., 1 g fat (trace sat. fat), 0 chol., 24 mg sodium, 35 g carb., 3 g fiber, 4 g pro.*

SUNDAY CHICKEN SUPPER

## Sunday Chicken Supper

This convenient slow-cooker dish makes a hearty meal for you and someone special, especially for a nice Sunday dinner.

—RUTHANN MARTIN LOUISVILLE, OH

**PREP:** 15 MIN. • **COOK:** 6 HOURS
**MAKES:** 2 SERVINGS

- 2 **small carrots, cut into 2-inch pieces**
- ½ **medium onion, chopped**
- ½ **celery rib, cut into 2-inch pieces**
- 1 **cup cut fresh green beans (2-inch pieces)**
- 2 **small red potatoes, halved**
- 2 **bone-in chicken breast halves (7 ounces each), skin removed**
- 2 **bacon strips, cooked and crumbled**
- ¾ **cup hot water**
- 1 **teaspoon chicken bouillon granules**
- ¼ **teaspoon salt**
- ¼ **teaspoon dried thyme**
- ¼ **teaspoon dried basil**
  **Pinch pepper**

In a 3-qt. slow cooker, layer the first seven ingredients in the order listed. Combine the water, bouillon, salt, thyme, basil and pepper; pour over the top. Do not stir. Cover and cook on low for 6-8 hours or until vegetables are tender and meat thermometer reads 170°. Remove chicken and vegetables. Thicken cooking juices for gravy if desired.
**PER SERVING** *304 cal., 7 g fat (2 g sat. fat), 94 mg chol., 927 mg sodium, 21 g carb., 5 g fiber, 37 g pro.*

## Portobello Burgers

These grilled portobello mushroom burgers make a savory and hearty meatless lunch or dinner.

—THERESA SABBAGH WINSTON-SALEM, NC

**PREP:** 10 MIN. + STANDING • **GRILL:** 15 MIN.
**MAKES:** 2 SERVINGS

- 2 **tablespoons balsamic vinegar**
- 1 **tablespoon olive oil**
- 3 **garlic cloves, minced**
- 1½ **teaspoons minced fresh basil or ½ teaspoon dried basil**
- 1½ **teaspoons minced fresh oregano or ½ teaspoon dried oregano**
  **Dash salt**
  **Dash pepper**
- 2 **large portobello mushrooms, stems removed**
- 2 **slices reduced-fat provolone cheese**
- 2 **hamburger buns, split**
- 2 **lettuce leaves**
- 2 **slices tomato**

**1.** In a small bowl, whisk the first seven ingredients. Add mushroom caps; let stand for 15 minutes, turning twice. Drain and reserve marinade.
**2.** Moisten a paper towel with cooking oil; using long-handled tongs, lightly rub the grill rack to coat. Grill mushrooms, covered, over medium heat or broil 4 in. from the heat for 6-8 minutes on each side or until tender, basting with reserved marinade. Top with cheese during the last 2 minutes.
**3.** Serve on buns with lettuce and tomato slices.
**PER SERVING** *280 cal., 13 g fat (3 g sat. fat), 10 mg chol., 466 mg sodium, 31 g carb., 3 g fiber, 11 g pro.* **Diabetic Exchanges:** *2 starch, 1½ fat, 1 medium-fat meat, 1 vegetable.*

### Did you know?

Portobello mushrooms are simply larger, more mature forms of common white mushrooms. They have a very memorable rich and meaty flavor, which makes them ideal substitutions for other proteins.

PORTOBELLO BURGERS

## Apple-Oat Bran Muffins F M

I love how light and tasty these muffins are. I often make the batter ahead of time because it keeps nicely in the fridge.

**—GRACE BRYANT** MERRITT ISLAND, FL

**PREP:** 20 MIN. • **BAKE:** 20 MIN. • **MAKES:** 6 MUFFINS (6 SERVINGS)

- ½ cup plus 2 tablespoons whole wheat flour
- ½ cup oat bran
- 3 tablespoons brown sugar
- 1¼ teaspoons baking powder
- ⅛ teaspoon baking soda
  Dash salt
- ¼ teaspoon ground cinnamon
- ⅛ teaspoon ground nutmeg
- 1 egg white
- ½ cup buttermilk
- 1 tablespoon canola oil
- ⅔ cup grated apple

**1.** In a small bowl, combine the first eight ingredients. In another bowl, whisk the egg white, buttermilk and oil. Stir into dry ingredients just until moistened. Fold in apple.
**2.** Coat muffin cups with cooking spray; fill three-fourths full with batter. Bake at 375° for 16-18 minutes or until a toothpick comes out clean. Cool for 5 minutes before removing from pan to a wire rack. Serve warm.
**PER SERVING** 128 cal., 3 g fat (trace sat. fat), 1 mg chol., 168 mg sodium, 24 g carb., 3 g fiber, 4 g pro. **Diabetic Exchange:** 1½ starch.

## Spicy Chicken Tenders F C

These quick chicken bites are juicy, delicious and have all the traditional East Indian flavors of cinnamon, ginger and curry. I serve this simple dish with rice and veggies for a tasty meal.

**—CAROL DODDS** AURORA, ON

**START TO FINISH:** 30 MIN. • **MAKES:** 2 SERVINGS

- 1 tablespoon water
- ¼ teaspoon salt
- ¼ teaspoon crushed red pepper flakes
- ¼ teaspoon curry powder
- ⅛ teaspoon each ground turmeric, ginger and cinnamon
- ⅛ teaspoon paprika
- ½ pound chicken tenderloins

**1.** In a small bowl, combine water and seasonings; brush over both sides of chicken tenders. Place in a large resealable plastic bag; seal bag and refrigerate for 15 minutes.
**2.** Place chicken on a broiler pan coated with cooking spray. Broil 3-4 in. from the heat for 3 minutes on each side or until meat is no longer pink.
**PER SERVING** 108 cal., 1 g fat (trace sat. fat), 67 mg chol., 343 mg sodium, 1 g carb., trace fiber, 26 g pro. **Diabetic Exchange:** 3 lean meat.

## Cranberry-Kissed Pork Chops for 2 S C

I like to serve this quick entree over golden cooked noodles or fluffy white rice. The cranberry sauce also tastes great drizzled over chicken breasts.

—**BETTY JEAN NICHOLS** EUGENE, OR

**START TO FINISH:** 25 MIN. • **MAKES:** 2 SERVINGS

- 2 **boneless pork loin chops (5 ounces each)**
  **Dash coarsely ground pepper**
- 2 **tablespoons jellied cranberry sauce**
- 1½ **teaspoons stone-ground mustard**
- 1 **tablespoon dried cranberries**
- 2 **teaspoons raspberry vinegar**

**1.** Sprinkle pork chops with pepper. In a large skillet coated with cooking spray, brown chops on both sides over medium-high heat. Combine cranberry sauce and mustard; spoon over chops. Reduce heat; cover and cook for 6-8 minutes or until a thermometer reads 160°.

**2.** Remove chops and keep warm. Add cranberries and vinegar to skillet, stirring to loosen browned bits from pan. Bring to a boil; cook until liquid is reduced to about 3 tablespoons. Serve with chops.

**PER SERVING** *232 cal., 8 g fat (3 g sat. fat), 68 mg chol., 120 mg sodium, 11 g carb., 1 g fiber, 27 g pro. **Diabetic Exchanges:** 4 lean meat, 1 starch.*

## High-Octane Pancakes M

Fluffy and healthy, these hotcakes are what I rely on to jump-start myself on frosty winter mornings and keep me fueled up all day long. This recipe is perfect for two people.

—**KELLY HANLON** STRASBURG, CO

**START TO FINISH:** 20 MIN. • **MAKES:** 4 PANCAKES (2 SERVINGS)

- ⅓ **cup plus 1 tablespoon all-purpose flour**
- ¼ **cup quick-cooking oats**
- 3 **tablespoons toasted wheat germ**
- 2 **teaspoons sugar**
- 1¼ **teaspoons baking powder**
- ⅛ **teaspoon salt**
- ⅔ **cup fat-free milk**
- ¼ **cup fat-free plain yogurt**
- 1 **tablespoon canola oil**

**1.** In a small bowl, combine the first six ingredients. In another bowl, combine the milk, yogurt and oil. Stir into dry ingredients just until moistened.

**2.** Pour batter by ⅓ cupfuls onto a hot nonstick griddle coated with cooking spray. Turn when bubbles form on top of pancake; cook until second side is golden brown.

**PER SERVING** *281 cal., 9 g fat (1 g sat. fat), 2 mg chol., 450 mg sodium, 41 g carb., 3 g fiber, 11 g pro. **Diabetic Exchanges:** 3 starch, 1½ fat.*

APPLE YOGURT PARFAITS

## Thanksgiving Turkey for Two C

One of the hardest meals to plan is a holiday meal for two. You want all the smells and feelings of the season, but you don't want leftovers that last until June! This recipe is the perfect solution.

**—JOYCE KRAMER** DONALSONVILLE, GA

**PREP:** 10 MIN. • **BAKE:** 30 MIN. • **MAKES:** 2 SERVINGS

- 2 turkey breast tenderloins (6 ounces each)
- ¼ cup white wine or chicken broth
- 1 tablespoon butter, melted
- ¼ teaspoon salt
- ¼ teaspoon dried tarragon
- ¼ teaspoon paprika
- ½ cup sliced fresh mushrooms

**1.** Place turkey in an 11-in. x 7-in. baking dish coated with cooking spray. In a small bowl, combine the wine, butter, salt, tarragon and paprika. Spoon over turkey. Arrange mushrooms around tenderloins.

**2.** Bake, uncovered, at 375° for 30-35 minutes or until a thermometer reads 170°, basting occasionally with pan drippings. Let stand for 5 minutes before slicing. Serve with remaining pan drippings.

**PER SERVING** *260 cal., 8 g fat (4 g sat. fat), 98 mg chol., 429 mg sodium, 2 g carb., trace fiber, 40 g pro.* **Diabetic Exchanges:** *5 lean meat, 1½ fat.*

THANKSGIVING TURKEY FOR TWO

## Apple Yogurt Parfaits S M

Get the morning started right with this super-simple four-ingredient parfait. Try chunky or flavored applesauce for easy variations.

**—REBEKAH RADEWAHN** WAUWATOSA, WI

**START TO FINISH:** 5 MIN. • **MAKES:** 2 SERVINGS

- ½ cup sweetened applesauce
  Dash ground nutmeg
- ¼ cup granola with raisins
- ⅔ cup vanilla yogurt

In a small bowl, combine applesauce and nutmeg. Spoon 1 tablespoon granola into each of two parfait glasses. Layer each with ⅓ cup yogurt and ¼ cup applesauce; sprinkle with remaining granola. Serve immediately.

**PER SERVING** *171 cal., 4 g fat (2 g sat. fat), 8 mg chol., 69 mg sodium, 30 g carb., 1 g fiber, 5 g pro.* **Diabetic Exchanges:** *1 starch, ½ whole milk.*

## Watermelon Cooler F S M

Cool down on a sweltering day with this special blend that features summer's favorite fruit. It's lovely and refreshing.

**—TASTE OF HOME TEST KITCHEN**

**START TO FINISH:** 10 MIN. • **MAKES:** 2 SERVINGS

- 1 cup ginger ale, chilled
- 2 fresh mint leaves
- 2 cups cubed seedless watermelon, frozen

In a blender, cover and process ginger ale and mint for 15 seconds or until finely chopped. Add watermelon; cover and process until slushy. Pour into chilled glasses; serve immediately.

**PER SERVING** *82 cal., 0 fat (0 sat. fat), 0 chol., 14 mg sodium, 24 g carb., 1 g fiber, 1 g pro.*

WATERMELON COOLER

## Vegetable Scrambled Eggs F C M

These scrambled eggs are packed with a variety of veggies, giving you an instant healthy start to your day.

**—MARILYN IPSON** ROGERS, AR

**START TO FINISH:** 10 MIN. • **MAKES:** 2 SERVINGS

- 1 cup egg substitute
- ½ cup chopped green pepper
- ¼ cup sliced green onions
- ¼ cup fat-free milk
- ¼ teaspoon salt
- ⅛ teaspoon pepper
- 1 small tomato, chopped and seeded

**1.** In a small bowl, combine the egg substitute, green pepper, onions, milk, salt and pepper.

**2.** Pour into a nonstick skillet coated with cooking spray. Cook and stir over medium heat until eggs are nearly set. Add tomato; cook and stir until completely set.

**PER SERVING** *90 cal., trace fat (trace sat. fat), 1 mg chol., 563 mg sodium, 8 g carb., 2 g fiber, 14 g pro.* **Diabetic Exchanges:** *2 lean meat, 1 vegetable.*

### ? Did you know?

Studies show that drinking watermelon juice before a tough workout can help reduce muscle soreness the next day. This is because watermelon is a rich source of L-citrulline, an amino acid that the body converts to L-arginine, which helps relax blood vessels.

## Turkey & Bow Ties

A splash of white wine and minced garlic go a long way in this Italian-influenced skillet dish. And it only takes 30 minutes.

—MARY RELYEA CANASTOTA, NY

**START TO FINISH:** 30 MIN.
**MAKES:** 2 SERVINGS

- 1¼ **cups uncooked bow tie pasta**
- 6 **ounces turkey breast tenderloin, cut into 1-inch cubes**
- 2 **teaspoons olive oil**
- 1 **cup fresh broccoli florets**
- 1 **garlic clove, minced**
- ¾ **cup canned Italian diced tomatoes**
- ⅓ **cup reduced-sodium chicken broth**
- 2 **tablespoons white wine or additional reduced-sodium chicken broth**
- ½ **teaspoon dried basil**
  **Dash cayenne pepper**
- 2 **tablespoons grated Parmesan cheese**

**1.** Cook pasta according to package directions. Meanwhile, in a large skillet, cook turkey in oil over medium heat until no longer pink. Add broccoli and garlic; cook until broccoli is tender.

**2.** Stir in the tomatoes, broth, wine, basil and cayenne. Bring to a boil. Reduce heat; simmer, uncovered, for 5-8 minutes or until heated through, stirring occasionally. Drain pasta; add to turkey mixture and toss to coat. Sprinkle with cheese.

**PER SERVING** *380 cal., 8 g fat (2 g sat. fat), 46 mg chol., 583 mg sodium, 45 g carb., 3 g fiber, 30 g pro.* **Diabetic Exchanges:** *3 lean meat, 2½ starch, 1 vegetable, 1 fat.*

LEMON-GARLIC BRUSSELS SPROUTS

TURKEY & BOW TIES

## Lemon-Garlic Brussels Sprouts C M

Even lifelong Brussels sprouts haters love these! For a heartier dish, sometimes I add crumbled bacon.

—JAN ROBERTS SAN PEDRO, CA

**START TO FINISH:** 30 MIN.
**MAKES:** 2 SERVINGS

- ½ **pound fresh Brussels sprouts**
- 1½ **teaspoons olive oil**
- 1½ **teaspoons lemon juice**
- ¼ **teaspoon salt**
- ¼ **teaspoon garlic powder**
  **Dash pepper**
- 1 **tablespoon shredded Parmesan cheese**

**1.** Cut an X in the core of each Brussels sprout. Place in a shallow baking pan coated with cooking spray. Drizzle with oil and lemon juice; sprinkle with salt, garlic powder and pepper.

**2.** Bake, uncovered, at 400° for 20-25 minutes or until tender, stirring once. Sprinkle with cheese.

**PER SERVING** *91 cal., 4 g fat (1 g sat. fat), 2 mg chol., 366 mg sodium, 11 g carb., 4 g fiber, 5 g pro.* **Diabetic Exchanges:** *2 vegetable, 1 fat.*

## Cocoa Meringues with Berries S M

**PREP:** 20 MIN. • **BAKE:** 50 MIN. + STANDING
**MAKES:** 2 SERVINGS

- 1 **egg white**
- ⅛ **teaspoon cream of tartar**
  **Dash salt**
- 3 **tablespoons sugar, divided**
- 1 **tablespoon baking cocoa**
- ¼ **teaspoon vanilla extract**
- 2 **tablespoons finely chopped bittersweet chocolate**

**BERRY SAUCE**

- 2 **tablespoons sugar**
- 1 **teaspoon cornstarch**
- 2 **tablespoons orange juice**
- 1 **tablespoon water**
- ½ **cup fresh or frozen blueberries, thawed**
- ½ **cup fresh or frozen raspberries, thawed**

**1.** Place egg white in a small bowl; let stand at room temperature for 30 minutes.

**2.** Preheat oven to 275°. Add cream of tartar and salt; beat on medium speed until soft peaks form. Gradually beat in 2 tablespoons sugar.

**3.** Combine cocoa and remaining sugar; add to meringue with vanilla. Beat on high until stiff glossy peaks form and sugar is dissolved. Fold in chopped chocolate.

**4.** Drop two mounds onto a parchment paper-lined baking sheet. Shape into 3-in. cups with the back of a spoon. Bake 50-60 minutes or until set and dry. Turn oven off; leave meringues in oven for 1 hour.

**5.** In a small saucepan, combine sugar, cornstarch, orange juice and water. Bring to a boil; cook and stir 1 minute or until thickened. Remove from heat; stir in berries. Cool to room temperature. Spoon into meringues.

**PER SERVING** *215 cal., 4 g fat (2 g sat. fat), 0 chol., 102 mg sodium, 46 g carb., 3 g fiber, 3 g pro.*

"Meringues can be challenging on a humid day, but if you're really craving one, they can be purchased at your favorite bakery. Add this sweet sauce, and you're all set!" —**RAYMONDE BOURGEOIS** SWASTIKA, ON

LEMON BASIL TEA

## Lemon Basil Tea F S C M

Our Test Kitchen experts sure know how to brew a great cup of tea! Infused with basil and lemon, this oh-so-drinkable recipe tastes as good as it smells.
—**TASTE OF HOME TEST KITCHEN**

**START TO FINISH:** 10 MIN.
**MAKES:** 2 SERVINGS

- 2 **cups water**
- 3 **tablespoons thinly sliced fresh basil leaves**
- 1 **tablespoon grated lemon peel**
- 2 **teaspoons English breakfast or other black tea leaves**

In a small saucepan, bring water to a boil. Remove from the heat. Add the basil, lemon peel and tea leaves; cover and steep for 4 minutes. Strain, discarding basil, lemon peel and tea leaves. Serve immediately.

**PER SERVING** *0 cal., 0 fat (0 sat. fat), 0 chol., 0 sodium, 0 carb., 0 fiber, 0 pro.* **Diabetic Exchange:** *Free food.*

**top tip**

## Tea Storage

When tea leaves are exposed to air, they begin to lose their flavor. Light, too, can strip tea leaves of their color and affect their taste. To prevent this from happening and to ensure freshness, store tea leaves in an airtight container (tea caddies and tea tins work well) away from light and at room temperature.

COCOA MERINGUES WITH BERRIES

# Orange Picante Pork Chops ©

These are no ordinary pork chops! I dress them up with picante sauce and a hint of orange juice. Grilling brings out the natural sweetness of the pork chops. They're delightful with rice or picnic salads.
—**LADONNA REED** PONCA CITY, OK

**PREP:** 15 MIN. + MARINATING • **GRILL:** 10 MIN. • **MAKES:** 2 SERVINGS

- 1 cup picante sauce
- ⅓ cup orange juice
- 2 garlic cloves, minced
- 2 boneless pork loin chops (½ inch thick and 5 ounces each)
  Hot cooked rice, optional

**1.** In a small bowl, combine the picante sauce, orange juice and garlic. Pour 1 cup marinade into a large resealable plastic bag; add pork. Seal bag and turn to coat; refrigerate for at least 4 hours. Cover and refrigerate remaining marinade.

**2.** Drain pork and discard marinade. Moisten a paper towel with cooking oil; using long-handled tongs, lightly rub the grill rack to coat. Grill pork, covered, over medium heat or broil 4-5 in. from the heat for 4-5 minutes on each side or until a thermometer reads 145°. Let stand for 5 minutes before serving.

**3.** Meanwhile, in a small saucepan, bring reserved marinade to a boil. Reduce heat; simmer, uncovered, for 5-7 minutes or until heated through. Serve chops with sauce and rice if desired.

**PER SERVING** *216 cal., 8 g fat (3 g sat. fat), 68 mg chol., 444 mg sodium, 6 g carb., trace fiber, 27 g pro.* **Diabetic Exchanges:** *4 lean meat, ½ starch.*

ORANGE PICANTE PORK CHOPS

## So-Easy Swiss Steak

Let your slow cooker simmer up this fuss-free and flavorful Swiss steak. It's perfect for busy days—the longer it cooks, the better it tastes!

—**SARAH BURKS** WATHENA, KS

**PREP:** 10 MIN. • **COOK:** 6 HOURS
**MAKES:** 2 SERVINGS

- 1 **tablespoon all-purpose flour**
- ¼ **teaspoon salt**
- ⅛ **teaspoon pepper**
- ¾ **pound beef top round steak, cut in half**
- ½ **medium onion, cut into ¼-inch slices**
- ⅓ **cup chopped celery**
- 1 **can (8 ounces) tomato sauce**

**1.** In a large resealable plastic bag, combine the flour, salt and pepper. Add beef; seal bag and shake to coat.
**2.** Place onion in a 3-qt. slow cooker coated with cooking spray. Layer with the beef, celery and tomato sauce. Cover and cook on low for 6-8 hours or until meat is tender.
**PER SERVING** *272 cal., 5 g fat (2 g sat. fat), 96 mg chol., 882 mg sodium, 13 g carb., 2 g fiber, 41 g pro.*

PHILLY CHEESE FAKES FOR TWO

## Philly Cheese Fakes for Two M

Mushrooms are the key to making these comforting Philly "steak" sandwiches into a nice meatless meal option that's tangy and tasty.

—**VERONICA VICHIT-VADAKAN**
PORTLAND, OR

**PREP:** 30 MIN. • **BROIL:** 5 MIN.
**MAKES:** 2 SERVINGS

- 2 **tablespoons lemon juice**
- 2 **garlic cloves, minced**
- 1½ **teaspoons olive oil**
- ¼ **teaspoon smoked paprika**
- ⅛ **teaspoon salt**
- ⅛ **teaspoon pepper**
- ½ **pound sliced fresh shiitake mushrooms**
- 1 **medium green pepper, sliced**
- ¼ **cup thinly sliced onion**
- 2 **hoagie buns, split**
- 2 **slices reduced-fat provolone cheese**

**1.** In a small bowl, whisk the first six ingredients. In a large bowl, combine the mushrooms, green pepper and onion. Pour dressing over vegetables; toss to coat.
**2.** Transfer to a 15-in. x 10-in. x 1-in. baking pan coated with cooking spray. Bake at 450° for 15-20 minutes or until crisp-tender, stirring once.
**3.** Divide mushroom mixture among buns and top with cheese. Broil 3-4 in. from the heat for 2-3 minutes or until cheese is melted.
**PER SERVING** *344 cal., 12 g fat (4 g sat. fat), 10 mg chol., 681 mg sodium, 47 g carb., 4 g fiber, 17 g pro.*

SO-EASY SWISS STEAK

223

228

231

# Cookies, Bars & More

"There's sweetness from the honey, chewiness from the raisins, a hint of cinnamon and a bit of crunch in these granola bars. To save a few for later, wrap individual bars in plastic wrap and place in a resealable freezer bag. When you want a satisfying treat on short notice, just grab one and let it thaw for a few minutes."

—**TASHA LEHMAN** WILLISTON, VT
*about her recipe, Chewy Honey Granola Bars, on page 228*

## Raspberry Oat Bars F S M

These sweet, fruity bars are wonderful with hot coffee or cold milk and make a tasty breakfast or sweet snack.
—**MARY NOURSE** SOUTH DEERFIELD, MA

**PREP:** 20 MIN. • **BAKE:** 25 MIN. + COOLING • **MAKES:** 2 DOZEN

- 2 **tablespoons sugar**
- 2 **tablespoons cornstarch**
- 1 **package (10 ounces) frozen sweetened raspberries, thawed**
- ¼ **teaspoon almond extract**
- 1 **cup quick-cooking oats**
- ¾ **cup all-purpose flour**
- ⅔ **cup packed brown sugar**
- ¼ **cup whole wheat flour**
- ¼ **teaspoon salt**
- 1 **teaspoon vanilla extract**
- ⅓ **cup cold butter, cubed**

**1.** In a small saucepan, combine sugar and cornstarch. Gradually stir in raspberries until blended. Bring to a boil; cook and stir for 1-2 minutes or until thickened. Remove from the heat; stir in extract. Cool.

**2.** In a large bowl, combine the oats, flour, brown sugar, wheat flour, salt and vanilla. Cut in butter until mixture resembles coarse crumbs. Press 2½ cups crumb mixture into a 9-in. square baking pan coated with cooking spray. Spread with cooled berry mixture. Sprinkle with remaining crumb mixture.

**3.** Bake at 350° for 25-30 minutes or until golden brown. Cool on a wire rack. Cut into bars.

**PER SERVING** *95 cal., 3 g fat (2 g sat. fat), 7 mg chol., 45 mg sodium, 17 g carb., 1 g fiber, 1 g pro.* **Diabetic Exchanges:** *1 starch, ½ fat.*

## Old-Fashioned Crackle Cookies F S C M

This recipe falls in the "oldie but goodie" category. My family loves them! Kids can help by rolling the balls in confectioners' sugar and placing them on the baking sheets.
—**RUTH CAIN** HARTSELLE, AL

**PREP:** 15 MIN. + CHILLING • **BAKE:** 10 MIN./BATCH
**MAKES:** ABOUT 3 DOZEN

- 1 **cup sugar**
- ¼ **cup canola oil**
- 2 **eggs**
- 2 **ounces unsweetened chocolate, melted and cooled**
- 1 **teaspoon vanilla extract**
- 1 **cup all-purpose flour**
- 1 **teaspoon baking powder**
- ¼ **teaspoon salt**
  **Confectioners' sugar**

**1.** In a large bowl, beat sugar and oil until blended. Beat in eggs, chocolate and vanilla. Combine the flour, baking powder and salt; gradually add to sugar mixture and mix well. Cover and refrigerate dough for at least 2 hours.

**2.** With sugared hands, shape dough into 1-in. balls. Roll in confectioners' sugar. Place 2 in. apart on baking sheets coated with cooking spray. Bake at 350° for 10-12 minutes or until set. Remove to wire racks to cool.

**MOCHA CRACKLE COOKIES** *Add 1½ teaspoons instant coffee granules to the sugar mixture.*

**PER SERVING** *63 cal., 3 g fat (1 g sat. fat), 12 mg chol., 32 mg sodium, 10 g carb., trace fiber, 1 g pro.* **Diabetic Exchanges:** *½ starch, ½ fat.*

## Molasses Crackle Cookies F S C M

You can treat yourself to one or two of my crackle cookies without any pang of guilt. Most molasses cookies are loaded with butter and have way too much sugar, but not mine. You would never know these are so low in fat.

—**JEAN ECOS** HARTLAND, WI

**PREP:** 20 MIN. + CHILLING • **BAKE:** 10 MIN./BATCH
**MAKES:** 2½ DOZEN

- ⅔ **cup sugar**
- ¼ **cup canola oil**
- 1 **egg**
- ⅓ **cup molasses**
- 2 **cups white whole wheat flour**
- 1½ **teaspoons baking soda**
- 1 **teaspoon ground cinnamon**
- ½ **teaspoon salt**
- ¼ **teaspoon ground ginger**
- ¼ **teaspoon ground cloves**
- 1 **tablespoon confectioners' sugar**

**1.** In a small bowl, beat sugar and oil until blended. Beat in egg and molasses. Combine the flour, baking soda, cinnamon, salt, ginger and cloves; gradually add to sugar mixture and mix well. Cover and refrigerate for at least 2 hours.

**2.** Shape dough into 1-in. balls; roll in confectioners' sugar. Place 2 in. apart on baking sheets coated with cooking spray; flatten slightly. Bake at 350° for 7-9 minutes or until set. Remove to wire racks to cool.

**PER SERVING** *77 cal., 2 g fat (trace sat. fat), 7 mg chol., 106 mg sodium, 14 g carb., 1 g fiber, 1 g pro.* ***Diabetic Exchange:*** *1 starch.*

## Chewy Whole Wheat Snickerdoodles F S C M

My cookies get coated with sugar, spice and everything nice! They turn out soft on the inside and a little crunchy on the outside. The dough is easy to work with and they taste fantastic. What more could you ask for in a cookie?

—**ASHLEY WISNIEWSKI** CHAMPAIGN, IL

**PREP:** 30 MIN. • **BAKE:** 10 MIN./BATCH • **MAKES:** 3 DOZEN

- ¼ **cup butter, softened**
- 1 **cup plus 2 tablespoons sugar, divided**
- 1 **egg**
- 1 **tablespoon agave nectar**
- 1 **teaspoon vanilla extract**
- 1¾ **cups white whole wheat flour**
- ½ **teaspoon baking soda**
- ½ **teaspoon cream of tartar**
- 2 **teaspoons ground cinnamon**

**1.** In a large bowl, cream butter and 1 cup sugar until blended. Beat in the egg, agave nectar and vanilla. Combine the flour, baking soda and cream of tartar; gradually add to creamed mixture and mix well. In a small bowl, combine cinnamon and remaining sugar.

**2.** Shape dough into 1-in. balls; roll in cinnamon-sugar. Place 2 in. apart on baking sheets coated with cooking spray. Bake at 375° for 9-11 minutes or until lightly browned. Cool on racks for 2 minutes before removing from pans to wire racks.

**PER SERVING** *52 cal., 1 g fat (1 g sat. fat), 8 mg chol., 24 mg sodium, 10 g carb., 1 g fiber, 1 g pro.* ***Diabetic Exchange:*** *½ starch.*

## Full-of-Goodness Oatmeal Cookies F S C M

**PREP:** 35 MIN. • **BAKE:** 10 MIN./BATCH
**MAKES:** 6 DOZEN

- 2 **tablespoons hot water**
- 1 **tablespoon ground flaxseed**
- 1 **cup pitted dried plums, chopped**
- 1 **cup chopped dates**
- ½ **cup raisins**
- ⅓ **cup butter, softened**
- ¾ **cup packed brown sugar**
- 1 **egg**
- 2 **teaspoons vanilla extract**
- ½ **cup unsweetened applesauce**
- ¼ **cup maple syrup**
- 1 **tablespoon grated orange peel**
- 3 **cups quick-cooking oats**
- 1 **cup all-purpose flour**
- ½ **cup whole wheat flour**
- 1 **teaspoon baking soda**
- 1 **teaspoon ground cinnamon**
- ½ **teaspoon salt**
- ¼ **teaspoon ground nutmeg**
- ¼ **teaspoon ground cloves**

**1.** In a small bowl, combine water and flaxseed. In a large bowl, combine the plums, dates and raisins; cover with boiling water. Let flaxseed and plum mixtures stand for 10 minutes.

**2.** Meanwhile, in a large bowl, cream butter and brown sugar until light and fluffy. Beat in egg and vanilla. Beat in the applesauce, maple syrup and orange peel. Combine the oats, flours, baking soda, cinnamon, salt, nutmeg and cloves; gradually add to creamed mixture and mix well. Drain plum mixture; stir plum mixture and flaxseed into dough.

**3.** Drop by rounded teaspoonfuls 2 in. apart onto lightly greased baking sheets. Bake at 350° for 8-11 minutes or until set. Cool for 2 minutes before removing from pans to wire racks.

**PER SERVING** *56 cal., 1 g fat (1 g sat. fat), 5 mg chol., 40 mg sodium, 11 g carb., 1 g fiber, 1 g pro.* **Diabetic Exchange:** *1 starch.*

COCONUT KISSES

"I love to bake, and bring in extra treats to leave in the faculty lounge for my colleagues. To avoid being blamed for ruining their healthy diets, I came up with this healthier version of the classic oatmeal cookie to make snacking on these a good choice, instead of a guilty indulgence."

—**SHARON BALESTRA** BLOOMFIELD, NY

FULL-OF-GOODNESS OATMEAL COOKIES

## Coconut Kisses F S C M

Chewy on the inside and crisp on the outside, these meringue cookies are a sweet reward. They add a light touch to the cookie platter, not only during the holidays but all year round.

—**DOROTHY BEAUDRY** ALBERTVILLE, MN

**PREP:** 15 MIN. • **BAKE:** 20 MIN.
**MAKES:** 1 DOZEN

- 1 **egg white**
- ½ **cup confectioners' sugar**
- 1 **cup flaked coconut**

**1.** Place egg white in a small bowl; let stand at room temperature for 30 minutes. Beat on medium speed until soft peaks form. Gradually beat in confectioners' sugar, 1 tablespoon at a time, on high until stiff peaks form. Fold in coconut.

**2.** Drop by rounded tablespoonfuls 2 in. apart onto a parchment paper-lined baking sheet. Bake at 325° for 18-20 minutes or until firm to the touch. Cool for 1 minute before removing to a wire rack. Store in an airtight container.

**PER SERVING** *60 cal., 3 g fat (2 g sat. fat), 0 chol., 25 mg sodium, 9 g carb., trace fiber, 1 g pro.* **Diabetic Exchange:** *½ starch.*

## Almond Crispies FSCM

The trio of almond flavors (almond extract, ground almonds and blanched almonds) makes these cookies extra tasty, but I sometimes make them with toasted pecans and place a pecan half in the center of each cookie.

—TRISHA KRUSE EAGLE, ID

**PREP:** 20 MIN. + CHILLING
**BAKE:** 20 MIN./BATCH • **MAKES:** 3 DOZEN

- 3 tablespoons plus 1 cup sugar, divided
- 1/8 teaspoon ground cinnamon
- 1/3 cup butter, softened
- 1 egg
- 1/4 cup fat-free milk
- 1/2 teaspoon almond extract
- 1/2 teaspoon vanilla extract
- 2 1/2 cups all-purpose flour
- 1/4 cup ground almonds
- 1/8 teaspoon salt
- 36 blanched almonds

**1.** In a small bowl, combine 3 tablespoons sugar and cinnamon; set aside.

**2.** In a large bowl, beat butter and remaining sugar until crumbly. Beat in the egg, milk and extracts. Combine the flour, ground almonds and salt; add to the creamed mixture and mix well. Cover and refrigerate for at least 1 hour.

**3.** Roll into 1-in. balls. Place 2 in. apart on ungreased baking sheets. Coat bottom of glass with cooking spray, then dip in cinnamon-sugar mixture. Flatten cookies with prepared glass, redipping in cinnamon-sugar mixture as needed. Top each cookie with a blanched almond.

**4.** Bake at 325° for 16-18 minutes or until lightly browned. Remove to wire racks.

**PER SERVING** *86 cal., 3 g fat (1 g sat. fat), 10 mg chol., 23 mg sodium, 14 g carb., trace fiber, 2 g pro.* **Diabetic Exchanges:** *1 starch, 1 fat.*

CRANBERRY OAT COOKIES

## Cranberry Oat Cookies FSCM

Dotted with sweet dried cranberries, these chewy oatmeal treats are perfect for fall and winter but can be made with just about any dried fruit.

—HEATHER BREEN CHICAGO, IL

**PREP:** 15 MIN. • **BAKE:** 10 MIN./BATCH
**MAKES:** 2 1/2 DOZEN

- 1/2 cup plus 2 tablespoons packed brown sugar
- 1/4 cup sugar
- 1/3 cup canola oil
- 1 egg
- 1 tablespoon fat-free milk
- 3/4 teaspoon vanilla extract
- 1 1/4 cups quick-cooking oats
- 3/4 cup plus 2 tablespoons all-purpose flour
- 1/2 teaspoon baking soda
- 1/2 teaspoon salt
- 1/2 cup dried cranberries

**1.** In a large bowl, combine sugars and oil until blended. Beat in egg, milk and vanilla. Combine the oats, flour, baking soda and salt; gradually add to sugar mixture and mix well. Stir in cranberries.

**2.** Drop by tablespoonfuls onto baking sheets coated with cooking spray. Bake at 375° for 10-12 minutes or until lightly browned. Remove to wire racks.

**PER SERVING** *79 cal., 3 g fat (trace sat. fat), 7 mg chol., 64 mg sodium, 13 g carb., 1 g fiber, 1 g pro.* **Diabetic Exchanges:** *1 starch, 1/2 fat.*

ALMOND CRISPIES

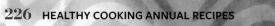

CINNAMON NUT BARS

## Cinnamon Nut Bars ⑤Ⓜ

Classic bar meets good-for-you ingredients in this updated recipe. If you have the patience, after the bars are cool, store them in a tin for a day to allow the flavors to meld. I think they taste even better the next day.

—**HEIDI LINDSEY** PRAIRIE DU SAC, WI

**PREP:** 20 MIN. • **BAKE:** 15 MIN. + COOLING
**MAKES:** 2 DOZEN

- ½ cup whole wheat flour
- ½ cup all-purpose flour
- ½ cup sugar
- 1½ teaspoons ground cinnamon
- 1¼ teaspoons baking powder
- ¼ teaspoon baking soda
- 1 egg, beaten
- ⅓ cup canola oil
- ¼ cup unsweetened applesauce
- ¼ cup honey
- 1 cup chopped walnuts

**ICING**

- 1 cup confectioners' sugar
- 2 tablespoons butter, melted
- 1 teaspoon vanilla extract
- 1 tablespoon water
- 2 tablespoons honey

**1.** In a large bowl, combine the flours, sugar, cinnamon, baking powder and baking soda. In another bowl, combine the egg, oil, applesauce and honey. Stir into dry ingredients just until moistened. Fold in walnuts.

**2.** Spread batter into a 13-in. x 9-in. baking pan coated with cooking spray. Bake at 350° for 15-20 minutes or until a toothpick inserted near the center comes out clean.

**3.** Combine icing ingredients; spread over warm bars. Cool completely before cutting.

**PER SERVING** *1 bar equals 142 cal., 7 g fat (1 g sat. fat), 11 mg chol., 44 mg sodium, 18 g carb., 1 g fiber, 2 g pro.* **Diabetic Exchanges:** *1 starch, 1 fat.*

 **Did you know?**

Even though they are easy to make at home, granola bars are a lucrative part of the prepared-food industry. In 2012 the best-selling granola bar, Nature Valley, recorded more than $385 million in sales.

## White Chip Cranberry Granola Bars ⑤Ⓜ

Tasty and nutritious, these chewy, high-energy snack bars are great for road trips, lunch boxes, late-night snacks or getting college kids through exams and into the Christmas spirit!

—**JANIS LOOMIS** MADISON, VA

**PREP:** 25 MIN. • **BAKE:** 20 MIN. + COOLING
**MAKES:** 2 DOZEN

- ¼ cup maple syrup
- ¼ cup honey
- ¼ cup packed brown sugar
- 2 tablespoons peanut butter
- 1 egg white
- 1 tablespoon evaporated milk
- 1 teaspoon vanilla extract
- 1 cup whole wheat flour
- ½ teaspoon baking soda
- ½ teaspoon ground cinnamon
- 2 cups old-fashioned oats
- 1½ cups crisp rice cereal
- ½ cup vanilla or white chips
- ½ cup dried cranberries
- ¼ cup chopped walnuts

**1.** In a large bowl, combine the maple syrup, honey, brown sugar, peanut butter, egg white, evaporated milk and vanilla; beat until smooth. Combine the flour, baking soda and cinnamon; stir into maple syrup mixture. Fold in the oats, cereal, vanilla chips, cranberries and walnuts.

**2.** Press into a greased 13-in. x 9-in. baking pan. Bake at 350° for 18-20 minutes or until golden brown. Cool on a wire rack. Cut into bars. Store in an airtight container.

**PER SERVING** *140 cal., 4 g fat (2 g sat. fat), 2 mg chol., 59 mg sodium, 24 g carb., 2 g fiber, 3 g pro.* **Diabetic Exchanges:** *1½ starch, ½ fat.*

WHITE CHIP CRANBERRY GRANOLA BARS

GINGERSNAP CREAM
COOKIE CUPS

## Gingersnap Cream Cookie Cups S C M

Whole wheat flour gives a rustic look to these little tassies that are big on flavor. The velvety, rich filling is a delectable contrast to the cookie cup.

**—REBEKAH RADEWAHN** WAUWATOSA, WI

**PREP:** 35 MIN. • **BAKE:** 10 MIN./BATCH • **MAKES:** 2½ DOZEN

- 1½ cups all-purpose flour
- ½ cup whole wheat flour
- ⅓ cup sugar
- 1½ teaspoons ground ginger
- 1 teaspoon baking soda
- 1 teaspoon ground cinnamon
- ½ teaspoon salt
- 1 egg
- ¼ cup canola oil
- ¼ cup unsweetened applesauce
- ¼ cup molasses

**FILLING**

- 4 ounces reduced-fat cream cheese
- ½ cup confectioners' sugar
- ¾ teaspoon vanilla extract
- ½ cup heavy whipping cream, whipped

**1.** In a large bowl, combine the flours, sugar, ginger, baking soda, cinnamon and salt. In another bowl, combine the egg, oil, applesauce and molasses; add to dry ingredients. Stir until dough forms a ball. Roll into 1-in. balls. Press onto the bottoms and up the sides of miniature muffin cups greased with cooking spray.

**2.** Bake at 350° for 10-12 minutes or until golden brown. Cool for 5 minutes before removing from pans to wire racks to cool completely.

**3.** For filling, in a small bowl, beat the cream cheese, confectioners' sugar and vanilla until smooth; fold in whipped cream. Spoon 2 teaspoons into each cup.

**PER SERVING** *97 cal., 4 g fat (2 g sat. fat), 15 mg chol., 102 mg sodium, 13 g carb., trace fiber, 2 g pro.* **Diabetic Exchanges:** *1 starch, ½ fat.*

## Chewy Honey Granola Bars S M

There's sweetness from the honey, chewiness from the raisins, a hint of cinnamon and a bit of crunch in these granola bars. To save a few for later, wrap individual bars in plastic wrap and place in a resealable freezer bag. When you want a satisfying treat on short notice, just grab one and let it thaw for a few minutes.

**—TASHA LEHMAN** WILLISTON, VT

**PREP:** 10 MIN. • **BAKE:** 15 MIN. + COOLING • **MAKES:** 20 SERVINGS

- 3 cups old-fashioned oats
- 2 cups unsweetened puffed wheat cereal
- 1 cup all-purpose flour
- ⅓ cup chopped walnuts
- ⅓ cup raisins
- ⅓ cup miniature semisweet chocolate chips
- 1 teaspoon baking soda
- 1 teaspoon ground cinnamon
- 1 cup honey
- ¼ cup butter, melted
- 1 teaspoon vanilla extract

**1.** In a large bowl, combine the first eight ingredients. In a small bowl, combine the honey, butter and vanilla; pour over oat mixture and mix well. (Batter will be sticky.)

**2.** Press into a 13-in. x 9-in. baking pan coated with cooking spray. Bake at 350° for 14-18 minutes or until set and edges are lightly browned. Cool on a wire rack. Cut into bars.

**PER SERVING** *178 cal., 5 g fat (2 g sat. fat), 6 mg chol., 81 mg sodium, 32 g carb., 2 g fiber, 3 g pro.* **Diabetic Exchanges:** *2 starch, ½ fat.*

CHEWY HONEY GRANOLA BARS

APPLESAUCE BROWNIES

## Rhubarb Oat Bars S M

These soft rhubarb bars provide just the right amount of tartness and sweetness. They are simply unbeatable!

—**RENETTE CRESSEY** FORT MILL, SC

**PREP:** 20 MIN. • **BAKE:** 25 MIN. + COOLING • **MAKES:** 16 BARS

- 1½ cups chopped fresh or frozen rhubarb
- 1 cup packed brown sugar, divided
- 4 tablespoons water, divided
- 1 teaspoon lemon juice
- 4 teaspoons cornstarch
- 1 cup old-fashioned oats
- ¾ cup all-purpose flour
- ½ cup flaked coconut
- ½ teaspoon salt
- ⅓ cup butter, melted

**1.** In a large saucepan, combine the rhubarb, ½ cup brown sugar, 3 tablespoons water and lemon juice. Bring to a boil. Reduce heat to medium; cook and stir for 4-5 minutes or until rhubarb is tender.
**2.** Combine the cornstarch and remaining water until smooth; gradually stir into rhubarb mixture. Bring to a boil; cook and stir for 2 minutes or until thickened. Remove from the heat; set aside.
**3.** In a large bowl, combine the oats, flour, coconut, salt and remaining brown sugar. Stir in butter until mixture is crumbly.
**4.** Press half of the mixture into a greased 8-in. square baking dish. Spread with rhubarb mixture. Sprinkle with remaining oat mixture and press down lightly.
**5.** Bake at 350° for 25-30 minutes or until golden brown. Cool on a wire rack. Cut into squares.
**NOTE** *If using frozen rhubarb, measure rhubarb while still frozen, then thaw completely. Drain in a colander, but do not press liquid out.*
**PER SERVING** *145 cal., 5 g fat (3 g sat. fat), 10 mg chol., 126 mg sodium, 24 g carb., 1 g fiber, 2 g pro.* **Diabetic Exchanges:** *1½ starch, 1 fat.*

## Applesauce Brownies S M

Cinnamon-flavored brownies are a cinch to make, even from scratch. If you're making them for a crowd, this recipe can be doubled and baked in a jelly-roll pan.

—**BERNICE PEBLEY** COZAD, NE

**PREP:** 15 MIN. • **BAKE:** 25 MIN. + COOLING • **MAKES:** 16 BROWNIES

- ¼ cup butter, softened
- ¾ cup sugar
- 1 egg
- 1 cup all-purpose flour
- 1 tablespoon baking cocoa
- ½ teaspoon baking soda
- ½ teaspoon ground cinnamon
- 1 cup applesauce

**TOPPING**
- ½ cup chocolate chips
- ½ cup chopped walnuts or pecans
- 1 tablespoon sugar

**1.** In a large bowl, cream butter and sugar. Beat in egg. Combine the flour, cocoa, baking soda and cinnamon; gradually add to creamed mixture and mix well. Stir in applesauce. Pour into an 8-in. square baking pan coated with cooking spray.
**2.** Combine topping ingredients; sprinkle over batter. Bake at 350° for 25 minutes or until toothpick inserted near the center comes out clean. Cool on a wire rack. Cut into squares.
**PER SERVING** *154 cal., 7 g fat (3 g sat. fat), 21 mg chol., 65 mg sodium, 22 g carb., 1 g fiber, 2 g pro.* **Diabetic Exchanges:** *1½ starch, 1½ fat.*

RHUBARB OAT BARS

## Chocolate Amaretti F S M

With a touch of almond, these chewy treats are similar to those sold in Italian bakeries. My husband and children are always excited when I include these in my holiday baking lineup.

—**KATHY LONG** WHITEFISH BAY, WI

**PREP:** 15 MIN. • **BAKE:** 20 MIN./BATCH
**MAKES:** 3 DOZEN

- 1¼ **cups almond paste**
- ¾ **cup sugar**
- 2 **egg whites**
- ½ **cup confectioners' sugar**
- ¼ **cup baking cocoa**

**1.** In a large bowl, beat the almond paste, sugar and egg whites until combined. Combine confectioners' sugar and cocoa; gradually add to almond mixture and mix well.

**2.** Drop by tablespoonfuls 2 in. apart onto parchment paper-lined baking sheets. Bake at 350° for 17-20 minutes or until tops are cracked. Cool for 1 minute before removing from pans to wire racks. Store in an airtight container.

**PER SERVING** *69 cal., 3 g fat (trace sat. fat), 0 chol., 4 mg sodium, 11 g carb., 1 g fiber, 1 g pro.* **Diabetic Exchanges:** *1 starch, ½ fat.*

CHOCOLATE AMARETTI

ALMOND ESPRESSO BARS

## Almond Espresso Bars F S C M

If you like coffee, you'll love these mocha morsels dressed up with toasted almonds. Save a few bars for afternoon snack time or even breakfast, too.

—**TAIRE VAN SCOY** BRUNSWICK, MD

**PREP:** 15 MIN. • **BAKE:** 20 MIN. + COOLING
**MAKES:** 4 DOZEN

- ¼ **cup butter, softened**
- 1 **cup packed brown sugar**
- ½ **cup brewed espresso**
- 1 **egg**
- 1½ **cups self-rising flour**
- ½ **teaspoon ground cinnamon**
- ¾ **cup chopped slivered almonds, toasted**

**GLAZE**

- 1½ **cups confectioners' sugar**
- 3 **tablespoons water**
- ¾ **teaspoon almond extract**
- ¼ **cup slivered almonds, toasted**

**1.** In a large bowl, cream the butter, brown sugar and espresso until blended. Beat in egg. Combine flour and cinnamon; gradually add to creamed mixture and mix well. Stir in chopped almonds.

**2.** Spread into a greased 15-in. x 10-in. x 1-in. baking pan. Bake at 350° for 18-22 minutes or until lightly browned.

**3.** In a small bowl, combine the confectioners' sugar, water and extract until smooth; spread over warm bars. Sprinkle with slivered almonds. Cool on a wire rack. Cut into bars.

**NOTE** *As a substitute for 1½ cups self-rising flour, place 2¼ teaspoons baking powder and ¾ teaspoon salt in a measuring cup. Add all-purpose flour to measure 1 cup. Combine with an additional ½ cup all-purpose flour.*

**PER SERVING** *68 cal., 2 g fat (1 g sat. fat), 7 mg chol., 55 mg sodium, 11 g carb., trace fiber, 1 g pro.* **Diabetic Exchanges:** *1 starch, ½ fat.*

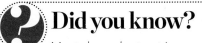 **Did you know?**

Most almond extract is not made from almonds. Often the almond flavor comes from benzaldehyde extracted from stone fruits such as peaches and apricots.

## Swirled Pumpkin Cheesecake Bars S C M

**PREP:** 30 MIN. • **BAKE:** 20 MIN. + CHILLING
**MAKES:** 16 SERVINGS

- 1 cup graham cracker crumbs
- 2 tablespoons sugar
- 2 tablespoons reduced-fat butter, melted

**FILLING**

- 11 ounces reduced-fat cream cheese
- ⅓ cup reduced-fat sour cream
- ⅓ cup sugar
- 2 teaspoons all-purpose flour
- ½ teaspoon vanilla extract
- 1 egg, lightly beaten
- ½ cup canned pumpkin
- 1 tablespoon brown sugar

**1.** In a small bowl, combine cracker crumbs and sugar; stir in butter. Press onto the bottom of a 9-in. square baking dish coated with cooking spray.

Bake at 325° for 7-10 minutes or until set. Cool on a wire rack.

**2.** For filling, in a large bowl, beat the cream cheese, sour cream, sugar, flour and vanilla until smooth. Add egg; beat on low just until combined. Remove ¾ cup batter to a small bowl; stir in pumpkin and brown sugar until well blended.

**3.** Pour plain batter over crust. Drop pumpkin batter by tablespoonfuls over plain batter. Cut through batter with a knife to swirl. Bake at 325° for 20-25 minutes or until center is almost set. Cool on a wire rack for 1 hour. Cover and refrigerate for at least 2 hours. Refrigerate leftovers.

**NOTE** *This recipe was tested with Land O'Lakes light stick butter.*

**PER SERVING** *117 cal., 6 g fat (4 g sat. fat), 31 mg chol., 135 mg sodium, 13 g carb., trace fiber, 3 g pro.* **Diabetic Exchanges:** *1 starch, 1 fat.*

ALMOND BLONDIES

SWIRLED PUMPKIN CHEESECAKE BARS

"Enjoy this holiday dessert without worrying about calories. Plus it is so luscious that no one will guess that it is light!"
—**JEAN ECOS** HARTLAND, WI

## Almond Blondies S M

Here's a sweet change from the typical chocolate brownie. When I bake up a batch, they never last long at my house.
—**CINDY PRUITT** GROVE, OK

**PREP:** 15 MIN. • **BAKE:** 25 MIN. + COOLING
**MAKES:** 16 SERVINGS

- 2 eggs
- ½ cup sugar
- ½ cup packed brown sugar
- ⅓ cup butter, melted
- 1 teaspoon vanilla extract
- ¼ teaspoon almond extract
- 1⅓ cups all-purpose flour
- ½ teaspoon baking powder
- ¼ teaspoon salt
- ¼ cup chopped almonds

**1.** In a large bowl, beat the eggs, sugar and brown sugar for 3 minutes. Add butter and extracts; mix well. Combine the flour, baking powder and salt. Gradually add to the creamed mixture, beating just until blended. Fold in almonds.

**2.** Pour into an 8-in. square baking pan coated with cooking spray. Bake at 350° for 25-30 minutes or until a toothpick inserted near the center comes out clean. Cool on a wire rack. Cut into squares.

**PER SERVING** *143 cal., 6 g fat (3 g sat. fat), 36 mg chol., 88 mg sodium, 21 g carb., 1 g fiber, 2 g pro.* **Diabetic Exchanges:** *1½ starch, 1 fat.*

235

241

242

# Cakes & Pies

❝Old-fashioned flavor comes through with the molasses, cinnamon, cloves and nutmeg in these light, fluffy cupcakes. The mocha frosting is a fresh touch that makes them extra special.❞

**—SARAH VAUGHAN** WATERVILLE, ME
*about her recipe, Spice Cupcakes with Mocha Frosting, on page 236*

STRAWBERRY MARBLE CAKE

## Strawberry Marble Cake F M

Perfect for special occasions, this strawberry swirl cake makes a pretty presentation. Besides serving it as a dessert at dinners, I've served it with afternoon tea. It's also been snapped up in minutes at bake sales.

—**MARGERY RICHMOND** FORT COLLINS, CO

**PREP:** 30 MIN. • **BAKE:** 45 MIN. + COOLING
**MAKES:** 12 SERVINGS

- 1½ cups egg whites (about 10)
- 1 package (10 ounces) frozen unsweetened strawberries, thawed and drained
- 1½ cups sugar, divided
- 1¼ cups cake flour
- 1½ teaspoons cream of tartar
- ½ teaspoon salt
- 1 teaspoon vanilla extract
- 1 teaspoon almond extract
  Red food coloring, optional
  Whipped topping and sliced fresh strawberries, optional

**1.** Let egg whites stand at room temperature for 30 minutes. In a food processor, puree strawberries; strain puree and discard seeds. Set aside.
**2.** Sift together ¾ cup sugar and the flour twice; set aside. Add cream of tartar and salt to egg whites; beat on medium speed until soft peaks form. Gradually beat in remaining sugar, 2 tablespoons at a time, on high until stiff glossy peaks form and sugar is dissolved. Gradually fold in flour mixture, about ½ cup at a time.
**3.** Transfer half of the batter to another bowl; fold in extracts. Fold ¼ cup strawberry puree into remaining batter; add food coloring if desired.
**4.** Gently spoon batters, alternating colors, into an ungreased 10-in. tube pan. Cut through with a knife to swirl. Bake on the lowest oven rack at 350° for 45-50 minutes or until lightly browned and top appears dry. Immediately invert pan; cool completely, about 1 hour.
**5.** Run a knife around side and center tube of pan. Serve cake with remaining puree; garnish with whipped topping and fresh strawberries if desired.
**PER SERVING** *176 cal., trace fat (trace sat. fat), 0 chol., 150 mg sodium, 39 g carb., 1 g fiber, 5 g pro.*

## Lemon Angel Cake Roll F S M

Tart and delicious, this pretty cake roll will tickle any lemon lover's fancy. Its feathery angel food texture is complemented with a lovely lemon filling and a dusting of sweet confectioners' sugar.

—**TASTE OF HOME TEST KITCHEN**

**PREP:** 30 MIN. • **BAKE:** 15 MIN. + COOLING
**MAKES:** 10 SERVINGS

- 9 egg whites
- 1½ teaspoons vanilla extract
- ¾ teaspoon cream of tartar
- 1 cup plus 2 tablespoons sugar
- ¾ cup cake flour
- 1 tablespoon confectioners' sugar

**FILLING**

- 1 cup sugar
- 3 tablespoons cornstarch
- 1 cup water
- 1 egg, lightly beaten
- ¼ cup lemon juice
- 1 tablespoon grated lemon peel
  Yellow food coloring, optional
  Additional confectioners' sugar

**1.** Place the egg whites in a large bowl; let stand at room temperature for 30 minutes. Meanwhile, line a 15-in. x 10-in. x 1-in. baking pan with waxed paper; lightly coat paper with cooking spray and set aside.
**2.** Preheat oven to 350°. Add vanilla and cream of tartar to egg whites; beat on medium speed until soft peaks form. Gradually beat in sugar, 2 tablespoons at a time, on high until stiff glossy peaks form and sugar is dissolved. Fold in flour, about ¼ cup at a time.
**3.** Carefully spread batter into prepared pan. Bake 15-20 minutes or until cake springs back when lightly touched. Cool 5 minutes.
**4.** Turn cake onto a kitchen towel dusted with 1 tablespoon confectioners' sugar. Gently peel off waxed paper. Roll up cake in the towel jelly-roll style, starting with a short side. Cool completely on a wire rack.
**5.** In a large saucepan, combine sugar and cornstarch; stir in water until smooth. Cook and stir over medium-high heat until thickened and bubbly. Reduce heat; cook and stir 2 minutes. Remove from heat. Stir a small amount of hot mixture into egg; return all to the pan, stirring constantly. Bring to a gentle boil; cook and stir 2 minutes.
**6.** Remove from heat. Gently stir in lemon juice, peel and food coloring if desired. Cool to room temperature without stirring.
**7.** Unroll cake; spread filling to within ½ in. of edges. Roll up again. Place seam side down on a serving plate; sprinkle with additional confectioners' sugar.
**PER SERVING** *243 cal., 1 g fat (trace sat. fat), 21 mg chol., 57 mg sodium, 55 g carb., trace fiber, 5 g pro.*

## Triple Chocolate Dream Pie Ⓜ

Creamy chocolate pie makes for an indulgent dessert, and my light version is every bit as good as the original. Sometimes I add a teaspoon of instant coffee granules to the sugar-cocoa mixture for a mocha pie.

—MARY ANN RING BLUFFTON, OH

**PREP:** 30 MIN. + CHILLING
**MAKES:** 8 SERVINGS

- 1½ cups graham cracker crumbs
- 2 tablespoons butter, melted
- 1 egg white

**FILLING**

- ⅔ cup sugar
- ⅓ cup baking cocoa
- 3 tablespoons cornstarch
- ⅛ teaspoon salt
- 2 cups fat-free milk
- 1 egg, beaten
- ¼ cup semisweet chocolate chips
- 1 teaspoon vanilla extract

**TOPPING**

- 1½ cups reduced-fat whipped topping
- 1 teaspoon grated chocolate

**1.** Combine the graham cracker crumbs, butter and egg white; press onto the bottom and up the sides of a greased 9-in. pie plate. Bake at 375° for 6-8 minutes or until lightly browned. Cool on a wire rack.

**2.** For filling, in a large saucepan, combine the sugar, cocoa, cornstarch and salt. Stir in milk until smooth. Cook and stir over medium-high heat until thickened and bubbly. Reduce heat to low; cook and stir 2 minutes longer.

**3.** Remove from the heat. Stir a small amount of hot mixture into egg; return all to the pan, stirring constantly. Bring to a gentle boil; cook and stir for 2 minutes. Remove from the heat; stir in chocolate chips and vanilla.

**4.** Pour into crust. Refrigerate for at least 2 hours or until firm. Spread whipped topping over filling; sprinkle with grated chocolate.

**PER SERVING** *268 cal., 9 g fat (5 g sat. fat), 35 mg chol., 195 mg sodium, 45 g carb., 2 g fiber, 5 g pro.*

FRESH BLUEBERRY PIE

## Fresh Blueberry Pie Ⓜ

We live in blueberry country, and this pie is a perfect way to showcase the luscious berries. A neighbor made this pie for us when we had a death in the family several years ago, and she shared the recipe, too. Our whole family enjoys it.

—R. RICKS KALAMAZOO, MI

**PREP:** 20 MIN. + CHILLING
**MAKES:** 8 SERVINGS

- ¾ cup sugar
- 3 tablespoons cornstarch
- ⅛ teaspoon salt
- ¼ cup water
- 4 cups fresh blueberries, divided
- 1 graham cracker crust (9 inches)
  Whipped cream

**1.** In a large saucepan, combine the sugar, cornstarch and salt. Gradually add water, stirring until smooth. Stir in 2 cups of blueberries. Bring to a boil; cook and stir for 1-2 minutes or until thickened. Remove from the heat; cool to room temperature.

**2.** Spoon remaining blueberries into the crust; top with cooled blueberry mixture. Cover and refrigerate for 1-2 hours or until chilled. Serve with whipped cream.

**PER SERVING** *230 cal., 6 g fat (1 g sat. fat), 0 chol., 159 mg sodium, 46 g carb., 2 g fiber, 1 g pro.*

TRIPLE CHOCOLATE DREAM PIE

## Spice Cupcakes with Mocha Frosting Ⓜ

Old-fashioned flavor comes through with the molasses, cinnamon, cloves and nutmeg in these light, fluffy cupcakes. The mocha frosting is a fresh touch that makes them extra special.

—SARAH VAUGHAN WATERVILLE, ME

**PREP:** 30 MIN. • **BAKE:** 20 MIN. + COOLING • **MAKES:** 15 CUPCAKES

- ½ **cup butter, softened**
- ½ **cup sugar**
- 1 **egg**
- ½ **cup molasses**
- 1½ **cups all-purpose flour**
- ½ **teaspoon baking soda**
- ¼ **teaspoon salt**
- ¼ **teaspoon each ground cinnamon, cloves and nutmeg**
- ½ **cup buttermilk**

**FROSTING**

- 1¾ **cups confectioners' sugar**
- 1 **tablespoon baking cocoa**
- 2 **tablespoons strong brewed coffee**
- 1 **tablespoon butter, softened**
- ¼ **teaspoon vanilla extract**
  **Chocolate-covered coffee beans and assorted candies, optional**

**1.** In a large bowl, cream butter and sugar until light and fluffy. Beat in egg and molasses. Combine the flour, baking soda, salt, cinnamon, cloves and nutmeg; add to creamed mixture alternately with buttermilk.

**2.** Fill paper-lined muffin cups two-thirds full. Bake at 350° for 20-25 minutes or until a toothpick inserted near the center comes out clean. Cool for 10 minutes before removing from pans to wire racks to cool completely.

**3.** In a small bowl, combine confectioners' sugar and cocoa. Stir in the coffee, butter and vanilla until smooth. Frost cupcakes. Garnish with coffee beans and candies if desired.

**NOTE** *Warmed buttermilk will appear curdled.*

**PER SERVING** *227 cal., 7 g fat (4 g sat. fat), 32 mg chol., 147 mg sodium, 39 g carb., trace fiber, 2 g pro.*

LEMON-BERRY SHORTCAKE

"Bake a simple cake using fresh strawberries and enjoy this summertime classic with a generous layer of whipped topping and berries." —MERYL HERR GRAND RAPIDS, MI

## Lemon-Berry Shortcake Ⓜ

**PREP:** 30 MIN. • **BAKE:** 20 MIN. + COOLING • **MAKES:** 8 SERVINGS

- 1⅓ **cups all-purpose flour**
- ½ **cup sugar**
- 2 **teaspoons baking powder**
- ¼ **teaspoon salt**
- 1 **egg**
- ⅔ **cup buttermilk**
- ¼ **cup butter, melted**
- 1 **tablespoon lemon juice**
- 1 **teaspoon grated lemon peel**
- 1 **teaspoon vanilla extract**
- 1 **cup sliced fresh strawberries**

**TOPPING**

- 1½ **cups sliced fresh strawberries**
- 1 **tablespoon lemon juice**
- 1 **teaspoon sugar**
- 2 **cups reduced-fat whipped topping**

**1.** In a large bowl, combine the flour, sugar, baking powder and salt. In another bowl, combine the egg, buttermilk, butter, lemon juice, lemon peel and vanilla. Stir into dry ingredients just until moistened. Fold in strawberries. Pour into a greased and floured 9-in. round baking pan.

**2.** Bake at 350° for 20-25 minutes or until a toothpick inserted near the center comes out clean. Cool for 10 minutes before removing from pan to a wire rack to cool completely.

**3.** For topping, in a large bowl, combine the strawberries, lemon juice and sugar. Cover and refrigerate until serving. Spread whipped topping over cake. Drain strawberries; arrange over top.

**PER SERVING** *252 cal., 9 g fat (6 g sat. fat), 42 mg chol., 245 mg sodium, 40 g carb., 2 g fiber, 4 g pro.*

SPICE CUPCAKES WITH MOCHA FROSTING

## Apple Butter Cake Roll M

This spicy gingerbread cake is a new take on a classic pumpkin roll. It might make you think back fondly to your grandma's Christmas cookies.

—**DEBBIE WHITE** WILLIAMSON, WV

**PREP:** 35 MIN. • **BAKE:** 15 MIN. + CHILLING
**MAKES:** 10 SERVINGS

- 3 **eggs, separated**
- 1 **cup all-purpose flour, divided**
- 2 **tablespoons plus ½ cup sugar, divided**
- 2 **teaspoons ground cinnamon**
- 1 **teaspoon baking powder**
- 1 **teaspoon ground ginger**
- 1 **teaspoon ground cloves**
- ¼ **teaspoon baking soda**
- ¼ **cup butter, melted**
- ¼ **cup molasses**
- 2 **tablespoons water**
- 1 **tablespoon confectioners' sugar**
- 2 **cups apple butter**

**1.** Place egg whites in a small bowl; let stand at room temperature for 30 minutes. Line a greased 15-in. x 10-in. x 1-in. baking pan with waxed paper and grease the paper. Sprinkle with 1 tablespoon flour and 2 tablespoons sugar; set aside.
**2.** In a large bowl, combine remaining flour and sugar; add the cinnamon, baking powder, ginger, cloves and baking soda. In another bowl, whisk the egg yolks, butter, molasses and water. Add to dry ingredients and beat until blended. Beat egg whites on medium speed until soft peaks form; fold into batter. Pour into prepared pan.
**3.** Bake at 375° for 12-14 minutes or until cake springs back when lightly touched. Cool for 5 minutes. Turn cake onto a kitchen towel dusted with confectioners' sugar. Gently peel off waxed paper. Roll up cake in the towel jelly-roll style, starting with a short side. Cool completely on a wire rack.

APPLE BUTTER CAKE ROLL

FRESH PEAR CAKE

**4.** Unroll cake; spread apple butter to within ½ in. of edges. Roll up again. Cover and chill for 1 hour before serving. Refrigerate leftovers.
**NOTE** *This recipe was tested with commercially prepared apple butter.*
**PER SERVING** *283 cal., 6 g fat (3 g sat. fat), 76 mg chol., 143 mg sodium, 54 g carb., 2 g fiber, 3 g pro.*

## Fresh Pear Cake M

Old-fashioned pear spice cake is a wonderful ending to any meal. This light treat is brimming with fresh fruit flavors, but it's not too heavy or too rich.

—**AUDREY GOLDEN** CARY, NC

**PREP:** 25 MIN. • **BAKE:** 45 MIN. + COOLING • **MAKES:** 16 SERVINGS

- 1½ **cups sugar**
- ¾ **cup (6 ounces) fat-free plain yogurt**
- ½ **cup canola oil**
- 4 **egg whites**
- 1 **egg**
- 3 **cups all-purpose flour**
- 1½ **teaspoons baking soda**
- 1½ **teaspoons ground cinnamon**
- 1 **teaspoon salt**
- ½ **teaspoon ground nutmeg**
- ½ **teaspoon ground cloves**
- 2 **cups chopped peeled fresh pears**
- ⅓ **cup chopped pecans**
- 1 **teaspoon confectioners' sugar**

**1.** Coat a 10-in. fluted tube pan with cooking spray and sprinkle with flour. In a large bowl, beat the sugar, yogurt, oil, egg whites and egg until well blended. Combine the flour, baking soda, cinnamon, salt, nutmeg and cloves; gradually beat into yogurt mixture until blended. Stir in pears and pecans.
**2.** Transfer to prepared pan. Bake at 350° for 45-55 minutes or until a toothpick inserted near the center comes out clean. Cool for 10 minutes before removing from pan to a wire rack to cool completely. Dust with confectioner's sugar.
**PER SERVING** *264 cal., 9 g fat (1 g sat. fat), 13 mg chol., 291 mg sodium, 42 g carb., 2 g fiber, 5 g pro.*

## Marmalade Pudding Cakes S M

For a light and elegant dessert, serve guests these cute custard treats. The fluffy cakes are accented with orange peel and glazed with marmalade sauce.

—**MARIAN PLATT** SEQUIM, WA

**PREP:** 20 MIN. • **BAKE:** 25 MIN.
**MAKES:** 8 SERVINGS

- 2 **tablespoons butter, softened**
- ¾ **cup sugar, divided**
- ¼ **cup all-purpose flour**
- 4 **eggs, separated**
- 1 **cup 2% milk**
- ¼ **cup orange juice**
- ¼ **cup lemon juice, divided**
- 1½ **teaspoons grated orange peel**
- ⅓ **cup orange marmalade, warmed**

**1.** In a small bowl, beat butter and ½ cup sugar until crumbly. Beat in flour and egg yolks until smooth. Gradually beat in milk, orange juice, 2 tablespoons lemon juice and orange peel.
**2.** In another small bowl, beat egg whites on high speed until soft peaks form. Add the remaining sugar; beat until stiff peaks form. Gently fold into orange mixture.
**3.** Pour into eight 6-oz. custard cups thoroughly coated with cooking spray.

Place the cups in two 13-in. x 9-in. baking pans; add 1 in. of boiling water to pans.
**4.** Bake at 325° for 25-30 minutes or until a knife inserted near the center comes out clean and tops are golden brown. Run a knife around the edges; carefully invert cakes onto dessert plates.
**5.** Combine marmalade and remaining lemon juice; drizzle over warm cakes.
**PER SERVING** 201 cal., 6 g fat (3 g sat. fat), 116 mg chol., 78 mg sodium, 34 g carb., trace fiber, 5 g pro. **Diabetic Exchanges:** 2 starch, 1 fat.

## Cranberry Cake Roll F S M

This low-fat angel food cake roll is a guilt-free indulgence that is much-appreciated during the Christmas season.

—**PAIGE KOWOLEWSKI** TOPTON, PA

**PREP:** 45 MIN. + CHILLING
**BAKE:** 15 MIN. + COOLING
**MAKES:** 12 SERVINGS

- 9 **egg whites**
- 1½ **teaspoons vanilla extract**
- ¾ **teaspoon cream of tartar**
- ¼ **teaspoon salt**
- 1 **cup plus 2 tablespoons sugar**
- ¾ **cup cake flour**

**FILLING**

- 2⅓ **cups fresh or frozen cranberries**
- 1 **cup sugar**
- 6 **tablespoons water, divided**
- 2 **tablespoons cornstarch**

**1.** Place egg whites in a large bowl; let stand at room temperature for 30 minutes. Meanwhile, line a greased 15-in. x 10-in. x 1-in. baking pan with waxed paper; grease the paper and set aside.
**2.** Add vanilla, cream of tartar and salt to egg whites; beat on medium speed until soft peaks form. Gradually beat in sugar, 2 tablespoons at a time, on high until stiff glossy peaks form and sugar is dissolved. Fold in flour, about ¼ cup at a time.
**3.** Carefully spread into prepared pan. Bake at 350° for 15-20 minutes or until cake springs back when lightly touched. Cool for 5 minutes. Turn cake onto a kitchen towel dusted with confectioners' sugar. Gently peel off waxed paper. Roll up cake in the towel jelly-roll style, starting with a long side. Cool completely on a wire rack.
**4.** For filling, in a large saucepan, combine the cranberries, sugar and ¼ cup water. Bring to a boil. Reduce heat; simmer, uncovered, for 5-6 minutes or until berries pop. Mash berries; strain, reserving juice and discarding pulp. Return juice to the pan. Combine cornstarch and remaining water until smooth; gradually add to cranberry juice. Bring to a boil; cook and stir for 2 minutes or until thickened. Chill.
**5.** Unroll cake and spread filling to within ½ in. of edges. Roll up again. Cover and refrigerate for 1 hour before serving. Refrigerate leftovers.
**PER SERVING** 196 cal., trace fat (trace sat. fat), 0 chol., 91 mg sodium, 46 g carb., 1 g fiber, 3 g pro.

MARMALADE PUDDING CAKES

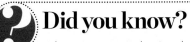

## Did you know?

When it comes to having the most disease-fighting antioxidants, cranberries beat out strawberries, red grapes, raspberries and nearly every other fruit.

CRANBERRY CAKE ROLL

FRESH PUMPKIN PIE

## Fresh Pumpkin Pie M

In my opinion, there's no contest as to which pie is best. No matter how good your canned pumpkin is, it will never match fresh pie filling made with traditional spices.

—**CHRISTY HARP** MASSILLON, OH

**PREP:** 30 MIN. • **BAKE:** 55 MIN. + COOLING
**MAKES:** 8 SERVINGS

- 1 **medium pie pumpkin**
  **Pastry for single-crust pie (9 inches)**
- 2 **eggs**
- ¾ **cup packed brown sugar**
- 1 **teaspoon ground cinnamon**
- ½ **teaspoon salt**
- ½ **teaspoon ground ginger**
- ¼ **teaspoon ground cloves**
- 1 **cup 2% milk**

**1.** Cut pumpkin in half lengthwise; discard seeds. Place cut side down in a microwave-safe dish; add 1 in. of water. Cover and microwave on high for 15-18 minutes or until very tender.
**2.** Meanwhile, roll out pastry to fit a 9-in. pie plate. Transfer pastry to pie plate. Trim pastry to ½ in. beyond edge of plate; flute edges. Set aside.
**3.** Drain pumpkin. When cool enough to handle, scoop out pulp and mash. Set aside 1¾ cups (save remaining pumpkin for another use).

**4.** In large bowl, combine the mashed pumpkin, eggs, brown sugar, cinnamon, salt, ginger and cloves; beat until smooth. Gradually beat in milk. Pour into crust.
**5.** Bake at 425° for 15 minutes. Reduce heat to 350°; bake 40-45 minutes longer or until a knife inserted near the center comes out clean. Cover edges with foil during the last 30 minutes to prevent overbrowning if necessary. Cool on a wire rack. Refrigerate leftovers.
**PER SERVING** *239 cal., 9 g fat (4 g sat. fat), 60 mg chol., 289 mg sodium, 37 g carb., trace fiber, 4 g pro.*

## Orange Dream Angel Food Cake F S M

A basic angel food cake becomes a heavenly indulgence thanks to a hint of orange flavor swirled into every bite.

—**LAUREN OSBORNE** HOLTWOOD, PA

**PREP:** 25 MIN. • **BAKE:** 30 MIN. + COOLING
**MAKES:** 16 SERVINGS

- 12 **egg whites**
- 1 **cup all-purpose flour**
- 1¾ **cups sugar, divided**
- 1½ **teaspoons cream of tartar**
- ½ **teaspoon salt**
- 1 **teaspoon almond extract**
- 1 **teaspoon vanilla extract**
- 1 **teaspoon grated orange peel**

- 1 **teaspoon orange extract**
- 6 **drops red food coloring, optional**
- 6 **drops yellow food coloring, optional**

**1.** Place egg whites in a large bowl; let stand at room temperature for 30 minutes. Sift flour and ¾ cup sugar together twice; set aside.
**2.** Add the cream of tartar, salt and almond and vanilla extracts to egg whites; beat on medium speed until soft peaks form. Gradually add remaining sugar, about 2 tablespoons at a time, beating on high until stiff glossy peaks form and sugar is dissolved. Gradually fold in flour mixture, about ½ cup at a time.
**3.** Gently spoon half of batter into an ungreased 10-in. tube pan. To the remaining batter, stir in the orange peel, orange extract and food colorings if desired. Gently spoon orange batter over white batter. Cut through both layers with a knife to swirl the orange and remove air pockets.
**4.** Bake on the lowest oven rack at 375° for 30-35 minutes or until lightly browned and entire top appears dry. Immediately invert pan; cool completely, about 1 hour.
**5.** Run a knife around side and center tube of pan. Remove cake to a serving plate.
**PER SERVING** *130 cal., trace fat (trace sat. fat), 0 chol., 116 mg sodium, 28 g carb., trace fiber, 4 g pro. **Diabetic Exchange:** 2 starch.*

ORANGE DREAM ANGEL FOOD CAKE

> "This pie is a rite of spring at our house, and many people have enjoyed sharing it with us. We love that it's both sweet and tart, with a mild almond accent."
> —JESSIE GREARSON-SAPAT FALMOUTH, ME

STRAWBERRY-RHUBARB MERINGUE PIE

## Strawberry-Rhubarb Meringue Pie M

**PREP:** 45 MIN. • **BAKE:** 50 MIN. + CHILLING
**MAKES:** 8 SERVINGS

- ½ cup all-purpose flour
- ¼ cup whole wheat pastry flour
- ¼ cup ground almonds
- ½ teaspoon salt
- ¼ cup cold butter, cubed
- 2 tablespoons cold water

**FILLING**

- 1 egg, lightly beaten
- ¾ cup sugar
- 2 tablespoons all-purpose flour
- ¼ teaspoon ground cinnamon
- 2 cups chopped fresh or frozen rhubarb, thawed
- 1½ cups sliced fresh strawberries

**MERINGUE**

- 3 egg whites
- ¼ teaspoon almond extract
- 6 tablespoons sugar

**1.** In a food processor, combine the all-purpose flour, pastry flour, almonds and salt; cover and pulse until blended. Add butter; cover and pulse until mixture resembles coarse crumbs. While processing, gradually add water until dough forms a ball.

**2.** Roll out pastry to fit a 9-in. pie plate. Transfer pastry to pie plate. Trim pastry to ½ in. beyond edge of plate; flute edges.

**3.** In a large bowl, combine the egg, sugar, flour and cinnamon; stir in rhubarb and strawberries. Transfer to prepared crust. Bake at 375° for 35-40 minutes or until filling is bubbly. Place pie on a wire rack; keep warm. Reduce heat to 350°.

**4.** In a large bowl, beat egg whites and extract on medium speed until soft peaks form. Gradually beat in sugar, 1 tablespoon at a time, on high until stiff peaks form. Spread over hot filling, sealing edges to crust.

**5.** Bake for 15 minutes or until golden brown. Cool on a wire rack for 1 hour; refrigerate for 1-2 hours before serving.

**PER SERVING** 255 cal., 8 g fat (4 g sat. fat), 41 mg chol., 219 mg sodium, 42 g carb., 2 g fiber, 5 g pro.

## Chipotle Peach Pie S M

This daring recipe takes peach pie to a new level. You might be surprised at the combination of ingredients, but don't judge it until you taste it.
—**TASTE OF HOME TEST KITCHEN**

**PREP:** 20 MIN. • **BAKE:** 30 MIN. + COOLING
**MAKES:** 8 SERVINGS

- 1 sheet refrigerated pie pastry
- 2 cans (15 ounces each) sliced peaches in extra-light syrup/juice
- ¼ cup cornstarch
- 2 tablespoons finely chopped chipotle peppers in adobo sauce

**TOPPING**

- ¼ cup sour cream
- 1 tablespoon sugar
- ½ teaspoon lime juice

**1.** Unroll pastry into a 9-in. pie plate; flute edges. Line unpricked pastry with a double thickness of heavy-duty foil. Bake at 450° for 8 minutes. Remove foil; bake 5 minutes longer.

**2.** Meanwhile, drain peaches, reserving juice. In a small saucepan, stir cornstarch and peach juice until smooth. Bring to a boil; cook and stir for 2 minutes or until thickened. Remove from the heat; stir in peaches and chipotle peppers. Pour into crust.

**3.** Bake at 350° for 30-35 minutes or until crust is golden brown and filling is bubbly (cover edges with foil during the last 20 minutes to prevent overbrowning if necessary). Cool on a wire rack.

**4.** In a small bowl, whisk the topping ingredients. Serve with pie. Refrigerate leftovers.

**PER SERVING** 210 cal., 8 g fat (4 g sat. fat), 10 mg chol., 136 mg sodium, 32 g carb., 1 g fiber, 1 g pro.

### top tip No Rainy-Day Meringue

When it comes to making meringue pies and cookies, don't save the baking for a rainy day. On humid days, meringues can absorb moisture and become limp and sticky.

## Dutch Apple Pie Tartlets F S C M

These adorable mini apple-pie pastries make a delightful addition to a dessert buffet or snack tray. The combination of baked apples and sweet-tart lemon curd is like getting two pies in one.
—**MARY ANN LEE** CLIFTON PARK, NY

**PREP:** 15 MIN • **BAKE:** 20 MIN • **MAKES:** 2½ DOZEN

- 1 cup finely chopped peeled apple
- ¼ cup lemon curd
- 2 packages (1.9 ounces each) frozen miniature phyllo tart shells

**TOPPING**
- ½ cup all-purpose flour
- 3 tablespoons sugar
- ½ teaspoon ground cinnamon
- ¼ cup cold butter
  Confectioners' sugar

**1.** In a small bowl, combine apples and lemon curd. Spoon into tart shells.
**2.** In another bowl, combine the flour, sugar and cinnamon; cut in butter until mixture resembles fine crumbs. Spoon over apple mixture. Place on an ungreased baking sheet.
**3.** Bake at 350° for 18-20 minutes or until golden brown. Cool on wire racks for 5 minutes. Dust with confectioners' sugar. Serve warm or at room temperature. Refrigerate leftovers.
**PER SERVING** *57 cal., 3 g fat (1 g sat. fat), 6 mg chol., 22 mg sodium, 7 g carb., trace fiber, 1 g pro.* **Diabetic Exchanges:** *½ starch, ½ fat.*

## Upside-Down Berry Cake

This cake is good warm or cold and served with whipped topping or ice cream. It soaks up loads of flavor from the berries and can be whipped up in just minutes.
—**CANDICE SCHOLL** WEST SUNBURY, PA

**PREP:** 20 MIN. • **BAKE:** 35 MIN. + COOLING • **MAKES:** 15 SERVINGS

- ½ cup chopped walnuts
- 1 cup fresh or frozen blueberries
- 1 cup fresh or frozen raspberries, halved
- 1 cup sliced fresh strawberries
- ¼ cup sugar
- 1 package (3 ounces) raspberry gelatin
- 1 package yellow cake mix (regular size)
- 2 eggs
- 1¼ cups water
- 2 tablespoons canola oil
- 1½ cups miniature marshmallows

**1.** In a well-greased 13-in. x 9-in. baking pan, layer the walnuts and berries; sprinkle with sugar and gelatin. In a large bowl, combine the cake mix, eggs, water and oil; beat on low speed for 30 seconds. Beat on medium for 2 minutes. Fold in marshmallows. Pour over top.
**2.** Bake at 350° for 35-40 minutes or until a toothpick inserted near the center comes out clean. Cool for 5 minutes before inverting onto a serving platter. Refrigerate leftovers.
**PER SERVING** *276 cal., 7 g fat (2 g sat. fat), 28 mg chol., 249 mg sodium, 51 g carb., 1 g fiber, 3 g pro.*

## Three-Fruit Shortcakes 🅼

Biscuit mix makes this dessert a snap. It's livened up with miniature chocolate chips and the summer's freshest berries and fruits.

**—TASTE OF HOME TEST KITCHEN**

**START TO FINISH:** 30 MIN. • **MAKES:** 4 SERVINGS

- 1 cup biscuit/baking mix
- ¼ cup miniature semisweet chocolate chips
- ⅓ cup 2% milk
- ½ teaspoon sugar
- 1 cup sliced fresh strawberries
- 1 cup sliced peeled peaches
- 1 cup fresh blueberries
- 1 teaspoon lemon juice
- 1 tablespoon confectioners' sugar
  Whipped topping, optional

**1.** In a small bowl, combine baking mix and chocolate chips; stir in milk until a soft dough forms. Drop by tablespoonfuls 2 in. apart onto a baking sheet coated with cooking spray. Sprinkle with sugar.

**2.** Bake at 425° for 12-14 minutes or until golden brown. Remove to a wire rack to cool. Meanwhile, in a large bowl, combine fruits and lemon juice. Add confectioners' sugar; toss to coat.

**3.** To assemble, split shortcakes in half. Place cake bottoms on dessert plates. Spoon fruit over bottom halves. Replace shortcake tops. Serve with whipped topping if desired.

**PER SERVING** *245 cal., 8 g fat (3 g sat. fat), 2 mg chol., 390 mg sodium, 42 g carb., 4 g fiber, 4 g pro.*

## Rhu-berry Pie 🆂🅼

I cook in a coffee shop, so I'm always looking for new and unique pies to serve my customers. The combination of blueberries and rhubarb in this recipe caught my eye, and it was an instant best-seller.

**—KAREN DOUGHERTY** FREEPORT, IL

**PREP:** 20 MIN. • **BAKE:** 45 MIN. • **MAKES:** 8 SERVINGS

  Pastry for single-crust pie (9 inches)
- ½ cup sugar
- ¼ cup cornstarch
- 1 cup unsweetened apple juice
- 3½ cups diced fresh rhubarb
- 2½ cups fresh blueberries

**1.** Roll out pastry to fit a 9-in. pie plate. Transfer pastry to pie plate. Trim pastry to ½ in. beyond edge of plate; flute edges.

**2.** In a large heavy saucepan, combine sugar and cornstarch. Stir in apple juice until smooth. Cook and stir over medium heat until thickened. Add rhubarb; cook and stir gently 2-3 minutes or just until heated through. Stir in blueberries. Spoon mixture into pie shell.

**3.** Place a foil-lined baking sheet on a rack below the pie to catch any spills. Bake at 375° for 45-50 minutes or until bubbly. Cool completely on a wire rack.

**PER SERVING** *231 cal., 7 g fat (3 g sat. fat), 5 mg chol., 104 mg sodium, 41 g carb., 2 g fiber, 2 g pro.*

## Lemon-Yogurt Tea Cakes Ⓜ

Light, tender and tangy, these little lemon cakes will be a hit at a brunch. They're also great for lunch, supper or snacking.

—**RUTH BURRUS** ZIONSVILLE, IN

**PREP:** 20 MIN. • **BAKE:** 20 MIN. + COOLING
**MAKES:** ABOUT 1 DOZEN

- 2¼ cups all-purpose flour
- 1 cup sugar
- ¾ teaspoon baking powder
- ½ teaspoon baking soda
- ½ teaspoon salt
- ½ cup cold butter
- 1 cup (8 ounces) fat-free plain yogurt
- 3 egg whites
- 2 tablespoons lemon juice
- 4 teaspoons grated lemon peel
- 1 teaspoon lemon extract

**1.** In a large bowl, combine the flour, sugar, baking powder, baking soda and salt; cut in butter until mixture resembles coarse crumbs. Whisk the yogurt, egg whites, lemon juice, peel and extract; stir into crumb mixture just until moistened.

**2.** Fill greased or paper-lined muffin cups three-fourths full. Bake at 350° for 18-22 minutes or until a toothpick inserted near the center comes out clean. Cool for 10 minutes before removing from pan to a wire rack to cool completely.

**PER SERVING** *232 cal., 8 g fat (5 g sat. fat), 20 mg chol., 255 mg sodium, 37 g carb., 1 g fiber, 4 g pro.*

PUMPKIN-CITRUS BUNDT CAKE

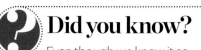
LEMON-YOGURT TEA CAKES

## Pumpkin-Citrus Bundt Cake Ⓜ

I was determined to make a healthier version of this pumpkin- and spice-laden cake. Judging by the compliments, it worked. Even a picky 4-year-old eater asked for more.

—**KRISTA FRANK** RHODODENDRON, OR

**PREP:** 20 MIN. • **BAKE:** 55 MIN. + COOLING
**MAKES:** 14 SERVINGS

- 2 cups canned pumpkin
- 1⅓ cups sugar
- 1¼ cups fat-free milk
- 2 eggs
- ½ cup orange juice
- ⅓ cup canola oil
- 1½ teaspoons maple flavoring
- 1½ teaspoons vanilla extract
- 1½ cups all-purpose flour
- 1½ cups whole wheat flour
- ¼ cup ground flaxseed
- 2 tablespoons grated orange peel
- 4 teaspoons baking powder
- 1 tablespoon cornstarch
- 1 tablespoon poppy seeds
- 2 teaspoons pumpkin pie spice
- 1 teaspoon salt
- ½ teaspoon baking soda

GLAZE
- 1 cup confectioners' sugar
- 1 teaspoon grated orange peel
- 1 to 2 tablespoons orange juice

**1.** In a large bowl, beat the pumpkin, sugar, milk, eggs, orange juice, oil, maple flavoring and vanilla until well blended. Combine the flours, flaxseed, orange peel, baking powder, cornstarch, poppy seeds, pie spice, salt and baking soda; gradually beat into pumpkin mixture until blended.

**2.** Transfer to a greased and floured 10-in. fluted tube pan. Bake at 350° for 55-60 minutes or until a toothpick inserted near the center comes out clean. Cool for 10 minutes before removing from pan to a wire rack to cool completely.

**3.** In a small bowl, whisk the confectioners' sugar, orange peel and enough juice to achieve desired consistency. Drizzle over cake.

**PER SERVING** *301 cal., 8 g fat (1 g sat. fat), 31 mg chol., 351 mg sodium, 54 g carb., 4 g fiber, 6 g pro.*

### ? Did you know?

Even though we know it as a type of squash, the word pumpkin comes from the Greek word *pepon,* meaning "large melon."

## Cherry Jubilee Cake M

An upside-down cherry cake is a fun alternative to pineapple. The cake portion turns out light and tender—perfect for soaking up the sweet cherry juice.
—DORIS HEATH FRANKLIN, NC

**PREP:** 30 MIN. • **BAKE:** 30 MIN. + COOLING
**MAKES:** 8 SERVINGS

- 2 **egg whites**
- 2 **tablespoons butter, melted**
- 3 **tablespoons brown sugar**
- 2 **cans (15 ounces each) pitted dark sweet cherries, drained**
- 3 **tablespoons butter, softened**
- ⅔ **cup sugar**
- 1 **cup cake flour**
- 1 **teaspoon baking powder**
- ¼ **teaspoon salt**
- ⅓ **cup 2% milk**
- ½ **teaspoon almond extract**
- ¼ **cup slivered almonds, toasted**
  **Whipped cream**

**1.** Let egg whites stand at room temperature for 30 minutes. Pour melted butter into a 9-in. round baking pan; sprinkle with brown sugar. Arrange cherries in a single layer over sugar.

**2.** In a large bowl, beat softened butter and sugar until crumbly, about 2 minutes. Combine the flour, baking powder and salt; add to the butter mixture alternately with milk. Stir in extract. In another bowl, beat egg whites until stiff peaks form; fold into batter. Spoon over cherries.

**3.** Bake at 350° for 30-35 minutes or until a toothpick inserted near the center comes out clean. Cool for 10 minutes before inverting onto a serving plate. Sprinkle with almonds. Serve warm with whipped cream.
**PER SERVING** *288 cal., 9 g fat (5 g sat. fat), 20 mg chol., 197 mg sodium, 49 g carb., 2 g fiber, 4 g pro.*

CHERRY JUBILEE CAKE

## Lemon Meringue Cupcakes M

"Classic lemon meringue pie inspired these gorgeous little cupcakes. The tangy treats hide a surprise lemon pie filling and are topped with fluffy toasted meringue." —ANDREA QUIROZ CHICAGO, IL

**PREP:** 30 MIN. • **BAKE:** 25 MIN. + COOLING
**MAKES:** 2 DOZEN

- 1 **package lemon cake mix (regular size)**
- 1⅓ **cups water**
- ⅓ **cup canola oil**
- 3 **eggs**
- 1 **tablespoon grated lemon peel**
- 1 **cup lemon creme pie filling**

**MERINGUE**
- 3 **egg whites**
- ½ **teaspoon cream of tartar**
- ½ **cup sugar**

**1.** In a large bowl, combine the cake mix, water, oil, eggs and lemon peel; beat on low speed for 30 seconds. Beat on medium for 2 minutes.

**2.** Fill paper-lined muffin cups two-thirds full. Bake at 350° for 18-22 minutes or until a toothpick inserted near the center comes out clean.

**3.** Cut a small hole in the corner of a pastry or plastic bag; insert a very small tip. Fill with pie filling. Push the tip into the top of each cupcake to fill.

**4.** In a large bowl, beat egg whites and cream of tartar on medium speed until soft peaks form. Gradually beat in sugar, 1 tablespoon at a time, on high until stiff glossy peaks form and sugar is dissolved. Pipe over tops of cupcakes.

**5.** Bake at 400° for 5-8 minutes or until meringue is golden brown. Cool for 10 minutes before removing from pans to wire racks to cool completely. Store in an airtight container in the refrigerator.
**PER SERVING** *153 cal., 5 g fat (1 g sat. fat), 28 mg chol., 176 mg sodium, 25 g carb., trace fiber, 2 g pro.* **Diabetic Exchanges:** *1½ starch, 1½ fat.*

248

251

258

# Treat Yourself

"My family loves cannoli, but I don't love making the shells. These parfaits are an easy way to enjoy the flavor without spending time baking the shells."

—**ANNA GINSBERG** AUSTIN, TX
*about her recipe, Black Forest Cannoli Parfaits, on page 254*

## Spiced Peach Cobbler M

When you dig into this warm and comforting fresh peach cobbler, you won't miss the extra fat and calories a bit!

—MARY RELYEA CANASTOTA, NY

**PREP:** 20 MIN. • **BAKE:** 30 MIN.
**MAKES:** 8 SERVINGS

- 12 medium peaches, peeled and sliced
- ¾ cup sugar, divided
- 3 tablespoons cornstarch
- 1 tablespoon lemon juice
- ½ teaspoon ground cinnamon
- ¼ teaspoon ground cardamom
- 1 cup all-purpose flour
- 2 teaspoons grated orange peel
- ¾ teaspoon baking powder
- ¼ teaspoon salt
- ¼ teaspoon baking soda
- 3 tablespoons cold butter
- ¾ cup buttermilk

1. In a large bowl, combine the peaches, ½ cup sugar, cornstarch, lemon juice, cinnamon and cardamom. Transfer to a 2-qt. baking dish coated with cooking spray.
2. In a small bowl, combine the flour, orange peel, baking powder, salt, baking soda and remaining sugar; cut in butter until mixture resembles coarse crumbs. Stir in buttermilk just until moistened. Drop by tablespoonfuls onto peach mixture.

SPICED PEACH COBBLER

CHOCOLATE LOVER'S PUDDING

3. Bake, uncovered, at 375° for 30-35 minutes or until golden brown. Serve warm.
**PER SERVING** *246 cal., 5 g fat (3 g sat. fat), 12 mg chol., 206 mg sodium, 49 g carb., 3 g fiber, 4 g pro.*

## Chocolate Lover's Pudding M

I made this for the first time when my husband asked me, "Why don't you ever make chocolate pudding?" It's not too rich, but it has an amazing chocolate flavor. It's nice knowing you can enjoy a from-scratch pudding in just 30 minutes.

—CHARIS O'CONNELL MOHNTON, PA

**PREP:** 20 MIN. • **COOK:** 10 MIN. + CHILLING
**MAKES:** 6 SERVINGS

- ½ cup sugar, divided
- 3 cups 2% milk
- 3 tablespoons cornstarch
- ¼ teaspoon salt
- 2 egg yolks, beaten
- ⅓ cup baking cocoa
- 2 ounces semisweet chocolate, chopped

- 1 tablespoon butter
- 2 teaspoons vanilla extract
  Fresh raspberries, optional

1. In a large heavy saucepan, combine ¼ cup sugar and milk. Bring just to a boil, stirring occasionally. Meanwhile, in a large stainless steel bowl, combine cornstarch, salt and remaining sugar; whisk in egg yolks until smooth.
2. Slowly pour hot milk mixture in a thin stream into egg yolk mixture, whisking constantly. Whisk in cocoa. Return mixture to saucepan and bring to a boil, stirring constantly until thickened, about 1 minute. Immediately remove from the heat.
3. Stir in the chocolate, butter and vanilla until melted. Whisk until completely smooth. Cool for 15 minutes, stirring occasionally. Transfer to dessert dishes. Cover and refrigerate for 1 hour. Just before serving, top with raspberries if desired.
**PER SERVING** *239 cal., 9 g fat (5 g sat. fat), 82 mg chol., 176 mg sodium, 35 g carb., 2 g fiber, 7 g pro.*

## Pear Gingerbread Cobbler M

**PREP:** 25 MIN. • **BAKE:** 20 MIN.
**MAKES:** 8 SERVINGS

- 4 **cups sliced peeled fresh pears (about 4 medium)**
- ½ **cup packed brown sugar**
- ½ **cup water**
- 1 **tablespoon orange juice**
- ¼ **teaspoon ground cinnamon**
- 2 **tablespoons cornstarch**
- 2 **tablespoons cold water**
- 2 **tablespoons finely chopped crystallized ginger**

**GINGERBREAD LAYER**

- ½ **cup buttermilk**
- ¼ **cup sugar**
- ¼ **cup molasses**
- 1 **egg**
- 2 **tablespoons canola oil**
- 1 **cup all-purpose flour**
- ½ **teaspoon baking soda**
- ½ **teaspoon baking powder**
- ½ **teaspoon ground ginger**
- ¼ **teaspoon salt**
- ¼ **teaspoon ground nutmeg**

1. Preheat oven to 350°. In a large saucepan, combine the first five ingredients; bring to a boil. Reduce heat; simmer, uncovered, 10 minutes or until pears are tender, stirring occasionally.
2. In a small bowl, mix cornstarch and cold water until smooth; stir into pears. Bring to a boil; cook and stir 2 minutes or until thickened. Stir in crystallized ginger. Transfer to a greased 8-in.-square baking dish.
3. In a large bowl, beat buttermilk, sugar, molasses, egg and oil until sugar is dissolved. In another bowl, whisk the remaining ingredients; gradually beat into buttermilk mixture. Pour over pear mixture.
4. Bake 20-25 minutes or until filling is bubbly and a toothpick inserted into center comes out clean.

**PER SERVING** *277 cal., 5 g fat (1 g sat. fat), 27 mg chol., 215 mg sodium, 58 g carb., 3 g fiber, 3 g pro.*

> "Cobblers are often associated with summer baking, but this autumn-inspired dessert will have you looking forward to fall."
> —**CHERYL PETERMAN** PRESCOTT, AZ

**SUMMER BREEZE FRUIT TARTLETS**

## Summer Breeze Fruit Tartlets F S M

Here's a lighter fruit tart that substitutes baked wonton wrappers for rich pastry shells. Friends and family enjoy this easy-to-prepare dessert!

—**FRAN FEHLING** STATEN ISLAND, NY

**START TO FINISH:** 25 MIN.
**MAKES:** 1 DOZEN

- 1 **medium mango, peeled and chopped**
- 1 **cup sliced fresh strawberries**
- ½ **cup fresh blueberries**
- 12 **wonton wrappers**
  **Cooking spray**
- ¼ **cup apple jelly**
- 2 **tablespoons sugar**
- ½ **teaspoon ground cinnamon**

1. In a small bowl, combine the mango, strawberries and blueberries.
2. Press wonton wrappers into miniature muffin cups coated with cooking spray; spritz each wrapper with additional cooking spray. Bake at 350° for 7-9 minutes or until lightly browned.
3. In a small saucepan, combine the jelly, sugar and cinnamon. Cook and stir over medium heat until sugar is dissolved. Spoon fruit into cups; brush with jelly mixture.

**PER SERVING** *69 cal., trace fat (trace sat. fat), 1 mg chol., 46 mg sodium, 16 g carb., 1 g fiber, 1 g pro.* **Diabetic Exchange:** *1 starch.*

PEAR GINGERBREAD COBBLER

LEMONY COCONUT FROZEN YOGURT

## Lemony Coconut Frozen Yogurt S M

Whenever I crave something cold to beat the heat, I whip this yogurt together and share with family. Everyone enjoys the sweet relief.

**—CAITLYN HEINZ** OVID, NY

**PREP:** 15 MIN. + CHILLING
**PROCESS:** 15 MIN. • **MAKES:** 10 SERVINGS

- 4 cups (32 ounces) plain yogurt
- ¾ cup sugar
- ½ cup lemon juice
- 3 tablespoons grated lemon peel
- 1 cup half-and-half cream
- ½ cup flaked coconut, toasted
  Ice cream waffle bowls, optional
  Fresh blueberries and raspberries, optional

1. Line a strainer or colander with four layers of cheesecloth or one coffee filter; place over a bowl. Place yogurt in prepared strainer; refrigerate, covered, 3 hours. Remove yogurt from cheesecloth and place in a large bowl; discard drained liquid.

2. Whisk sugar, lemon juice and lemon peel into yogurt until sugar is dissolved. Stir in cream. Pour into cylinder of ice cream freezer; freeze according to the manufacturer's directions, adding coconut during the last 5 minutes of processing time. If desired, serve in waffle bowls and top with berries.

**NOTE** *To toast coconut, spread in a 15-in. x 10-in. x 1-in. baking pan. Bake at 350° for 5-10 minutes or until golden brown, stirring frequently.*
**PER SERVING** *177 cal., 7 g fat (5 g sat. fat), 25 mg chol., 69 mg sodium, 24 g carb., trace fiber, 4 g pro. Diabetic Exchanges: 1½ starch, 1½ fat.*

## top tip
### Orange Zest

Before you peel and eat your next orange, zest the skin. Place it in a freezer bag and pop it into the freezer. That way you'll have it on hand to add a punch of flavor to your favorite recipes. The same can be done for limes and lemons.

SWEET POTATO PUDDING

## Sweet Potato Pudding F S M

I've made this recipe for the holidays for years. I came up with this low-fat version and nobody noticed the difference. My family prefers this dish served cold, but it's also nice served warm.

**—TRISHA KRUSE** BOISE, ID

**PREP:** 1¼ HOURS
**BAKE:** 1¼ HOURS + CHILLING
**MAKES:** 8 SERVINGS

- 2 pounds sweet potatoes (about 4 medium)
- 1 cup fat-free milk
- ½ cup egg substitute
- ¾ cup packed brown sugar
- ¼ cup all-purpose flour
- ¼ cup raisins
- 2 teaspoons grated orange peel
- 1 teaspoon pumpkin pie spice
- 1 teaspoon vanilla extract
- ⅛ teaspoon salt
- 8 tablespoons fat-free whipped topping in a can

1. Scrub and pierce sweet potatoes. Bake at 350° for 1 to 1¼ hours or until very tender.

2. Cut potatoes in half; scoop out pulp and place in a large bowl. Mash with milk and egg substitute. Stir in the brown sugar, flour, raisins, orange peel, pumpkin pie spice, vanilla and salt until blended.

3. Transfer to a 1½-qt. baking dish coated with cooking spray. Cover and bake at 350° for 1¼ to 1½ hours or just until top is set. Cool on a wire rack for 1 hour. Refrigerate for at least 2 hours. Serve with whipped topping.

**PER SERVING** *205 cal., trace fat (trace sat. fat), 1 mg chol., 102 mg sodium, 46 g carb., 2 g fiber, 4 g pro.*

CINNAMON BLUEBERRY CRUMBLE

## Cinnamon Blueberry Crumble F M

This is my favorite blueberry recipe. Its unique cookie topping tastes delicious with the warm berry filling.
—**LORI SULEWSKI** RINGOES, NJ

**PREP:** 20 MIN. • **BAKE:** 40 MIN. • **MAKES:** 6 SERVINGS

- 4 **cups fresh blueberries**
- ½ **cup sugar**
- 2 **tablespoons cornstarch**
- 1 **tablespoon all-purpose flour**
- 1 **teaspoon ground cinnamon**
- 1 **teaspoon grated lemon peel**
- 1 **teaspoon lemon juice**
- ½ **teaspoon ground nutmeg**
- ¼ **teaspoon salt**

**TOPPING**
- ⅔ **cup crushed reduced-fat vanilla wafers (about 20 wafers)**
- 1 **tablespoon all-purpose flour**
- 2 **teaspoons packed brown sugar**
- ¾ **teaspoon ground cinnamon**
- 1 **tablespoon butter, melted**
  **Whipped cream and shredded lemon peel, optional**

1. Place blueberries in a large bowl. Combine the sugar, cornstarch, flour, cinnamon, lemon peel and juice, nutmeg and salt; sprinkle over blueberries and toss to coat. Transfer to a greased 8-in.-square baking dish.
2. For topping, in a small bowl, combine the wafer crumbs, flour, brown sugar and cinnamon. Stir in butter until blended. Sprinkle over blueberry mixture.
3. Bake at 350° for 40-50 minutes or until filling is bubbly and topping is golden brown. Serve warm. Garnish with whipped cream and lemon peel if desired.
**PER SERVING** *215 cal., 3 g fat (1 g sat. fat), 5 mg chol., 158 mg sodium, 47 g carb., 3 g fiber, 1 g pro.*

## Strawberry Yogurt Pops F S M

**PREP:** 20 MIN. + FREEZING • **MAKES:** 6 POPS

- 1 **cup chopped fresh strawberries**
- 2 **tablespoons balsamic vinegar**
- 2 **tablespoons strawberry preserves**
- 2 **fresh rosemary sprigs**
- 1½ **cups (12 ounces) vanilla yogurt**
- 6 **freezer pop molds or paper cups (3 ounces each) and wooden pop or lollipop sticks**

1. In a small bowl, mix strawberries, vinegar, preserves and rosemary. Let stand 30 minutes; discard rosemary.
2. Spoon 2 tablespoons yogurt and 1 tablespoon strawberry mixture into each mold or paper cup. Repeat layers. Top molds with holders. If using cups, top with foil and insert sticks through foil. Freeze until firm.
**PER SERVING** *81 cal., 1 g fat (trace sat. fat), 3 mg chol., 42 mg sodium, 16 g carb., 1 g fiber, 3 g pro.* **Diabetic Exchange:** *1 starch.*

STRAWBERRY YOGURT POPS

"We planted strawberries a few years ago and my very favorite treat to make with them is these tangy-sweet frozen yogurt pops! The options are endless: Try using other yogurt flavors like lemon, raspberry or blueberry. You may also use your favorite herb instead of the rosemary, or simply omit the latter altogether."
—**CARMELL CHILDS** FERRON, UT

BANANA PUDDING

## Banana Pudding

I didn't see my son for more than two years after he enlisted in the Marines. When I saw him for the first time at the airport, I just grabbed hold of him and burst out crying. When we got home, the first thing he ate was two bowls of my banana pudding.
—**STEPHANIE HARRIS** MONTPELIER, VA

**PREP:** 15 MIN. + CHILLING • **COOK:** 20 MIN. + COOLING
**MAKES:** 9 SERVINGS

- ¾ cup sugar
- ¼ cup all-purpose flour
- ¼ teaspoon salt
- 3 cups 2% milk
- 3 eggs
- 1½ teaspoons vanilla extract
- 58 vanilla wafers (about 8 ounces), divided
- 4 large ripe bananas, cut into ¼-inch slices

1. In a large saucepan, mix sugar, flour and salt. Whisk in milk. Cook and stir over medium heat until thickened and bubbly. Reduce heat to low; cook and stir 2 minutes longer. Remove from heat.
2. In a small bowl, whisk eggs. Whisk a small amount of hot mixture into eggs; return all to pan, whisking constantly. Bring to a gentle boil; cook and stir 2 minutes. Remove from heat. Stir in vanilla. Cool 15 minutes, stirring occasionally.
3. In an ungreased 8-in.-square baking dish, layer 25 vanilla wafers, half of the banana slices and half of the pudding. Repeat layers.
4. Press plastic wrap onto surface of pudding. Refrigerate 4 hours or overnight. Just before serving, crush remaining wafers and sprinkle over top.
**PER SERVING** *302 cal., 7 g fat (2 g sat. fat), 80 mg chol., 206 mg sodium, 55 g carb., 2 g fiber, 7 g pro.*

## Almond-Pistachio Dandy Dessert Roll-Ups ⓢ ⓒ Ⓜ

With a flavor and texture similar to baklava, this delightful dessert appeals to young and old alike. It's especially delicious with honey drizzled over the top.
—**MARIE RIZZIO** INTERLOCHEN, MI

**PREP:** 25 MIN. • **BAKE:** 20 MIN. • **MAKES:** 1½ DOZEN

- ½ cup shelled pistachios, toasted
- ¼ cup unblanched whole almonds, toasted
- 1 tablespoon sugar
- 1 tablespoon butter, softened
- ½ teaspoon ground cinnamon
- 12 sheets phyllo dough (14 inches x 9 inches)
  Butter-flavored cooking spray
- ¼ cup honey, divided

1. Place pistachios and almonds in a food processor; cover and process until finely chopped. Add the sugar, butter and cinnamon; cover and process until blended.
2. Place one sheet of phyllo dough on a work surface. Spray with butter-flavored cooking spray. Repeat with second layer. Keep remaining phyllo dough covered with plastic wrap and a damp towel to avoid drying out. Spread ⅓ cup nut mixture over phyllo to within 1 in. of sides; drizzle with 1 tablespoon honey. Layer with two more sheets of phyllo, spraying each layer with cooking spray.
3. Roll up jelly-roll style, starting from the short side. Repeat with remaining phyllo, nut mixture and honey.
4. With a sharp knife, cut each roll into six pieces; place seam side down on a greased baking sheet. Spray with cooking spray. Bake at 325° for 16-20 minutes or until golden; drizzle with remaining honey.
**PER SERVING** *83 cal., 4 g fat (1 g sat. fat), 2 mg chol., 50 mg sodium, 10 g carb., 1 g fiber, 2 g pro.* **Diabetic Exchanges:** *1 fat, ½ starch.*

ALMOND-PISTACHIO
DESSERT ROLL-UPS

## Black Forest Cannoli Parfaits 🅜

My family loves cannoli, but I don't love making the shells. These parfaits are an easy way to enjoy the flavor without spending time baking the shells.
—**ANNA GINSBERG** AUSTIN, TX

**PREP:** 25 MIN. + CHILLING
**MAKES:** 8 SERVINGS

- 1 **package (16 ounces) frozen pitted tart cherries, thawed**
- 2 **tablespoons sugar**
- 1 **tablespoon cornstarch**
- 2 **teaspoons lemon juice**

**PARFAIT**

- 1 **carton (15 ounces) reduced-fat ricotta cheese**
- 1 **package (8 ounces) fat-free cream cheese**
- ¼ **cup sugar**
- 2 **tablespoons maple syrup**
- 2 **teaspoons lemon juice**
- 2 **teaspoons vanilla extract**
- 2 **cups reduced-fat whipped topping**
- ⅓ **cup miniature semisweet chocolate chips**
- 20 **chocolate wafers, crushed**

1. Drain cherries, reserving liquid in a measuring cup. Add enough water to measure ⅓ cup; set aside.
2. In a small saucepan, combine sugar and cornstarch; stir in reserved cherry juice mixture until smooth. Bring to a boil; cook and stir for 2 minutes or until thickened. Remove from the heat; stir in cherries and lemon juice. Cool.
3. Place the ricotta, cream cheese and sugar in a food processor; cover and process until smooth. Add the syrup, lemon juice and vanilla; process until combined. Gently fold in whipped topping and chocolate chips.
4. Place 1 tablespoon crushed wafers in each of eight parfait glasses. Top with ⅓ cup cheese mixture and a heaping tablespoonful of cherry sauce. Repeat layers. Refrigerate for at least 2 hours before serving.
**PER SERVING** *300 cal., 9 g fat (6 g sat. fat), 15 mg chol., 291 mg sodium, 46 g carb., 2 g fiber, 10 g pro.*

CHOCOLATE HAZELNUT SOY POPS

## Chocolate Hazelnut Soy Pops 🆂 🅒 🅜

I love Nutella, and I'm always looking for ways to use it. These pops are a great way to stay cool in the summer, but also make a tasty treat in the winter.
—**BONITA SUTER** LAWRENCE, MI

**PREP:** 10 MIN. + FREEZING
**MAKES:** 8 POPS

- 1 **cup vanilla soy milk**
- ½ **cup fat-free milk**
- ¾ **cup fat-free vanilla Greek yogurt**
- ⅓ **cup Nutella**
- 8 **freezer pop molds or 8 paper cups (3 ounces each) and wooden pop sticks**

Place milks, yogurt and Nutella in a blender; cover and process until smooth. Pour into molds or paper cups. Top molds with holders, If using cups, top with foil and insert sticks through foil. Freeze until firm.
**PER SERVING** *94 cal., 4 g fat (1 g sat. fat), trace chol., 33 mg sodium, 11 g carb., trace fiber, 4 g pro.* **Diabetic Exchanges:** *1 starch, ½ fat*

### ❓ Did you know?

Nutella lovers, this one's for you. Feb. 5 is celebrated as World Nutella Day. It's no surprise such a day exists, considering a jar of Nutella is sold every 2.5 seconds throughout the world.

BLACK FOREST CANNOLI PARFAITS

## Patriotic Pops F S C M

My kids love homemade ice pops, and I love knowing that the ones we make are good for them. We whip up a big batch with multiple flavors so they have many choices, but these patriotic red, white and blue ones are always a favorite!

—**SHANNON CARINO** FRISCO, TX

**PREP:** 15 MIN. + FREEZING
**MAKES:** 1 DOZEN

- 1¼ cups sliced fresh strawberries, divided
- 1¾ cups (14 ounces) vanilla yogurt, divided
- 1¼ cups fresh or frozen blueberries, divided
- 12 freezer pop molds or 12 paper cups (3 ounces each) and wooden pop sticks

**1.** In a blender, combine 1 cup strawberries and 2 tablespoons yogurt; cover and process until blended. Transfer to a small bowl. Chop remaining strawberries; stir into strawberry mixture.

**2.** In same blender, combine 1 cup blueberries and 2 tablespoons yogurt; cover and process until blended. Stir in remaining blueberries.

**3.** Layer 1 tablespoon strawberry mixture, 2 tablespoons yogurt and 1 tablespoon blueberry mixture in each of 12 molds or paper cups. Top molds with holders. If using cups, top with foil and insert sticks through foil. Freeze until firm.

**PER SERVING** *45 cal., 1 g fat (trace sat. fat), 2 mg chol., 24 mg sodium, 9 g carb., 1 g fiber, 2 g pro.* **Diabetic Exchange:** *½ starch.*

**WATERMELON SORBET**

## Watermelon Sorbet F S M

Using vodka in this fruity treat is the secret to soft sorbet. Alcohol does not freeze, and adding a little bit keeps the sorbet from completely freezing.

—**REBEKAH BEYER** SABETHA, KS

**PREP:** 15 MIN. + FREEZING
**MAKES:** 5 CUPS

- 1 cup sugar
- ½ cup water
- 8 cups cubed seedless watermelon
- 2 tablespoons lemon juice
- 2 tablespoons vodka

**1.** In a small saucepan, bring sugar and water to a boil. Cook and stir until sugar is dissolved; set aside to cool.

**2.** In batches, process the watermelon in a food processor for 2-3 minutes or until smooth. Transfer puree to a large bowl; stir in the lemon juice, vodka and sugar syrup. Pour into a 13-in. x 9-in. dish. Freeze for 1 hour or until edges begin to firm; stir. Freeze 2 hours longer or until firm.

**3.** Process watermelon mixture in batches for 2-3 minutes or until smooth. Serve immediately or transfer to freezer containers and freeze until serving.

**PER SERVING** *117 cal., 0 fat (0 sat. fat), 0 chol., 4 mg sodium, 31 g carb., 1 g fiber, trace pro.*

**PATRIOTIC POPS**

## Summertime Fruit Cones 🅂 🅼

Here's a simple summer dessert that appeals to kids and adults alike. You could also assemble this treat in parfait glasses instead of ice cream cones.
**—TASTE OF HOME TEST KITCHEN**

**START TO FINISH:** 20 MIN. • **MAKES:** 4 SERVINGS

- 2 **medium nectarines, chopped**
- 1 **cup whole small fresh strawberries**
- 1 **cup fresh blueberries**
- 2 **tablespoons mashed fresh strawberries**
- 1 **teaspoon finely chopped crystallized ginger**
- ¼ **teaspoon ground cinnamon**
- 1 **cup reduced-fat whipped topping**
- 4 **ice cream waffle cones**

1. In a small bowl, combine the nectarines, whole strawberries and blueberries. In another bowl, combine the mashed strawberries, ginger and cinnamon. Fold in whipped topping.
2. Fill each waffle cone with ¼ cup fruit mixture; top with 2 tablespoons whipped topping mixture. Repeat layers. Serve immediately.
**PER SERVING** *162 cal., 4 g fat (2 g sat. fat), 1 mg chol., 18 mg sodium, 31 g carb., 3 g fiber, 2 g pro.* **Diabetic Exchanges:** *1 starch, 1 fruit, ½ fat.*

## Grilled Stone Fruits with Balsamic Syrup 🅵 🅂 🅼

Get ready to experience another side of stone fruits. Hot off the grill, this late-summer dessert practically melts in your mouth.
**—SONYA LABBE** WEST HOLLYWOOD, CA

**START TO FINISH:** 20 MIN. • **MAKES:** 4 SERVINGS

- ½ **cup balsamic vinegar**
- 2 **tablespoons brown sugar**
- 2 **medium peaches, peeled and halved**
- 2 **medium nectarines, peeled and halved**
- 2 **medium plums, peeled and halved**

1. In a small saucepan, combine vinegar and brown sugar. Bring to a boil; cook until liquid is reduced by half.
2. Moisten a paper towel with cooking oil; using long-handled tongs, rub the grill rack to lightly coat. Grill peaches, nectarines and plums, covered, over medium heat or broil 4 in. from the heat for 3-4 minutes on each side or until tender.
3. Slice fruits; arrange on a serving plate. Drizzle with sauce.
**PER SERVING** *114 cal., 1 g fat (trace sat. fat), 0 chol., 10 mg sodium, 28 g carb., 2 g fiber, 2 g pro.* **Diabetic Exchanges:** *1 starch, 1 fruit.*

## Star-Spangled Parfaits S M

The best time for this dessert is midsummer, when the blueberries are thick in our northern woods. Red raspberries can be added to the mixed berries, too, to brighten up the patriotic colors.
—**ANNE THERIAULT** WELLESLEY, MA

**START TO FINISH:** 15 MIN. • **MAKES:** 4 SERVINGS

- 2 **cups fresh strawberries, cut into ½-inch pieces**
- 2 **cups fresh blueberries**
- 4 **teaspoons reduced-fat raspberry walnut vinaigrette**
- ¾ **cup (6 ounces) fat-free strawberry Greek yogurt**
- 2 **teaspoons minced fresh mint**
  **Finely shredded unsweetened coconut, optional**

1. Place strawberries and blueberries in separate bowls. Drizzle each with 2 teaspoons vinaigrette; toss to coat. In a small bowl, mix yogurt and mint.
2. Spoon strawberries into four parfait glasses. Layer each with yogurt mixture and blueberries. If desired, top with coconut.
**NOTE** *Look for unsweetened coconut in the baking or health food section.*
**PER SERVING** *172 cal., 7 g fat (5 g sat. fat), 0 chol., 41 mg sodium, 24 g carb., 5 g fiber, 5 g pro.* **Diabetic Exchanges:** *1 fruit, 1 fat, ½ starch.*

## Cherry & Spice Rice Pudding S M

Cinnamon and cherries sweeten the deal in this homey dessert. If you've never tried rice pudding, this an excellent place to start.
—**DEB PERRY** TRAVERSE CITY, MI

**PREP:** 10 MIN. • **COOK:** 2 HOURS • **MAKES:** 12 SERVINGS

- 4 **cups cooked long grain rice**
- 1 **can (12 ounces) evaporated milk**
- 1 **cup 2% milk**
- ⅓ **cup sugar**
- ¼ **cup water**
- ¾ **cup dried cherries**
- 3 **tablespoons butter, softened**
- 2 **teaspoons vanilla extract**
- ½ **teaspoon ground cinnamon**
- ¼ **teaspoon ground nutmeg**

1. In a large bowl, combine the rice, evaporated milk, milk, sugar and water. Stir in the remaining ingredients. Transfer to a 3-qt. slow cooker coated with cooking spray.
2. Cover and cook on low for 2-3 hours or until mixture is thickened. Stir lightly before serving. Serve warm or cold. Refrigerate leftovers.
**PER SERVING** *193 cal., 5 g fat (4 g sat. fat), 19 mg chol., 61 mg sodium, 31 g carb., trace fiber, 4 g pro.* **Diabetic Exchanges:** *2 starch, 1 fat.*

## Strawberry-Hazelnut Meringue Shortcakes [S] [M]

**PREP:** 25 MIN. • **BAKE:** 45 MIN. + COOLING
**MAKES:** 8 SERVINGS

- **2 egg whites**
- **½ cup sugar**
- **¼ cup finely chopped hazelnuts, toasted**
- **6 cups fresh strawberries, hulled and sliced**
- **4 cups low-fat frozen yogurt**

1. Place egg whites in a small bowl; let stand at room temperature 30 minutes.
2. Preheat oven to 250°. Beat egg whites on medium speed until foamy. Gradually add sugar, 1 tablespoon at a time, beating on high after each addition until sugar is dissolved. Continue beating until stiff glossy peaks form.
3. Drop meringue into eight mounds on a parchment paper-lined baking sheet. With the back of a spoon, shape into 3-in. cups. Sprinkle with hazelnuts. Bake 45-50 minutes or until set and dry. Turn off oven (do not open oven door); leave meringues in oven 1 hour. Remove from oven; cool completely on baking sheets. Remove meringues from paper.
4. Place 3 cups strawberries in a large bowl; mash slightly. Stir in remaining strawberries. Just before serving, top meringues with frozen yogurt and strawberries.

**NOTE** *To toast nuts, spread in a 15-in. x 10-in. x 1-in. baking pan. Bake at 350° for 5-10 minutes or until lightly browned, stirring occasionally. Or, spread in a dry nonstick skillet and heat over low heat until lightly browned, stirring occasionally.*

**PER SERVING** *212 cal., 4 g fat (1 g sat. fat), 5 mg chol., 74 mg sodium, 40 g carb., 3 g fiber, 7 g pro.*

"In summer the strawberry farms are open for picking. I serve strawberries with a crunchy hazelnut meringue cookie."
—**BARBARA ESTABROOK** RHINELANDER, WI

## Chocolate Eclair Delight [M]

It's amazing how the layers soften overnight into a cake-like texture. Just before serving this dessert, I like to dust the top with cocoa.
—**AGNES WARD** STRATFORD, ON

**PREP:** 15 MIN. • **COOK:** 15 MIN. + CHILLING
**MAKES:** 9 SERVINGS

- **½ cup sugar**
- **⅓ cup baking cocoa**
- **2 tablespoons plus 1 teaspoon cornstarch**
- **⅛ teaspoon salt**
- **⅛ teaspoon ground cinnamon**
- **1 can (12 ounces) fat-free evaporated milk**
- **1 cup fat-free milk**
- **½ cup egg substitute**
- **1 teaspoon vanilla extract**

TOPPING
- **2 cups reduced-fat whipped topping**
- **1 tablespoon plus ½ teaspoon baking cocoa, divided**
- **9 whole graham crackers, halved**

1. In a large heavy saucepan, combine the first five ingredients. Gradually whisk in evaporated milk and milk until smooth. Cook and stir over medium heat until mixture comes to a boil. Reduce heat; cook and stir 2 minutes longer or until thickened.
2. Remove from the heat. Stir a small amount of hot filling into egg substitute; return all to pan, stirring constantly. Bring to a gentle boil; cook and stir 2 minutes longer. Remove from the heat. Gently stir in vanilla. Press plastic wrap onto surface of filling; cover and refrigerate until cooled.
3. Meanwhile, in a small bowl, combine whipped topping and 1 tablespoon cocoa; set aside. Arrange half of the crackers in a 9-in. square pan coated with cooking spray. Layer half of the filling and topping over the crackers. Repeat layers. Cover and refrigerate overnight. Just before serving, sprinkle with ½ teaspoon of cocoa.

**PER SERVING** *209 cal., 4 g fat (2 g sat. fat), 2 mg chol., 213 mg sodium, 37 g carb., 1 g fiber, 7 g pro.*

STRAWBERRY-HAZELNUT
MERINGUE SHORTCAKES

CHOCOLATE ECLAIR DELIGHT

BROWN RICE PUDDING

## Brown Rice Pudding M

Brown rice gives this creamy pudding a deep, nutty flavor, while lemon and mango make it subtly sweet and refreshing. It's a healthy snack or dessert any time of the year.
—**LORIE MINER** KAMAS, UT

**PREP:** 15 MIN. • **COOK:** 1½ HOURS + CHILLING • **MAKES:** 4 SERVINGS

1¼ cups water
½ cup uncooked brown rice
3 teaspoons grated lemon peel, divided
¼ teaspoon salt
3 cups 2% milk
3 tablespoons brown sugar
1 teaspoon vanilla extract
Optional toppings: fresh mango, ground cinnamon and flaked coconut

1. In a large saucepan, combine the water, rice, 1½ teaspoons lemon peel and salt. Bring to a boil. Reduce heat; cover and simmer for 30-45 minutes or until tender.
2. Stir in milk and brown sugar. Cook, uncovered, for 40-50 minutes or until desired consistency, stirring occasionally. Remove from the heat; stir in vanilla and remaining lemon peel. Chill if desired.
3. Spoon into dessert dishes. Add toppings as desired.
**PER SERVING** 235 cal., 5 g fat (3 g sat. fat), 14 mg chol., 250 mg sodium, 40 g carb., 1 g fiber, 8 g pro.

## Sweet-Tart Rhubarb Crepes M

This recipe's name speaks true to its well-balanced flavor from tart rhubarb and sweet orange. It's a wonderful, unique breakfast or brunch dish.
—**BETSY KING** DULUTH, MN

**START TO FINISH:** 25 MIN. • **MAKES:** 8 SERVINGS

5 cups finely chopped fresh or frozen rhubarb, thawed
¾ cup sugar
2 tablespoons all-purpose flour
2 tablespoons orange juice
1 tablespoon butter
1 teaspoon grated orange peel
16 prepared crepes (9 inches)
Confectioners' sugar and additional grated orange peel, optional

1. In a large saucepan, combine the first five ingredients. Cook, stirring occasionally, over medium heat for 15-18 minutes or until tender. Remove from the heat; stir in orange peel.
2. Spread 2 tablespoons filling down the center of each crepe; roll up. Sprinkle with confectioners' sugar and additional orange peel if desired.
**NOTE** *If using frozen rhubarb, measure rhubarb while still frozen, then thaw completely. Drain in a colander, but do not press liquid out.*
**PER SERVING** *200 cal., 4 g fat (2 g sat. fat), 15 mg chol., 175 mg sodium, 40 g carb., 1 g fiber, 3 g pro.*

SWEET-TART RHUBARB CREPES

AUTUMN HARVEST COBBLER

## Autumn Harvest Cobbler Ⓜ

Saying goodbye to summer peach crisp doesn't have to be sorrowful when there's a delicious fall cobbler waiting to comfort you.
—**NANCY FOUST** STONEBORO, PA

**PREP:** 35 MIN. • **BAKE:** 15 MIN. • **MAKES:** 12 SERVINGS

- ½ cup sugar
- 1 teaspoon ground cinnamon
- ½ teaspoon salt
- ½ teaspoon ground nutmeg
- 2 cups cold water, divided
- 6 large tart apples, peeled and thinly sliced
- 1 cup golden raisins
- 1 cup dried apricots, halved
- 1 tablespoon lemon juice
- 2 tablespoons cornstarch

**TOPPING**
- 2 cups biscuit/baking mix
- ¾ cup 2% milk
- 1 tablespoon coarse sugar
- 2 teaspoons grated lemon peel
  Whipped cream

**1.** In a large saucepan combine the sugar, cinnamon, salt, nutmeg and 1¾ cups water. Bring to a boil. Stir in the apples, raisins, apricots and lemon juice. Return to a boil. Reduce heat; simmer, uncovered, for 10 minutes, stirring occasionally.

**2.** Combine the cornstarch and remaining water until smooth. Stir into pan. Bring to a boil; cook and stir for 2 minutes or until thickened. Transfer to a greased 13-in. x 9-in. baking dish.

**3.** In a small bowl combine biscuit mix and milk just until blended. Drop by tablespoonfuls onto hot apple mixture. Sprinkle with coarse sugar and lemon peel.

**4.** Bake at 400° for 15-20 minutes or until topping is golden brown. Serve warm with whipped cream.

**PER SERVING** 245 cal., 4 g fat (1 g sat. fat), 1 mg chol., 359 mg sodium, 53 g carb., 3 g fiber, 3 g pro.

## Sweet Potato Frozen Yogurt Pops Ⓢ Ⓒ Ⓜ

Once I had my little girl I quickly became really creative in the kitchen, needing to have healthy foods on hand. These frozen treats turned out to be a favorite and are a staple in our home.
—**JENN TIDWELL** FAIR OAKS, CA

**PREP:** 10 MIN. + FREEZING • **MAKES:** 6 SERVINGS

- 2 cartons (6 ounces each) honey Greek yogurt
- 1 cup mashed sweet potatoes
- ½ teaspoon ground cinnamon
- ¼ cup fat-free milk
- 6 freezer pop or paper cups (3 ounces each) and wooden pop sticks

Place the first four ingredients in a food processor; process until smooth. Pour into molds or paper cups. Top molds with holders. If using cups, top with foil and insert sticks through foil. Freeze until firm.

**PER SERVING** 111 cal., 6 g fat (4 g sat. fat), 15 mg chol., 54 mg sodium, 13 g carb., 1 g fiber, 3 g pro. *Diabetic Exchanges: 1 starch, ½ fat.*

SWEET POTATO
FROZEN YOGURT POPS

# General Recipe Index

This handy index lists every recipe by food category, major ingredient and/or cooking method, so you can easily locate recipes that suit your needs.

# Alphabetical Index

This handy index lists every recipe alphabetically,
so you can easily find the dishes you enjoy most.